PROVERBS

Proverbes

Sprichwörter

Proverbi

Proverbios

Пословицы

PROVERBS

Proverbes
Sprichwörter
Proverbi
Proverbios
Пословицы

A Comparative Book of English, French, German, Italian, Spanish and Russian Proverbs with a Latin Appendix

Compiled and Edited by
JERZY GLUSKI

ELSEVIER PUBLISHING COMPANY
Amsterdam / London / New York 1971

ELSEVIER PUBLISHING COMPANY
335 JAN VAN GALENSTRAAT
P.O. BOX 211, AMSTERDAM, THE NETHERLANDS

ELSEVIER PUBLISHING CO. LTD.
BARKING, ESSEX, ENGLAND

AMERICAN ELSEVIER PUBLISHING COMPANY, INC.
52 VANDERBILT AVENUE
NEW YORK, NEW YORK 10017

LIBRARY OF CONGRESS CARD NUMBER: 75-135483

ISBN: 0-444-40904-1

PRINTED IN THE NETHERLANDS

Publisher's note

We regret to say that the author of this work, Jerzy Gluski, died before the final stages of production of the book had been completed. He had the satisfaction, however, of knowing that this volume, the fruit of many years' work, was about to be published. The various proverbs were collected throughout a period of fourteen years. No attempt has been made to bring them into line with present idiom since their origin is so often traditional if not Biblical or Shakespearian.

1897- 146817

Preface

The famous English philosopher Francis Bacon (1561–1626) said: "The genius, wit and spirit of a nation are discovered in its proverbs." The comparative paroemiography shows that in this respect the European nations have much in common, despite the frontiers and distances which divide them, and that they are all like one great family notwithstanding the various conditions of their development, or the different forms of their political and economical systems. The comparative paroemiography may also be considered, in some measure, as a contributive factor to a better mutual understanding and rapprochement between nations.

The beginnings of comparative paroemiography date back to the 16th century. Since Erasmus of Rotterdam published his collection of proverbial locutions from Latin authors (*Adagiorum Collectanea*, Paris 1515), attempts have been made in several countries to compile comparative collections of proverbs of various nations.

Among others, James Howell, Historiographer Royal to Charles II, published his *Lexicon Tetraglotton* (1660). This work contains in several chapters English, French, Italian, Spanish and British (i.e. Welsh) proverbs–mostly in bilingual arrangement. Howell availed himself of the collections of proverbs issued before him, but as he did not apply any system in compiling his lexicon, it is very difficult to find there any given proverb.

The most comprehensive collection of this kind (in two volumes) appeared in Leipzig: *Sprichwörter der germanischen und romanischen Sprachen, vergleichend zusammengestellt* (1872–75). Its authors were Mrs. Ida von Düringsfeld and her husband, baron Otto von Reinsberg-Düringsfeld. Their collection contains 2,000 German proverbs along with their equivalents in other languages. Notwithstanding some deficiencies, it is the most important work in the field of comparative paroemiography for Germanic and Romance languages and dialects.

Besides, it is to be mentioned that in the monumental *Deutsches*

Sprichwörter-Lexicon by C. F. W. Wander (Leipzig 1863–80) are quoted sometimes equivalents in other languages.

In our century, there was published among others the *Dizionario Comparato di Proverbi e Modi Proverbiali* by Augusto Arthaber (Milan 1929, 2nd edition 1952) in seven languages: Italian, Latin, French, Spanish, German, English and Old Greek. This collection contains 1,483 entries, partly based on the work of Düringsfeld. Not in all cases are equivalents in all the seven languages given.

Among the publications of late years in this field is to be mentioned the collection of Gérard Ilg: *Proverbes français suivis des équivalents en allemand, anglais, espagnol, italien, néerlandais* (Amsterdam 1960). It contains 607 entries; in some cases the missing equivalents are replaced by translations.

As for comparative paroemiography in Slavonic languages, there appeared as early as 1632 the collection *Adagia Polonica* by the Rev. Jesuit father Gregor Knapski (Cnapius). It quotes Latin and Old Greek equivalents to each Polish proverb. In the 17th and 18th centuries further similar collections of proverbs were issued in Poland.

At the end of the 19th century there appeared in Warsaw a comparative collection of Russian, Polish, French and German proverbs, compiled by Mark Fabian Zamenhof (2nd edition 1905).

In Russia, M. Masson published in 1868 the first part of his collection, conceived on a wide scale, which was to contain a large number of Russian, German, French, Latin, Polish, English, Italian, Spanish, Serbian and Ukrainian proverbs. Unfortunately, it was only a part of the whole that was published.

In 1896 there appeared in St. Petersburg a book of *Volatile Words* by M. Michelson. It contained quotations and proverbs in Russian and some West-European languages.

In the Soviet Union collections of English, German and French proverbs were brought out, each of them containing about 500–600 entries along with Russian equivalents or translations. More proverbs by far are to be found in the bilingual phraseological dictionaries (English-Russian, German-Russian, French-Russian), which were issued after 1950.

A pretty comprehensive collection *6000 deutsche und russische*

Sprichwörter, compiled by A. E. Graf, was published 1956 in Halle/ Saale (G.D.R.).

A remarkable multilingual book of proverbs of all Slav nations was compiled by the Czech poet Fr. L. Čelakovský (Prague 1851, 3rd edition 1949).

A few remarks regarding the method used in compiling the present collection of proverbs in the six universal languages. In each of these languages over 1,100 proverbs and proverbial phrases, more or less current, are quoted. English is the basic language of the collection which, as a whole, is divided into 48 topical sections.

There are certain proverbs which are to be found, in one or another language, in two or more variants. In this book there is given, in principle, only one variant in each language, the most closely connected equivalents having been selected. In some cases, however, it was expedient to give two variants in one or another language. Then again, when it was possible to find out in all six languages the diverse variants of a given proverb, they are cited as separate entries respectively.

The proverbs marked by *(B)* are gathered from the Bible. A few entries taken from Shakespeare's works are marked by *(Sh)* accordingly. To proverbs with an asterisk* equivalents are to be found in the appendix "Latin Origins of Certain Proverbs".

Préface

Le célèbre philosophe anglais Francis Bacon (1561–1626) a dit: "Le génie, la sagesse et l'esprit d'une nation se révèlent dans ses proverbes." La parémiographie comparée prouve que les peuples européens ont à cet égard, malgré les frontières et les distances qui les séparent, beaucoup de traits communs, qu'ils constituent comme une grande famille indépendamment des conditions différentes de développement ou de systèmes sociaux et économiques différents. On peut aussi admettre que la parémiographie comparée contribue en quelque sorte à une meilleure compréhension réciproque et au rapprochement entre les peuples.

Les débuts de la parémiographie comparée remontent au XVIe siècle. Depuis qu'Érasme de Rotterdam a publié son recueil d'expressions proverbiales d'auteurs latins (*Adagiorum Collectanea*, Paris 1515), on a tenté dans plusieurs pays de comparer les proverbes de divers peuples.

C'est ainsi notamment que James Howell, historiographe du roi d'Angleterre Charles II, a publié son *Lexicon Tetraglotton* (1660). Cette œuvre contient dans plusieurs chapitres des proverbes anglais, français, italiens, espagnols et britanniques (c'est-à-dire gallois), cités pour la plupart dans une présentation bilingue. Howell avait puisé dans les recueils de proverbes édités avant lui, mais comme il n'appliquait dans son Lexicon aucune méthode de classement, il est difficile d'y retrouver un proverbe précis.

Le recueil le plus vaste de ce genre (en 2 tomes) est paru à Leipzig sous le titre *Sprichwörter der germanischen und romanischen Sprachen, vergleichend zusammengestellt*. Ses auteurs sont: Ida von Düringsfeld et son mari, le baron Otto von Reinsberg-Düringsfeld. Ce recueil comprend 2000 proverbes allemands et leurs équivalents en d'autres langues. Malgré certaines lacunes, c'est l'œuvre la plus importante de parémiographie comparée dans les langues et dialectes germaniques et romans.

Mentionnons encore que dans l'œuvre monumentale *Deutsches*

Sprichwörter-Lexicon de C. F. W. Wander (Leipzig 1863–80) on trouve parfois des équivalents dans d'autres langues.

Au cours de notre siècle a paru notamment un recueil d'Augusto Arthaber intitulé *Dizionario comparato di Proverbi e Modi Proverbiali* (Milan 1929, IIe édition 1952) en 7 langues: italien, latin, français, espagnol, allemand, anglais et grec ancien. Cet ouvrage contient 1483 proverbes et expressions proverbiales, basés en partie sur l'œuvre des Düringsfeld. Les équivalents ne sont pas donnés dans tous les cas en sept langues.

Parmi les publications plus récentes de ce domaine, citons le recueil de Gérard Ilg: *Proverbes français suivis des équivalents en allemand, anglais, espagnol, italien, néerlandais* (Amsterdam 1960). Ce recueil contient 607 proverbes; dans certains cas, les équivalents manquants ont été remplacés par leur traduction.

Quant à la parémiographie comparée en langues slaves, dès 1632 est paru le recueil *Adagia Polonica* élaboré par l'abbé Gregor Knapski (Cnapius), jésuite, qui fait suivre chaque proverbe polonais ses équivalents latins et grecs. Au XVIIe et XVIIIe siècles, d'autres recueils de ce genre ont été édités en Pologne.

Vers la fin du dernier siècle est paru à Varsovie un recueil de proverbes russes, polonais, français et allemands, élaboré par Marc Fabian Zamenhof (IIe édition 1905).

En Russie, M. Masson a publié en 1868 une partie de son recueil conçu à une grande échelle et qui devait contenir de nombreux proverbes russes, allemands, français, latins, polonais, anglais, italiens, espagnols, serbes et ukrainiens. Malheureusement, seule une partie de ce recueil a été éditée.

En 1896 est paru à St.-Pétersbourg le livre des *Paroles ailées* de M. Michelson qui contenait des citations et des proverbes en russe et dans plusieurs langues ouest-européennes.

En U.R.S.S. ont été édités des recueils de proverbes anglais, allemands et français avec leurs équivalents russes ou leur traduction (de 500 à 600 proverbes). Les dictionnaires phraséologiques bilingues (anglo-russe, germano-russe, franco-russe), édités après 1950, contiennent un nombre bien plus considérable de proverbes.

Un recueil assez vaste d'A. E. Graf intitulé *6000 deutsche und*

russische Sprichwörter est paru en 1956 à Halle/Saale (R.D.A.).
Il convient de citer encore le recueil multilingue de proverbes de tous les peuples slaves, élaboré par le poète tchèque Fr. L. Čelakovský (Prague 1851, IIIe édition 1949).

Quelques remarques concernant la méthode appliquée pour l'élaboration du présent recueil de proverbes dans les six langues universelles. Dans chacune d'elles sont cités plus de mille-cent proverbes et expressions proverbiales, plus ou moins courantes. Les proverbes anglais servent de point de départ. La totalité est divisée en 48 parties thématiques.

Il est des proverbes qui possèdent dans telle ou autre langue 2 variantes et même plus. Une seule variante par proverbe dans chaque langue, avec choix des équivalents les plus proches possible, a été prise en principe en considération dans ce recueil. Dans certains cas néanmoins, il était préférable de donner dans telle ou autre langue deux variantes. D'autre part, lorsqu'il était possible de trouver diverses variantes d'un proverbe déterminé dans les six langues, elles ont été citées séparément.

Les proverbes indiqués par la lettre *(B)* sont puisés dans la Bible. Plusieurs proverbes provenants des œuvres de Shakespeare ont été indiqués respectivement par *(Sh)*. Pour les proverbes avec astérisque,* les équivalents se trouvent dans l'appendice "Origines latines de certains proverbes".

Vorwort

Der berühmte englische Philosoph Francis Bacon (1561–1626) sagte: "Das Genie, die Klugheit und der Geist eines Volkes offenbaren sich in seinen Sprichwörtern." Die vergleichende Parömiographie beweist, dass in dieser Hinsicht die europäischen Völker viel Gemeinsames haben, trotz der sie trennenden Grenzen und Entfernungen, und dass sie gleichsam eine einzige grosse Familie bilden, ungeachtet der verschiedenen Entwicklungsbedingungen oder abweichenden Gesellschaftsordnung und Wirtschaftsform. Es ist auch anzunehmen, dass die vergleichende Parömiographie gewissermassen zu einer besseren gegenseitigen Verständigung und Annäherung zwischen Völkern beiträgt.

Die Anfänge der vergleichenden Parömiographie reichen ins 16. Jahrhundert zurück. Seitdem Erasmus von Rotterdam seine Sammlung von sprichwörtlichen Wendungen aus lateinischen Autoren (*Adagiorum Collectanea*, Paris 1515) herausgab, wurden in manchen Ländern Versuche gemacht, Sprichwörter verschiedener Völker vergleichend zusammenzustellen.

Unter anderen hat James Howell, königlicher Historiograph Karls II. von England, das *Lexicon Tetraglotton* (1660) veröffentlicht. Dieses Werk enthält in einigen Kapiteln englische, französische, italienische, spanische und britische (d.h. walisische) Sprichwörter, meistens in zweisprachiger Fassung. Howell benutzte die früheren Sprichwörtersammlungen, da er aber kein System in die Anordnung seines Lexicons brachte, ist es recht schwierig, ein bestimmtes Sprichwort darin aufzufinden.

Die reichhaltigste Sammlung dieser Art (in 2 Bänden) erschien in Leipzig 1872–75: *Sprichwörter der germanischen und romanischen Sprachen, vergleichend zusammengestellt*. Die Verfasser sind Ida von Düringsfeld und ihr Mann Otto Frh. von Reinsberg-Düringsfeld. Ihre Sammlung umfasst rund 2000 deutsche Sprichwörter und deren Gegenstücke in anderen Sprachen. Trotz gewisser Unzulänglichkeiten ist es das bedeutendste Werk der vergleichenden Parömiographie für germanische und romanische Sprachen und Dialekte.

Hier ist noch zu erwähnen, dass im monumentalen *Deutsches Sprichwörter-Lexicon* von C. F. W. Wander (Leipzig 1863–80) manchmal anderssprachige Gegenstücke angegeben sind.

In unserem Jahrhundert erschien u.a. Arthur Arthabers *Dizionario Comparato di Proverbi e Modi Proverbiali* (Mailand 1929, Neuauflage 1952) in 7 Sprachen: italienisch, lateinisch, französisch, spanisch, deutsch, englisch und altgriechisch. Die Sammlung enthält 1483 Eintragungen, teilweise in Anlehnung an das Werk von Düringsfeld. Nicht in allen Fällen jedoch sind Gegenstücke in sämtlichen sieben Sprachen angeführt.

Zu den neueren Veröffentlichungen auf diesem Gebiet gehört die Sammlung von Gérard Ilg: *Proverbes français suivis des équivalents en allemand, anglais, espagnol, italien, néerlandais* (Amsterdam 1960). Die Sammlung enthält 607 Nummern, wobei in manchen Fällen die fehlenden Gegenstücke durch Übertragungen ersetzt worden sind.

Was die vergleichende Parömiographie in slawischen Sprachen betrifft, so erschien bereits im Jahre 1632 eine vom Jesuitenpater Gregor Knapski (Cnapius) zusammengestellte Sammlung *Adagia Polonica*, in der bei jedem polnischen Sprichwort die lateinischen und altgriechischen Gegenstücke zitiert werden. Im 17. und 18. Jahrhundert wurden in Polen weitere ähnliche Sammlungen herausgegeben.

Ende des 19. Jahrhunderts erschien in Warschau eine russisch-polnisch-französisch-deutsche Sprichwörtersammlung (Neuauflage 1905) von Mark Fabian Zamenhof.

In Russland veröffentlichte M. Masson einen Teil seiner grossangelegten Sammlung (1868), die viele russische, deutsche, französische, lateinische, polnische, englische, italienische, spanische, serbische und ukrainische Sprichwörter enthalten sollte. Leider wurde nur ein Teil davon herausgegeben.

Im Jahre 1896 erschien in Petersburg M. Michelsons Sammlung von *Geflügelten Worten*, die Zitaten und Sprichwörter in Russisch und einigen westlichen Sprachen enthielt.

In der Sowjetunion wurden Sammlungen von englischen, deutschen und französischen Sprichwörtern mit russischen Gegenstücken oder Übersetzungen (je 500-600 Eintragungen) herausgegeben. Eine weitaus grössere Anzahl von Sprichwörtern enthalten die nach 1950 erschienenen zweisprachigen phraseologischen Wörterbücher (englisch-russisch, deutsch-russisch, französisch-russisch).

Eine ziemlich umfangreiche Sammlung von A. E. Graf *6000 deutsche und russische Sprichwörter* erschien 1956 in Halle/Saale (D.D.R.). Eine bemerkenswerte vielsprachige Sammlung von Sprichwörtern aller slawischen Völker bearbeitete der tschechische Dichter Fr. L. Čelakovský (Prag 1851, dritte Auflage 1949).

Ein paar Bemerkungen zur Methode, die bei der Zusammenstellung der vorliegenden Sprichwörtersammlung in 6 Weltsprachen angewendet wurde. In jeder Sprache sind über 1100 Sprichwörter und sprichwörtliche Redensarten, mehr oder weniger gebräuchliche, angeführt. Den Ausgangspunkt bilden die englischen Sprichwörter. Das Ganze ist in 48 Themengruppen eingeteilt.

Es gibt manche Sprichwörter, die in der einen oder anderen Sprache in zwei oder mehr Varianten vorkommen. In dieser Sammlung wird grundsätzlich nur je eine Variante in jeder Sprache zitiert, wobei die am meisten nahestehenden Gegenstücke gewählt wurden. In einigen Fällen jedoch war es zweckmässig, in dieser oder jener Sprache zwei Varianten anzugeben. Anderseits, wenn es möglich war, in allen sechs Sprachen verschiedene Varianten eines bestimmten Sprichworts ausfindig zu machen, wurden dieselben als entsprechende besondere Eintragungen angeführt.

Die mit dem Buchstaben *(B)* bezeichneten Sprichwörter sind der Bibel entnommen. Ein paar Eintragungen, die aus Shakespeares Werken stammen, sind entsprechend mit *(Sh)* bezeichnet. Für die mit einem Sternchen* bezeichneten Sprichwörter sind Gegenstücke im Anhang "Lateinische Ursprünge mancher Sprichwörter" angegeben.

Anmerkung des Verlages

Auf ausdrücklichen Wunsch des Autors, wurden im Deutschen die "ß" durch "ss" ersetzt.

Prefazione

Il celebre filosofo inglese Francesco Bacone (1561–1626) disse: "Il genio, la saggezza e lo spirito di una nazione si scoprono nei suoi proverbi." La paremiografia comparata dimostra che sotto questo aspetto i popoli europei hanno molti elementi in comune, nonostante i confini e le distanze che li dividono, e costituiscono quasi un'unica grande famiglia indipendentemente dalle condizioni di sviluppo o dai sistemi sociali ed economici. Si può anche ritenere che la paremiografia comparata contribuisca, in un certo modo, ad una maggiore comprensione e ad un reciproco avvicinamento fra i popoli.

Le origini della paremiografia comparata risalgono al XVI secolo. Da quando Erasmo di Rotterdam pubblicò la sua raccolta delle locuzioni proverbiali degli autori latini (*Adagiorum Collectanea*, Parigi 1515), in vari paesi si tentò di confrontare i proverbi delle varie nazioni.

Tra l'altro James Howell, storiografo del re d'Inghilterra Carlo II, pubblicò nel 1660 il suo *Lexicon Tetraglotton*. Quest'opera contiene, suddivisi in alcuni capitoli, i proverbi inglesi, francesi, italiani, spagnuoli e britannici (cioè in gaelico)–per lo più nella versione bilingue. Howell si servì delle raccolte dei proverbi edite prima di lui, ma poichè non seguì alcun sistema nell'ordinare il suo lessico, è assai difficile trovarvi un dato proverbio.

La più ampia raccolta di questo genere (in 2 volumi) *Sprichwörter der germanischen und romanischen Sprachen, vergleichend zusammengestellt*, venne pubblicata a Lipsia. Gli autori sono: Ida von Düringsfeld e suo marito, il barone Otto von Reinsberg-Düringsfeld. La raccolta comprende 2000 proverbi tedeschi e i loro corrispettivi in altre lingue. Nonostante alcune deficienze si tratta della principale opera di paremiografia comparata nelle lingue e nei dialetti germanici e romanzi.

Si deve qui inoltra ricordare che nella monumentale raccolta *Deutsches Sprichwörter-Lexicon* di C. F. W. Wander (Lipsia 1863–80) furono riportati, a volte, i corrispettivi in altre lingue.

Nel nostro secolo è uscita, tra l'altro, la raccolta di Augusto Arthaber *Dizionario Comparato di Proverbi e Modi Proverbiali* (Milano 1929, II ed. 1952) pubblicata in sette lingue: italiano, latino, francese, spagnuolo, tedesco, inglese e greco antico. Questa raccolta comprende 1483 posizioni e si basa, in parte, sull'opera dei Düringsfeld. Non in tutti i casi sono stati riportati corrispettivi nelle sette lingue.

Tra le pubblicazioni più recenti si deve ricordare la raccolta di Gérard Ilg: *Proverbes français suivis des équivalents en allemand, anglais, espagnol, italien, néerlandais* (Amsterdam 1960). La raccolta contiene 607 posizioni; in alcuni casi i corrispettivi mancanti sono stati sostituiti da traduzione.

Quanto alla paremiografia comparata nelle lingue slave, già nel 1632 venne pubblicata dal gesuita Gregor Knapski (Cnapius) la raccolta intitolata *Adagia Polonica*, dove presso ogni proverbio polacco erano riportati i corrispettivi latini e greco antichi. Nei secoli XVII e XVIII vennero pubblicate in Polonia anche altre raccolte di questo tipo.

Verso la fine dello scorso secolo venne pubblicata a Varsavia una raccolta di proverbi russi, polacchi, francesi e tedeschi a cura di Marco Fabian Zamenhof (II ed. 1905).

In Russia M. Masson pubblicò nel 1868 una parte della sua monumentale raccolta che doveva comprendere numerosi proverbi russi, tedeschi, francesi, latini, polacchi, inglesi, italiani, spagnuoli, serbi ed ucraini. Purtroppo solo una parte di quella raccolta venne pubblicata.

Nel 1896 uscì a Pietroburgo il libro delle *Facezie Correnti* di M. Michelson, contenente citazioni e proverbi nella lingua russa e in alcune lingue dell'Europa occidentale.

Nell'U.R.S.S. sono state pubblicate raccolte di proverbi inglesi, tedeschi e francesi con i corrispettivi o con le traduzioni russe (500–600 posizioni). Molto più ricchi di proverbi sono i dizionari fraseologici (inglese-russo, tedesco-russo, francese-russo) pubblicati dopo il 1950.

Abbastanza ampia è la raccolta di A. E. Graf *6000 deutsche und russische Sprichwörter* pubblicata a Halle/Saale (R.D.T.) nel 1956.

Merita attenzione la raccolta multilingue dei proverbi dei popoli slavi elaborata a cura del poeta cecoslovacco Fr. L. Čelakovský (Praga 1851, III ed. 1949).

Facciamo ora alcune osservazioni sul metodo seguito nella elaborazione della presente raccolta nelle 6 principali lingue. In ognuna di queste lingue sono stati riportati più di 1100 proverbi e modi proverbiali, più o meno correnti. Si è preso l'avvio dai proverbi inglesi. L'insieme è diviso in 48 capitoli tematici.

Vi sono alcuni proverbi che, in una o in un'altra lingua, appaiono in due o più varianti. Nella presente raccolta è stata riportata, in linea di massima, una sola variante in ogni lingua e sono stati scelti, possibilmente, i corrispettivi più vicini. In alcuni casi è stato però opportuno riportare, in una o in un'altra lingua, due varianti. D'altra parte, dove è stato possibile trovare diverse varianti di un determinato proverbio in tutte e sei lingue, si è avuto cura di riportarle come posizioni a parte.

I proverbi contrassegnati con la lettera *(B)* sono stati tratti dalla Bibbia. Alcune posizioni tratte dalle opere di Shakespeare sono adeguatamente contrassegnate con la sigla *(Sh)*. I proverbi marcati dall'asterisco* hanno i loro corrispettivi nell'appendice "Origini latine di alcuni proverbi".

Prefacio

El célebre filósofo inglés Francis Bacon (1561–1626) dijo: "El genio, la agudeza y el espíritu de una nación se revelan en sus proverbios." La paremiografía comparada demuestra que en este aspecto los pueblos europeos tienen mucho en común, pese a las fronteras y las distancias que los separan, y que forman algo como una gran familia, no obstante las diferentes condiciones de su desarrollo y sus diversas sistemas sociales o económicos. Puede también decirse que la paremiografía comparada contribuye en cierto modo a un mejor entendimiento mutuo entre los pueblos y a su acercamiento.

Los comienzos de la paremiografía comparada se remontan al siglo XVI. Desde que Erasmo de Rotterdam publicó su compilación de locuciones proverbiales de los autores latinos (*Adagiorum Collectanea*, París 1515), en muchos paises se han emprendido ensayos de compilación comparada de proverbios de diversos pueblos.

Entre otros, James Howell, historiógrafo del rey Carlos II de Inglaterra, publicó su *Lexicon Tetraglotton* (1660). Esta obra reune en varios capítulos refranes ingleses, franceses, italianos, castellanos y británicos (es decir, galeses), ateniéndose generalmente al orden bilingüe. Howell aprovechó los refraneros publicados anteriormente, pero dado que no siguió ningún sistema en la composición de su léxico, resulta difícil encontrar allí un proverbio determinado.

La recopilación más amplia de este género (en dos tomos) apareció en Leipzig, bajo el título *Sprichwörter der germanischen und romanischen Sprachen, vergleichend zusammengestellt* (1872–75). Sus autores son: Ida von Düringsfeld y su esposo, el barón Otto von Reinsberg-Düringsfeld. Esta colección incluye 2000 proverbios alemanes y sus equivalentes en otras lenguas. A pesar de ciertas deficiencias, es la obra más importante de paremiografía comparada en lenguas y dialectos germánicos y romances.

Debe mencionarse también que en la obra monumental *Deutsches Sprichwörter-Lexicon* de C. F. W. Wander (Leipzig 1863–80) se citan a veces los equivalentes en otras lenguas.

En nuestro siglo apareció, entre otros, la colección de Augusto Arthaber, titulada *Dizionario Comparato di Proverbi e Modi Proverbiali* (Milán 1929, 2a ed. 1952) en siete idiomas: italiano, latino, francés, español, alemán, inglés y griego clásico. Esta colección incluye 1483 artículos y está basada parcialmente en la obra de los Düringsfeld. Los equivalentes no aparecen en todos los casos en siete lenguas.

Entre las publicaciones más recientes en este dominio, mencionaemos la recopilación de Gérard Ilg: *Proverbes français suivis des équivalents en allemand, anglais, espagnol, italien, néerlandais* (Amsterdam 1960). Esta colección contiene 607 artículos; en algunos casos la falta de equivalentes ha sido suplida por traducciones.

En cuanto a la paremiografía comparada en lenguas eslavas, merece recordarse que ya en 1632 apareció la recopilación *Adagia Polonica*, obra del sacerdote jesuita Gregor Knapski (Cnapius), en la cual, junto a cada proverbio polaco, se citan los correspondientes proverbios latinos y griegos. En los siglos XVII y XVIII fueron publicados en Polonia otros refraneros de este tipo.

Al final del siglo pasado apareció en Varsovia una colección de refranes rusos, polacos, franceses y alemanes, elaborada por Marc Fabian Zamenhof (2a ed. 1905).

En Rusia, M. Masson publicó en 1868 una parte de su colección, concebida en gran escala y que debía incluir muchos proverbios rusos, alemanes, franceses, latinos, polacos, ingleses, italianos, españoles, servios y ucranianos. Desgraciadamente, sólo una parte de esta colección fué publicada.

En 1896 apareció en San Petersburgo el libro de *Locuciones Corrientes* de M. Michelson, con citas y proverbios en ruso y varias lenguas de Europa Occidental.

En la Unión Soviética fueron publicadas colecciones (de 500 a 600 artículos cada una) de proverbios ingleses, alemanes y franceses con los equivalentes rusos o traducciones. Un acervo de proverbios mucho mayor contienen los diccionarios fraseológicos bilingües (inglés-ruso, alemán-ruso, francés-ruso), editados después del año 1950.

Una colección bastante amplia de A. E. Graf *6000 deutsche und russische Sprichwörter* apareció en 1956 en Halle/Saale (R.D.A.). Merece también atención la recopilación plurilingüe de proverbios de todos los pueblos eslavos, elaborada por el poeta checo Fr. L. Čelakovský (Praga 1851, 3a ed. 1949).

Algunas observaciones sobre el método aplicado en la elaboración de la presente recopilación de proverbios en las seis lenguas universales. En cada uno de estos idiomas se citan más de 1100 proverbios y frases proverbiales, más o menos corrientes. Los proverbios ingleses sirven de punto de partida. El todo está dividido en 48 capítulos temáticos.

Hay algunos proverbios que aparecen en una u otra lengua en dos o más variantes. En esta colección se cita, por principio, sólo una variante de cada lengua, habiéndose escogido en lo posible los equivalentes más próximos. Sin embargo, en algunos casos ha sido preferible dar en una u otra lengua dos variantes. Por otra parte, cuando ha sido posible encontrar diversas variantes de un proverbio determinado en los seis idiomas, éstas han sido incluidas en artículos aparte.

Los proverbios marcados con la letra *(B)* han sido sacados de la Biblia. Algunos proverbios, recogidos de las obras de Shakespeare, han sido señalados con *(Sh)*. Los proverbios marcados con el asterisco* tienen sus equivalentes en el apéndice "Orígenes latinos de algunos proverbios".

Предисловие

Знаменитый английский философ Фрэнсис Бэкон (1561–1626) сказал: "Гениальность, мудрость и дух народа проявляются в его пословицах." Сравнительная паремиография доказывает, что в этом отношении европейские народы имеют много общего, несмотря на разделяющие их границы и расстояния, что они составляют как бы одну большую семью, независимо от разных условий их развития или различных форм общественного строя и хозяйственной системы. Можно также считать, что сравнительная паремиография способствует в некоторой степени лучшему взаимопониманию и сближению между народами.

Начала сравнительной паремиографии относятся к 16 веку. С тех пор, как Эразм Роттердамский издал свой сборник провербиальных выражений из латинских авторов (Париж 1515), в разных странах предпринимались попытки составлять сравнительные сборники пословиц и поговорок различных народов.

Между прочим, Джемс Хауэлль, надворный историограф английского короля Карла II, издал свой *Лексикон тетраглоттон* (1660). Этот труд содержит в нескольких главах английские, французские, итальянские, испанские и британские (т.е. валлийские) пословицы–большей частью в двуязычном сопоставлении. Хауэлль пользовался изданными до него сборниками пословиц, но ввиду того, что он не применил никакого метода при составлении своего лексикона, очень трудно отыскать в нём какую-нибудь определённую пословицу.

Самый обширный сборник этого рода (в двух томах) был издан в Лейпциге под заглавием: *Пословицы германских и романских языков в сравнительном сопоставлении* (1872–75). Авторами его были: Ида фон Дюрингсфельд и её муж, барон Отто фон Рейнсберг-Дюрингсфельд. Этот лексикон содержит в общем 2000 немецких пословиц с их эквивалентами на других языках. Несмотря на некоторые недостатки, это самый крупный труд по сравнительной паремиографии в области германских и романских языков и диалектов.

Следует ещё отметить, что в монументальном *Лексиконе немецких пословиц* К. Ф. В. Вандера (Лейпциг 1863–80) приведены местами эквивалентные пословицы на других языках.

В нашем столетии вышел из печати м.пр. сборник Августа Артхабера под заглавием: *Сравнительный словарь пословиц и поговорок* (Милан 1929, 2 изд. 1952) на семи языках: итальянском, латинском, французском, испанском, немецком, английском и древнегреческом. Этот словарь содержит 1483 пословиц и поговорок. Он составлен частично на базе труда Дюрингсфельдов; не во всех случаях приведены соответствующие пословицы на семи языках.

К новейшим изданиям в этой области принадлежит сборник Жерара Ильга: *Французские пословицы с эквивалентами на немецком, английском, испанском, итальянском и голландском языках* (Амстердам 1960). Этот сборник содержит 607 пословиц, при чём в некоторых случаях недостающие эквиваленты замещены переводами.

Что касается сравнительной паремиографии по славянским языкам, то уже в 1632 г. был издан под латинским заглавием сборник польских пословиц, составленный ксендзом-иезуитом Гр. Кнапским и содержащий латинские и древнегреческие эквиваленты каждой названной польской пословицы. В 17 и 18 веках были изданы в Польше дальнейшие сборники этого рода.

В конце минувшего столетия вышел из печати в Варшаве сборник русских, польских, французских и немецких пословиц, составленный Марком Фабианом Заменгофом (2 изд. 1905).

В России М. Массон издал в 1868 г. часть своего широко задуманного лексикона, который должен был содержать большое количество русских, немецких, французских, латинских, польских, английских, итальянских, испанских, сербских и украинских пословиц. К сожалению, только часть этого труда была издана.

В 1896 г. вышла из печати в Петербурге книга М. Михельсона под заглавием *Ходячие и меткие слова*, содержащая цитаты и пословицы на русском и нескольких западноевропейских языках.

В Советском Союзе были изданы сборники английских, немецких и французских пословиц с русскими эквивалентами или переводами (по 500–600 пословиц). Гораздо большее количество пословиц и поговорок содержат изданные после 1950 г. двуязычные фразеологические словари (англо-русский, немецко-русский, французско-русский).

Довольно обширный сборник, составленный А. Е. Графом, под загла
вием *6000 немецких и русских пословиц* был издан в Германской
Демократической Республике (г. Галле 1956).

Примечательный многоязычный лексикон пословиц всех славянских
народов был составлен чешским поэтом Фр. Л. Челяковским (Прага
1851, 3 изд. 1949).

А вот несколько замечаний, касающихся метода, применённого при
составлении данного сборника пословиц на шести главных языках
мира. В каждом из этих языков приведено свыше 1100 пословиц и
поговорок, более или менее употребляемых. Исходным языком являет-
ся английский. Всё содержание подразделено на 48 тематических глав.

Некоторые пословицы встречаются на том или ином языке в двух
или нескольких вариантах. В данном сборнике приведено, в основном,
по одной пословице на каждом языке, при чём подобраны наиболее
приближённые по смыслу эквиваленты. Однако, в некоторых случаях
было целесообразно привести на том или ином языке два варианта.
С другой стороны, когда возможно было найти разные варианты опре-
делённой пословицы на всех шести языках, они приведены соответственно как отдельные единицы.

Пословицы, отмеченные буквой *(Б)*, позаимствованы из Библии.
Несколько единиц, взятых из произведений Шекспира, обозначено
соответственно *(Ш)*. К пословицам со звёздочкой* эквиваленты на-
ходятся в приложении "Латинские источники некоторых пословиц".

Bibliography
Bibliographie
Literaturverzeichnis
Bibliografia
Bibliografía
Библиография

James Howell, Lexicon Tetraglotton. London 1660.

W. C. Hazlitt, English Proverbs and Proverbial Phrases. London 1869.

W. G. Smith, The Oxford Dictionary of English Proverbs. Oxford 1957.

A. Johnson, Common English Proverbs. London 1956.

A. Johnson, Common English Sayings. London 1958.

V. H. Collins, A Book of English Proverbs. London 1959.

D. C. Browning, Everyman's Dictionary of Quotations and Proverbs. London 1951.

H. Davidoff, A World Treasury of Proverbs. London 1953.

A. Taylor and B. J. Whiting, A Dictionary of American Proverbs and Proverbial Phrases 1820–80. Cambridge, Mass. 1958.

G. Cumberlege, The Oxford Dictionary of Quotations. London 1954.

Brewer's Dictionary of Phrase and Fable. London 1959.

Chamber's Twentieth Century Dictionary. London 1959.

B. L. K. Henderson, A Dictionary of English Idioms. London 1954.

A. Pasquier, English Idiomatic Phrases and French, German, Italian Equivalents. Bulle 1946.

W. J. Ball, A Practical Guide to Colloquial Idioms. London 1958.

W. McMordie, English Idioms. London 1959.

R. Benham, Everyday English Idioms. Bombay 1959.

V. H. Collins, A Book of English Idioms. London 1957.

V. H. Collins, A Second Book of English Idioms. London 1958.

V. H. Collins, A Third Book of English Idioms. London 1960.

A. Blass, English Idioms. Bamberg 1959.

E. Partridge, A Dictionary of Slang and Unconventional English. London 1956.

The Holy Bible (King James Version). New York.

The Works of William Shakespeare (Odhams Press). London 1947.

Loewe-Breul, Deutsch-englische Phraseologie. Berlin 1926.

Muret-Sanders, Enzyklopädisches englisch-deutsches und deutsch-englisches Wörterbuch. Berlin 1931.

H. Messinger, Langenscheidts Handwörterbuch Deutsch-Englisch. Berlin 1959.

R. Wykeham, 1000 idiomatische englische Redensarten. Berlin 1956.

Leroux de Lincy, Le Livre des Proverbes français. Paris 1859.

J. Pineaux, Proverbes et Dictons français. Paris 1958.

M. Rat, Dictionnaire des Locutions françaises. Paris 1957.

E. Genest, Dictionnaire des Citations. Paris 1955.

A. Syreychtchikova, Locutions Idiomatiques françaises. Moscou 1948.

M. Maloux, Dictionnaire des Proverbes, Sentences et Maximes. Paris 1960.

M. Kalma et C. Tarpel, Trésor des Proverbes et Locutions du Monde. Paris 1961.

G. Ilg, Proverbes français suivis des équivalents en allemand, anglais, espagnol, italien, néerlandais. Amsterdam 1960.

J. E. Mansion, Harrap's Standard French and English Dictionary. London 1956.

Sachs-Villatte, Enzyklopädisches französisch-deutsches und deutsch-französisches Wörterbuch. Berlin 1927.

H. W. Klein, 1000 idiomatische französische Redensarten. Berlin 1957.

A. Blass, Französische Redewendungen und Sprichwörter. Bamberg 1959.

J. Humbert, L'Interprète (500 phrases). Bienne 1959.

Nouveau Larousse Classique. Paris 1959.

Petit Larousse. Paris 1960.

La Sainte Bible (par Louis Segond). Paris 1958.

Shakespeare, Théâtre Complet. Paris 1938.

E. Littré/A. Beaujean, Dictionnaire de la Langue française. Paris 1958.

B. Tougan-Baranovskaia, Proverbes et Dictons russes avec leurs équivalents français. Moscou 1963.

C. F. W. Wander, Deutsches Sprichwörter-Lexicon. Leipzig 1863–80.

Ida von Düringsfeld und Otto von Düringsfeld-Reinsberg, Sprichwörter der germanischen und romanischen Sprachen, vergleichend zusammengestellt. Leipzig 1872–75.

K. Simrock, Die deutschen Sprichwörter. Basel 1881.

W. Borchardt, Die sprichwörtlichen Redensarten im deutschen Volksmunde. Leipzig 1895.

F. Lipperheide, Sprichwörterbuch. München 1909.

G. Büchmann, Geflügelte Worte. Berlin 1925.

Duden, Stilwörterbuch der deutschen Sprache. Mannheim 1956.

Kürschner, Lexikon der sechs Weltsprachen. Salzburg.

I. Pawlowsky, Deutsch-russisches Wörterbuch. Riga 1902.

A. Boecklen, Sprichwörter in sechs Sprachen. Stuttgart 1947.

Die Heilige Schrift (M. Luther). London 1954.

Die Heilige Schrift (F. E. Schlachter). Genf-Zürich 1951.

Shakespeares Sämtliche Werke (A. W. Schlegel, Fr. Bodenstedt u.a.). Stuttgart.

A. E. Graf, 6000 deutsche u. russische Sprichwörter. Halle/Saale 1956.

G. di Castro, Proverbi italiani. Milano 1858.

P. Petrocchi, Nuovo Dizionario Universale della Lingua Italiana. Milano 1887–91.

A. Arthaber, Dizionario Comparato di Proverbi e Modi Proverbiali. Milano 1952.

Lysle-Gualteri, Nuovo Dizionario Moderno delle Lingue Italiana e Inglese. Torino 1951.

N. Spinelli, Dizionario Italiano-Inglese, Inglese-Italiano. Torino 1955.

M. Bergomi, Vocabolario delle Lingue Italiano e Tedesca. Livorno 1942.

G. Sacerdote, Taschenwörterbuch der italienischen und deutschen Sprache. Berlin 1956.

Frenzel-Ross, 1000 italienische Redensarten. Berlin 1957.

La Sacra Bibbia. Roma 1955.

Fr. Rodríguez Marín, Refranes Castellanos. Madrid 1926.

Fr. Rodríguez Marín, 6666 Refranes Castellanos. Madrid 1934.

Diccionario de la Lengua Española (Real Academia Española).
Madrid 1925.

F. del Valle Abad, Diccionario Francés-Español y Español-Francés.
Granada.

V. Salva/M. de Toro y Gómez, Nouveau Dictionnaire Espagnol-
Français. Paris 1905.

Cassell's Spanish-English and English-Spanish Dictionary. London
1955.

L. de Baeza, Brush Up Your Spanish. London 1946.

Yvonne P. de Dony, Léxico del Lenguaje Figurado, en cuatro idiomas.
Buenos Aires 1951.

Schoen-Noeli, Taschenwörterbuch der spanischen und deutschen
Sprache. Berlin 1955.

W. Beinhauer, 1000 spanische Redensarten. Berlin 1955.

Crocker-Noble, The Traveler's Phrase Book English-Spanish. New
York 1961.

Nuevo Pequeño Larousse Ilustrado. Paris 1957.

New Revised Velázquez Spanish and English Dictionary. Chicago
1960.

La Santa Biblia. Londres 1957.

В. И. Даль, Пословицы русского народа. Москва 1957.

В. И. Даль, Толковый словарь живого великорусского языка. Москва
1955 (1880–82).

С. И. Ожегов, Словарь русского языка. Москва 1960.

Н. Колпакова, Золотые зёрна. Загадки и пословицы народов СССР.
Москва 1950.

А. А. Разумов, Мудрое слово. Русские пословицы и поговорки. Москва
1957.

Н. Колпакова, М. Мельц, Т. Шаповалова, Избранные пословицы и
поговорки русского народа. Москва 1957.

А. М. Жигулев, Русские народные пословицы и поговорки. Москва
1965.

М. Михельсон, Ходячие и меткие слова. Петербург 1896.

С. Максимов, Крылатые слова. Петербург 1899.

М. Булатов, Крылатые слова. Москва 1958.

А. И. Соболев, Народные пословицы и поговорки. Москва 1961.

В. К. Мюллер, Англо-русский словарь. Москва 1953.

А. Смирницкий, О. Ахманова, Русско-английский словарь. Москва 1958.

К. А. Ганшина, Французско-русский словарь. Москва 1957.

Л. Щерба, М. Матусевич, Русско-французский словарь. Москва 1959.

А. Лепинг, Н. Страхова, Немецко-русский словарь. Москва 1958.

А. Лепинг, Н. Страхова, А. Лоховиц, Русско-немецкий словарь. Москва 1961.

С. Герье, Н. Скворцова, Б. Грифцов, Итальянско-русский словарь. Москва 1947.

Н. Скворцова, Б. Майзель, Итальянско-русский словарь. Москва 1963.

С. Герье, Н. Скворцова, Русско-итальянский словарь. Москва 1953.

Ф. В. Кельин, Испанско-русский словарь. Москва 1954.

Ю. С. Ясельман, Русско-испанский словарь. Москва 1948.

Х. Ногейра и Г. Я. Туровер, Русско-испанский словарь. Москва 1967.

А. В. Кунин, Англо-русский фразеологический словарь. Москва 1956.

Л. Э. Бинович, Немецко-русский фразеологический словарь. Москва 1956.

Я. И. Рецкер, Французско-русский фразеологический словарь. Москва 1963.

В. Шекспир, Собрание сочинений под ред. С. А. Венгерова. Петербург 1902–04.

В. Шекспир, Трагедии (перевод Б. Пастернака). Москва 1951.

Библия в русском переводе. Нью-Йорк.

Table of Contents
Table des Matières
Inhaltsverzeichnis
Tàvola delle Matèrie
Índice
Оглавление

Topical sections

Parties thématiques

Themengruppen

Capitoli tematici

Capítulos temáticos

Тематических глав

1 Words and Deeds
  Paroles et Actes
  Wort und Tat
  Parole e Fatti
  Palabras y Hechos
  Слова и дела

1 *En* No sooner said than done.*
   Fr Aussitôt dit, aussitôt fait.
   De Gesagt–getan.
   It Detto–fatto.
   El Dicho y hecho.
   Ru Сказано–сделано.

2 *En* Actions speak louder than words.
   Fr Bien dire fait rire, bien faire fait taire.
   De Tatsachen sind stärker als Worte.
   It Detto senza fatto ad ognun par misfatto.
   El Dicho sin hecho no trae provecho.
   Ru Дела сильнее слов.

3 *En* Saying is one thing, and doing another.*
   Fr Dire et faire sont deux.
   De Reden und tun sind zweierlei.
   It Altra cosa è il dire, altra il fare.
   El Decir y hacer, dos cosas suelen ser.
   Ru Дела словом не заменишь.

4 *En* From words to deeds is a great space.*
   Fr Du dit au fait il y a un grand trait.
   De Von Worten zu Werken ist ein weiter Weg.

It   Dal detto al fatto c'è un gran tratto.
El   Del dicho al hecho hay gran trecho.
Ru   От слова до дела целая верста (сто перегонов).

5   *En*   The greatest talkers are the least doers.
     Fr   Les grands diseurs ne sont pas les grands faiseurs.
     De   Wer viel redet, tut am wenigsten.
     It   Chi troppo parla, poco agisce.
     El   El que mucho habla, poco obra.
     Ru   Кто много говорит, тот мало делает.

6   *En*   Fair words and foul deeds.
     Fr   Belles paroles et mauvais faits.
     De   Schöne Worte, faule Taten.
     It   Belle parole e cattivi fatti.
     El   Buenas palabras y ruines hechos.
     Ru   Слова гладкие, а дела гадкие

7   *En*   Good words and ill deeds deceive wise and fools.
     Fr   Belles paroles et mauvais jeu trompent les jeunes et les
          vieux.
     De   Mit guten Worten fängt man die Leute.
     It   Belle parole e cattivi fatti ingannano savi e matti.
     El   Buenas palabras y ruines hechos engañan sabios y locos.
     Ru   Птицу кормом, а человека словом обманывают.

8   *En*   It is one thing to promise and another to perform.
     Fr   Promettre et tenir sont deux.
     De   Versprechen und halten ist zweierlei.
     It   Altro è promettere, altro è mantenere.
     El   Prometer no es dar.
     Ru   Одно дело обещать, другое–выполнять.

9   *En*   He that promises too much, means nothing.
     Fr   Grand prometteur, petit donneur.

De   Wer viel verspricht, hält selten etwas.
It   Chi promette molto, attiene poco.
El   Quien mucho promete, con poco cumple.
Ru   Много обещают–ничего не дают.

10   En   Out of the abundance of the heart the mouth speaketh. *(B)*
     Fr   C'est de l'abondance du cœur que la bouche parle.
     De   Wes das Herz voll ist, des geht der Mund über.
     It   Della pienezza del cuore parla la bocca.
     El   De la abundancia del corazón habla la boca.
     Ru   От избытка сердца уста глаголют. *(Б)*

11   En   He who says what he likes shall hear what he does not
          like.*
     Fr   Qui dira tout ce qu'il voudra, ouïra ce que lui ne plaira.
     De   Wer alles sagt, was er will, der hört auch das, was er
          nicht will.
     It   Chi dice quel che vuole, ode quel che non vorrebbe.
     El   Quien dice lo que quiere, oye lo que no quiere.
     Ru   Кто говорит всё, что хочет, тот услышит то, чего не хочет.

12   En   First think, and then speak.
     Fr   Il faut tourner sept fois sa langue avant de parler.
     De   Überlege dir hundertmal, ehe du sprichst.
     It   Pensare tre volte prima di parlare!
     El   Antes de hablar, un padrenuestro rezar.
     Ru   Сперва подумай, потом говори.

13   En   Hear much, speak little.
     Fr   Écoute beaucoup et parle peu.
     De   Rede wenig, höre viel.
     It   Parla poco, e ascolta assai.
     El   Habla poco, escucha mucho, y no errarás.
     Ru   Больше слушай, меньше говори.

14   *En*   Speech is silvern, silence is golden.
      Fr   La parole est d'argent, le silence est d'or.
      De   Reden ist Silber, Schweigen ist Gold.
      It   La parola è d'argento, il silenzio è d'oro.
      El   La palabra es de plata, el silencio es de oro.
      Ru   Слово–серебро, молчание–золото.

15   *En*   Speak fitly, or be silent wisely.
      Fr   Mieux vaut se taire que mal parler.
      De   Besser schweigen als das Maul verbrannt.
      It   Chi sa tacer all'occasione, guadagna più che col parlare.
      El   Cállate o di algo mejor que el silencio.
      Ru   Не стыдно молчать, когда нечего сказать.

16   *En*   More have repented speech than silence.
      Fr   On se repent souvent de parler, jamais de se taire.
      De   Reden schadet oft, Schweigen nie.
      It   Mai nocque il tacere, ma l'aver parlato.
      El   Del callar ningún se arrepiente, del hablar muchos.
      Ru   Лишнее говорить–только себе вредить.

17   *En*   Silence does seldom harm.*
      Fr   Qui de tout se tait, de tout a paix.
      De   Schweigen und Denken kann niemand kränken.
      It   Un bel tacere non fu mai scritto.
      El   El callar es cosa muy virtuosa.
      Ru   Молчанием никого не обидишь.

18   *En*   Silence gives consent.*
      Fr   Qui ne dit mot, consent.
      De   Wer schweigt, stimmt zu.
      It   Chi tace, acconsente.
      El   Quien calla, otorga.
      Ru   Молчание–знак согласия.

19 *En*   A word spoken is past recalling.*
   Fr   Parole lâchée ne revient jamais.
   De   Ein gesprochen Wort ist nicht wieder einzufangen.
   It   Parola detta e sasso tirato non torna indietro.
   El   Palabra y piedra suelta no tienen vuelta.
   Ru   Слово скажешь–не воротишь.

20 *En*   No wisdom like silence.
   Fr   Parle peu et tu seras estimé.
   De   Schweigen ist auch eine Kunst.
   It   Chi parla rado, è stimato.
   El   Vale más callarse que hablar.
   Ru   Молчи–за умного сойдёшь.

21 *En*   Lip-honour costs little, yet may bring in much.
   Fr   Les belles paroles ont bien de force et coûtent peu.
   De   Ein gut Wort ist besser denn eine grosse Gabe.
   It   Buone parole valgono tanto e costano poco.
   El   Cortesía de boca mucho vale y poco cuesta.
   Ru   Доброе слово лучше мягкого пирога.

22 *En*   Kind words go a long way.
   Fr   Bonne parole bon lieu tient.
   De   Ein gutes Wort findet einen guten Ort.
   It   Le buone parole trovano buon luogo.
   El   El hablar bien no cuesta dinero.
   Ru   Доброе слово не пропадает даром.

23 *En*   Such answer as a man gives, such will he get.
   Fr   Telle demande, telle réponse.
   De   Wie die Frage, so die Antwort.
   It   Qual proposta, tal risposta.
   El   Cual pregunta harás, tal respuesta habrás.
   Ru   Каков вопрос, таков и ответ.

24 *En* The lame tongue gets nothing.
   Fr Qui ne veut parler, ne veut gagner.
   De Einem schweigenden Maul ist nicht zu helfen.
   It Chi non chiede, non ottiene.
   El Quien no habla, no le oye Dios.
   Ru Молчанием прав не будешь.

25 *En* Better the foot slip than the tongue.*
   Fr Il vaut mieux glisser du pied que de la langue.
   De Es ist besser mit dem Fusse auszugleiten als mit der Zunge.
   It È meglio sdrucciolar coi piedi che colla lingua.
   El Más daño hace una mala palabra que una mala patada.
   Ru Лучше споткнуться ногою, чем словом.

26 *En* An ox is taken by the horns, and a man by the tongue.
   Fr On prend les bêtes par les cornes et les hommes par les paroles.
   De Den Mann fasst man beim Wort, den Ochsen bei den Hörnern.
   It L'uomo per la parola e il bue per le corna.
   El Al buey por el cuerno, y al hombre por la palabra.
   Ru Быка берут за рога, а человека ловят на слове.

27 *En* The bird is known by his note, the man by his words.*
   Fr A la plume et au chant l'oiseau, et au parler le bon cerveau.
   De An der Rede erkennt man den Mann.
   It Al cantare l'uccello, al parlare il cervello.
   El El cántaro se conoce por el sueno, y el hombre por el verbo.
   Ru Видна птица по перьям, а человек по речам.

28 *En* Words cut (hurt) more than swords.*
   Fr Coup de langue est pire que coup de lance.

De   Wörter schneiden schärfer als Schwerter.

It   Cattive lingue tagliano più che spade.

El   Duras palabras más hieren que espada.

Ru Слово пуще стрелы разит.

29 *En* Fair words fill not the belly.*

     Fr   Le ventre ne se rassasie pas de paroles.

     De Von schönen Worten wird man nicht satt.

     It   Il ventre non si sazia di parole.

     El   Con palabras solas nadie pone olla.

     Ru Брюхо не насыщается словами.

30 *En* Fine words butter no parsnips.

     Fr   Les belles paroles ne font pas bouiller la marmite.

     De Schöne Worte machen den Kohl nicht fett.

     It   Le parole non empiono il corpo.

     El   Con buenos apellidos nadie ha comido.

     Ru Соловья баснями не кормят.

31 *En* A honey tongue, a heart of gall.*

     Fr   Langue de miel et cœur de fiel.

     De Honig auf der Zunge, Galle im Herzen.

     It   Volto di miele, cuor di fiele.

     El   Boca de miel, corazón de fiel.

     Ru На языке мёд, а в сердце лёд.

32 *En* Talk of the devil, and he is sure to appear.*

     Fr   Quand on parle du loup, on en voit la queue.

     De Wenn man den Wolf nennt, kommt er gerennt.

     It   Chi ha il lupo in bocca, l'ha sulla groppa.

     El   Háblate del lobo, y veréis su pelleja.

     Ru О волке речь, а он навстречь.

        Лёгок на помине.

33 *En* There is a time to speak, and a time to be silent. *(B)*
   Fr Il y a un temps pour parler, et un temps pour se taire.
   De Reden hat seine Zeit, und Schweigen hat seine Zeit.
   It Vi è tempo di parlare, e tempo di tacere.
   El Hay tiempos de hablar, y tiempos de callar.
   Ru Есть время говорить, и время молчать. *(Б)*

2 **Truth–Lie**
Vérité–Mensonge
Wahrheit–Lüge
Verità–Bugia
Verdad–Mentira
Правда–Ложь

1 *En* Truth and oil are ever above.
   Fr La vérité comme l'huile vient au dessus.
   De Wahrheit will an den Tag.
   It L'olio e la verità tornano alla sommità.
   El La verdad y el aceite nadan siempre encima.
   Ru Правда–елей: везде наверх всплывает.

2 *En* Truth needs not many words.*
   Fr Les paroles de la vérité sont simples.
   De Wahrheit gibt kurzen Bescheid.
   It La verità è senza varietà.
   El El lenguaje de la verdad es sencillo.
   Ru На правду немного слов надобно.

3 *En* Truth may be blamed, but cannot be shamed.*
   Fr La vérité est souvent éclipsée, mais jamais éteinte.
   De Die Wahrheit leidet wohl Not, aber nie den Tod.
   It La verità può languire, ma non perire.
   El Zozobra la verdad, mas nunca ahogada la verás.
   Ru Правда на огне не горит, на воде не тонет.

4 *En* Many a true word is spoken in jest.
   Fr On dit souvent la vérité en riant.
   De Im Scherz gesagt, im Ernst gemeint.

It	Burlando si dice il vero.
El	En broma se dice la verdad.
Ru	В каждой шутке есть доля правды.

5 *En* In wine there is truth.*
   Fr La vérité est dans le vin.
   De Im Wein ist Wahrheit.
   It La verità è nel vino.
   El En el vino está la verdad.
   Ru Вся правда в вине.

6 *En* Children and fools speak the truth.*
   Fr Enfants et fous disent la vérité.
   De Kinder und Narren sagen die Wahrheit.
   It I fanciulli e i pazzi dicono la verità.
   El Los niños y los locos dicen la verdad.
   Ru Глупый да малый правду говорят.

7 *En* Nothing hurts like the truth.
   Fr Il n'y a que la vérité qui offense.
   De Die Wahrheit ist eine bittere Pille.
   It Non c'è niente che offenda come la verità.
   El Las verdadas amargan.
   Ru Правда глаза колет.

8 *En* Truth finds foes, where it makes none.*
   Fr La vérité engendre la haine.
   De Wahrheit bringt Hass.
   It La verità genera odio.
   El Quien dice las verdades, pierde las amistades.
   Ru Правда ненависть родит.

9 *En* All truths are not to be told.*
   Fr Toute vérité n'est pas bonne à dire.

De   Es ist nicht immer klug, die Wahrheit zu sagen.

It   Ogni verità non è da dire.

El   No todas las verdades son para dichas.

Ru Не всякую правду сказывай.

10 *En* Follow not truth too near the heels, lest it dash out thy teeth.

     Fr Qui talonne la vérité trop près pourra avoir les dents brisés.

     De Mit der Wahrheit schlägt man den Leuten die Geige um den Kopf.

     It   Chi segue la verità troppo presso potrà aver gli denti spezzati.

     El Quien sigue la verdad muy cerquita, podrá haber los dientes quebrados.

     Ru За правдивую погудку смычком по рылу бьют.

11 *En* Lies have short legs.

     Fr Les mensonges ont les jambes courtes.

     De Lügen haben kurze Beine.

     It   Le bugie hanno le gambe corte.

     El La mentira tiene piernas cortas.

     Ru У лжи ноги коротки.

12 *En* Liars have need of good memories.*

     Fr Il faut qu'un menteur ait bonne mémoire.

     De Lügner müssen ein gutes Gedächtnis haben.

     It   Forza è tenga ben a mente, un bugiardo quando mente.

     El Al mentiroso conviene ser memorioso.

     Ru Лживому надо памятным быть.

13 *En* Great talkers are great liars.

     Fr Grand parleur, grand menteur.

     De Wer viel redet, lügt viel.

It Gran parlatore, gran mentitore.
El Hablar mucho sin mentir, nunca lo ví.
Ru Большой болтун–большой лгун.

14 *En* A liar is not believed when he speaks the truth.*
    Fr Un menteur n'est point écouté, même en disant la vérité.
    De Wer einmal lügt, dem glaubt man nicht, und wenn er
         auch die Wahrheit spricht.
    It Al bugiardo non è creduto il vero.
    El En boca del mentiroso lo cierto se halla dudoso.
    Ru Кто солжёт раз, тому больше не поверят.

15 *En* One lie makes many.
    Fr Un mensonge en entraîne un autre.
    De Eine Lüge schleppt zehn andere nach sich.
    It Una bugia ne fa cento.
    El De una mentira nacen ciento.
    Ru Ложь ложью погоняет.

16 *En* Murder will out (cannot be hid).
    Fr Tout finit par se savoir.
    De Die Sonne bringt es an den Tag.
    It La verità vien sempre a galla.
    El Todo termina por saberse.
    Ru Шила в мешке не утаишь.

17 *En* A traveller may lie with authority.*
    Fr A beau mentir qui vient de loin.
    De Aus der Fern' lügt man gern.
    It Egli ha bel dir bugie chi vien da lontano.
    El De luengas vías luengas mentiras.
    Ru Тому врать легко, кто был далеко.

18 *En* Lying and thieving go together.*
    Fr Les voleurs sont des menteurs.

De Wer lügt, der stiehlt.

It Chi è bugiardo, è ladro.

El El mentiroso es hurtadoso.

Ru Кто лжёт, тот и крадёт.

19 *En* It is true that all men say.

    Fr Il faut bien qu'il soit vrai ce que tout le monde dit.

    De Um nichts munkelt man nicht.

    It Bisogna che sia vero quel che tutti dicono.

    El Es menester que sea verdadero lo que cada uno dice.

    Ru Что люди говорят, то и правда.

20 *En* Common fame is seldom to blame.*

    Fr Le cri public sert quelquefois de preuve, ou du moins fortifie la preuve.

    De Allgemeiner Ruf ist selten grundlos.

    It Non si dice mai tanto una cosa, che non ne sia qualche cosa.

    El Lo que todos dicen, o es, o quiere ser.

    Ru Народ недаром говорит.

21 *En* Paper won't blush.*

    Fr Le papier souffre tout.

    De Papier ist geduldig.

    It La carta non diventa rossa.

    El El papel todo lo aguanta.

    Ru Бумага всё терпит.

3 Honesty–Dishonesty
Honnêteté–Malhonnêteté
Ehrlichkeit–Unehrlichkeit
Probità–Improbità
Honestidad–Deshonestidad
Честность–Нечестность

1   *En* Honesty is the best policy.
    Fr Avec l'honnêteté on va le plus loin.
    De Ehrlich währt am längsten.
    It Onestà è la miglior moneta.
    El La honradez es el mejor capital.
    Ru Честный путь–лучший путь.

2   *En* A good name is better than riches.*
    Fr Mieux vaut bonne renommée que grandes richesses.
    De Ein guter Name ist besser als Silber und Gold.
    It E meglio il buon nome che tutte le ricchezze del mondo.
    El Más vale buena fama que oro ni plata.
    Ru Добрая слава дороже богатства.

3   *En* A good conscience is a soft pillow.
    Fr Une bonne conscience est un doux oreiller.
    De Ein gutes Gewissen ist ein sanftes Ruhekissen.
    It Una buona coscienza è un buon guanciale.
    El Una buena conciencia es una suave almohada.
    Ru У кого совесть чиста, у того подушка под головой не вертится.

4   *En* A guilty conscience needs no accuser.
    Fr Pécheur a toujours peur.

De Der Schuldige verrät sich selbst.
It Al ladro fa paura anche un sorcio.
El Al que mal vive, el miedo le sigue.
Ru На воре шапка горит.
    Злая совесть стоит палача.

5 *En* Do right and have well.*
  Fr Fais ce que dois, advienne que pourra!
  De Tue recht und scheue niemand.
  It Fa il dovere e non temere.
  El Haz bien sin mirar a quien.
  Ru За правое дело стой смело.

6 *En* Better go to heaven in rags than to hell in embroidery.
  Fr Il vaut mieux vivre pauvre que injuste et dans les honneurs.
  De Besser arm in Ehren als reich in Schanden.
  It È meglio povertà onorata che ricchezza svergognata.
  El Comer arena antes que hacer vileza.
  Ru Лучше убожество с добром, нежели богатство с грехом.

7 *En* Evil-gotten goods (gains) never prosper.*
  Fr Bien mal acquis ne profite jamais.
  De Unrecht Gut gedeihet nicht.
  It I beni mal acquistati non arricchiscono.
  El Bien mal adquirido a nadie ha enriquecido.
  Ru Неправдой нажитое впрок не идёт.

8 *En* What is got over the devil's back is spent under his belly.*
  Fr Ce qui vient du diable retourne au diable.
  De Böser Gewinn fährt bald dahin.
  It Roba mal acquistata non dura un'annata.
  El Quien lleva lo ajeno, en la calle le dejan sin ello.
  Ru Пришло махом–ушло прахом.

9 *En* Opportunity makes the thief.*
   Fr L'occasion fait le larron.
   De Gelegenheit macht Diebe.
   It L'occasione fa l'uomo ladro.
   El La ocasión hace el ladrón.
   Ru Плохо не клади, вора в грех не вводи.

10 *En* An open door may tempt a saint.
    Fr Un coffre ouvert fait pécher le juste même.
    De Offene Tür verführt auch den Heiligen.
    It A porta aperta anche il giusto vi pecca.
    El Puerta abierta al santo tienta.
    Ru Открытая дверь может соблазнить и святого.

11 *En* To a crafty man a crafty and a half.*
    Fr A malin, malin et demi.
    De Auf einen Schelmen anderthalbe.
    It A un furbo, un furbo e mezzo.
    El A ruin, ruin y medio.
    Ru Наскочил плут на тройного плута.

12 *En* Set a thief to catch a thief.
    Fr A voleur, voleur et demi.
    De Den Fuchs muss man mit Füchsen fangen.
    It Con la volpe convien volpeggiare.
    El A pillo, pillo y medio.
    Ru Вор у вора дубинку украл.

13 *En* The receiver is as bad as the thief.*
    Fr Le receleur ne vaut pas mieux que le voleur.
    De Der Hehler ist nicht besser als der Stehler.
    It Tanto è ladro chi ruba, che chi tiene il sacco.
    El No hay ladrón sin encubridor.
    Ru Утайщик–тот же вор.

14 *En* Ill doers are ill deemers (dreaders).
   Fr Le larron pense que tous soient de sa condition.
   De Der Dieb meint, es stehlen alle.
   It Pensa il ladrone che tutti siano di sua condizione.
   El Piensa el ladrón que todos son de su condición.
   Ru Вор думает, что все на свете воры.

15 *En* When thieves fall out honest men come to their own.
   Fr Quand les larrons se battent, les larcins se découvrent.
   De Wenn Diebe sich zanken, bekommen ehrliche Leute das Ihrige.
   It Quando i ladri contrastanno, gli uomini da bene riscuoteranno lor beni.
   El Pelean los ladrones y descúbrense los hurtos.
   Ru Два вора дерутся–честному польза.

16 *En* Once a knave, and ever a knave.
   Fr Une fois coquin, et toujours coquin.
   De Wer einmal stiehlt, bleibt immer ein Dieb.
   It Una volta forfante, e sempre forfante.
   El El que roba una vez, ladrón es.
   Ru Раз украл–навек вором стал.

17 *En* He that will steal an egg will steal an ox.
   Fr Qui vole un œuf vole un bœuf.
   De Wer nur erst die Kälber stiehlt, der stiehlt auch bald die Kühe.
   It Chi ruba una spilla, ruba una libbra.
   El Ladroncillo de agujeta después sube a barjuleta.
   Ru Кто украдёт яйцо, украдёт и быка.

18 *En* Little thieves are hanged, but great ones escape.*
   Fr On pend les petits voleurs et on laisse courir les grands.
   De Kleine Diebe hängt man, grosse lässt man laufen.

It   I ladroncelli s'appiccano, non i ladri.

El   Para los desgraciados se hizo la horca.

Ru Что сходит с рук ворам, за то воришек бьют.

19 *En* Great thieves hang little ones.

Fr   Les gros larrons pendent les petits.

De   Grosse Diebe hängen die kleinen.

It   I ladri grandi fanno impiccare i piccoli.

El   Los grandes ladrones ahorcan a los menores.

Ru Большой вор малого воришку вешает.

20 *En* He is a thief indeed that robs a thief.*

Fr   Il est bien larron qui un larron dérobe.

De   Bei einem Dieb ist nicht gut stehlen.

It   In casa di ladri non ci si ruba.

El   Al cuco no cuques, y al ladrón no hurtes.

Ru У вора воровать–только время терять.

21 *En* He hath a conscience like a cheverel's skin.

Fr   Il a la conscience large comme la manche d'un cordelier.

De   Mancher hat ein breites Gewissen wie ein Franziskanerärmel.

It   Ha la coscienza come una nave di sughero.

El   Tiene la manga demasiado ancha.

Ru У него совесть–мешок: что хочешь, положи.

22 *En* Better known than trusted.

Fr   Il est connu comme le loup blanc.

De   Er ist bekannt wie ein bunter Hund.

It   È più conosciuto che la bettonica.

El   Es más conocido que la ruda.

Ru Все его знают, как серого волка.

23 *En* The biter bit.

Fr   Le trompeur trompé.

De Der betrogene Betrüger.

It Il truffatore truffato.

El El engañador engañado.

Ru Попался, который кусался.

24 *En* The fox preys farthest from home.

    Fr Un bon renard ne mange point les poules de son voisin.

    De Wo der Fuchs sein Lager hat, da raubt er nicht.

    It La volpe in vicinato non fa mai danno.

    El Cuando el lobo va a hurtar, lejos de casa va a cazar.

    Ru Близ норы лиса на промыслы не ходит.

25 *En* Forbidden fruit is sweet.

    Fr Les fruits défendus sont les plus doux.

    De Verbotene Frucht schmeckt süss.

    It Frutto proibito, più saporito.

    El Fruto vedado, el más deseado.

    Ru Запретный плод сладок.

26 *En* To fish in troubled waters.*

    Fr Pêcher en eau trouble.

    De Im trüben fischen.

    It Pescare nel torbido.

    El Pescar en río revuelto.

    Ru Ловить рыбу в мутной воде.

4 **Shadow and Substance**
Apparence et Fond
Schein und Wesen
Apparenza e Realtà
Apariencias y Realidad
Видимость и сущность

1 *En* Appearances are deceitful.*
  Fr Les apparences sont trompeuses.
  De Der Schein trügt.
  It L'Apparenza inganna.
  El Las apariencias engañan.
  Ru Наружный вид обманчив.

2 *En* All is not gold that glitters.*
  Fr Tout ce qui reluit n'est pas or.
  De Es ist nicht alles Gold, was glänzt.
  It Non è oro tutto quel che luce.
  El No es oro todo lo que reluce.
  Ru Не всё то золото, что блестит.

3 *En* Fair without, foul within.
  Fr Souvent la plus belle pomme est véreuse.
  De Von aussen fix und innen nix.
  It Bella in vista, dentro trista.
  El La apariencia hermosa, y por dentro es otra cosa.
  Ru Снаружи мило, а внутри гнило.

4 *En* The cowl does not make the monk.*
  Fr L'habit ne fait pas le moine.

De   Die Kutte macht nicht den Mönch.
It   L'abito non fa il monaco.
El   El hábito no hace al monje.
Ru   Не всяк монах, на ком клобук.

5   En   All are not hunters that blow the horn.*
    Fr   Ne sont pas tous chasseurs qui sonnent du cor.
    De   Es sint nicht alle Jäger, die das Horn blasen.
    It   Non tutti sono cacciatori quelli che suonano il corno.
    El   El cazar, en más que tocar el cuerno ha de estribar.
    Ru   Не все те повара, у кого ножи длинные.

6   En   All are not saints that go to church.
    Fr   Tous ne sont pas saints qui vont à l'église.
    De   Es sind nicht alle Heilige, die in die Kirche gehen.
    It   Non son tutti santi quelli che vanno in chiesa.
    El   Todos los que estudian no son letrados.
    Ru   Не всяк праведник, кто ходит в церковь.

7   En   It is not the beard that makes the philosopher.*
    Fr   La barbe ne fait pas le philosophe.
    De   Nicht jeder, der einen Bart trägt, ist ein Philosoph.
    It   La barba non fa il filosofo.
    El   Seda y raso no dan estado.
    Ru   Мудрость в голове, а не в бороде.

8   En   Still waters run deep.
    Fr   Il n'est pas pire eau que l'eau qui dort.
    De   Stille Wasser gründen tief.
    It   Acqua cheta rompe i ponti.
    El   Agua que corre silenciosa, agua peligrosa.
    Ru   Тихая вода берега подмывает.
         В тихом омуте черти водятся.

9   *En*   Barking dogs seldom bite.*
    Fr   Chien qui aboie ne mord pas.
    De   Ein Hund, der bellt, beisst nicht.
    It   Can che abbaia, non morde.
    El   Perro que ladra, no muerde.
    Ru   Не всякая собака кусает, которая лает.

10 *En*   A creaking door hangs long on its hinges.*
    Fr   Les pots fêlés durent longtemps.
    De   Die knarrigen Karren gehen am längsten.
          Gesprungene Töpfe halten am längsten.
    It   Dura più un carro rotto che uno nuovo.
    El   Carro que canta a su dueño avanza.
          No cae todo lo que bambolea.
    Ru   Битая посуда два века живёт.
          Скрипучее дерево дольше стоит.

11 *En*   The garment makes the man.*
    Fr   L'habit fait l'homme.
    De   Kleider machen Leute.
    It   L'abito fa l'uomo.
          I vestimenti fanno onore.
    El   Según te verán, así te tratarán.
    Ru   По одёжке встречают (а по уму провожают).

12 *En*   An ape's an ape, a varlet's a varlet, though they be clad
          in silk or scarlet.*
    Fr   Le singe est toujours singe, et fût-il déguisé en prince.
    De   Affen bleiben Affen, wenn man sie auch in Sammet kleidet.
    It   La scimmia è sempre scimmia, anco vestita di seta.
    El   Aunque la mona se vista de seda, mona se queda.
    Ru   Чёрт во что ни нарядится, всё чёртом останется.

13 *En*   There are more men threatened than stricken.
    Fr   Qui menace son ennemi, combattre ne veut contre lui.

De Wer lange droht, macht dich nicht tot.
It Molte minacce non ammazzano la gente.
El Mas son los amenazados que los heridos.
Ru Кто много грозит, тот мало вредит.

14 *En* You cackle often, but never lay an egg.
   Fr Brebis qui bêle a moins de lait.
   De Hühner, die viel gackern, legen keine Eier.
   It Gallina che schiamazza non fa uova.
   El Gallina que mucho canta, pocos huevos pone.
   Ru Много кудахтанья, да яиц нет.

15 *En* Handsome is that handsome does.
   Fr Beau est qui bien fait.
      Beauté sans bonté ne vaut pas un dé.
   De Adel sitzt im Gemüt, nicht im Geblüt.
   It Bello è chi bello fa.
   El El varón es quien ennoblece.
   Ru Не тот пригож, кто лицом хорош, а кто на деле гож.

16 *En* Dress up a stick, and it does not appear to be a stick.
   Fr Habillez un bâton, il aura l'air d'un baron.
   De Ein schöner Rock ziert den Stock.
   It Se vesti una colonna, ella pare una donna.
   El Palo compuesto no parece palo.
      Afeita un cepo, parecerá mancebo.
   Ru Наряди пень в вешний день, и тот будет красив.

17 *En* He that cannot beat the horse, beats the saddle.*
   Fr Qui ne peut battre le cheval, bat la selle.
   De Auf den Sack schlägt man, den Esel meint man.
   It Chi non può battere il cavallo, batte la sella.
   El Quien no puede dar en el asno, da en la albarda.
   Ru Кошку бьют, а невестке наветки дают.

18 *En* Many kiss the child for the nurse's sake.
 Fr Pour l'amour du chevalier baise la dame l'écuyer.
 De Man küsst das Kind oft um der Mutter willen.
 It Si bacia il fanciullo a cagion della madre.
 El Por la madre se besa al infante.
 Ru Дитятко за ручку, а матку за сердечко.

5 **Falsehood–Hypocrisy**
Fausseté–Hypocrisie
Falschheit–Heuchelei
Falsità–Ipocrisia
Falsedad–Hipocresía
Ложность–Лицемерие

1 *En* The cross on the breast, and the devil in the heart.
   Fr Habit de béat a souvent ongles de chat.
   De Worte eines Heiligen, Klauen einer Katze.
   It Parole di santo e unghie di gatto.
   El La cruz en los pechos, y el diablo en los hechos.
   Ru Борода апостольская, а усок дьявольский.

2 *En* A snake in the grass.*
   Fr Le serpent est caché sous les fleurs.
   De Die Schlange lauert im Grase.
   It Il serpe tra' fiori e l'erba giace.
   El La serpiente se oculta en la yerba.
   Ru Таится змея в траве.

3 *En* Snake (Viper) in the bosom.
   Fr Nourrir un serpent dans son sein.
   De Eine Schlange am Busen nähren.
   It Allevarsi la serpe in seno.
   El Dar de comer al diablo.
   Ru Выкормить змею на своей груди.

4 *En* He has brought up a crow to pick out his own eyes.
   Fr Nourris un corbeau, il te crèvera les yeux.

De	Erziehst du dir einen Raben, wird er dir die Augen ausgraben.
It	Nutrisci il corvo, alla fin ti caverà gli occhi.
El	Cría el cuervo, y sacarte ha el ojo.
Ru	Вскорми ворона–он тебе очи выклюет.

5
En	Beware of false prophets. *(B)*
Fr	Gardez-vous des faux prophètes.
De	Hütet euch vor den falschen Propheten.
It	Guardatevi da' falsi profeti.
El	Guardaos de los falsos profetas.
Ru	Берегитесь лжепророков. *(Б)*

6
En	A wolf in sheep's clothing.
Fr	Le loup qui s'est fait agneau.
De	Ein Wolf im Schafspelz.
It	Lupo in pelle d'agnello.
El	Un lobo con piel de oveja.
Ru	Волк в овечьей шкуре.

7
En	He covers me with his wings and bites me with his bill.*
Fr	Gardez-vous des gens qui font patte de velours.
De	Hüte dich vor den Katzen, die vorne lecken und hinten kratzen.
It	Dio ti guardi da quella gatta che davanti ti lecca e di dietro ti graffia.
El	Reniega del amigo que cubre con sus alas y muerde con su pico.
Ru	Спереди ноги лижет, а сзади за пятки хватает.

8
En	Many kiss the hand they wish cut off.*
Fr	Tel pied baise-t-on qu'on voudrait qu'il fût coupé.
De	Viele küssen die Hände, die sie abgehauen zu sehen wünschten.

It   Tal mano si bacia che si vorrebbe veder tagliata.
El   Muchos besan los manos que querrían ver cortadas.
Ru Руки лижет, а зубы на оскале.

9 *En* When the fox preacheth, then beware your geese.
   Fr   Quand le renard se met à prêcher, gare aux poules.
   De Wenn der Fuchs predigt, hüte die Gänse.
   It   Quando la volpe predica, guardatevi galline.
   El   Cuando la zorra predica, no están seguros los pollos.
   Ru Когда лиса читает проповеди, загоняй своих гусей.

10 *En* To run with the hare and hunt with the hounds.
    Fr   Nager entre deux eaux.
    De Auf beiden Achseln tragen.
    It   Tener l'orto salvo e la capra sazia.
    El   Nadar entre dos aguas.
    Ru Служить и нашим и вашим.

6 **Work–Industry–Idleness**
Travail–Assiduité–Paresse
Arbeit–Fleiss–Faulheit
Lavoro–Assiduità–Pigrizia
Trabajo–Diligencia–Pereza
Труд–Усердие–Леность

1 *En* As the work, so the pay.*
   Fr Tel travail, tel salaire.
   De Wie die Arbeit, so der Lohn.
   It Quale il lavoro, tale il salario.
   El A tal trabajo, tal salario.
   Ru Какова работа, такова и плата.

2 *En* As you sow, you shall mow.*
   Fr Comme tu auras semé, tu moissonneras.
   De Wie die Saat, so die Ernte.
   It Ognuno raccoglie quel che ha seminato.
   El Según siembras, así recogerás.
   Ru Что посеешь, то и пожнёшь.

3 *En* You must sow ere you reap.
   Fr Il faut semer pour recueillir.
   De Wer nicht sät, wird auch nicht ernten.
   It Chi non semina, non raccoglie.
   El Quien no siembra, no coge.
   Ru Не посеяв, не жнут.

4 *En* No pains, no gains.*
   Fr Nul bien sans peine.
   De Ohne Fleiss kein Preis.

It Ogni agio porta seco il suo disagio.
El No hay atajo sin trabajo.
Ru Без труда нет плода.

5 *En* Many hands make light work.*
   Fr A plusieurs mains l'ouvrage avance.
   De Viele Hände machen bald ein Ende.
   It Molte mani fanno l'opera leggiera.
   El Muchas bocas vacian el platón.
   Ru Когда рук много, работа спорится.

6 *En* Strike while the iron is hot.*
   Fr Il faut battre le fer pendant qu'il est chaud.
   De Man muss das Eisen schmieden, solange es heiss ist.
   It Batti il ferro quando è caldo.
   El Al hierro caliente, batir de repente.
   Ru Куй железо, пока горячо.

7 *En* Make hay while the sun shines.
   Fr Récolter le blé quand il est mûr.
   De Man muss Heu machen, während die Sonne scheint.
   It Bisogna macinare fin che piove.
   El Mientras hace calor, se pelan los árboles.
   Ru Коси, коса, пока роса.

8 *En* The morning hour has gold in its mouth.*
   Fr L'aurore est l'amie des Muses.
   De Morgenstunde hat Gold im Munde.
   It L'aurora ha l'oro in bocca.
   El A quien madruga, Dios le ayuda.
   Ru Утренний час дарит золотом нас.

9 *En* The early bird catches the worm.
   Fr Heure du matin, heure du gain.

De   Morgenrot schafft Brot.
It   L'uccello mattiniero si becca il verme.
El   Los asuntos importantes–para mañana.
Ru   Ранняя птичка носок прочищает.

10   *En*   After the work is done, repose is sweet.*
     Fr   Après besogne faite le repos est doux.
     De   Nach getaner Arbeit ist gut ruhen.
     It   Dopo il lavoro è dolce il riposo.
     El   El trabajo es padre del descanso.
     Ru   Кончил дело–гуляй смело.

11   *En*   Never put off till tomorrow what may be done today.
     Fr   Ce qu'aujourd'hui tu peux faire, au lendemain ne diffère.
     De   Was du heute kannst besorgen, das verschiebe nicht auf
           morgen.
     It   Non rimandare a domani quel che puoi far oggi.
     El   No dejes para mañana lo que puedes hacer hoy.
     Ru   Не откладывай на завтра то, что можешь сделать сегодня.

12   *En*   By the work one knows the workman.*
     Fr   A l'œuvre on connaît l'artisan.
     De   Am Werke erkennt man den Meister.
     It   All'opera si conosce il maestro.
     El   El obrero se conoce por el trabajo.
     Ru   По работе и мастера знать.

13   *En*   The work shows the workman.*
     Fr   L'œuvre l'ouvrier découvre.
     De   Das Werk lobt den Meister.
     It   L'opera loda il maestro.
     El   La buena obra al maestro honra.
     Ru   Всякая работа мастера хвалит.
           Дело мастера боится.

14 *En* A bad workman quarrels with his tools.
    Fr Mauvais ouvrier ne trouve jamais bon outil.
    De Schlechter Arbeiter wird nie gutes Gerät finden.
    It Ai cattivi marinari tutti i venti sono contrari.
    El Lavandera mala no encuentra jamás buena piedra.
    Ru У плохого мастера и пила плохая.

15 *En* A cat in gloves catches no mice.
    Fr Jamais chat emmitouflé ne prit souris.
    De Die Katze fängt die Mäuse nicht in Handschuhen.
    It Gatta inguantata non piglia mai sorci.
    El Gato con guantes no coge ratón.
    Ru Без труда не вытащишь и рыбки из пруда.

16 *En* The sleeping fox catches no poultry.
    Fr A renard endormi rien ne tombe dans la gueule.
    De Ein schlafender Fuchs fängt kein Huhn.
    It Volpe che dorme, vive sempre magra.
    El A la vulpeja dormida no le cae nada en la boca.
    Ru Лёжа пищи не добудешь.

17 *En* By doing nothing we learn to do ill.
    Fr Qui ne fait rien, fait mal.
    De Nichtstun lehrt Übles tun.
    It Niente facendo s'impara a far male.
    El Si nada haces, mal haces.
    Ru Праздный на грех натолкнётся.

18 *En* An idle brain is the devil's shop.
    Fr Une tête oisive est l'atelier du diable.
    De Müssiggang ist des Teufels Ruhebank.
    It Un uomo ozioso è il capezzale del diavolo.
    El Un hombre ocioso es la oreja del diablo.
    Ru Праздный мозг–мастерская дьявола.

19 *En* Idleness is the root (mother) of all evil.*
   Fr L'oisiveté est la mère de tous les vices.
   De Müssiggang ist aller Laster Anfang.
   It L'ozio è il padre di tutti i vizi.
   El La ociosidad es madre de los vicios.
   Ru Праздность–мать всех пороков.

20 *En* Idleness is the key of beggary.*
   Fr Le paresseux est le frère du mendiant.
   De Faulheit ist der Schlüssel zur Armut.
   It La pigrizia è la chiave della povertà.
   El El perezoso siempre es menesteroso.
   Ru Леность наводит на бедность.

21 *En* He that will not work shall not eat. *(B)*
   Fr Celui qui ne veut pas travailler ne doit pas manger.
   De Wer nicht arbeitet, soll auch nicht essen.
   It Chi non lavora, non mangia.
   El El que no trabaja, no come.
   Ru Кто не работает, тот не ест. *(Б)*

22 *En* If you want a thing well done, do it yourself.
   Fr On n'est jamais si bien servi que par soi-même.
   De Selbst getan ist gut (bald) getan.
   It Chi fa da sè, fa per tre.
   El Si quieres ser bien servido, sírvete a ti mismo.
   Ru Всякий сам себе лучший слуга.

23 *En* If thou thyself canst do it, attend no other's help or hand.*
   Fr De ce que tu pourras faire, jamais n'attends à autrui.
   De Mit dem, was du selbst tun kannst, bemühe nie andere.
   It Quel che tu stesso puoi fare, che altri il faccia mai non
         aspettare.
   El A lo que puedes hacer solo, no esperes a otro.
   Ru Непочто гонца, где рукой подать до конца.

24 *En* The cat would eat fish and would not wet her feet.*

   Fr Le chat aime le poisson, mais il n'aime pas à mouiller la patte.

   De Die Katze frisst gern Fische, sie will aber nicht ins Wasser.

   It La gatta vorrebbe mangiar pesci, ma non pescare.

   El Peces qiuere la gata, mas no entrar en el agua.

   Ru Лакома кошка до рыбки, да в воду лезть не хочется.

25 *En* He thinks that roasted larks will fall into his mouth.*

   Fr Il attend que les alouettes lui tombent toutes rôties.

   De Tauben fliegen einem nicht gebraten ins Maul.

   It A nessuno piovono le lasagne in bocca.

   El Al raposo durmiente no le amanece la gallina en el vientre.

   Ru Печёные голубки не прилетят до губки.

26 *En* Omelets are not made without breaking of eggs.

   Fr On ne peut pas faire des omelettes sans casser les œufs.

   De Wer Eierkuchen will, muss Eier einschlagen.

   It Non si fanno frittate senza rompere le uova.

   El No se hacen tortillas sin huevos.

   Ru Не разбивши яиц, не сделаешь яичницы.

27 *En* To take the chestnuts out of the fire with the cat's paw.

   Fr Tirer les marrons du feu avec la patte du chat.

   De Es ist leicht, mit Katzenpfoten die Kastanien aus dem Feuer zu holen.

   It Cavar la bruciata col zampino del gatto.

   El Con ajena mano sacar la culebra del horado.

   Ru Чужими руками жар загребать.

14 6817

7 Business and Trade
Commerce–Métier
Handel und Gewerbe
Commercio–Mestiere
Comercio–Arte
Торговля–Ремесло

1 *En* Business is business.
   Fr Les affaires sont les affaires.
   De Geschäft ist Geschäft.
   It Gli affari sono affari.
   El El negocio es el negocio.
   Ru Честь честью, а дело делом.

2 *En* Good wine needs no bush.*
   Fr A bon vin il ne faut point d'enseigne.
   De Guter Wein bedarf keines Kranzes.
   It Il buon vino non ha bisogno di frasca.
   El Vino que es bueno, no ha menester pregonero.
   Ru Хороший товар сам себя хвалит.

3 *En* Good ware makes quick markets.*
   Fr La bonne marchandise se recommande elle-même.
   De Gute Ware braucht man nicht anzupreisen.
   It La buona mercanzia trova presto recapito.
   El El buen paño en el arca se vende.
   Ru На хороший товар и купцов много.

4 *En* Every pedlar praises his needles.
   Fr Chacon mercier prise ses aiguilles et son panier.
   De Jeder Krämer lobt seine Ware.

34

It	Ogni mercante loda la sua mercanzia.
El	Cada buhonero alaba sus agujas.
Ru	Всякий купец свой товар хвалит.

5
En	Every cook praises his own broth.
Fr	Chacun loue son œuvre.
De	Jeder lobt das Seine.
It	Ognun parla ben del suo mestiere.
El	Cada ollero su olla alaba.
Ru	Всякий кулик своё болото хвалит.

6
En	An handful of trade is an handful of gold.*
Fr	Un métier est un fond assuré.
De	Handwerk hat einen goldenen Boden.
It	Chi ha un mestiere in man, dappertutto trova pan.
El	El oficial tiene oficio y ál.
Ru	Ремесло–золотой кормилец.

7
En	He who has an art has everywhere a part.
Fr	Tout métier fait vivre son maître.
	Qui art a, partout part a.
De	Jegliches Handwerk nährt seinen Mann.
It	Chi ha un'arte, ha digià una parte.
El	Quien tiene arte, va por toda parte.
Ru	Ремеслу везде почёт.
	С ремеслом не пропадёшь.

8
En	Trade is the mother of money.
Fr	Qui a métier a pain (a rente).
De	Mit einem Handwerk kommt man weiter als mit tausend Gulden.
It	Tutti i mestieri danno il pane.
El	Quien ha oficio, ha beneficio.
Ru	Не просит ремесло хлеба, а само кормит.

9   *En*   A man of many trades begs his bread on Sunday.*
              Jack of all trades is of no trade.

      Fr   Douze métiers, quatorze malheurs.

      De   Wer viele Handwerke kann, wird zuletzt ein Bettelmann.
              Vierzehn Handwerke, fünfzehn Unglücke.

      It   Quattordici mestieri, quindici infortuni.

      El   Hombre de siete oficios, hombre sin oficio.

      Ru   За всё браться, ничего не сделать.

10   *En*   A good bargain is a pick-purse.

      Fr   Bon marché tire argent de bourse.

      De   Wohlfeile Ware leert den Beutel.

      It   Buon mercato sfonda la borsa.

      El   Lo que mucho vale, mucho cuesta.

      Ru   Дёшево, да гнило, дорого, да мило.

11   *En*   Good cheap is dear.

      Fr   Le bon marché coûte cher.

      De   Das Billigste ist immer das Teuerste.

      It   Buon mercato diventa qualche volta caro.

      El   Lo barato es caro.

      Ru   Где дёшево, там и дорого.

12   *En*   He that buys what he does not want, must often sell
              what he does want.

      Fr   Qui achète ce qu'il ne peut, vend après ce qu'il ne veut.

      De   Wer Unnötiges kauft, wird bald Notwendiges verkaufen.

      It   Chi compra il superfluo, venderà il necessario.

      El   Quien compra lo que no puede, vende lo que le duele.

      Ru   Купишь лишнее–продашь нужное.

13   *En*   Change is no robbery.

      Fr   Change n'est pas vol.

      De   Tausch ist kein Raub.

It Cambio non è furto.
El Trueque no es robo.
Ru Обмен не обман.

14 *En* To buy a pig in a poke.
    Fr Acheter chat en poche.
    De Die Katze im Sack kaufen.
    It Comprar la gatta nel sacco.
    El Comprar gato en saco.
    Ru Купить кота в мешке.

8 **Knowledge–Experience**
   Science–Expérience
   Wissen–Erfahrung
   Scienza–Esperienza
   Ciencia–Experiencia
   Знание–Опыт

1 *En* Knowledge is power.*
   Fr Savoir, c'est pouvoir.
   De Wissen ist Macht.
   It Intendere è potere.
   El Saber es poder.
   Ru Знание–сила.

2 *En* Know thyself.*
   Fr Connais-toi toi-même.
   De Erkenne dich selbst.
   It Conosci te stesso.
   El Conócete ti mismo.
   Ru Познай самого себя.

3 *En* Live and learn.*
   Fr On s'instruit à tout âge.
   De Man lernt, solange man lebt.
   It Si impara tanto, quanto si vive.
   El Todos los días se aprende algo.
   Ru Век живи, век учись.

4 *En* Never too old (late) to learn.*
   Fr On n'est jamais trop vieux pour apprendre.
   De Zum Lernen ist niemand zu alt.

It   Non si è mai vecchio per imparare.
El   Nunca es tarde para aprender.
Ru   Учиться никогда не поздно.

5   *En*   Experience is the mother of knowledge.*
      Fr   Expérience est mère de science.
      De   Erfahrung ist die beste Lehrmeisterin.
      It   L'esperienza è ottima maestra.
      El   La experiencia es madre de la ciencia.
      Ru   Опыт–лучший учитель.

6   *En*   Practice makes perfect.*
      Fr   Usage rend maître.
      De   Übung macht den Meister.
      It   L'esercizio è buon maestro.
      El   El ejercicio hace maestro.
      Ru   Навык мастера ставит.

7   *En*   Years know more than books.
      Fr   Les années en savent plus que les livres.
      De   Jahre lehren mehr als Bücher.
      It   Molto più fanno gli anni che i libri.
      El   Los libros no enseñan mucho: los años dan experiencia.
      Ru   Поживи подольше, узнаешь побольше.

8   *En*   One learns in teaching.*
      Fr   En enseignant, on apprend.
      De   Durch Lehren lernt man.
      It   Chi altri insegna, se stesso ammaestra.
      El   Enseñando aprendemos.
      Ru   Учи других–и сам поймёшь.

9   *En*   He that travels far knows much.
      Fr   On s'instruit en voyageant.

De	Weite Reise macht weise.
It	Viaggiando s'impara.
El	Viajando se instruye la gente.
Ru	Чужая сторона прибавит и ума.

10	*En*	He that nothing questioneth nothing learneth.
	Fr	Qui demande, apprend.
	De	Durch Fragen wird man klug.
	It	Quando non sai, frequenta in domandare.
	El	Quien pregunta, más sabe que duda.
	Ru	Спрос всё укажет.

11	*En*	He that knows nothing doubts nothing.*
	Fr	Qui rien ne sait, de rien ne doute.
	De	Mit dem Wissen wächst der Zweifel.
	It	Il dubbio è padre del sapere.
	El	Quien no duda, no acierta en cosa alguna.
	Ru	Сомнение–мать учения.

12	*En*	Whoso learneth young forgets not when he is old.
	Fr	Ce qu'on apprend au berceau, dure jusqu'au tombeau.
	De	Am längsten behält man, was man in der Jugend gelernt hat.
	It	Quel che si impara in gioventù, non si dimentica mai più.
	El	Lo que se aprende en la cuna, siempre dura.
	Ru	Чему научишься в молодости, то знаешь и в старости.

13	*En*	No man is his craft's master the first day.*
	Fr	On ne naît pas savant.
	De	Es fällt kein Meister von Himmel.
	It	Nessuno nasce maestro.
	El	Nadie nace sabiendo.
	Ru	С мастерством люди не родятся.

14 *En* Mistakes are often the best teachers.*
   Fr C'est en faisant des fautes qu'on apprend.
   De Aus den Fehlern lernt man.
   It Sbagliando s'impara.
   El El errar es maestro del acertar.
   Ru На ошибках мы учимся.

9 **Time–Weather**
Temps
Zeit–Wetter
Tempo
Tiempo
Время–Погода

1 *En* Everthing hath its time.*
  Fr Chaque chose à son temps.
  De Jedes Ding hat seine Zeit.
  It Ogni cosa ha il suo tempo.
  El Cada cosa en su tiempo.
  Ru Всякой вещи своё время.

2 *En* Time is money.
  Fr Le temps, c'est de l'argent.
  De Zeit ist Geld.
  It Il tempo è denaro.
  El El tiempo es dinero.
  Ru Время–деньги.

3 *En* Time flies.*
  Fr Le temps fuit.
  De Die Zeit hat Flügel.
  It Il tempo fugge.
  El El tiempo vuela.
  Ru Время летит.

4 *En* Time and tide wait for no man.
  Fr Le temps et la marée n'attendent personne.
  De Zeit, Ebbe und Flut warten auf niemand.

It   Tempo e marea non aspettan a nessuno.

El   El tiempo y la marea no esperan al rey.

Ru   Попутный ветер ждать не любит.

5   *En*   Time lost cannot be won again.

     Fr   Le temps perdu ne se retrouve jamais.

     De   Verlorene Zeit kommt niemals wieder.

     It   Il tempo perso non si ritrova più.

     El   El tiempo perdido hasta los santos lo lloran.

     Ru   Потерянного времени не воротишь.

6   *En*   Time cures (softens) all griefs.

     Fr   Le temps guérit les douleurs et les querelles.

     De   Die Zeit heilt alle Wunden.

     It   Il tempo mitiga ogni gran piaga.

     El   El tiempo todo lo cura.

     Ru   Время всё излечит.

7   *En*   Time is the best healer.*

     Fr   Le temps est le meilleur médecin.

     De   Die Zeit ist der beste Arzt.

     It   Il tempo è il miglior medico.

     El   El tiempo es el mejor médico.

     Ru   Время–лучший врач.

8   *En*   Times change, and we change with them.*

     Fr   Les temps changent et nous changeons avec eux.

     De   Die Zeiten ändern sich, und wir ändern uns in ihnen.

     It   Mutansi i tempi e noi con loro.

     El   Mudan los tiempos, y nosotros con ellos.

     Ru   Меняются времена, меняются и люди.

9   *En*   Time will show.

         All in good time.

Fr Vient jour, vient conseil.

De Kommt Zeit, kommt Rat.

It Il tempo dà consiglio.

El Al tiempo el consejo.

Ru Время–лучший советчик.

Время покажет.

10 *En* He that hath time, and looks for time, loseth time.

Fr   Qui a le temps et attend le temps perd son temps.

De Wer auf die Zeit wartet, dem fehlt die Zeit.

It Chi tempo ha e tempo aspetta, tempo perde.

El Quien tiempo tiene y tiempo atiende, tiempo viene que se arrepiente.

Ru Кто временем не дорожит, у того всегда убытки.

11 *En* Better late than never.*

Fr Mieux vaut tard que jamais.

De Besser spät als nie.

It Meglio tardi che mai.

El Más vale tarde que nunca.

Ru Лучше поздно, чем никогда.

12 *En* It happens in an hour that happens not in seven years.*

Fr Il advient souvent en un jour ce qui n'advient en cent ans.

De Ein Tag kann bringen, was ein Jahr nicht bringen mag.

It Arriva in un momento quello che non accade in un anno.

El Lo que no sucede en un año, sucede en un instante.

Ru Пропущенный час годом не нагонишь.

13 *En* Rome was not built in a day.*

Fr Paris n'a pas été bâti en un jour.

De Rom ist nicht in einem Tage gebaut worden.

It Roma non fu fatta in un giorno.

El No se ganó Zamora en una hora.

Ru Не в один день Москва строилась.

14 *En* Other times, other manners.
  Fr Autres temps, autres mœurs.
  De Andere Zeiten, andere Sitten.
  It Altri tempi, altri costumi.
  El A otros tiempos, otras costumbres.
  Ru Другие времена–другие нравы.

15 *En* Night is the mother of counsel.*
  Fr La nuit porte conseil.
  De Guter Rat kommt über Nacht.
  It La notte è la madre dei consigli.
  El Antes de hacello, dormir sobre ello.
  Ru Утро вечера мудренее.

16 *En* Much water has run under the bridge since then.
  Fr Il a passé bien de l'eau sous les ponts.
  De Seitdem ist schon viel Wasser vom Berge geflossen.
  It È passata molt'acqua sotto il ponte.
  El Mucha agua corrió bajo los puentes.
  Ru Много воды утекло с тех пор.

17 *En* The longest day must have an end.
  Fr Il n'y a si long jour qui ne vienne à la nuit.
  De Es ist kein Tag, er bringt seinen Abend mit.
  It Non v'è si lungo giorno che nol segua la notte.
  El No hay día sin noche.
  Ru Каков ни будь грозен день, а вечер настанет.

18 *En* Every day is not Sunday (no Yule-day).*
  Fr Ce n'est pas tous les jours fête.
  De Es ist nicht alle Tage Sonntag.
  It Ogni giorno non si fanno nozze.
  El Agosto y vendimia no es cada día.
  Ru Не всё коту масленица.

19 *En* Fair and softly goes far.
   Fr Qui va doucement, va loin.
   De Allgemach kommt man auch weit.
   It Chi va piano, va lontano.
   El Poco a poco se va lejos.
   Ru Тише едешь, дальше будешь.

20 *En* Make haste slowly.*
   Fr Hâtez-vous lentement.
   De Eile mit Weile.
   It Chi ha fretta, indugi.
   El Date prisa lentamente.
   Ru Торопись (Поспешай) медленно.

21 *En* Haste makes waste.
   Fr Trop presser nuit.
   De Eilen tut nicht gut.
   It Troppa fretta nuoce.
   El Cosa hecha aprisa, cosa de risa.
   Ru Поспешишь, людей насмешишь.

22 *En* The more haste, the less speed.
   Fr Trop grande hâte est cause de retard.
   De Wer zu sehr eilt, kommt langsam heim.
   It Chi fa in fretta, ha disdetta.
   El A gran priesa, gran vagar.
   Ru Скорость нужна, а поспешность вредна.

23 *En* Who cometh late lodgeth ill.*
   Fr Qui tard arrive, mal loge.
   De Wer zu spät kommt, hat das Nachsehen.
   It Chi tardi arriva, male alloggia.
   El Quien tarde llega, mal escoge.
   Ru Кто поздно приходит, тот ничего не находит.

24 *En* First come, first served.*
    Fr Premier arrivé, premier servi.
    De Wer zuerst kommt, mahlt zuerst.
    It Chi primo arriva, primo macina.
    El El primer venido, primer servido.
    Ru Первому гостю первое место.

25 *En* It will be all one a hundred years hence.
    Fr Les races de petits et grands seront égales en mille ans.
    De Leid oder Freud'–in fünfzig Jahren ist's alles eins.
    It In cento anni e cento mesi l'acqua torna a' suoi paesi.
    El Después de los años mil torna el agua a su carril.
    Ru Не нами свет начался, не нами и кончится.

26 *En* After a storm comes a calm.*
    Fr Après la pluie le beau temps.
    De Auf Regen kommt Sonnenschein.
    It Dopo la pioggia il sereno.
    El Tras la tempestad llega la calma.
    Ru После дождика–солнышко.

27 *En* A snow year, a rich year.
    Fr Années neigeuse, année fructueuse.
    De Schneejahr–gut Jahr.
    It Anno di neve, anno di bene.
    El Año de nieves, año de bienes.
    Ru Много снегу–много хлеба.

28 *En* Green Christmas brings white Easter.
    Fr A Noël au balcon, à Pâques au tison.
    De Grüne Weihnacht, weisse Ostern.
    It Verde Natale, bianca Pasqua.
    El La de Navidad al sol, y la florida al tizón.
    Ru Зелёное Рождество–белая пасха.

29   *En*   A dry March, wet April and cool May, fill barn and cellar
         and bring much hay.

     Fr   Mars poudreux, avril pluvieux, mai joli, gai et
         venteux, dénotent l'an fertil et plantureux.

    De   Trockener März, nasser April und kühler Mai–füllen
         Keller und Boden.

     It   April piovoso, maggio ventoso–anno fruttuoso.

    El   Lluvioso abril, si mayo ventea, ya te puedes reír.

    Ru   Март сухой да мокрый май–будет каша и каравай.

30   *En*   April and May are the keys of the year.

     Fr   Avril et mai de l'année font tous seuls la destinée.

    De   April und Mai sind die Schlüssel zum ganzen Jahr.

     It   Aprile e maggio son la chiave di tutto l'anno.

    El   Abril y mayo, llaves de todo el año.

    Ru   Вешний день целый год кормит.

10 Beginning–End
Commencement–Fin
Anfang–Ende
Principio–Fine
Principio y Fin
Начало–Конец

1   *En*   Everthing must have a beginning.
    Fr   Il y a un commencement à tout.
    De   Jedes Ding will seinen Anfang haben.
    It   Ogni cosa ha il suo inizio.
    El   Todo requiere un principio.
    Ru   Всё имеет начало.

2   *En*   A good beginning makes a good ending.*
    Fr   De bon commencement bonne fin.
    De   Guter Anfang–gutes Ende.
    It   Buon principio fa buon fine.
    El   A buen principio, buen fin.
    Ru   Путному началу благой конец.

3   *En*   Well begun is half done.*
    Fr   A moitié fait qui a bien commencé.
    De   Wohl angefangen ist halb getan.
    It   Chi ben comincia, ha la metà dell' opra.
    El   Buen principio, la mitad es hecho.
    Ru   Доброе начало полдела откачало.

4   *En*   A good lather is half a shave.
    Fr   Barbe bien étuvé est à demi rasée.
    De   Ein gut geseifter Bart ist halb geschoren.

49

It   Barba bagnata è mezza fatta.
El   Barba bien remojada, medio rapada.
Ru   Хорошее начало–половина дела.
      (Хорошо намылишь–половина бритья).

5   *En*   Such beginning, such end.*
      Fr   De tel commencement telle fin.
      De   Wie der Anfang, so das Ende.
      It   Qual principio, tal fine.
      El   Quien bien ata, bien desata.
      Ru   Каково начало, таков и конец.

6   *En*   All beginnings are hard (difficult).*
      Fr   Ce qu'il y a de plus difficile, c'est le commencement.
      De   Aller Anfang ist schwer.
      It   Ogni principio è difficile.
      El   El comienzo es duro.
      Ru   **Всякое начало трудно.**
      Лиха беда–начало.

7   *En*   The first step is the only difficulty.
      Fr   Il n'y a que le premier pas qui coûte.
      De   Der erste Schritt ist immer der schwerste.
      It   Il primo scudo è il più difficile a fare.
      El   Todo lo difícil está en el comenzar.
      Ru   Только первый шаг труден.

8   *En*   The greatest step is that out of doors.
      Fr   Tout dépend du premier pas.
      De   Der grösste Schritt ist immer der über die Schwelle.
      It   Il passo più difficile è quello dell'uscio.
      El   El salir de la posada es la mayor jornada.
      Ru   Почин дороже всего.
      Страшно дело до начину.

9 *En* He who commences many things finishes but few.
   Fr Qui commence plusieurs choses en achève peu.
   De Wer viel anfängt, beendet wenig.
   It Chi troppo intraprende, poco finisce.
   El Demasiado y demasiado poco pierde todo juego.
   Ru Кто за всё хватается, тот ничего не сделает.

10 *En* Better is the end of a thing than the beginning thereof. *(B)*
   Fr Mieux vaut la fin d'une chose que son commencement.
   De Besser ist der Ausgang einer Sache als ihr Anfang.
   It Meglio vale il fin della cosa, che il principio di essa.
   El Mejor es el fin del negocio que su principio.
   Ru Конец дела лучше начала его. *(Б)*

11 *En* Better never to begin than never to make an end.
   Fr C'est folie de commencer ce qu'on ne peut achever.
   De Besser unbegonnen als unvollendet.
   It Meglio è non dire, che cominciar e non finire.
   El Más vale no empezar que lo empezado no acabar.
   Ru Не бойся начала, а бойся конца.

12 *En* Look to (Mark) the end.*
   Fr Dans tout ce que tu fais, considère la fin.
   De Was du auch tust, bedenke das Ende.
   It Chi da savio operar vuole, pensi al fine.
   El Mira que ates que desates.
   Ru Начиная дело, о конце помышляй.

13 *En* The end crowns the work.*
   Fr La fin couronne l'œuvre.
   De Das Ende krönt das Werk.
   It La fine corona l'opera.
   El El fin corona la obra.
   Ru Конец–делу венец.

14 *En* All is well that ends well.*
   Fr Tout est bien qui finit bien.
   De Ende gut–alles gut.
   It Tutto è bene quel che finisce bene.
   El Es bien lo que acaba bien.
   Ru Всё хорошо, что хорошо кончается.

15 *En* Everything hath an end.
   Fr Il y a une fin à tout.
   De Alles hat einmal ein Ende.
   It Tutto ha una fine.
   El Todo tiene fin en este mundo.
   Ru Сколько верёвку ни вить, а концу быть.

16 *En* There is a limit to everything.
   Fr Il y a une limite à tout.
   De Alles hat seine Grenzen.
   It C'è un limite a ogni cosa.
   El Todo tiene sus límites.
   Ru Всему есть свой предел.

17 *En* He laughs best who laughs last.
   Fr Rira bien qui rira le dernier.
   De Wer zuletzt lacht, lacht am besten.
   It Ride bene chi ride l'ultimo.
   El Quien ríe último, ríe mejor.
   Ru Хорошо смеётся тот, кто смеётся последним.

18 *En* You cannot say A without saying B.
   Fr Qui dit A doit dire B.
   De Wer A sagt, muss auch B sagen.
   It Chi dice A, bisogna che dica B.
   El Quien dice A, debe decir B.
   Ru Кто сказал А, должен сказать и Б.

19 *En* In for a penny, in for a pound.
 Fr Quand le vin est tiré il faut le boire.
 De Man muss die Suppe auslöffeln, die man sich eingebrockt hat.
 It Beva la feccia chi ha bevuto il vino.
 El Preso por mil, preso por mil quinientos.
 Ru Взялся за гуж, не говори, что не дюж.

20 *En* It is not good praising a ford till a man be over.*
 Fr Il ne faut pas chanter triomphe avant la victoire.
 De Singe nicht Viktoria, bevor der Sieg erfochten ist.
 It Non convien cantare trionfo prima della vittoria.
 El No cantes victoria antes de estar seguro.
 Ru Хвали горку, как перевалишься.

21 *En* Do not halloo till you are out of the wood.
 Fr Il ne faut pas se moquer des chiens avant d'être sorti du village.
 De Rufe nicht "Juch!", bevor du über den Graben bist.
 It Non dir quattro se non l'hai nel sacco.
 El Antes de acabar, nadie se debe alabar.
 Ru Не говори "гоп", пока не перескочишь.

22 *En* All roads lead to Rome.
 Fr Tous les chemins mènent à Rome.
 De Alle Wege führen nach Rom.
 It Tutte le strade conducono a Roma.
 El Todos los caminos llevan a Roma.
 Ru Все дороги ведут в Рим.

23 *En* At length the fox is brought to the furrier.
 Fr A la fin les renards se trouvent chez le pelletier.
 De Alle Füchse kommen endlich beim Kürschner zusammen.
 It Tutte le volpi alla fine si riveggono in pellicceria.

El   Allá nos veremos en el corral de los pellejeros.
Ru   Таскал волк, потащили и волка.

24   En   Look before you leap.
     Fr   Regardez à deux fois avant de sauter.
     De   Habe Rat vor der Tat.
         Erst wägen, dann wagen.
     It   Pensarci prima per non pentirsi poi.
     El   Mirar antes de saltar.
     Ru   Погляди, прежде чем прыгнуть.

25   En   An oak is not felled at one stroke.
     Fr   D'un seul coup ne s'abat un chêne.
     De   Von einem Streiche fällt keine Eiche.
     It   Al primo colpo non cade l'albero.
     El   Un solo golpe no derriba el roble.
     Ru   С одного удара дуба не свалишь.

26   En   When a thing is done, advice comes too late.*
     Fr   A parti pris point de conseil.
     De   Begangene Tat leidet keinen Rat.
     It   Dopo il fatto il consiglio non vale.
     El   Hecho el hecho, huelga el consejo.
     Ru   Решённого дела советом не поправишь.

27   En   He that endureth to the end shall be saved. *(B)*
     Fr   Celui qui persévérera jusqu'à la fin sera sauvé.
     De   Wer bis ans Ende beharrt, der wird gerettet werden.
     It   Chi avrà sostenuto fino alla fine, sarà salvato.
     El   El que soportará hasta el fin, éste será salvo.
     Ru   Перетерпевший до конца спасётся. *(Б)*

28   En   To cut the Gordian knot.
     Fr   Trancher le nœud gordien.

De   Den gordischen Knoten zerhauen.

It   Tagliare il nodo gordiano.

El   Cortar el nudo gordiano.

Ru   Разрубить гордиев узел.

29 En   To shut up shop windows.

Fr   Fermer boutique.

De   Die Bude schliessen.

It   Farla finita con qualcosa.

El   Cerrar el boliche.

Ru   Закрыть лавочку.

30 En   Praise day at night, and life at the end.*

Fr   Loue le beau jour au soir, et la vie à la mort.

De   Man soll den Tag nicht vor dem Abend loben.

It   Non lodar il bel giorno innanzi sera.

El   Al fin loa a la vida, y a la tarde loa al día.

Ru   Хвали жизнь при смерти, а день вечером.

11 Wisdom–Foolishness
  Sagesse–Sottise
  Weisheit–Torheit
  Saggezza–Stupidità
  Sabiduría–Necedad
  Мудрость–Глупость

1 *En* Older and wiser.*
  Fr Avec l'âge on devient sage.
  De Mit der Zeit wird man klug.
  It Gli anni dan senno.
  El Tras los años viene el seso.
  Ru Время разум даёт.

2 *En* Adversity makes men wise.
  Fr Dommage rend sage.
  De Durch Schaden wird man klug.
  It Danno fa far senno.
  El Dolorosa experiencia es la mejor ciencia.
  Ru Беды научают человека мудрости.

3 *En* Wisdom goes beyond strength. *(B)*
  Fr La sagesse vaut mieux que la force.
  De Weisheit ist besser als Stärke.
  It Meglio val sapienza che forza.
  El Mejor es la sabiduría que la fortaleza.
  Ru Разум силу победит. *(Б)*

4 *En* A word is enough to the wise.*
  Fr Le sage entend à demi-mot.
  De Den Gelehrten ist gut predigen.

It A buon intenditor poche parole.
El Al buen entendedor media palabra basta.
Ru Умный с полслова речь понимает.

5 *En* Wise men learn by other men's harms; fools, by their own.*
   Fr Après dommage le fou est sage.
   De Des Narren Unfall ist des Weisen Warnung.
   It Impara a vivere lo sciocco a sue spese, il savio a quelle
        altrui.
   El El loco por la pena es cuerdo.
   Ru Дураку вред–умному навет.

6 *En* The wise head gives in.
   Fr Le plus sage se tait.
   De Der Klügere gibt nach.
   It Al più potente cede il più prudente.
   El El sabio dice al fuerte: Adelántate.
   Ru Умный уступает.

7 *En* It is easy to be wise after the event.
   Fr Après dommage chacun est sage.
   De Nach der Tat sind alle klug.
   It Dopo il fatto ognuno è savio.
   El El conejo ido, el consejo venido.
   Ru Задним умом крепок (всяк догадлив).

8 *En* He has heard something, but is no wiser through it.
   Fr Il écoute, mais n'entend pas.
   De Er hat läuten hören, weiss aber nicht, wo die Glocken
        hängen.
   It Ha sentito, ma non ha capito.
   El Oye campanas, y no sabe donde.
   Ru Слышал звон, да не знает, где он.

9   *En*   No man is wise at all times.*

     Fr   Il n'est si sage qui ne folie quelquefois.

     De   Kluge Hühner legen auch in die Nesseln.

     It   Niuno è savio d'ogni tempo.

     El   Nadie es sabio en todas ocasiones.

     Ru   И умный иногда делает глупости.

10   *En*   Great wits jump.

     Fr   Les grands esprits se rencontrent.

     De   Grosse Geister treffen sich.

     It   Le grandi menti si assomigliano.

     El   Los grandes ingenios se encuentran.

     Ru   Великие умы сходятся.

11   *En*   Every one hath a fool in his sleeve.

     Fr   Chacun a un fou dans sa manche.

     De   Jedermann hat einen Narren in seinem Ärmel.

     It   Ognuno ha un ramo di pazzia.

     El   Cada uno lleva un loco en la manga.

     Ru   На всякого мудреца довольно простоты.

12   *En*   A fool may give a wise man counsel.

     Fr   Un fou avise bien un sage.

     De   Ein Weiser kann von einem Narren lernen.

     It   Anche il pazzo dice talvolta parole da savio.

     El   De hombre necio a veces buen consejo.

     Ru   Иной дурак может умному посоветовать.

13   *En*   A fool may ask more questions in an hour than a wise man can answer in seven years.

     Fr   Un fou fait plus de questions qu'un sage de raisons.

     De   Ein Narr kann mehr fragen als sieben (zehn) Weise antworten.

     It   Un matto sa più domandare che sette savi rispondere.

El Más fácil es al burro preguntar, que al sabio contestar.

Ru Один дурак может больше спрашивать, чем десять умных ответить.

14 *En* Fools make feasts, and wise men eat them.
    Fr Les fous donnent de grands repas et les sages les mangent
    De Die Narren machen Gastereien, die Weisen essen drauf.
    It I matti fanno le feste ed i savi le godono.
    El Los locos hacen los banquetes, y los sabios los comen.
    Ru Дурак пир устроил, а умница наелся.

15 *En* A fool, unless he knows Latin, is never a great fool.
    Fr Un sot savant est sot plus qu'un sot ignorant.
    De Je gelehrter, desto verkehrter.
    It I pazzi per lettera sono i maggiori pazzi.
    El Necio letrado, necio doblado.
    Ru Переученный хуже недоученного.

16 *En* He who is born a fool is never cured.
    Fr Qui naît fou n'en guérit jamais.
    De Der Narr bleibt ein Narr.
    It Chi nasce matto, non guarisce mai.
    El El mal que no tiene cura, es locura.
    Ru Дурак дураком остаётся.

17 *En* If an ass goes a-travelling he'll not come home a horse.
    Fr Qui bête va à Rome, tel en retourne.
    De Ein Esel bleibt ein Esel, und käm' er nach Rom.
    It Chi bestia va a Roma, bestia ritorna.
    El Fuíme a Palacio, fuí bestia y vine asno.
    Ru Осла хоть в Париж, всё будет рыж.

18 *En* A fool and his money are soon parted.
    Fr Le fol et son argent sont bientôt séparés.

De Ein Narr und sein Geld sind nicht lange Freund' in der Welt.

It Il pazzo e il suo danaro sono presto separati.

El El tonto y su dinero son luego apartados.

Ru У дурака деньги долго не держатся.

19 *En* He will not set the Thames on fire.

Fr Il n'a pas inventé la poudre.

De Er hat das Pulver nicht erfunden.

It Non è quello che inventò la polvere.

El No descubre la pólvora.

Ru Он пороха не выдумает.

20 *En* Long hair and short wit.

Fr Longs cheveux, courte cervelle.

De Langes Haar, kurzer Verstand.

It I capelli lunghi, i cervelli corti.

El Cabello luengo, y corto el seso.

Ru Волос долог, да ум короток.

21 *En* Too much laughter discovers folly.*

Fr Qui rit trop, a nature de sot.

De Am vielen Lachen erkennt man den Narren.

It Dal riso molto conosci lo stolto.

El La risa demasiada es señal de cabeza vana.

Ru Дураку всё смех на уме.

22 *En* One fool makes a hundred.

Fr Un fou en fait cent.

De Ein Narr macht hundert Narren.

It Un pazzo ne fa cento.

El Un loco hace ciento.

Ru Глупость заразительна.

23   *En*   One fool praises another.*
      Fr   A l'âne l'âne semble très beau.
      De   Ein Narr gilt dem andern für gescheit.
      It   Un asino par bello ad un altro asino.
      El   No hay un tonto a quien no admire otro tonto.
      Ru   Дурак дурака и хвалит.

24   *En*   No fool to the old fool.
      Fr   Un vieux fou est le pire des fous.
      De   Alter schützt vor Torheit nicht.
      It   A testa bianca spesso cervello manca.
      El   La cabeza blanca, y el seso por venir.
      Ru   Старые дураки глупее молодых.

25   *En*   Knaves and fools divide the world.
      Fr   Les fous depuis Adam sont en majorité.
      De   Die Narren werden nicht alle.
      It   Al mondo ci sono più pazzi che briciole di pane.
      El   Tontos y locos nunca fueron pocos.
      Ru   Дураками свет стоит.

26   *En*   He that sends a fool expects one.*
      Fr   Qui fou envoie, fou attend.
      De   Wer einen Narren schickt, empfängt einen Toren.
      It   Chi matto manda, matto aspetta.
      El   El que tonto va a la guerra, tonto viene de ella.
      Ru   Пошлёшь дурного, а за ним другого.

27   *En*   Every fool likes his own bauble best.
      Fr   A chaque fou plaît sa marotte.
      De   Jedem Narren gefällt seine Kappe.
      It   Ad ogni pazzo piace il suon del suo sonaglio.
      El   A cada necio agrada su porrada.
      Ru   Всяк дурак хвалит свой колпак.

28   *En*   Every man is mad on some point.
      Fr   Chacun a sa marotte.
      De   Jeder hat seinen Splitter (seine Schelle).
      It   Ognun ha il suo ramicello.
      El   Sin un ramito de locura no hay humana criatura.
      Ru   У всякого своя дурь в голове.

29   *En*   A white wall is a fool's paper.
      Fr   La muraille blanche est le papier des sots.
      De   Narrenhände beschmieren Tisch' und Wände.
      It   Muro bianco, carta de'pazzi.
      El   Las señas de los simples se encuentran en todas partes.
      Ru   Белая стена–дуракам бумага.

30   *En*   Little wit in the head makes much work for the feet.*
      Fr   Quand on n'a pas une bonne tête il faut avoir de bonnes jambes.
      De   Was man nicht im Kopfe hat, muss man in den Beinen haben.
      It   Chi non ha cervello, abbia gambe.
      El   Quien no tiene cabeza, debe tener piernas.
      Ru   За плохой головой и ногам не покой.

12 Cause and Effect
Cause et Effet
Ursache und Wirkung
Causa ed Effetto
Causa y Efecto
Причины и последствия

1 *En* A little spark kindles a great fire.*
   Fr Petite étincelle engendre grand feu.
   De Kleiner Funken–grosses Feuer.
   It Piccola favilla accende gran fuoco.
   El De chica centella gran hoguera.
   Ru От малой искры, да большой пожар.

2 *En* A bow long bent at last waxeth weak.*
   Fr L'arc trop tendu tôt lâché ou rompu.
   De Wer den Bogen überspannt, der sprengt ihn.
   It Quando si tende troppo l'arco, si rompe.
   El Arco siempre armado, o flojo o quebrado.
   Ru Что больше натягивать, то скорее лопнет.

3 *En* He that toucheth pitch shall be defiled.
   Fr Qui touche de la poix souille ses doigts.
   De Wer Pech angreift, besudelt sich.
   It Chi tocca la pece, s'imbratta le mani.
   El Quien anda con pez, se manchará los dedos.
   Ru С грязью играть–лишь руки марать.

4 *En* As you make your bed, so you must lie on it.
   Fr Comme on fait son lit, on se couche.
   De Wie man sich bettet, so liegt man.

It   Come uno si fa il letto, così dorme.

El   Según se hace uno la cama, así se acuesta.

Ru Как постелешь, так и поспишь.

5   *En* He that lies down with dogs must rise up with fleas.

     Fr Qui se couche avec des chiens, se lève avec des puces.

     De Wer mit Hunden ins Bett geht, steht mit Flöhen auf.

     It Chi va a letto co' cani, si leva colle pulci.

     El Quien con perros se acuesta, con pulgas se levanta.

     Ru С собакой ляжешь–с блохами встанешь.

6   *En* From chipping come chips.

     Fr Où il pleut, il y dégoutte.

     De Wo man Holz haut, da fallen Späne.

     It Dove piove, ci sono gocciole.

     El Cuando llueve, hay gotas de lluvia.

     Ru Лес рубят–щепки летят.

7   *En* When the cat's away, the mice will play.

     Fr Absent le chat, les souris dansent.

     De Wenn die Katze fort ist, tanzen die Mäuse.

     It Dove non è la gatta, il topo balla.

     El Cuando el gato no está, los ratones bailan.

     Ru Где кошки нет, там мыши резвятся.

         Без кота мышам раздолье.

8   *En* No smoke without some fire.*

     Fr Il n'y a pas de fumée sans feu.

     De Kein Rauch ohne Feuer.

     It Non c'è fumo senza fuoco.

     El Donde fuego se hace, humo sale.

     Ru Нет дыма без огня.

9   *En* Who sows the wind will reap the whirlwind. *(B)*

     Fr Qui sème le vent, récolte la tempête.

De	Wer Wind sät, wird Sturm ernten.
It	Chi semina il vento, raccoglie la tempesta.
El	El que siembra vientos, recoge tempestades.
Ru	Кто посеет ветер, пожнёт бурю. *(Б)*

10 *En* The cask savours of the first fill.*
    Fr La caque sent toujours le hareng.
    De Das Fass riecht nach dem ersten Wein.
    It Il mortaio sente sempre d'aglio.
    El La cuba huele al vino que tenía.
        A la vasija nueva dura el resabio.
    Ru Бочка пахнет тем, что в ней раньше было.

11 *En* He who excuses himself, accuses himself.
    Fr Qui s'excuse s'accuse.
    De Wer sich entschuldigt, klagt sich an.
    It Chi si scusa s'accusa.
    El Quien se excusa, se acusa.
    Ru Кто извиняется, тот сам себя обвиняет.

12 *En* As they brew, so let them drink.
    Fr Qui fait la faute, la boit.
    De Wie man's einbrockt, muss man's essen.
    It Chi l'ha fatta, la beva.
    El El que hace la soma, éste la coma.
    Ru Как заварили, так и расхлёбывайте.
        Заварил кашу, сам и расхлёбывай.

13 *En* Wheresoever the carcase is, there will the eagles be
        gathered together. *(B)*
    Fr En quelque lieu que soit le cadavre, là s'assembleront les
        aigles.
    De Wo das Aas ist, da sammeln sich die Adler.
    It Dovunque sarà il carname, quivi si accoglieranno le
        aquile.

El   Donde quiera que estuviere el cuerpo muerto, allí se
     juntarán las águilas.

Ru   Где будет труп, там соберутся орлы. *(Б)*

14 En   One scabbed sheep will mar a whole flock.*
    Fr   Une brebis galeuse gâte tout le troupeau.
    De   Ein räudiges Schaf steckt die ganze Herde an.
    It   Una pecora marcia ne guasta un branco.
    El   Oveja infestada, infesta a la manada.
         Una oveja mala estropea el rebaño.
    Ru   Одна паршивая овца всё стадо испортит.

15 En   One drop of poison infects the whole tun of wine.
    Fr   Un peu de fiel gâte beaucoup de miel.
    De   Ein wenig Galle macht viel Honig bitter.
         Eine Fliege verdirbt den ganzen Brei.
    It   Una goccia d'assenzio guasta un vaso di miele.
    El   Poca hiel hace amarga mucha miel.
    Ru   Ложка дёгтю испортил бочку мёду.

16 En   The rotten apple injures its neighbours.
    Fr   Une pomme gâtée en gâte cent.
    De   Ein fauler Apfel steckt den andern an.
    It   Una mela marcia ne guasta cento.
    El   La manzana podrida pierde a su compañía.
    Ru   От одного порченого яблока целый воз загнивает.

17 En   He who digs a pit for others falls in himself. *(B)*
    Fr   Tel qui creuse une fosse à un autre y tombe souvent
         lui-même.
    De   Wer andern eine Grube gräbt, fällt selbst hinein.
    It   Chi scava la fossa agli altri, vi cade dentro egli stesso.
    El   Quien hace un hoyo para otro, él cae en el hoyo.
    Ru   Не рой другому яму–сам в неё попадёшь. *(Б)*

18 *En* Constant dropping wears the stone. *(B)**
    Fr Les gouttes qui tombent sans cesse usent le rocher.
          La goutte creuse la pierre.
    De Steter Tropfen höhlt den Stein.
    It A goccia a goccia s'incava la pietra.
    El Continua gotera cava la piedra.
    Ru Капля по капле и камень долбит. *(Б)*

19 *En* The pitcher goes so often to the well (water) that it is
          broken at last.*
    Fr Tant va la cruche à l'eau, qu'à la fin elle se brise.
    De Der Krug geht so lange zum Brunnen, bis er bricht.
    It Tante volte al pozzo va la seccia, ch'ella vi lascia il
          manico o l'orecchia.
    El Tanto va el cántaro a la fuente, que al fin se rompe.
    Ru Повадился кувшин по воду ходить, тут ему и голову
          сломить.

20 *En* For want of a nail the shoe is lost; for want of a shoe the
          horse is lost.
    Fr Faute d'un point Martin perdit son âne.
    De Wer den Nagel am Hufeisen nicht achtet, der verliert
          auch das Pferd.
    It Per un chiodo si perde un ferro, e per un ferro un cavallo.
    El Por un clavo se pierde una herradura.
    Ru Не было гвоздя, подкова пропала; не было подковы,
          лошадь захромала.

21 *En* Rust eats up iron.*
    Fr La rouille ronge le fer.
    De Rost frisst Eisen.
    It La ruggine mangia il ferro.
    El El orín roe el hierro.
    Ru Ржа железо ест.

(12) 22

22 *En* Who spits against heaven, it falls in his face.
   Fr Qui crache contre le ciel, il lui tombe sur la tête.
   De Wer nach dem Himmel speit, dem fällt der Speichel in den
        eigenen Bart.
   It Chi sputa in su, lo sputo gli torna sul viso.
   El Quien al cielo escupe, en la cara le cae.
   Ru Кверху плевать–свою бороду заплевать.

23 *En* Trust is the mother of deceit.*
   Fr Confiance est mère de dépit.
        Il est tôt déçu qui mal ne pense.
   De Wer leicht glaubt, wird leicht betrogen.
   It Chi spesso fida, spesso grida.
   El Si no quieres ser engañado, no seas confiado.
   Ru Кто легко верит, легко и пропадает.

24 *En* Hasty climbers have sudden falls.
   Fr Qui trop se hâte, reste en chemin.
   De Eilesehr brach den Hals.
   It La fretta fa romper la pentola.
   El El que mucho corre, pronto para.
   Ru Поспешишь–упадёшь, последним придёшь.

25 *En* Bound is he that gifts taketh.*
   Fr Qui d'autrui prend, sujet se rend.
   De Geschenke binden die Gelenke.
   It Chi dono prende, libertà vende.
   El Merced recibida, libertad vendida.
   Ru Дадут ломоть, да заставят неделю молоть.

26 *En* The fairer the hostess, the fouler the reckoning.
   Fr Belle hôtesse c'est un mal pour la bourse.
   De Je schöner die Wirtin, je schwerer die Zeche.
   It Bella ostessa, brutti conti.

El Cuando es hermosa la huéspeda, la cuenta es fea.
Ru Хозяйка красна–и каша дорога.

27 *En* Make yourself all honey, and the flies will devour you.
   Fr Faites-vous miel, les mouches vous mangeront.
   De Wer sich zu Honig macht, den benaschen die Fliegen.
   It Fatti di miele, e ti mangeranno le mosche.
   El A quien se hace miel, moscas se le comen.
   Ru Будь лишь мёд, много мух нальнёт.

28 *En* He that makes himself a sheep shall be eaten by the wolf.
   Fr Qui se fait brebis, le loup le mange.
   De Wer sich zum Lamm macht, den fressen die Wölfe.
   It Chi pecora si fa, lupo la mangia.
   El Hace os miel, y comeros han moscas.
   Ru Не прикидывайся овцой–волк съест.

29 *En* Here lies the rub!
   Fr C'est là que gît le lièvre!
   De Da liegt der Hase im Pfeffer!
      Da liegt der Hund begraben!
   It Qui giace la lepre!
   El ¡Aquí hay gato encerrado!
   Ru Вот где собака зарыта!

13 Conditioned–Relativity
Conditionnellement–Relativité
Bedingtheit–Relativität
Condizionatezza–Relatività
Condicionalidad–Relatividad
Условность–Относительность

1 *En* When the tree is fallen, every one runs to it with his axe.
  Fr Quand l'arbre est tombé chacun court aux branches.
  De Wenn der Baum gefallen ist, so macht ein jeder Holz.
  It Sopra l'albero caduto ognuno corre a far legna.
  El Del árbol caído todos hacen leña.
  Ru Павшее дерево рубят на дрова.

2 *En* If the blind lead the blind, both shall fall into the ditch. *(B)*
  Fr Si un aveugle conduit un aveugle, ils tomberont tous deux dans une fosse.
  De Wenn ein Blinder den andern führt, so fallen sie beide in die Grube.
  It Se un cieco guida un altro cieco, ambedue cadranno nella fossa.
  El Si el ciego guiare al ciego, ambos caerán en el hoyo.
  Ru Если слепой ведёт слепого, то оба упадут в яму. *(Б)*

3 *En* If the sky falls we shall catch larks.*
  Fr Si le ciel tombait, il y aurait des alouettes prises.
  De Wenn der Himmel einstürzt, sind alle Vögel gefangen.
  It Se il cielo rovinasse, si piglierebbero molti uccelli.
  El Si el cielo se cae, nos cogerá debajo.
  Ru Если небо упадёт, мы будем ловить жаворонков.

4   *En* If the cap fits, wear it.
      Fr Qui se sent galeux se gratte.
      De Wen's juckt, der kratze sich.
      It Chi ha la rogna, se la gratta.
      El Quien tiene roña rásquese.
      Ru У кого свербит, тот и чешись.

5   *En* If the lion's skin cannot, the fox's shall.*
      Fr Coudre la peau du renard à celle du lion.
      De Wo die Löwenhaut nicht reicht, muss man den Fuchsbalg annähen.
      It Dove non basta la pelle del leone, bisogna attaccarvi quella della volpe.
      El Donde no valen cuñas, aprovechan uñas.
      Ru Где силой не возьмёшь, там хитрость на подмогу.
          Где волчьи зубы, а где лисий хвост.

6   *En* He that is surety for a stranger shall smar for it. *(B)*
      Fr Celui qui cautionne autrui s'en trouve mal.
      De Wer für einen Fremden bürgt, dem geht es gar übel.
      It L'uomo certamente sofferirà del male, se fa sicurità per lo strano.
      El Con ansiedad será afligido él que fiare al extraño.
      Ru Зло причиняет себе, кто ручается за постороннего. *(Б)*
          Кто поручится, тот и помучится.

7   *En* The moon's not seen where the sun shines.
      Fr Où le soleil luit, la lune n'y a que faire.
      De Wem die Sonne scheint, der fragt nicht nach den Sternen.
      It Quando il sol ti splende, non ti curar della luna.
      El El sol me luzca, pues de la luna no me curo.
      Ru Луны не видно, когда светит солнце.

8   *En* In the kingdom of blind men the one-eyed is king.*
      Fr Au royaume des aveugles les borgnes sont rois.

De Unter den Blinden ist der Einäugige König.
It In terra di ciechi chi ha un occhio è signore
El En el país de los ciegos el tuerto es rey.
Ru Меж слепых и кривой зрячий.

9 *En* In a long journey straw weighs.
Fr A long chemin paille pèse.
De Die Länge trägt die Last.
It In lungo viaggio anche una paglia pesa.
El En luengo camino paja pesa.
Ru На большом пути и малая ноша тяжела.

10 *En* If Ifs and Ans were pots and pans, there'd be no trade
for tinkers.
Fr Si ce n'était le "si" et le "mais", nous serions tous
riches à jamais.
De Wenn die "aber" und "wenn" nicht wären, würde niemand
sich beschweren.
It Se non ci fosse il "se" e il "ma", no' saremmo ricchi
sempre mai.
El Si el cielo cae, quebrarse han las ollas.
Si todo fuera orégano.
Ru Если бы да кабы во рту росли бобы, –был бы не рот,
а целый огород.

11 *En* The thread breaks where it is weakest.
Fr On tombe toujours du côté où l'on penche.
De Wo der Faden dünn ist, da reisst er.
It Il filo se rompe nel punto più debole.
El Se rompe la cuerda por lo más fino.
Ru Где верёвка тонка, там и рвётся.

12 *En* Men leap over where the hedge is lowest.
Fr Où la haie est basse tout le monde passe.

De Wo der Zaun am niedrigsten ist, springt jeder über.
It Dove la siepe è bassa, ognuno passa.
El Adonde el seto es bajo todos pasan.
Ru Через низкий забор и овца прыгает.

13 *En* All cats are alike grey in the night.*
   Fr La nuit tous les chats sont gris.
   De Bei Nacht sind alle Katzen grau.
   It Di notte tutti i gatti sono neri.
   El De noche todos los gatos son pardos.
   Ru Ночью все кошки серы.

14 *En* Standing pools gather filth.
   Fr L'eau dormant vaut pire que l'eau courant.
       L'eau arrêtée devient impure.
   De Stehendes Wasser stinkt.
   It Acqua che stagna, o puzza o magagna.
   El Agua estancada no vale nada.
   Ru Стоячая вода гниёт.

15 *En* A gift long waited for is sold, not given.
   Fr Un présent trop attendu n'est point donné, mais bien vendu.
   De Langsame Gabe verliert den Dank.
   It Dono molto aspettato è venduto e non donato.
   El Quien promete y en dar se tarda, pierde las gracias.
   Ru Поздно дать–всё равно что отказать.

16 *En* A little pot is soon hot.
   Fr Un petit pot est bientôt échauffé.
   De Ein kleiner Topf kocht bald über.
   It Picciola pentola si scalda presto.
   El Olla chiquita se calienta luego.
   Ru Маленькие горшки быстрее кипят.

17 *En* A house built by the wayside is either too low or too high.*

He who builds by the roadside has many masters.

    Fr Qui édifie en grande place fait maison trop haute ou trop basse.

    De Wer am Wege baut, hat viele Meister.

    It Chi fa in piazza la casa, o l'è tropp'alta o troppo bassa.

    El Haz casa en la plaza, y unos dirán que es alta, y otros que es baja.

    Ru При дороге жить–всем не угодить.

18 *En* A rolling stone gathers no moss.

    Fr Pierre qui roule n'amasse pas mousse.

    De Am rollenden Stein wächst kein Moos.

    It Pietra mossa non fa muschio.

    El Piedra movediza, nunca el moho la cobija.

    Ru Катучий камень мохнат не будет.

19 *En* A stitch in time saves nine.

    Fr Un point fait à temps en épargne cent.

    De Ein Stich zur Zeit erhält das Kleid.

    It Piccol rimedio a tempo, salva gran male.

    El Una puntada a tiempo ahorra ciento.

    Ru Один стежок, сделанный вовремя, стоит девяти.

20 *En* As the call, so the echo.

    Fr Tel voix, tel écho.

    De Wie es fällt, so bullert es.

    It Tal sonata, tal ballata.

    El Según es la voz, es el eco.

    Ru Как аукнется, так и откликнется.

21 *En* Forewarned, forearmed.*

    Fr Un homme averti en vaut deux.

De Gewarnter Mann ist halb gerettet.
It Uomo avvisato è mezzo salvato.
El Hombre prevenido vale por dos.
Ru Кто предупреждён, тот наполовину спасён.

22 *En* He who greases his wheels helps his oxen.
    Fr Pour faire aller le chariot il faut graisser les roues.
    De Wer gut schmeert (schmiert), der gut fährt.
    It La carrucola non frulla, se non è unta.
    El Quien su carro unta, sus bueyes ayuda.
    Ru Хорошо смазал, хорошо и поехал.

23 *En* Great honours are great burdens.*
    Fr Trop d'honneurs pèsent.
    De Grosse Würde–grosse Bürde.
    It Troppo onori, troppo oneri.
    El Como me crecieron los favores, me crecieron los dolores.
    Ru Чем больше почёт, тем больше хлопот.

24 *En* A prophet has no honour in his own country. *(B)**
    Fr Nul n'est prophète en son pays.
    De Der Prophet gilt nichts in seinem Vaterland.
    It Niuno è profeta nella sua patria.
    El Nadie es profeta en su tierra.
    Ru Нет пророка в своём отечестве. *(Б)*

25 *En* No great loss but some small profit.
    Fr A quelque chose malheur est bon.
    De Kein Schaden ohne Nutzen.
    It Tutto il male non vien per nuocere.
    El No hay mal sin bien, cata para quien.
    Ru Нет худа без добра.

26 *En* Nothing so bad in which there is not something of good.*
    Fr Il n'est pas mal dont bien ne vienne.

De Es ist nichts so böse, es findet sich etwas Gutes dabei.
Kein Unglück so gross, es trägt ein Glück im Schoss.

It Non c'è cosa così cattiva, che non sia buona a qualche cosa.

El Males hay que por bien vienen, y por mal no pocos bienes.

Ru Во всяком худе не без добра.

27 *En* Every cloud has a silver lining.

Fr Dans toute chose il y a un bon côté.

De Auch das Unglück hat sein Gutes.

It Non c'è male senza bene.

El No hay mal que por bien no venga.

Ru При несчастьи и счастье.

28 *En* Every man to his taste.

Fr Chacun à son goût.

De Jeder nach seinem Geschmack.

It Ciascuno a modo suo.

El Cada cual a su manera.

Ru У каждого свой вкус.

29 *En* Tastes differ.

Fr Les goûts sont différents.

De Geschmack ist verschieden.

It Ognuno ha i suoi gusti.

El Sobre gustos no hay nada escrito.

Ru На вкус и цвет товарища нет.

30 *En* There is no accounting for tastes.*

Fr Il ne faut pas disputer des goûts.

De Über den Geschmack lässt sich nicht streiten.

It Dei gusti non se ne disputa.

El Sobre gustos no hay disputa.

Ru О вкусах не спорят.

31 *En* To measure another man's foot by one's own last.

    Fr Mesurer les autres à son aune.

    De Mit eigenem Massstab messen.

    It Misurare gli altri col suo metro.

    El Medir con su rasero.

    Ru Мерить других на свой аршин.

32 *En* Thou art a bitter bird, said the raven to the starling.*

    Fr Un âne appelle l'autre rogneux.

    De Ein Esel schilt den andern Langohr.

    It Il bove chiama cornuto l'asino.

    El Dijo el asno al mulo: Anda para orejudo.

    Ru Не смейся, горох, ты не лучше бобов.

33 *En* The pot calls the kettle black.

    Fr La poêle se moque du chaudron.

    De Der Kessel schimpft immer den Ofentopf.

    It La padella dice al paiuolo: Fatti in là che mi tingi.

    El Dijo la sartén a la caldera: Quítate de allá, culinegra.

    Ru Горшок над котлом смеётся, а оба чёрны.

34 *En* There is no general rule without some exception.*

    Fr Il n'y a pas de règle sans exception.

    De Keine Regel ohne Ausnahme.

    It Ogni regola patisce eccezione.

    El No hay regla sin excepción.

    Ru Нет правила без исключения.

35 *En* The exception proves the rule.*

    Fr L'exception confirme la règle.

    De Ausnahmen bestätigen die Regel.

    It L'eccezione conferma la regola.

    El La excepción confirma la regla.

    Ru Исключение подтверждает правило.

36 *En* Every man hath his faults.*
    Fr Chacun a ses défauts.
    De Niemand ist ohne Fehler.
    It Nessun uomo senza difetti.
    El Ninguno ha nacido sin defectos.
       No hay hombre sin pero.
    Ru Нет человека без недостатков.

37 *En* Standers-by see more than gamesters.
    Fr Les spectateurs voient plus que les joueurs.
    De Die Zuschauer sehen mehr als die Spieler.
    It Lo spettatore vede più ch'il giocatore.
    El El que está mirando cerca, ve más que el jugador
    Ru Со стороны виднее.

14 Impossibility
   Impossibilité
   Unmögliches
   Impossibilità
   Imposibilidad
   Невозможность

1 *En* Things done cannot be undone.*
   Fr A chose faite point de remède.
   De Geschehenes kann nicht ungeschehen gemacht werden.
   It Il fatto non si può disfare.
   El No se puede desandar lo andado.
   Ru Сделанного не воротишь.

2 *En* No one is bound to do impossibilities.*
   Fr A l'impossible nul n'est tenu.
   De Unmögliches kann man von niemand verlangen.
   It Nessuno è tenuto all' impossibile.
   El Nadie està obligado a lo imposible.
   Ru Чего нет, того и не спрашивай.

3 *En* No naked man is sought after to be rifled.
   Fr Quarante bien vêtus ne dépouilleraient un nu.
   De Den Nackten kann man nicht ausziehen.
   It Cento ladri non possono spogliare un uomo nudo.
   El Desnudo nací, desnudo me hallo, ni pierdo ni gano.
   Ru Мокрый дождя, а нагой разбоя не боится.

4 *En* No man can serve two masters. *(B)*
   Fr Nul ne peut servir deux maîtres.
   De Niemand kann zwei Herren dienen.

It   Niuno può servire due signori.
El   Ninguno puede servir a dos señores.
Ru Никто не может служить двум господам. *(Б)*

5   En One cannot be in two places at once.*
     Fr On ne peut pas être à la fois au four et au moulin.
     De Wir können nicht zugleich hier sein und dort.
     It Non si può essere in due luoghi.
     El No se puede estar en dos lugares diferentes a la vez.
     Ru На двух свадьбах сразу не танцуют.

6   En A man cannot whistle and drink at the same time.
     Fr On ne peut à la fois souffler et avaler.
     De Man kann nicht zugleich blasen und schlucken.
     It Non si può bere e fischiare.
     El No se puede hacer a la par sorber y soplar.
     Ru Всего вдруг не сделаешь.

7   En A carrion kite will never make a good hawk.
     Fr D'une buse on ne saurait faire un épervier.
     De Aus dem Esel wird kein Reitpferd, magst ihn zäumen wie du willst.
     It Chi nasce mulo, non diventa mai cavallo.
     El Quien mulo nace, caballo no se hace.
     Ru Вороне соколом не быть.

8   En Good and quickly seldom meet.
     Fr Vite et bien se trouvent rarement ensemble.
     De Schnell und gut sind selten beisammen.
     It Presto e bene non stanno insieme.
     El Pronto y bien, rara vez juntos se ven.
     Ru Что хорошо, то не скоро.

9   En It is hard to please all parties.*
     Fr On ne peut pas plaire à tout le monde.

On ne peut contenter tout le monde et son père.

De   Man kann es nicht allen recht machen.

It   Nessuno può piacere a tutti.

El   No se puede gradar a todos.

Ru   На весь мир не угодишь.

10 *En*   He that all men will please shall never find ease.

    Fr   C'est chose ardue et trop profonde que d'agréer à tout le monde.

    De   Allen Leuten recht getan, ist eine Kunst, die niemand kann.

    It   Non si può fare a modo di tutti.

    El   Gran trabajo tiene quien contentar a todos quiere.

    Ru   На всех угодить–себя истомить.

11 *En*   He who pleased everybody died before he was born.

    Fr   Qui veut plaire à tout le monde, doit se lever de bonne heure.

    De   Der lebt nicht, glaub'ich, auf der Welt, der allen Leuten gut gefällt.

    It   Magari si potesse accontentare tutti!

    El   Nunca llueve a gusto de todos.

    Ru   На всех угождать–самому в дураках сидеть.

12 *En*   There is no building a bridge across the ocean.

    Fr   On ne saurait chanter plus haut que la bouche.

    De   Es ist dafür gesorgt, dass die Bäume nicht in den Himmel wachsen.

    It   Nessuno può fare i passi più lunghi che le gambe.

    El   Ninguno sabe subirse a las estrellas.

    Ru   Выше лба уши не растут.

13 *En*   He that will not be counselled cannot be helped.

    Fr   Pour néant demande conseil qui ne le veut croire.

De Wem nicht zu raten ist, dem ist auch nicht zu helfen.

It   Chi non vuol esser consigliato, non può esser aiutato.

El   Quien no toma consejo, no merece remedio.

Ru Кто не слушает советов, тому бесполезно помогать.

14 En You may take a horse to the water, but you can't make him drink.

Fr   On ne saurait pas faire boire un âne qui n'a pas soif.

De Pferde lassen sich zum Wasser bringen, aber nicht zum Trinken zwingen.

It   Trenta monaci ed un abate non farebbero bere un asino per forza.

El   Trenta monjes y un abad no pueden hacer cagar un asno contra su voluntad.

Ru Не всего можно добиться силой.

15 En You cannot make a silk purse of a sow's ear.*

Fr   D'un sac à charbon ne saurait sortir de blanche farine.

De Aus des Esels Wedel wird kein Sieb.
Grobes Tuch gibt keine feinen Kleider.

It   Di coda d'asino non si può fare staccio.

El   De rabo de puerco nunca buen virote.

Ru Из собачьей шерсти одеяла не сделаешь.

16 En You cannot catch old birds with chaff.

Fr   On ne prend pas les vieux moineaux avec de la paille.

De Alte Spatzen fängt man nicht mit Spreu.

It   Nuova rete non piglia uccello vecchio.

El   Pájaro viejo no entra en jaula.

Ru Старого воробья на мякине не проведёшь.

17 En There comes nought out of the sack but what was there.

Fr   Il ne saurait sortir d'un sac que ce qui y est.

De Man kann nichts aus dem Sack herausnehmen, als was drinnen ist.

It Dal sacco non può uscir, se non quel che vi è.

El De donde no hay, no se puede sacar.

Rn Из порожнего ни пьют, ни едят.

18 *En* To look for a needle in a haystack.

   Fr Chercher un épingle dans une botte de foin.

   De Eine Stecknadel in einem Fuder Heu suchen.

   It Cercare uno spillo in un mucchio di fieno.

       Cercare un ago in un pagliaio.

   El Buscar una aguja en un pajar.

   Ru Искать иголку в стоге сена.

19 *En* That which is crooked cannot be made straight. *(B)*

   Fr Ce qui est courbé ne peut se redresser.

   De Krumme Sachen kann man nicht gerademachen.

   It Le cose torte non si possono dirizzare.

   El Lo torcido no se puede enderezar.

   Ru Кривое не может сделаться прямым. *(Б)*

       Горбатого могила исправит.

20 *En* Hard with hard makes not the stone wall.*

   Fr Dur contre dur ne font pas bon mur.

   De Zwei harte Steine mahlen selten kleine.

   It Duro con duro non fa buon muro.

   El Duro con duro no hace buen muro.

   Ru Два жёстких жёрнова хорошей муки не намелят.

15 **Uselessness**
   Inutilité
   Nutzlosigkeit
   Inutilità
   Inutilidad
   Бесполезность

1   *En*   After meat, mustard.*
    Fr   De la moutarde après dîner.
    De   Das kommt einen Posttag zu spät.
    It   Arrivare a piatti lavati.
    El   Después de vendimias, cuévanos.
    Ru   После ужина горчица.

2   *En*   After death the doctor.*
    Fr   Après la mort le médecin.
    De   Nach dem Tode braucht man keine Arznei mehr.
    It   Dopo la morte non val medicina.
    El   Al asno muerto la cebada al rabo.
    Ru   После пожара, да за водой.

3   *En*   A fifth wheel to a coach.
    Fr   Une cinquième roue à la carrosse.
    De   Ein fünftes Rad am Wagen.
    It   La quinta ruota del carro.
    El   La quinta rueda del carro.
    Ru   Пятое колесо в телеге.

4   *En*   A blind man has no need of a looking-glass.*
    Fr   Un aveugle ne vous remerciera pas pour un miroir.
    De   Was soll der Blinde mit dem Spiegel?

El   ¿Qué hará el ciego con los anteojos?
Ru   Нужно, как слепому зеркало.

5   *En*   Blind men can (should) judge no colours.*
    Fr   L'aveugle ne doit pas juger des couleurs.
    De   Der Blinde soll nicht von Farben urteilen.
    It   Il cieco non giudichi dei colori.
    El   Que el ciego no juzgue de colores.
    Ru   Судит, как слепой о красках.

6   *En*   If you run after two hares, you will catch neither.*
    Fr   Qui court deux lièvres n'en prend aucun.
    De   Wer zwei Hasen zugleich jagt, fängt keinen.
    It   Chi due lepri caccia, l'una non piglia e l'altra lascia.
    El   Quien corre tras dos liebres, ninguna prenda.
    Ru   за двумя зайцами погонищъся, ни одного не поймаещъ.

7   *En*   It is too late to shut the stable-door when the steed is stolen.
    Fr   Il n'est plus temps de fermer l'étable quand les chevaux n'y sont plus.
    De   Wenn das Kind in den Brunnen gefallen ist, deckt man ihn zu.
    It   È inutile chiudere la stalla quando i buoi sono fuggiti.
    El   Cuando se fueron los bueyes, cierran el establo.
    Ru   Незачем запирать конюшню, когда лошадь уже украдена.

8   *En*   Honey is not for the ass's mouth.
    Fr   Le miel n'est pas fait pour les ânes.
    De   Was soll der Honig im Esels Munde?
    It   Il miele non è fatto per gli asini.
    El   No se hizo la miel para la boca del asno.
    Ru   Не свиным рылом апельсины нюхать.

9 *En* A sow to a fiddle.*
   Fr Qu'a de commun l'âne avec la lyre?
   De Was soll dem Esel die Leier?
   It Come l'asino al suono della lira.
   El Meter a músico a un jumento es falta de discernimiento.
   Ru Знает вкус, как свинья в апельсинах.

10 *En* The braying of an ass does not reach heaven.
   Fr Prière de fou n'est point écoutée.
   De Katzengebet geht nicht in den Himmel.
   It Raglio d'asino non entrò mai in cielo.
   El Oración de perro no va al cielo.
   Ru Собака лает, ветер носит.

11 *En* The moon does not heed the barking of dogs.
   Fr La lune ne se soucie pas des aboiements du chien.
   De Was kümmert es den Mond, dass ihn die Hunde anbellen?
   It La luna non cura l'abbaiar de'cani.
   El En vano ladran los perros a la luna.
   Ru Вольно собаке на месяц лаять.

12 *En* He that washes an ass's head, loseth both his soap and
        his labour.*
   Fr A laver la tête d'un âne on ne perd que la lessive.
   De Auf einen Eselskopf sind Laugen umsonst.
   It Chi lava la testa all'asino, perde il sapone.
   El El que lava de un asno la testa, pierde el jabón y la
        apuesta.
   Ru Чёрного кобеля не отмоешь добела.

13 *En* Drumming is not the way to catch a hare.
   Fr On ne prend pas le lièvre au tambourin.
   De Es ist übel, Hasen mit Trommeln zu fangen.
   It Le lepri non si pigliano col tamburo.

El Tañendo cencerros no se cogen liebres ni conejos.

Ru Зайца на барабан не выманишь.

14 *En* Gold plate does not fill your belly.

    Fr La belle cage ne nourrit pas l'oiseau.

    De Schöner Käfig nährt den Vogel nicht.

    It La gabbia d'oro non sazia l'uccello.

    El Con la hermosura no se come.

    Ru Золотая клетка соловью не потеха.

15 *En* To do good to an ingrateful man is to throw rose-water in the sea.

    Fr Obliger un ingrat c'est perdre le bienfait.

    De Was man dem Undankbaren tut, ist immer ein verloren Gut.

    It Chi fa del bene agli ingrati, fa onta a Dio.

    El Quien al ingrato favorece, su bueno acción pierde.

    Ru Чёрное сердце не знает благодарности.

16 *En* The voice of one crying in the wilderness. *(B)**

    Fr La voix de celui qui crie dans le désert.

    De Die Stimme eines Predigers in der Wüste.

    It Voce di chi grida nel deserto.

    El Voz que clama en el desierto.

    Ru Глас вопиющего в пустыне. *(Б)*

17 *En* In at one ear and out at the other.

    Fr Ce qui entre par une oreille sort par l'autre.

    De Zu einem Ohr hinein, zum andern heraus.

    It Per un orecchio entra e per l'altro esce.

    El Entrar por un oído, y salir por otro.

    Ru В одно ухо вошло, в другое вышло.

18 *En* The game is not worth the candle.

    Fr Le jeu ne vaut pas la chandelle.

De Das Spiel lohnt nicht den Einsatz (ist nicht des Lichtes wert).

It È più la spesa che la presa.

El El juego no vale la pena.

Ru Игра не стоит свеч.

19 En Look not for musk in a dog's kennel.*

Fr Demander de la laine à un âne.

De Beim Esel Wolle suchen.

It Dall'asino non cercar lana.

El Comprar del lobo carne.

Ru Захотел молочка от бычка.

20 En You must not teach fish to swim.*

Fr Enseigner à nager aux poissons.

De Die Fische das Schwimmen lehren.

It Insegnare a nuotare ai pesci.

El A perro viejo no hay tus tus.

Ru Не учи рыбу плавать.

21 En To sell the bear's skin before one has caught the bear.

Fr Vendre la peau de l'ours avant de l'avoir tué.

De Die Bärenhaut verkaufen, bevor man den Bären erlegt hat.

It Vender la pelle dell'orso prima d'averlo preso.

El Jugarse el sol antes que nace.
   Repartirse la piel del oso antes de cazarlo.

Ru Медведь в лесу, а шкура продана.

22 En To flog a dead horse.

Fr Battre l'eau avec un bâton.

De Leeres Stroh dreschen.

It Pestar acqua nel mortaio.

El Martillar en hierro frío.

Ru Напрасная работа–солому молотить.
   Толочь воду в ступе.

23 *En* To draw water in a sieve.*
    Fr Puiser l'eau dans un crible.
    De Wasser mit einem Sieb schöpfen.
    It Andar per acqua col vaglio.
    El Coger agua en cesto.
    Ru Черпать воду решетом.

24 *En* To run one's head against a stone wall.
    Fr Donner de la tête contre les murs.
    De Mit dem Kopfe gegen die Wand rennen.
    It Batter la testa contro il muro.
    El Golpear contra la pared.
    Ru Стены лбом не прошибёшь.

25 *En* To dispute about the shadow of an ass.*
    Fr Disputer sur la pointe d'une aiguille.
    De Um des Kaisers Bart streiten.
    It Disputare dell'ombra dell'asino.
    El Discutir sobre la lana de la cabra.
    Ru О пустяках спорить–дело упустить.

26 *En* To cast pearls before swine. *(B)*
    Fr Jeter des perles devant les pourceaux.
    De Perlen vor die Schweine werfen.
    It Gettare le perle dinanzi a' porci.
    El Echar perlas delante los puercos.
    Ru Метать бисер перед свиньями. *(Б)*

27 *En* To build castles in the air (in Spain).
    Fr Faire des châteaux en Espagne.
    De Luftschlösser bauen.
    It Fare castelli in aria.
    El Hacer castillos en el aire.
    Ru Строить воздушные замки.

28   *En*   To break a butterfly upon the wheel.
      Fr   Tirer sa poudre aux moineaux.
      De   Mit Kanonen nach Spatzen schiessen.
      It   Tirar cannonate contro i passeri.
      El   Gastar la pólvora en salvas.
      Ru   Стрелять из пушек по воробьям.

29   *En*   To set the wolf to keep the sheep.*
      Fr   Donner la brebis à garder au loup.
      De   Dem Wolf die Schafe anbefehlen.
           Den Bock zum Gärtner setzen.
      It   Dar le pecore in guardia al lupo.
      El   Dar las ovejas en guardia al lobo.
      Ru   Волка в пастухи поставить.
           Пустить козла в огород.

30   *En*   To fight with (tilt at) windmills.
      Fr   Combattre les moulins à vent.
      De   Gegen Windmühlen kämpfen.
      It   Battersi contro mulini a vento.
      El   Pelear con molinos de viento.
      Ru   Сражаться с ветряными мельницами.

31   *En*   To reckon without one's host.
      Fr   Compter sans son hôte.
      De   Die Rechnung ohne den Wirt machen.
      It   Fare i conti senza l'oste.
      El   Echar la cuenta sin la huéspeda.
      Ru   Рассчитать без хозяина.

32   *En*   To carry owls to Athens.*
      Fr   Porter des chouettes à Minerve.
      De   Eulen nach Athen tragen.
      It   Portare nottole ad Atene.
      El   Vender miel al colmenero.
      Ru   Ехать в Тулу со своим самоваром.

33 *En*   To carry coals to Newcastle.*
   Fr   Montrer le soleil avec un flambeau.
   De   Holz nach dem Wald tragen.
   It   Portare vasi a Samo.
   El   Llevar hierro a Vizcaya.
   Ru   Возить дрова в лес.

34 *En*   To cast water into the sea.*
   Fr   Porter de l'eau à la mer.
   De   Wasser ins Meer tragen.
   It   Portare acqua in mare.
   El   Llevar agua al mar.
   Ru   Морю воды прибавлять.

16 **Good–Evil**
   Bien et Mal
   Gutes–Böses
   Bene e Male
   Bien y Mal
   Добро и зло

1 *En* A good deed is never lost.
   Fr Un bienfait n'est jamais perdu.
   De Guter Dienst bleibt unverloren.
   It Piacer fatto non va perduto.
   El Hacer bien nunca se pierde.
   Ru Доброе дело без награды не остаётся.

2 *En* Good councel has no price.
   Fr Un bon avis vaut un œil dans la main.
   De Guter Rat ist Goldes wert.
   It A buon consiglio non si trova prezzo.
   El Al buen consejo no se halla precio.
   Ru Хороший совет дороже золота.

3 *En* A good example is the best sermon.*
   Fr Il faut prêcher d'exemple.
   De Ein gutes Beispiel ist die beste Predigt.
   It Non vale predicar bene e razzolar male.
   El No hay tal maestro como el buen ejemplo.
   Ru Хороший пример–лучшая проповедь.

4 *En* Example is better than precept.
   Fr L'exemple vaut mieux que le précepte.
   De Beispiele tun oft mehr als viele Wort' und Lehr'.

It Contanto più gli esempi che le parole.
El Es más eficaz el ejemplo que la doctrina.
Ru Пример лучше наставления.

5 *En* A good horse should be seldom spurred.
Fr Cheval bon n'a pas besoin d'éperon.
De Ein williges Pferd soll man nicht spornen.
It Caval che corre, non ha bisogno di sprone.
El Caballo que vuela, no quiere espuela.
Ru На послушного коня и кнута не надо.

6 *En* A curst dog must be tied short.
Fr A méchant chien court lien.
De Böse Hunde muss man kurz anbinden.
It A cattivo cane corto legame.
El A bestia loca recuero modorro.
Ru Куслив пёс, да на цепь попал.

7 *En* The wolf may lose his teeth, but never his nature.*
Fr Les loups peuvent perdre leurs dents, mais non leur naturel.
De Der Wolf ändert das Haar und bleibt, wie er war.
It Il lupo cangia il pelo, ma non il vizio.
El Muda el lobo los dientes y no las mientes.
Ru Волк каждый год линяет, а нрава не меняет.

8 *En* The good is the enemy of the best.
Fr Le mieux est l'ennemi du bien.
De Das Bessere ist des Guten Feind.
It Il meglio è nemico del bene.
El Lo mejor es enemigo de lo bueno.
Ru Лучшее–враг хорошего.

9 *En* Of two evils (harms, ills) choose the least.*
Fr De deux maux il faut choisir le moindre.

De Von zwei Übeln muss man das kleinere wählen.
It Di due mali bisogna scegliere il minore.
El De dos males, el menor (has de escoger).
Ru Из двух зол выбирай меньшее.

10 *En* Of one ill come many.
Fr Un péché attire l'autre.
De Ein Bube macht mehr Buben.
It Da colpa nasce colpa.
El Tras un yerro, una runfla de ellos.
Ru Дурные примеры заразительны.

11 *En* Ill news is too often true.
Fr Mauvaises nouvelles sont toujours vraies.
De Schlimme Nachrichten sind immer wahr.
It Le male nuove son sempre vere.
El Las malas nuevas siempre son ciertas.
Ru Худые вести не лежат на месте.

12 *En* Bad news has wings.
    Ill news comes apace.
Fr Les mauvaises nouvelles ont des ailes.
De Böse Botschaft bringt man bald.
It Novella cattiva presto arriva.
El Las malas nuevas no corren: vuelan.
Ru Плохая молва на крыльях летит.

13 *En* Ill weeds wax well.*
Fr Mauvaise herbe ne meurt point.
De Unkraut verdirbt nicht.
It La mal erba non si spegne mai.
El Hierba mala nunca muere.
Ru Злое зелье не уйдёт в землю.

14 *En* Ill weeds grow apace (fast).*
    Fr La mauvaise herbe croît vite.
    De Böses Kraut wächst bald.
    It La cattiva erba cresce presto.
    El La yerba mala presto crece.
    Ru Сорная трава хорошо растёт.

15 *En* Better be alone than in bad company.
    Fr Mieux vaut être seul que mal accompagné.
    De Besser allein als in böser Gemein.
    It È meglio star solo che mal accompagnato.
    El Más vale andarse soltero que con mal compañero.
    Ru Плохой товарищ пуще одиночки.

16 *En* Evil communications corrupt good manners. *(B)*
    Fr Les mauvaises compagnies corrompent les bonnes mœurs.
    De Schlechte Gesellschaften verderben gute Sitten.
    It Cattive conversazioni corrompono buoni costumi.
    El Las malas conversaciones corrompen las buenas costum-
         bres.
    Ru Худые сообщества развращают добрые нравы. *(Б)*

17 *En* There are black sheep in every flock.
    Fr Chaque troupeau a sa brebis galeuse.
    De In jeder Herde findet sich mal ein schwarzes Schaf.
    It In ogni grecce c'è una pecora nera.
    El En cada rebaño hay una oveja descarriada.
    Ru В семье не без урода.

18 *En* Envy shoots at others and wounds herself.
    Fr L'envie ronge les envieux.
         L'envieux maigrit de l'embonpoint des autres.
    De Der blasse Neid tut sich selber Leid.
    It L'invidia rode se stessa.
    El El orín se come el hierro, y la envidia al mal sujeto.
    Ru Завистливый от зависти погибает.

19 *En* When you are well hold yourself so.*
   Fr Quand on est bien il faut s'y tenir.
   De Wer gut sitzt, der rücke nicht.
   It Chi sta bene, non si muova.
   El El que bien está, no se mueva.
   Ru Ладно уселся, так сиди.

20 *En* Leave (Let) well alone.
   Fr Ne touchez pas à ce qui est bien.
   De Lass die Sache schlafen!
   It Lasciamo correre.
   El A lo bueno, dejarlo estar.
   Ru От добра добра не ищут.

21 *En* The treason is loved, but the traitor is hated.
   Fr On aime la trahison, mais le traître est odieux.
   De Den Verrat liebt man, den Verräter hasst man.
   It Tradimento piace assai, traditor non piacque mai.
   El La traición aplace, mas no él que la hace.
   Ru Перебежчик нужен на час, а там–не знай нас.

22 *En* Treachery will come home to the traitor.
   Fr Souvent la perfidie retourne sur son auteur.
   De Untreue schlägt ihren eigenen Herrn.
   It L'inganno va a casa dell'ingannatore.
   El A las veces donde cazar pensamos, cazados quedamos.
   Ru Думаешь–поймал, а тут сам попался.

23 *En* A good tree cannot bring forth evil fruit. *(B)*
   Fr Un bon arbre ne peut porter de mauvais fruits.
   De Ein guter Baum kann nicht schlechte Früchte bringen.
   It L'albero buono non può far frutti cattivi.
   El No puede el buen árbol llevar malos frutos.
   Ru От доброго дерева добрый и плод.

17 Law–Justice
Droit–Justice
Recht–Gerechtigkeit
Legge–Giustizia
Ley–Justicia
Закон–Справедливость

1 *En* All men are equal in the eyes of the law.
   Fr Tous les hommes sont égaux devant la loi.
   De Vor dem Gesetz sind alle gleich.
   It Siamo tutti eguali davanti alla legge.
   El Todos son iguales ante la ley.
   Ru Перед законом все равны.

2 *En* Ignorance of the law excuses no man.*
   Fr Nul n'est censé ignorer la loi.
   De Unkenntnis des Gesetzes schützt nicht vor Strafe.
   It L'ignoranza della legge non scusa nessuno.
   El La ley no admite ignorancia de derecho.
   Ru Незнанием закона никто не отговаривайся!

3 *En* Law-makers should not be law-breakers.
   Fr Celui qui établit la loi, garder la doit.
   De Wer ein Gesetz gibt, muss es zuerst selbst befolgen.
   It Chi fa la legge, servarla degge.
   El El respeto a la ley comience por el rey.
   Ru Кто законы пишет, пусть их не ломает.

4 *En* The law is good, if a man use it lawfully. *(B)*
   Fr La loi est bonne, pourvu qu'on en fasse un usage légitime.
   De Das Gesetz ist gut, wenn man es gesetzmässig braucht.

It   La legge è buona, se alcuno l'usa legittimamente.

El   La ley es buena, si alguno usa de ella legítimamente.

Ru Закон добр, если кто законно употребляет его. *(Б)*

5   En Every law has a loophole.*

     Fr On réussit toujours à éluder la loi.

     De Kein Gesetz, es findet sein Loch.

     It   Fatta la legge, pensata la malizia.

     El   Hecha la ley, hecha la trampa.

     Ru Нет закона без обхода.

6   En New lords, new laws.*

     Fr De nouveau roi nouvelle loi.

     De Neuer Herr, neues Recht.

     It   Nuovo principe, nuove leggi.

     El   Nuovo rey, nueva ley.

     Ru Новые господа–новые законы.

7   En Judge nothing before the time. *(B)*

     Fr Ne jugez de rien avant le temps.

     De Richtet nichts vor der Zeit.

     It   Non giudicate di nulla innanzi al tempo.

     El   No juzguéis nada antes de tiempo.

     Ru Не судите никак прежде времени. *(Б)*

8   En A fault confessed is half redressed.

     Fr Une faute avouée est à demi pardonnée.

     De Bekannt ist halb gebüsst.

     It   Peccato confessato è mezzo perdonato.

     El   Pecado confesado es medio perdonado.

     Ru Признание вины–полвины.

9   En Custom rules the law.*

     Fr Les lois doivent leur force aux mœurs.

         L'usage fait la loi.

De Gewohnheit will Recht werden.
It L'uso fa legge.
El Costumbre hace ley.
Ru Обычай старше (крепче) закона.

10 *En* Extreme right is extreme wrong.*
    Fr Justice extrême est extrême injustice.
    De Das strengste Recht–das grösste Unrecht.
    It Gran giustizia, grande offesa.
    El Justicia extrema, extrema injusticia.
    Ru Строгий закон велику вину творит.

11 *En* Might overcomes right.*
    Fr La force prime le droit.
    De Gewalt geht vor Recht.
    It La forza opprime la ragione.
    El Donde fuerza viene, derecho se pierde.
    Ru Где сила, там и закон.

12 *En* The absent are always in the wrong.
    Fr Les absents ont toujours tort.
    De Die Abwesenden haben immer Unrecht.
    It Gli assenti hanno sempre torto.
    El Nunca los ausentes se hallaron justos.
    Ru Отсутствующие всегда неправы.

13 *En* Pardoning the bad is injuring the good.*
    Fr Qui épargne le méchant nuit au bon.
    De Wer den Bösen schont, schadet den Frommen.
    It Chi perdona ai tristi, nuoce ai buoni.
    El Quien perdona al malo, al bueno hace agravio.
    Ru Вора помиловать–доброго погубить.

14 *En* He that soon deemeth, shall soon repent.
    Fr Juge hâtif est périlleux.

De Schnell Urteil hat Reue feil.
It Chi tosto giudica, tosto si pente.
El Juzgué de ligero, y arrepentime presto.
Ru Без рассуждения не делай осуждения.

15 *En* As a man sinneth, so is his punishment.
   Fr Par tel membre est corrigé l'homme dont il a péché.
   De Womit einer sündigt, damit wird er gestraft.
   It Con quel che uno pecca, è castigato.
   El El pecador por el pecado, donde pecó allí es penado.
   Ru Каков грех, такова и расправа.

16 *En* Punishment is lame, but it comes.
   Fr La punition boîte, mais elle arrive.
   De Strafe um Sünde bleibt nicht aus.
   It La pena è zoppa, ma pure arriva.
   El Dios tarda, pero no olvida.
   Ru Пуля виноватого найдёт.

17 *En* A suit at law and a urinal bring a man to the hospital.
   Fr Procès, taverne et urinal chassent l'homme à l'hôpital.
   De Wer einen Prozess führt um eine Kuh, gibt noch eine
       zweite hinzu.
   It Processo, taverna e orinale mandan l'uomo all' ospedale.
   El Pleito y urinal llevan el hombre al hospital.
   Ru За малое не судись–большое потеряешь.

18 *En* Honour to whom honour is due.
   Fr A tout seigneur tout honneur.
   De Ehre, dem Ehre gebührt.
   It Onore a chi onore è dovuto.
   El A gran señor, gran honor.
   Ru По заслугам и честь.

18 Necessity–Emergency
Nécessité–Besoin
Notfall–Bedarf
Necessità–Bisogno
Necesidad–Menester
Нужда–Необходимость

1   *En* A drowning man will catch at a straw.
Fr Un noyé s'accroche à un brin de paille.
De Der Ertrinkende klammert sich an einen Strohhalm.
It Chi sta per affogare si attacca anche ad un filo di paglia.
El Quien se ahoga, se agarra a un clavo ardiendo.
Ru Утопающий и за соломинку хватается.

2   *En* Do as you may if you can't do as you would.
Fr Quand on ne peut faire comme on veut, il faut faire comme on peut.
De Wer nicht kann, wie er will, muss wollen, wie er kann.
It Chi non può fare come vuole, faccia come può.
El Si no pudieres cuanto quisieres, conténtate con lo que pudieres.
Ru Не живи, как хочется–живи, как можется.

3   *En* Necessity is a hard dart.*
Fr La nécessité est une dure loi.
De Muss ist eine harte Nuss.
It È dura cosa la necessità.
El La necesidad tiene cara hereje.
Ru Нужда научит горшки обжигать.

4   *En* Necessity is the mother of invention.*
Fr La nécessité est mère de l'invention.

De Not macht erfinderisch.
It Necessità è madre dell'invenzione.
El La necesidad aguza el ingenio.
Ru Голь на выдумки хитра.
　　Нужда–отец догадки.

5 *En* Necessity knows no law.*
　Fr Nécessité n'a pas de loi.
　De Not kennt kein Gebot.
　It Necessità non conosce legge.
　El La necesidad carece de ley.
　Ru Нужда закона не знает.

6 *En* Need makes the old wife trot.
　Fr Le besoin fait la vieille trotter.
　De Not lehrt alte Weiber traben.
　It Il bisogno fa trottar la vecchia.
　El La necesidad hace a la vieja trotar.
　Ru Нужда и голод погонят на холод.

7 *En* What can't be cured must be endured.*
　Fr Ce qui ne peut être évité, il le faut embrasser.
　De Was man nicht kann ändern, muss man lassen schlendern.
　It Sopporta e non biasimare quel che non puoi cambiare.
　El Buen remedio es olvidar lo que no puedes enmendar.
　Ru Приходится мириться с тем, чего нельзя исправить.

8 *En* If thou hast not a capon, feed on an onion.
　Fr A faute de chapon, pain et oignon.
　De Man muss sich mit dem Brot behelfen, bis man Fleisch bekommt.
　It Chi non può avere la carne, beva il brodo.
　El A falta de olla, bueno es pan y una cebolla.
　Ru Ешь щи с мясом, а нет–так хлеб с квасом.

9   *En* Better bend (bow) than break.
     Fr Mieux vaut plier que rompre.
     De Lieber biegen als brechen.
     It È meglio piegare che rompere.
     El Antes doblar que quebrar.
     Ru Лучше гнуться, чем переломиться.

10 *En* As the wind blows, you must set your sail.
     Fr Il faut tendre la voile selon le vent.
     De Man muss sein Segel nach dem Winde aufspannen.
     It Bisogna navigare secondo il vento.
     El Ponte la capa según viniere el viento.
     Ru Парусы да снасти не в нашей власти.

11 *En* Better give the wool than the sheep.
     Fr Mieux vaut perdre la laine que le mouton.
     De Besser die Wolle geben als das Schaf.
     It È meglio perdere la lana che la pecora.
     El Más vale perder la silla que el caballo.
     Ru Лучше отдать шерсть, чем овцу.

12 *En* Who hath no horse may ride on a staff.
     Fr Faute de bœuf on fait labourer l'âne.
     De Hast du kein Pferd, so brauche den Esel.
     It Chi non ha letto, dorma sulla paglia.
     El A falta de bueyes labra con burros.
     Ru Когда нет лошади, и осёл скотина.

13 *En* Sink or swim.*
     Fr Il faut s'y tenir ou périr.
     De Friss, Vogel, oder stirb.
     It O bere, o affogare.
     El O bebe, o vete.
     Ru Хоть умри, но сделай!

14 *En* The belly teaches all arts.*
   Fr De tout s'avise à qui pain faut.
   De Der Bauch lehrt alle Künste.
   It La fame insegna tutte le arti.
   El La hambre es madre de las artes.
   Ru Нужда многому научит.

15 *En* Between the hammer and the anvil.
   Fr Entre le marteau et l'enclume.
   De Zwischen Hammer und Amboss.
   It Tra l'incudine ed il martello.
   El Entre la espada y la pared.
   Ru Между молотом и наковальней.

16 *En* To put a good face on a bad business.
   Fr Faire bonne mine à mauvais jeu.
   De Gute Miene zum bösen Spiel machen.
   It Far buon viso a cattivo gioco.
   El Poner buena cara al mal tiempo.
   Ru Сделать хорошую мину при плохой игре.

17 *En* To make a virtue of necessity.*
   Fr Faire de nécessité vertu.
   De Aus der Not eine Tugend machen.
   It Far di necessità virtù.
   El Hacer de necesidad virtud.
   Ru Сделать из нужды добродетель.

18 *En* If the mountain will not come to Mahomet, Mahomet must go to the mountain.
   Fr Si la montagne ne va pas à Mahomet, Mahomet va à la montagne.
   De Wenn der Berg nicht zum Propheten kommt, muss der Prophet zum Berg kommen.

It Se la montagna non va a Maometto, Maometto viene alla montagna.

El Si la montaña no va a Mahoma, Mahoma irá a la montaña.

Ru Если гора не идёт к Магомету, то Магомет идёт к горе.

19 Happiness–Misfortune
Bonheur–Malheur
Glück–Unglück
Felicità–Disgrazia
Felicidad–Desgracia
Счастье–Несчастье

1 *En* Every man is the architect of his own fortune.*
  Fr Chacun est l'artisan de sa fortune.
  De Jeder ist seines Glückes Schmied.
  It Ognuno è artefice della propria fortuna.
  El Cada uno es forjador de su fortuna.
  Ru Всяк своего счастья кузнец.

2 *En* He dances well to whom fortune pipes.
  Fr Bien danse à qui la fortune chante.
  De Wem das Glück pfeift, der tanzet wohl.
  It Assai ben balla, a chi fortuna suona.
  El Harto bien baila a quien la fortuna suena.
  Ru Кому счастье служит, тот ни о чём не тужит.

3 *En* Fortune is blind.*
  Fr La fortune est aveugle.
  De Das Glück ist blind.
  It La fortuna è cieca.
  El La fortuna es ciega.
  Ru Судьба слепа.

4 *En* Fortune is like glass.*
  Fr Bien de fortune passe comme la lune.
  De Glück und Glas, wie leicht bricht das.

It La fortuna ha i piedi di vetro.

El La felicidad es tan frágil como el cristal.

Ru Счастье–что солнышко: улыбнётся и скроется.

5 *En* Fortune is variant.

   Fr La fortune est un sable mouvant.

   De Das Glück ist wankelmütig.

   It Non sempre la fortuna un luogo tiene.

   El La buena ventura no siempre dura.

   Ru Судьба изменчива.

6 *En* Fortune's wheel is never stopped.

   Fr La roue de la fortune n'est pas toujours une.

   De Das Glückesrad geht um.

   It La ruota della fortuna non è sempre una.

   El La rueda de la fortuna nunca es una.

   Ru Колесо фортуны не стоит на одном месте.

7 *En* Fortune favours fools.*

   Fr La fortune rit aux sots.

   De Dumm hat's meiste Glück.

   It La fortuna aiuta i matti ed i fanciulli.

   El Ventura hayas, hijo, que poco saber te basta.

   Ru Дуракам счастье.

8 *En* Whom God loves, his bitch brings forth pigs.*

   Fr A qui la fortune est belle son bœuf vêle.

   De Wer's Glück hat, dem legt der Hahn Eier (dem kälbert
         der Ochs).

   It A chi ha fortuna, il bue gli fa un vitello.

   El A quien Dios quiere bien, la perra le pare puercos.

   Ru У кого счастье поведётся, у того и петух несётся.

9 *En* Good things come to some when they are asleep.

   Fr La fortune vient en dormant.

De Den Seinen gibt's der Herr im Schlaf.
It Chi ha d'aver bene, dormendo gli viene.
El Si la breva para ti está, en la boca te caerá.
Ru Счастье придёт–и на печи найдёт.

10 *En* Call no man happy till he dies.*
   Fr Nul avant mourir ne peut être dit heureux.
   De Niemand ist vor seinem Tode glücklich zu preisen.
   It Avanti la morte non lice chiamar alcun felice.
   El Nadie se alabe hasta que acabe.
   Ru Покуда кто жив, не говори, что счастлив.

11 *En* An ounce of good fortune is worth a pound of discretion.*
   Fr Mieux vaut une once de fortune qu'une livre de sagesse.
   De Ein Quentlein Glück ist besser als ein Pfund Weisheit.
   It Val più un'oncia di fortuna che una libbra di senno.
   El Más vale puñado de natural que almorzada de ciencia.
   Ru Не родись ни умён, ни красив, а родись счастлив.

12 *En* A land flowing with milk and honey. *(B)*
   Fr Une terre découlante de lait et de miel.
   De Ein Land, das von Milch und Honig fliesst.
   It Un paese stillante latte e mele.
   El Una tierra que fluye leche y miel.
   Ru Земля, где течёт молоко и мёд. *(Б)*
      Молочные реки и кисельные берега.

13 *En* Take occasion (time) by the forelock.
   Fr Il faut saisir l'occasion aux cheveux.
   De Das Glück muss man beim Schopfe fassen.
   It La fortuna va afferrata pei capelli.
   El Si el bien por tu calle pasa, mételo en tu casa.
   Ru Случай надо ловить за волосы.

14 *En* Flies hunt (go to) lean horses.
   Fr Aux chevaux maigres vont les mouches.
   De Fliegen setzen sich immer auf ein mageres Pferd.
   It Le mosche si posano sempre ai cavalli magri.
   El Al perro flaco todas son pulgas.
   Ru К мокрому телёнку все мухи льнут.
      На бедного Макара все шишки валятся.

15 *En* An unfortunate man would be drowned in a tea-cup.
   Fr Un homme malheureux se noyerait dans son crachat.
   De Wer Unglück haben soll, bricht den Finger im Hirsebrei.
   It Chi nasce sfortunato, s'ei va indietro a cader si rompe il naso.
   El El hombre desdichado, lo es en cuanto pone mano.
   Ru Кому не повезёт, тот и на ровном месте упадёт.

16 *En* He that is down, down with him.
   Fr Quand le loup est pris, tous les chiens lui lardent les fesses.
   De Wer da fällt, über den läuft alle Welt.
   It Quand'un'è per terra, ognun grida: dagli, dagli!
   El A moro muerto, gran lanzada.
   Ru Свались только с ног, а за тычками дело не станет.

17 *En* Every man has his cross to bear.
   Fr Chacun porte sa croix en ce monde.
   De Jeder hat sein Kreuz zu tragen.
   It Ognuno porta la sua croce.
   El Cada cual lleva su cruz.
   Ru Тяжёл крест, да надо несть.

18 *En* Losers are always in the wrong.
      Loss embraceth shame.
   Fr Les battus payent l'amende.
      Les malheureux ont toujours tort.

De Wer den Schaden hat, darf für den Spott nicht sorgen.
It Chi ha il danno, ha pur le beffe.
El Tras de cornudo, apaleado.
Ru Чья беда, того и грех.

19 *En* Whom fortune wishes to destroy, she first makes mad.*
   Fr La fortune rend fou celui qu'elle veut perdre.
   De Wen das Glück vernichten will, den macht es zum Narren.
   It Fortuna istupidisce, colui ch'ella troppo favorisce.
   El La fortuna enloquece a los mismos que favorece.
   Ru Кого счастье захочет погубить, у того оно отнимает разум.

20 *En* Two in distress makes sorrow less.*
   Fr Au malheureux fait confort avoir compagnie dans son sort.
   De Geteilter Schmerz ist halber Schmerz.
   It Mal comune, mezzo gaudio.
   El Mal de muchos, gozo es.
   Ru Горе на двоих-полгоря.

21 *En* The comforter's head never aches.*
   Fr Le mal d'autrui n'est que songe.
   De Fremder Schmerz geht nicht ans Herz.
   It È più facile il confortare che l'essere confortato.
   El Tu duelo de muelo, el ajeno de pelo.
       Por dolor ajeno ninguno pierde el sueño.
   Ru За чужой щекой зуб не болит.

22 *En* Small sorrows speak, great ones are silent.
   Fr Les grandes douleurs sont muettes.
   De Stummer Schmerz–grosser Schmerz.
   It I gran dolori sono muti.
   El Las grandes penas no se quejan.
   Ru Лёгкое горе болтливо, тяжёлое-молчаливо.

23 *En* Misfortunes never come alone.*
   Fr Un maleur n'arrive jamais seul.
   De Ein Unglück kommt selten allein.
   It Un malanno non vien mai solo.
   El Un mal nunca viene solo.
   Ru Беда никогда не приходит одна.

24 *En* One misfortune comes on the neck of another.
   Fr Un malheur en amène un autre.
   De Ein Unglück tritt dem andern auf die Fersen.
   It Un male tira l'altro.
   El Una desgracia trae consigo otra.
   Ru Беда семь бед приводит.

25 *En* Mischief comes by the pound and goes away by the ounce.
   Fr Le mal vient à charretée et s'en retourne once à once.
   De Böses kommt im Ritt und geht im Schritt.
   It Il male viene a carrate e va via a oncie.
   El El mal entra a brazadas y sale a pulgaradas.
   Ru Беда приходит пудами, а уходит золотниками.

26 *En* Out of the frying-pan into the fire.
   Fr Tomber de la poêle dans la braise.
   De Aus dem Regen in die Traufe kommen.
       Aus der Pfanne ins Feuer fallen.
   It Cascar dalla padella nella brace.
   El Saltar de la sartén y dar en las brasas.
   Ru Попасть из огня да в полымя.

27 *En* Running from Charybdis he rushed upon Scylla.
   Fr Tomber de Charybde en Scylla.
   De Aus der Charybdis in die Szylla geraten.
   It Cader di Cariddi in Scilla.

El   Salir de Caribdis para caer en Escila.

Ru   От волка бежал, да на медведя попал.

28 En To stew in one's own juice.

     Fr Cuire dans son jus.

     De In seinem eigenen Fett schmoren.

     It Crogiolare nel suo brodo.

     El Cocerce en su propia salsa.

     Ru Вариться в собственном соку.

29 En There shall be weeping and gnashing of teeth. *(B)*

     Fr Il y aura des pleurs et des grincements des dents.

     De Dort wird Heulen und Zähneknirschen sein.

     It Quivi sarà il pianto e lo stridor de denti.

     El Allí será el lloro y el crujir de dientes.

     Ru Там будет плач и скрежет зубов. *(Б)*

20 Joy–Sorrow
Joie–Chagrin
Freude–Sorge
Gioia–Tristezza
Gozo–Tristeza
Радость–Печаль

1   *En*   No joy without annoy (alloy).
     Fr   Pas de joie sans mélange.
     De   Keine Freud' ohne Leid.
     It   Non v'è gioia senza noia.
     El   No hay miel sin hiel.
     Ru   Ни печали без радости, ни радости без печали.

2   *En*   After joy comes annoy.*
     Fr   Plaisirs mondains finissent en pleurs.
     De   Auf Lachen folgt Weinen.
     It   La fine del riso è il pianto.
     El   No hay dulzura sin amargura.
     Ru   После смеха бывают слёзы.

3   *En*   Sadness and gladness succeed each other.*
     Fr   Après bon temps on se repent.
     De   Nach Freud' kommt Leid.
     It   Dopo il contento vien il tormento.
     El   La mucha alegría del pesar es víspera.
     Ru   Где радость, там и горе.

4   *En*   Sorrow treads upon the heels of mirth.
     Fr   Aise et mal se suivent de près.
     De   Keine Freude ohne Wehmutstropfen.

It   Dopo il dolce ne vien l'amaro.
El La alegría tiene a la tristeza por vecina.
Ru За радостью горе по пятам ходит.

5 *En* One day of pleasure is worth two of sorrow.
    Fr Qui a une heure de bien, il n'est pas toujours malheureux.
    De Eine selige Stunde wiegt ein Jahr Schmerzen auf.
    It Un'ora di contento sconta cent'anni di tormento.
    El Una hora de contento vale por ciento.
    Ru Час в добре побудешь–всё горе позабудешь.

6 *En* Laugh and grow fat.
        Laughter, the best medicine.
    Fr C'est demie vie que de rire.
    De Fröhliche Laune erhält gesund.
    It L'allegria è d'ogni male il rimedio universale.
    El La alegría es el mayor bien de la vida.
    Ru Кто в радости живёт, того и кручина неймёт.
        Смех силе брат.

7 *En* Laugh before breakfeast, you'll cry before supper.
    Fr Tel qui rit le matin, le soir pleurera.
    De Wer früh lacht, der weint gern abends.
    It Spesso chi ride la mattina, piange la sera.
    El Tú que riendo estás, mañana llorarás.
    Ru Рано пташечка запела, как бы кошечка не съела.

8 *En* He that sings on Friday will weep on Sunday.
    Fr Tel qui rit vendredi, dimanche pleurera.
    De Wer heute lacht, kann morgen weinen.
    It Chi ride in sabato, piange la domenica.
    El Día de placer, víspera de pesar.
    Ru Кто в субботу смеётся, в воскресенье плакать будет.

9   *En* Play, women, and wine undo men laughing.
     Fr Qui entretient femme et dé, mourra en pauvreté.
     De Weiber, Wein und Würfelspiel verderben Menschen viel.
     It Fuggi donne, vino, dado; se no, il tuo fato è spacciato.
     El Naipes, mujeres, bailes y vino, al más asesado quitan el tino.
     Ru Девки, винцо да игра не доведут до добра.

10 *En* Every heart hath its own ache.*
     Fr Chacune maison a sa croix et passion.
     De Jedes Häuschen hat sein Kreuzchen.
     It Ogni magione ha la sua passione.
     El No hay casa ninguna sin punta de mala fortuna.
     Ru У всякого своя забота.

11 *En* Care is no cure.
        Care killed the cat.
     Fr Les soucis font blancher les cheveux de bonne heure.
     De Sorge macht vor Zeiten grau.
        Sorge tötet eine Katze.
     It I pensieri fanno mettere i peli canuti.
     El Quien se apura, su muerte apresura.
     Ru Печаль беде не помощник.
        Заботы серебрят бороду.

12 *En* That which was bitter to endure may be sweet to remember.*
     Fr Ce qui est grief à supporter est après doux à raconter.
     De Überstandener Leiden gedenkt man gern.
     It Quel che fu duro a patire, è dolce a ricordar.
     El Alegre nos el recuerdo de las desgracias que han pasado.
     Ru Приятно вспомнить то, что было тяжело переживать.

13 *En* No rose without a thorn.*
     Fr Il n'y a pas de rose sans épines.

De Keine Rose ohne Dornen.
It Non vi è rosa senza spine.
El No hay rosa sin espinas.
Ru Нет розы без шипов.

14 *En* There is a time to weep, and a time to laugh. *(B)*
    Fr Il y a un temps pour pleurer, et un temps pour rire.
    De Weinen hat seine Zeit, und Lachen hat seine Zeit.
    It Vi è tempo di piangere, e tempo di ridere.
    El Hay tiempos de llorar, y tiempos de reír.
    Ru Есть время плакать, и время смеяться. *(Б)*

21 Will–Courage–Fear
Volonté–Courage–Peur
Wille–Mut–Angst
Volontà–Coraggio–Paura
Voluntad–Coraje–Miedo
Воля–Мужество–Страх

1   *En*   Where there's a will there's a way.*
      Fr   A bonne volonté ne faut faculté.
      De   Wo ein Wille ist, da ist auch ein Weg.
      It   A buona volontà non manca facoltà.
      El   Donde hay gana, hay maña.
      Ru   Где хотение, там и умение.

2   *En*   A wilful man will have his way.
      Fr   Vouloir c'est pouvoir.
      De   Wer will, dem ist alles möglich.
      It   Volere è potere.
      El   Querer es poder.
      Ru   Кто хочет, тот добьётся.

3   *En*   Nothing is impossible to a willing heart.
      Fr   A cœur vaillant rien d'impossible.
      De   Einem kühnen Herzen ist nichts unmöglich.
      It   Cuor forte rompe cattiva sorte.
      El   Buen corazón quebranta mala ventura.
      Ru   Была бы охота, а возможность найдётся.

4   *En*   Perseverance overcomes all things.*
      Fr   Les tenaces gagnent la bataille.
      De   Beharrlichkeit überwindet alles.

117

It Chi la dura, la vince.

El La perseverancia todo lo alcanza.

Ru Терпение и труд всё перетрут.

5 *En* Fortune favours the bold.*

  Fr La fortune sourit aux braves.

  De Das Glück ist dem Kühnen hold.

  It La fortuna aiuta gli audaci.

  El La fortuna ayuda a los osados.

  Ru Храброму счастье помогает.

    Смелость города берёт.

6 *En* He that is afraid of leaves must not come in a wood.*

  Fr Qui a peur des feuilles ne va point au bois.

  De Wer das Laub fürchtet, bleibe aus dem Walde.

  It Chi ha paura d'ogni foglia, non vada al bosco.

  El Quien tema a los lobos, no vaya al monte.

  Ru Волков бояться–в лес не ходить.

7 *En* He that would sail without danger, must never come on the main sea.

  Fr Qui craint le danger ne doit pas aller sur mer.

  De Wer die Gefahr fürchtet, darf nicht aufs Meer.

  It Chi teme acqua e vento, non si metta in mare.

  El Quien no se osa aventurar, no pase la mar.

  Ru Распутья бояться, так и в путь не ходить.

8 *En* He that counts all costs will never put plough in the earth.

  Fr Qui prend garde à chaque nuage, ne fait jamais voyage.

  De Wer alle Gefährden will erwiegen, bleibt ewig hinter dem Ofen liegen.

  It Chi guarda ad ogni nuvola, non fa mai viaggio.

  El Quien no se aventura, no ande a caballo ni a mula.

  Ru Кто ничем не рискует, тот ничего не получает.

9   *En*   Nothing venture, nothing have.

      Fr   Qui ne risque rien, ne gagne rien.

      De   Wer nicht wagt, gewinnt nicht.

      It   Chi non s'avventura, non ha ventura.

      El   Quien no arrisca, no aprisca.

      Ru   Не рискуя, не добудешь.

          Риск–благородное дело.

10   *En*   The burnt child dreads the fire.

          A scalded cat fears cold water.

      Fr   Chat échaudé craint l'eau froide.

      De   Gebrannte Kinder fürchten das Feuer.

          Gebrühte Katze scheut auch kaltes Wasser.

      It   L'uomo scottato ha paura del fuoco.

          Gatto scottato dall'acqua calda, ha paura della fredda.

      El   Gato escaldado del augua fría ha miedo.

      Ru   Обжёгшись на молоке, дуешь и на воду.

          Пуганая ворона и куста боится.

11   *En*   A cock is bold on his own dunghill.*

      Fr   Le coq est bien fort sur son fumier.

      De   Der Hahn ist kühn auf seinem Mist.

      It   È ardito il gallo sopra il suo letame.

      El   Cada gallo canta en su muladar.

      Ru   И петух на своём пепелище храбрится.

12   *En*   Fear takes molehills for mountains.

      Fr   La peur grossit les objets.

      De   Die Furcht hat tausend Augen.

      It   La paura ha cent'occhi.

      El   El miedo abulta las cosas.

      Ru   У страха глаза велики.

13   *En*   Fear gives wings.*

      Fr   La peur donne des ailes.

De Furcht macht Beine.
It La paura fa i passi lunghi.
El El miedo da alas.
Ru Страх придаёт ногам крылья.

14 *En* Afraid of his own shadow.*
   Fr Avoir peur de son ombre.
   De Sich vor seinem eigenen Schatten fürchten.
   It Avere paura della propria ombra.
   El Al espantado la sombra le espanta.
   Ru Бояться собственной тени.

15 *En* Rats desert a sinking ship.
   Fr Les rats quittent le navire qui coule.
   De Die Ratten verlassen das sinkende Schiff.
   It I topi abbandonano la nave che affonda.
   El Las ratas abandonan el barco que se hunde.
   Ru Крысы покидают тонущий корабль.

22 **God–Faith**
   Dieu–la Foi
   Gott–Glaube
   Iddio–la Fede
   Dios–la Fe
   Бог–Вера

1 *En* Man proposes, God disposes.*
   Fr L'homme propose et Dieu dispose.
   De Der Mensch denkt, und Gott lenkt.
   It L'uomo propone e Dio dispone.
   El El hombre propone, y Dios dispone.
   Ru Человек предполагает, а Бог располагает.

2 *En* God helps them that help themselves.
   Fr Aide-toi, et le Ciel t'aidera.
   De Hilf dir selbst, so hilft dir Gott.
   It Chi s'aiuta, Iddio l'aiuta.
   El Ayúdate, y el Cielo te ayudará.
   Ru На Бога надейся, а сам не плошай.

3 *En* God hath leaden feet, but iron hands.
   Fr La justice de Dieu a des pieds de plomb.
   De Gott kommt langsam, aber gewiss.
   It La vendetta di Dio non piomba in fretta.
   El Dios no se queja, mas lo suyo no lo deja.
   Ru Бог долго ждёт, да больно бьёт.

4 *En* God provides for him that trusteth.
   Fr Qui aime Dieu est sûr en tout lieu.
   De Wer Gott vertraut, hat gut gebaut.

121

It A chi bene crede, Dio provvede.
El Aquél es rico, que está bien con Dios.
Ru Тот не унывает, кто на Бога уповает.

5 *En* God shapes the back for the burden.
Fr Dieu ne veut pas plus qu'on ne peut.
De Gott gibt Schultern nach der Bürde.
It Dio non manda se non quel che si può portare.
El Dios da la carga según las fuerzas.
Ru Бог по силе крест налагает.

6 *En* God tempers the wind to the shorn lamb.
Fr Dieu mesure le vent à la brebis tondue.
De Gott gibt leisen Wind, wenn die Schafe geschoren sind.
It Dio modera il vento all'agnello tosato.
El A rebaño esquilado, mándale Dios viento manso.
Ru После стрижки Господь на овец теплом пахнёт.

7 *En* God's mill grinds slow but sure.*
Fr La meule de Dieu moud lentement, mais fin.
De Gottes Mühlen mahlen langsam, aber sicher.
It I mulini di Dio macinano adagio.
El Dios castiga sin piedra y sin palo.
Ru Не скор Бог, да меток.

8 *En* When need is highest, God's help is nighest.
Fr A barque désespérée Dieu fait trouver le port.
De Wenn die Not am grössten, ist Gottes Hilfe am nächsten.
It Quando è maggiore il bisogno, l'aiuto di Dio è più vicino.
El En la mayor necesidad, Dios te acudirá.
Ru Грозную тучу Бог пронесёт.

9 *En* Whom God would ruin, he first deprives of reason.*
Fr Quand Dieu quelqu'un veut châtier, de bon sens le fait
varier.

De   Wenn strafen will die Gotteshand, so nimmt sie einem den Verstand.
It   A chi Dio vuol castigare, leva il cervello.
El   Da Dios alas a la hormiga, para se pierda más aína.
Ru   Кого Бог захочет наказать, того лишит разума.

10 En   Every man for himself, and God for us all.
    Fr   Chacun pour soi, et Dieu pour tous.
    De   Jeder für sich, und Gott für alle.
    It   Ognuno per sè, e Dio per tutti.
    El   Cada uno para sí, y Dios para todos.
    Ru   Всяк про себя, а Господь про всех.

11 En   There is no going to heaven in a sedan.
    Fr   L'entrée du ciel ne se fait qu'avec zèle.
    De   Man rutscht auf keinem Kissen in den Himmel.
    It   In paradiso non ci si va in carrozza.
    El   No es blando el camino del cielo.
    Ru   Как ни мостись, а на небо не влезешь.

12 En   Ye cannot serve God and mammon. *(B)*
    Fr   Vous ne pouvez servir Dieu et Mammon.
    De   Ihr könnt nicht Gott dienen und dem Mammon.
    It   Voi non potete servire a Dio ed a Mammona.
    El   No podéis servir a Dios y a Mammón.
    Ru   Не можете служить Богу и маммоне. *(Б)*

13 En   Short prayers rise up to Heaven.*
    Fr   Brève oraison pénètre les cieux.
    De   Kurzes Gebet, tiefe Andacht.
    It   Corta preghiera penetra in cielo.
    El   La oración breve sube al cielo.
    Ru   Коротка молитва "Отче наш", да спасает.

14   *En*   Bells call others, but themselves enter not into the church.
      Fr   La cloche appelle à l'église, mais elle n'y entre pas.
      De Die Glocke ruft zur Kirche, geht aber selbst nicht hinein.
      It   Le campane chiamano gli altri e non entrano in chiesa.
      El   No entra en misa la campana, y a todos llama.
      Ru Колокол в церковь сзывает, а сам в церкви не бывает.

15   *En*   The nearer the church, the farther from God.
      Fr   Près de l'église, loin de Dieu.
      De Je näher der Kirche, je weiter von Gott.
      It   Vicino alla chiesa, lontano da Dio.
      El   Cerca de la iglesia, pero lejos de Dios.
      Ru Близко церкви, да далеко от Бога.

16   *En*   Like priest, like people.*
      Fr   Tel chapelain, tel sacristain.
      De Wie der Hirt, so die Herde.
      It   Tale è il gregge, qual'è chi lo regge.
      El   Cual el rey, tal la grey.
      Ru Каков поп, таков и приход.

17   *En*   He that would learn to pray, let him go to sea.*
      Fr   Qui veut apprendre à prier, aille souvent sur la mer.
      De Wer nicht beten kann, werde ein Schiffsmann.
      It   Chi non sa orare, vada in mare a navigare.
      El   Si quieres aprender a orar, entra en la mar.
      Ru Кто в море не бывал, тот досыта Богу не молился.

18   *En*   Faith can remove mountains. *(B)*
      Fr   La foi transporte les montagnes.
      De Der Glaube kann Berge versetzen.
      It   La fede può smuovere le montagne.
      El   La fe muda los montes.
      Ru Вера и гору с места сдвинет. *(Б)*

19 *En* The just shall live by faith. *(B)*

   Fr Le juste vivra par la foi.

   De Der Gerechte wird seines Glaubens leben.

   It Il giusto viverà per fede.

   El El justo vivirá por la fe.

   Ru Праведный верою жив будет. *(Б)*

23 **Devil–Hell**
   Diable–Enfer
   Teufel–Hölle
   Diavolo–Inferno
   Diablo–Infierno
   Дьявол–Ад

1 *En* The devil lurks behind the cross.
   Fr Derrière la croix se tient le diable.
   De Hinter dem Kreuz versteckt sich der Teufel.
   It Il diavolo si nasconde dietro la croce.
   El Detrás de la cruz está el diablo.
   Ru Около святых черти водятся.

2 *En* The devil was sick, the devil a monk would be.*
   Fr Quand le diable devient vieux, il se fait ermite.
   De Ist der Teufel krank, so will er Mönch werden.
   It Il diavolo, quando è vecchio, si fa frate.
   El Después de viejo el diablo se hizo fraile.
   Ru И чёрт под старость в монахи пошёл.

3 *En* The devil is not so black as he is painted.*
   Fr Le diable n'est pas si noir qu'on le fait.
   De Der Teufel ist nicht so schwarz, wie man ihn mahlt.
   It Il diavolo non è così nero come lo si dipinge.
   El No es el diablo tan feo como lo pintan.
   Ru Не так страшен чёрт, как его малюют.

4 *En* Where the devil cannot come, he will send.
   Fr Où le diable ne peut aller, sa mère tâche d'y mander.
   De Wo der Teufel nicht hin mag, da schickt er ein altes Weib.

It   Dove il diavolo non può entrare, manda una vecchia.
El   En lo que el diablo no sabe hacer, pide consejo a la mujer.
Ru   Куда чёрт не поспеет, туда бабу пошлёт.

5   *En*   He should have a long spoon that sups with the devil.
    Fr   Quand on dîne avec le diable, il faut se munir d'une longue cuiller.
    De   Der muss einen langen Löffel haben, der mit dem Teufel essen will.
    It   Chi vuol' mangiar col diavolo bisogna aver cucchiaio lungo.
    El   Quien con el diablo haya de comer, larga cuchara ha menester.
    Ru   Кто с чёртом обедать хочет, должен запастись длинной ложкой.

6   *En*   The devil's meal is all (half) bran.
    Fr   La farine du diable n'est que bran.
    De   Das Mehl des Teufels wird zu Kleie.
    It   La farina del diavolo va tutta in crusca.
    El   Lo bien mal ganado se lo lleva el diablo.
    Ru   Много чёртовой ржи, да всё лебеда.

7   *En*   Give the devil his due.
    Fr   Il faut donner au diable son dû.
    De   Selbst dem Teufel sein Recht geben.
    It   Dare al diavolo ciò che gli spetta.
    El   Dale al diablo lo que es suyo.
    Ru   Воздавай должное и дьяволу.

8   *En*   To hold a candle to the devil.
    Fr   Brûler une chandelle au diable.
    De   Dem Teufel eine Kerze anzünden.
    It   Accendere una candela al diavolo.
    El   Encender una vela al diablo.
    Ru   Взывать к помощи нечистой силы.

9　*En*　Hell and destruction are never full. *(B)*

　　Fr　Le séjour des morts et l'abîme sont insatiables.

　　De　Hölle und Abgrund werden nimmer voll.

　　It　Il sepolcro e il luogo della perdizione non son giammai satolli.

　　El　El sepulcro y la perdición nunca se hartan.

　　Ru　Преисподняя и Аваддон–ненасытимы. *(Б)*

10　*En*　Hell is paved with good intentions.*

　　Fr　L'enfer est pavé de bonnes intentions.

　　De　Der Weg zur Hölle ist mit guten Vorsätzen gepflastert.

　　It　L'inferno è lastricato di buone intenzioni.

　　El　De buenas intenciones está lleno el infierno.

　　Ru　Ад вымощен благими намерениями.

24 **Much–Little–Nothing**
Beaucoup–Peu–Rien
Viel–Wenig–Nichts
Molto–Poco–Niente
Mucho–Poco–Nada
Много–Мало–Ничего

1   *En*   Many a little makes a mickle.*
     Fr   Plusieurs peu font un beaucoup.
     De   Wenig zu wenig macht zuletzt viel.
     It   Molti pochi fanno un assai.
     El   Muchos pocos hacen un mucho.
     Ru   Из многих малых выходит одно большое.
         С миру по нитке–голому рубашка.

2   *En*   Penny and penny laid up will be many.
     Fr   Denier sur denier bâtit la maison.
     De   Viele Pfennige machen einen Taler.
     It   Quattrino a quattrino si fa il fiorino.
     El   Florín con florín hace buen tintín.
     Ru   Копеечка к копеечке–рубль набегает.

3   *En*   Grain by grain, and the hen fills her belly.
     Fr   Goutte à goutte on remplit la cuve.
     De   Viele Körner machen einen Haufen.
     It   A granello a granello s'empie lo staio e si fa il monte.
     El   Grano a grano hinche la gallina el papo.
     Ru   Курочка по зёрнышку клюёт и сыта бывает.

4   *En*   Large streams from little fountains flow.
         Many drops make a shower.

(24) 5

Fr Les petits ruisseaux font les grandes rivières.
De Kleine Bäche machen einen Strom.
It I piccoli ruscelli fanno i grandi fiumi.
El De los arroyos chicos se hacen los grandes ríos.
Ru Из крошек кучка, из капель море.

5 *En* One shallow does not make a summer.*
Fr Une hirondelle ne fait pas le printemps.
De Eine Schwalbe macht keinen Sommer.
It Una rondine non fa primavera.
El Una golondrina no hace verano.
Ru Одна ласточка весны не делает.

6 *En* One flower makes no garland.*
Fr Une fleur ne fait pas une guirlande.
De Eine Blume macht keinen Kranz.
It Un fior non fa ghirlanda.
El Ni un dedo hace mano, ni una golondrina verano.
Ru Одно дерево–ещё не сад.

7 *En* Store is no sore.*
Fr On n'en a jamais trop.
De Vorrat nimmer schad't.
It Meglio troppo che troppo poco.
El Lo que sobra, no daña.
Ru Запас беды не чинит.

8 *En* Plenty is no plague.
Fr Abondance de biens ne nuit pas.
De Je mehr, desto besser.
    Lieber zuviel als zuwenig.
It Abbondanza di bene non nuoce.
El Más valen dos camisones que uno.
Ru От прибыли голова не болит.

130

9 *En* Much ado about nothing.

  Fr Beaucoup de bruit pour rien.

     Tant de bruit pour une omelette.

  De Viel Lärm um nichts.

  It Molto rumore per nulla.

  El Mucho ruido para nada.

  Ru Много шума из ничего.

10 *En* He cannot see the wood for trees.

  Fr Les arbres l'empêchent de voir la forêt.

  De Er sieht den Wald vor lauter Bäumen nicht.

  It Non può veder il bosco per gli alberi.

  El No puede ver el bosque por los árboles.

  Ru Из-за деревьев не видит леса.

11 *En* Once is no custom.

  Fr Une fois n'est pas coutume.

  De Einmal ist keinmal.

  It Una volta non fa usanza.

  El Un solo acto no hace hábito.

  Ru Один раз не в счёт.

12 *En* One and none is all one.*

  Fr Un homme, nul homme.

  De Ein Mann–kein Mann.

  It Uno e nessuno è tutt'uno.

  El Uno y ninguno todo es uno.

  Ru Один в поле не воин.

13 *En* Many hounds may soon worry one hare.*

  Fr Finalement on est accablé par le nombre.

  De Viele Hunde sind des Hasen Tod.

  It Molti cani sono la morte della lepre.

El   Muchos lobos a una oveja, pronto le quitan la pelleja.
Ru   Где много гончих, там зайцу смерть.

14   *En*   Ask much to have a little.
    Fr   Demande beaucoup pour en avoir un peu.
    De   Wer viel haben will, muss mehr fordern.
    It   Chi vuole assai, non domandi poco.
    El   Pide lo más, y algo te darán.
    Ru   Проси много, а бери, что дают.

15   *En*   Too much of one thing is good for nothing.*
        More than enough is too much.
    Fr   L'excès en tout est un défaut.
    De   Allzuviel ist ungesund.
    It   Ogni estremo è vizioso.
        Il troppo stroppia.
    El   Lo demasiado, siempre ha dañado.
        Bueno es lo bastante, y malo lo sobrante.
    Ru   Хорошего понемногу.

16   *En*   Too much breaks the bag.
    Fr   Le surplus rompt le couvercle.
    De   Allzuviel zerreisst den Sack.
    It   Ogni soverchio rompe il coperchio.
    El   La demasía rompe la talega.
    Ru   Всему есть счёт, мера и граница.

17   *En*   Enough and to spare.
    Fr   Assez et au delà.
        Il y en a à revendre.
    De   In Hülle und Fülle.
        Mehr als genug.
    It   A bizzeffe.
        Più che sufficiente.

El Basta y sobra.
    Más que suficiente.
Ru За глаза довольно.
    Хоть пруд пруди.

18 En Better aught than naught.*
    Fr Mieux vaut peu que rien.
    De Etwas ist besser denn nichts.
    It È meglio qualche cosa che niente.
    El Más vale algo que nada.
    Ru Лучше кое-что, чем ничего.

19 En Better some of a pudding than none of a pie.
    Fr Faute de grives, on mange des merles.
    De In der Not frisst der Teufel Fliegen.
    It Chi non può ber nell'oro, beva nel vetro.
    El Más vale pan duro que ninguno.
    Ru Съешь и морковку, коли яблочка нет.

20 En Better are small fish than an empty dish.
    Fr Faute de truites, on mange des barbeaux.
    De Besser ein kleiner Fisch als gar nichts auf dem Tisch.
    It È meglio tale e quale che senza nulla stare.
    El Buenos son barbos, cuando no hay truchas a mano.
    Ru Маленькая рыбка лучше большого таракана.
        На безрыбьи и рак рыба.

21 En Half a loaf is better than no bread.
    Fr Demi pain vaut mieux que rien du tout.
    De Ein halbes Brot ist besser als gar keins.
    It Più val' mezzo pan che niente.
    El Más vale medio pan que no nada.
    Ru Всё лучше того, как нет ничего.

22 *En* It is a drop in the ocean.
    Fr C'est une goutte d'eau dans la mer.
    De Das ist ein Tropfen ins Meer.
    It C'è una goccia nel mare.
    El Es una gota de agua en el mar.
    Ru Это капля в море.

23 *En* For one that is missing there's no spoiling a wedding.
    Fr Faute d'un moine, l'abbaye ne chôme pas.
    De Sechs oder sieben sollen nicht harren auf einen Narren.
    It Sette non devono aspettare uno.
    El Por un garbanzo no se descompone la olla.
    Ru Семеро одного не ждут.

24 *En* Nothing comes of (from) nothing.*
    Fr De rien, rien ne sort.
    De Aus Nichts wird Nichts.
    It Col nulla non si fa nulla.
    El De nada no se hace nada.
    Ru Из ничего не будет ничего.

25 *En* Where nothing is, nothing can be had.*
    Fr Nul ne peut donner ce qu'il n'a.
    De Wer nichts hat, kann nichts geben.
    It Nessun può dare quel che non ha.
    El Nadie puede dar lo que no tiene.
    Ru Чего нет, того негде взять.
          На нет и суда нет.

26 *En* Where nought's to be got, kings lose their scot.*
    Fr Où il n'y a rien, le roi perd ses droits.
    De Wo nichts ist, hat der Kaiser sein Recht verloren.
    It Dove non n'è, non ne toglie neanche la piena.
    El Al que no tiene, el rey lo hace libre.
    Ru Чего нет, того и Бог не возьмёт.

27 *En* Many are called, but few are chosen. *(B)*
   Fr Il y a beaucoup d'appelés, mais peu d'élus.
   De Viele sind berufen, aber wenige sind auserwählt.
   It Molti son chiamati, ma pochi eletti.
   El Muchos son llamados, y pocos escogidos.
   Ru Много званных, а мало избранных. *(Б)*

28 *En* No money, no Swiss.
   Fr Pas d'argent, pas de Suisse.
   De Kein Kreuzer, kein Schweizer.
   It Per nulla non canta un cieco.
   El Sin pecunia no lograrás cosa alguna.
   Ru Нет денег–нет слуг.
      Даром только воду пьют.

29 *En* No penny, no paternoster.
   Fr Sans deniers Georges ne chante pas.
   De Nimmer Geld, nimmer Gesell.
   It Senza denari non si hanno i paternostri.
   El Por dinero baila el perro.
   Ru Даром петь–горло дереть.

25 Wealth–Poverty
   Richesse–Pauvreté
   Reichtum–Armut
   Ricchezza–Povertà
   Riqueza–Pobreza
   Богатство–Бедность

1   *En*   Much coin, much care.
    Fr   Plus on a d'argent, plus on a de soucis.
    De   Viel Geld–viel Sorgen.
    It   Grandi ricchezze–mille pensieri.
    El   A más dinero, más cuidado.
    Ru   Много денег–много и хлопот.

2   *En*   Money is round and rolls away.
    Fr   Puisque l'argent est rond, c'est pour rouler.
    De   Geld ist rund, es rollt gern.
    It   I denari sono tondi e ruzzolano.
    El   El dinero se ha hecho redondo para que ruede.
    Ru   Деньги без ног, а уходят.

3   *En*   Where gold speaks every tongue is silent.
    Fr   Où l'or parle, toute langue se tait.
    De   Redet Geld, so schweigt die Welt.
    It   Dove l'oro parla, ogni lingue tace.
    El   Cuando el rico habla, todos callan.
    Ru   Когда деньги говорят, тогда правда молчит.

4   *En*   Gold is an orator.
          Money talks.
    Fr   Rien de plus éloquent que l'argent comptant.

De Wo Geld redet, da gilt andere Rede nicht.
It Nulla di più eloquente che il denaro contante.
El Nada más elocuente que el dinero contante.
Ru Коли богатый заговорит, так есть кому послушать.

5 *En* Money will do anything.*
   Fr L'argent fait tout.
   De Geld macht alles.
   It Coi quattrini si fa tutto.
   El Con mucho dinero, todo es hacedero.
      Todo lo alcanza el dinero.
   Ru Деньги много могут.

6 *En* All things are obedient to money.*
   Fr L'argent comptant l'emporte.
   De Geld regiert die Welt.
   It L'oro governa il mondo.
   El Todas las cosas obedecen a la pecunia.
   Ru И барину деньги господин.

7 *En* A golden key opens every door.*
   Fr La clef d'or ouvre toutes les portes.
   De Ein goldner Schlüssel öffnet alle Tore.
   It Chiave d'oro apre tutte le porte.
   El La llave de oro abre todas las puertas.
   Ru Золотой ключ любые ворота отпирает.

8 *En* No lock will hold against the power of gold.
   Fr L'or ouvre tous les verroux.
   De Goldener Hammer bricht eisernes Tor.
   It Vuoi tu aprir qualqunque porta? Chiavi d'oro teco porta.
   El A llave de oro no resiste cerradura de acero.
   Ru Золотой молоток и железные ворота отпирает.

9   *En*   Money opens all doors.
    Fr   L'argent ouvre toutes les portes.
    De   Geld öffnet alle Türen.
    It   Il denaro apre tutte le porte.
    El   El dinero abre todas las puertas.
    Ru   Денежка дорожку прокладывает.

10 *En*   Money is the sinews of war.*
    Fr   L'argent est le nerf de la guerre.
    De   Geld ist des Krieges Stärke.
    It   Il danaro è il nervo della guerra.
    El   El nervio de la guerra: dinero.
    Ru   Кто силён да богат, тому хорошо воевать.

11 *En*   Money has no smell.*
    Fr   L'argent n'a pas d'odeur.
    De   Geld stinkt nicht.
    It   Il denaro non puzza.
    El   El dinero no tiene olor.
    Ru   Деньги не пахнут.

12 *En*   Money begets money.*
    Fr   L'argent appelle l'argent.
    De   Wo Geld ist, will Geld hin.
    It   Soldo fa soldo.
    El   Dinero llama dinero.
    Ru   Деньга деньгу родит.

13 *En*   Money draws money.
    Fr   Le bien cherche le bien.
    De   Geld kommt zu Geld.
    It   La roba va alla roba.
    El   El dinero va al dinero.
    Ru   Деньги к деньгам идут.

14 *En* The rich hath many friends. *(B)*
   Fr Les amis du riche sont nombreux.
   De Die Reichen haben viel Freunde.
   It Molti son gli amici del ricco.
   El Muchos son los que aman el rico.
   Ru У богатого много друзей. *(Б)*

15 *En* Take care of the pence, and the pounds will take care of
      themselves.
   Fr Economisez les deniers, les louis auront soin d'eux-mêmes.
   De Wer den Pfennig nicht ehrt, ist des Talers nicht wert.
   It Chi non tien conto del poco, non acquista l'assai.
   El A quien sabe guardar una peseta, nunca le falta un duro.
   Ru Кто не бережёт копейки, сам рубля не стоит.

16 *En* When a knave is in a plum-tree, he hath neither friend
      nor kin.
   Fr Vilain enrichi ne connaît ni parent, ni ami.
   De Ein reicher Bauer kennt seine Verwandten nicht.
   It Il villan nobilitato non conosce il parentado.
   El Cuando el villano está rico, no tiene pariente ni amigo.
   Ru Залез в богатство–забыл и братство.

17 *En* A penny saved is a penny gained.
   Fr L'épargne est une grande richesse.
   De Ersparter Pfennig–verdienter Pfennig.
   It Quattrino risparmiato–due volte guadagnato.
   El El que guarda, halla.
   Ru Бережливость–лучшее богатство.

18 *En* Lightly gained, quickly lost.
   Fr Ce qui vient par la flûte s'en va par le tambour.
   De Wie gewonnen, so zerronnen.
   It La roba di mal acquisto se la porta il vento.
   El Lo que el agua trae, el agua lleva.
   Ru Легко добыто, легко и прожито.

19 *En* In spending lies the advantage.
    Fr L'usage seulement fait la possession.
    De Verborgener Schatz ist nichts wert.
    It Denaro sepolto non fa guadagno.
    El Plata guardada, no gana nada.
          Dinero guardado, dinero capado.
    Ru Дано добро и нажить, и прожить.

20 *En* Poverty is no sin.*
    Fr Pauvreté n'est pas vice.
    De Armut ist keine Sünde.
    It Povertà non è vizio.
    El Pobreza no es vileza.
    Ru Бедность не порок.

21 *En* Poverty is a hateful good.
    Fr De pauvreté fatigue et peine.
          La pauvreté humilie les hommes.
    De Armut tut weh.
    It La povertà è una cattiva compagnia.
    El Pobreza nunca alza cabeza.
    Ru Бедность всего хуже.
          Нищета пуще смерти.

22 *En* Poverty is the mother of all arts.*
    Fr Pauvreté est mère des arts.
    De Armut ist aller Künste Meister.
    It La povertà insegna tutte le arti.
    El La pobreza es madre de las artes.
    Ru Голь на выдумки хитра.

23 *En* Poverty parteth fellowship (friends).
    Fr Pauvreté n'a point de parenté.
    De Arme Leuten haben keine Verwandten.

It Povertà non ha parenti.

El No hay amigo ni hermano, si no hay dinero de mano.

Ru Привяжется сума–откажется родня.

24 *En* Nothing agreeth worse than a lord's heart and a beggar's purse.

Fr Un noble s'il n'est à la rose, vaut parfois peu de chose.

De Adel ohne Geld gilt wenig in der Welt.

It Nobiltà poco si prezza, se vi manca la ricchezza.

El Mucha soberbia y pocos bienes mal se avienen.

Ru Велика честь, да нечего есть.

Пуст карман, да красив кафтан.

25 *En* To live from hand to mouth.

Fr Vivre au jour le jour.

De Von der Hand in den Mund leben.

It Campare giorno per giorno.

Vivere alla giornata.

El Vivir al día.

Ru Живёт–из кулака да в рот.

26 *En* He whose belly is full believes not him who is fasting.*

Fr Qui a la panse pleine croit que les autres sont rassasiés.

De Ein Satter glaubt dem Hungrigen nicht.

It Corpo satollo non crede al digiuno.

El El harto del ayuno no tiene duelo.

Ru Сытый голодного не разумеет.

27 *En* A poor man's tale cannot be heard. *(B)*

Fr Les paroles du pauvre ne sont pas écoutées.

De Auf den Armen hört man nicht.

It Le parole del povero non son ascoltate.

El Las palabras del pobre no están escuchadas.

Ru Слов бедняка никто не слушает. *(Б)*

28   *En*   He is rich enough that wants nothing.*
      Fr   Est assez riche qui est content.
      De   Reich genug, wer sich genügen lässt.
      It   Assai è ricco, a chi nulla manca.
      El   Nada necesita quien tiene lo bastante.
      Ru   Тот и богат, кто нужды не знает.

29   *En*   Content is more than a kingdom.*
      Fr   Contentement passe richesse.
      De   Zufriedenheit ist der grösste Reichtum.
      It   La vera ricchezza è contentarsi.
      El   No hay mayor riqueza que contentamiento.
      Ru   Довольство–лучшее богатство.

30   *En*   Another's bread costs dear.
      Fr   Le pain d'autrui est toujours dur.
      De   Fremdes Brot, herbes Brot.
      It   Il pane degli altri è troppo salato.
      El   Pan ajeno, caro cuesta.
      Ru   Чужой хлеб горек.

31   *En*   A man without money is no man at all.*
      Fr   Un homme sans argent est un loup sans dents.
      De   Ein Mann ohne Geld ist eine Leiche.
      It   Uomo senza quattrini è un morto che cammina.
      El   Hombre sin dinero, pozo sin agua.
      Ru   Без денег–везде худенек.

32   *En*   Stretch your legs according to your coverlets.
      Fr   Il faut étendre ses pieds selon ses draps.
      De   Man muss sich nach der Decke strecken.
      It   Bisogna distendersi quanto il lenzuolo è lungo.
      El   Extender la pierna hasta donde llega la sábana.
      Ru   По одёжке протягивай ножки.

33 *En* Cut your coat according to your cloth.
   Fr Il faut tailler la robe selon le drap.
        Selon ta bourse gouverne ta bouche.
   De Man muss sich nach seinem Beutel richten.
   It Bisogna fare la veste secondo il panno.
   El Según el tejido córtate el vestido.
   Ru По приходу и расход держи.

26 **Covetousness–Avarice**
   Avidité–Avarice
   Habsucht–Geiz
   Avidità–Avarizia
   Avidez–Avaricia
   Жадность–Скупость

1 *En* The love of money is the root of all evil. *(B)*
   Fr L'amour de l'argent est une racine de tous les maux.
   De Geldgier ist die Wurzel aller Übel.
   It La radice di tutti i mali è l'avarizia.
   El El amor del dinero es la raíz de todos los males.
   Ru Корень всех зол есть сребролюбие. *(Б)*

2 *En* A covetous man serves his riches, not they him.*
   Fr L'avare ne possède pas son or, c'est son or qui le possède.
   De Nicht das Geld gehört dem Geizigen, sondern der
         Geizige dem Geld.
   It L'avaro non possiede l'oro, ma è posseduto dall'oro.
   El El avariento no tiene el tesoro, tiene el entendimiento.
   Ru Умный человек–хозяин деньгам, а скупой–слуга.

3 *En* A covetous man does nothing that he should till he
         dies.*
   Fr L'avare et le cochon ne sont bons qu'après leur mort.
   De Der Geizhals und ein fettes Schwein uns erst im Tode
         nützlich sein.
   It L'avaro è come il porco, che è buono dopo morto.
   El Hombre avaricioso, solo en la muerte es generoso.
   Ru Есть много богачей, которых смерть одна к чему-нибудь
         годна.

144

4   *En* Beggars mounted run their horse to death.*
     Fr Gueux en selle galope à crever sa monture.
     De Der Bettler, der Ritter worden, jagt sein Pferd zu Tod.
     It Quando la merda monta in scanno, o che la puzza, o che fa danno.
     El Cuando el villano està en el mulo, no conoce a Dios, ni al mundo.
     Ru Мужик богатый–что бык рогатый.
         Дай глупому лошадь, так он на ней и к чёрту уедет.

5   *En* He would skin a mouse, and send the hide to market.
     Fr Il écorcherait un pou pour en avoir la peau.
     De Er schindet die Laus des Balges wegen.
     It Scorticherebbe il pidocchio per aver la pelle.
     El En su casa no comen huevos para no tirar la cáscara.
     Ru Он готов шкуру с блохи содрать шерсти ради.

6   *En* The miser is always in want.*
     Fr L'homme avare n'est jamais riche.
     De Des Geizes Schlund ist ohne Grund.
     It L'uomo avaro e l'occhio sono insaziabili.
     El Al avaro siempre le falta.
     Ru Скупой всегда нуждается.
         Жадному всё мало.

7   *En* Poor though in the midst of wealth.
     Fr N'est pas riche qui est chiche.
     De Geiz ist die grösste Armut.
     It L'avarizia è la maggiore delle povertà.
     El No hay tal pobre como el avariento.
     Ru Скупой богач беднее нищего.

8   *En* Covetousness is the root of all evil.*
     Fr L'avarice est la mère de tous les vices.
     De Geiz ist die Wurzel alles Übels.

It L'avarizia è scuola d'ogni vizio.

El La raíz de todos los males es la avaricia.

Ru Скупость–мать пороков.

9 *En* Much would have more.*

 Fr Plus on a, plus on désire avoir.

 De Je mehr man hat, je mehr man will.

 It Chi più ha, più desidera.

 El Quien más tiene, más quiere.

 Ru Кто много имеет, больше ещё хочет.

10 *En* All covet, all lose.*

 Fr Qui tout convoite tout perd.

 De Wer alles will haben, soll nichts haben.

 It Chi tutto vuole, tutto perde.

 El Quien todo lo quiere, todo lo pierde.

 Ru Всего желать–всё потерять.

11 *En* Grasp all, lose all.

 Fr Qui trop embrasse, mal étreint.

 De Wer zuviel fasst, lässt viel fallen.

 It Chi troppo abbraccia, nulla stringe.

 El Quien mucho abarca, poco aprieta.

 Ru Тяжело нагребёшь–домой не донесёшь.

12 *En* To kill the goose that lays the golden eggs.

 Fr Tuer la poule aux œufs d'or.

 De Die Henne schlachten, die goldene Eier legt.

 It Uccidere la gallina che fa le uova d'oro.

 El Matar la gallina de los huevos de oro.

 Ru Убить курицу, несущую золотые яйца.

13 *En* Give him an inch, and he'll take an ell.

 Fr Si vous lui donnez un doigt, il en prend long comme le bras.

De Gib ihm eine Handbreit, so nimmt er die ganze Elle.
It Gli dai un dito e si prende la mano.
El Dale el pie, y se tomará la mano.
Ru Дай ему палец, он и всю руку откусит.

14 *En* The golden calf. *(B)*
  Fr Le veau d'or.
  De Das goldene Kalb.
  It Vitello d'oro.
  El Becerro de oro.
  Ru Золотой телец. *(Б)*

27 Borrowing–Debts
   Emprunt–Dette
   Borgen–Schulden
   Prestito–Debito
   Empréstito–Deuda
   Заём–Долги

1 *En* He that goes a-borrowing, goes a-sorrowing.
   Fr Argent emprunté porte tristesse.
   De Borgen macht Sorgen.
   It Chi presta, male annesta.
   El El que algo debe, no reposa como quiere.
   Ru Долг не ревёт, а спать не даёт.

2 *En* Creditors have better memories than debitors.*
   Fr Le prêteur a meilleure mémoire que l'emprunteur.
   De Gläubiger haben ein besseres Gedächtnis als Schuldner.
   It I creditori hanno miglior memoria dei debitori.
   El El acreedor es más memorioso que el deudor.
   Ru Долги помнит не тот, кто берёт, а кто даёт.

3 *En* A good borrower is a lazy payer.
   Fr Bon emprunteur, mauvais payeur.
   De Guter Borger, schlechter Zahler.
   It Prendere in prestito e rendere sono due.
   El Buen pagador, mal cobrador.
   Ru В долг брать легко, а платить тяжело.

4 *En* The borrower is servant to the lender. *(B)*
   Fr Celui qui emprunte est l'esclave de celui qui prête.
   De Wer borgt, ist des Leihers Knecht.

It   Chi prende in prestanza è servo del prestatore.

El   El que toma prestado, siervo es del que empresta.

Ru   Должник делается рабом заимодавца. *(Б)*

5   *En*   Over head and ears in debt.

   Fr   Avoir des dettes par-dessus la tête.

   De   Bis über die Ohren in Schulden stecken.

   It   Avere debiti fin sopra alla testa.

   El   Deber a todo el mundo.

   Ru   Быть по уши в долгах.

       В долгу, как в шелку.

6   *En*   Of ill debtors men take oats.

   Fr   D'un mauvais débiteur prends paille et foin.

   De   Für böse Schuld nimm Bohnenstroh.

   It   Da cattivo debitor togli paglia per lavor.

   El   A quien es de mal pagar, en paja le has de cobrar.

   Ru   От худого должника хоть мякиною бери.

7   *En*   Lend your money and lose your friend.

   Fr   Qui prête à l'ami s'en fait souvent un ennemi.

   De   Leihen macht Freundschaft, Mahnen–Feindschaft.

   It   Amico beneficato, nemico dichiarato.

   El   Quien presta a un amigo, compra un enemigo.

   Ru   В долг давать–дружбу терять.

8   *En*   Better go to bed supperless than to rise in debt.

   Fr   Il vaut mieux se coucher sans souper que de se lever avec dettes.

   De   Besser ohne Abendbrot zu Bette gehn als mit Schulden aufstehn.

   It   Meglio andare a letto senza cena che alzarsi con debiti.

   El   Más vale acostarse sin cena que levantarse con deuda.

   Ru   Лучше без ужина ложиться, чем с долгами вставать.

9   *En*   Out of debt, out of danger.*
    Fr   Qui paye ses dettes s'enrichit.
    De   Wer seine Schulden bezahlt, verbessert seine Güter.
    It   Chi paga debito, acquista credito.
    El   Quien paga sus deudas, se hará rico.
    Ru   Рад будешь, как долг избудешь.

10 *En*   Once paid and never craved.
    Fr   Le bon payeur est de bourse d'autrui seigneur.
    De   Lustig und geduldig, keinem Wirt was schuldig.
    It   Chi paga debiti, è padrone degli altri.
    El   El que paga lo que debe, lo que queda es suyo.
    Ru   Заплати долг скорее, так будет веселее.

11 *En*   Promise is debt.*
    Fr   Chose promise, chose due.
    De   Versprechen macht Schuld.
    It   Ogni promessa è debito.
    El   Lo prometido es deuda.
    Ru   Посулился, так и задолжал.

12 *En*   A hired horse tired never.
    Fr   On avance mieux avec un cheval emprunté qu'avec le sien propre.
    De   Ein Mietsgaul darf nicht müde werden.
    It   Sproni propri e cavalli d'altrui fanno corte le miglia.
    El   Caballo ajeno, ni come ni se cansa.
    Ru   Конь не свой–погоняй, не стой!

28 Mine and Thine
   Le Mien et le Tien
   Das Mein und Dein
   Mio e Tuo
   Mio y Tuyo
   Своё и чужое

1   *En*   A burden of one's own choice is not felt.
    Fr   Le fardeau qu'on aime n'est point pesant.
    De   Eigene Last wird nicht zu schwer.
    It   Il proprio fardello pesa poco.
    El   Carga que agrada, no es pesada.
    Ru   Своя ноша не тянет.

2   *En*   Near is my coat (shirt), but nearer is my skin.*
    Fr   Ma peau m'est plus proche que ma chemise.
    De   Das Hemd ist mir näher als der Rock.
    It   Stringe più la camicia che la gonnella.
    El   Primero es la carne que la camisa.
    Ru   Своя рубашка ближе к телу.
           Своя кожа рубахи дороже.

3   *En*   Charity begins at home.*
    Fr   Charité bien ordonnée commence par soi-même.
    De   Jeder ist sich selbst der Nächste.
    It   La prima carità comincia da sè.
    El   La caridad bien entendida empieza por uno mismo.
    Ru   Всяк сам себе ближе.

4   *En*   Let every pedlar carry his own burden.
    Fr   Chacun mercier portera son panier.
           Chacun ira au moulin avec son propre sac.

151

De Trage jeder seinen Sack zur Mühle.
It Ognuno va col suo sacco al mulino.
El Cada carnero de su pie cuelga.
Ru Живи всяк своим умом да своим горбом.

5 *En* Men cut large thongs of other men's leather.*
   Fr Du cuir d'autrui, large courroie.
   De Aus fremdem Leder ist gut Riemen schneiden.
   It Del cuoio d'altri si fanno larghe stringhe.
   El De cuero ajeno correas largas.
   Ru Из чужой спины ремешки кроить.
      Чужим добром подносить ведром.

6 *En* It is good to learn at other men's cost.
   Fr Sage et prudent celui qui apprend au dépens d'autrui.
   De In anderer Leute Küche ist gut kochen lernen.
   It Felice chi impara a spese d'altri.
   El Escarmentar en cabeza ajena, es lección barata.
   Ru На чужой спине легко.
      На чужие деньги запоем пьём.

7 *En* All men are free of other men's goods.*
   Fr Du bien d'autrui, bon jouet.
   De Aus anderer Leute Beutel ist gut zehren.
   It Della roba d'altri si spende senza risparmio.
   El De lo ajeno, todos somos generosos.
   Ru Из чужого кармана платить легко.

8 *En* It is easy to cry Yule at other men's cost.
   Fr A table d'autrui on mange de meilleur appétit.
   De Auf anderer Leute Kirchweih ist gut Gäste laden.
   It Si balla bene sulla sala degli altri.
   El De petaca ajena, la mano llena.
   Ru Чужим обедом гостей потчевать не убыточно.

9   *En*   Every man likes his own things best.*
     Fr   Chacun aime le sien.
     De   Jedem gefällt das Seine.
     It   A ciascun piace il suo.
          Ogni naso par bello alla sua faccia.
     El   No hay nariz fea para quien en su cara la lleva.
     Ru   Всякому своё мило.

10   *En*   Each bird loves to hear himself sing.
     Fr   Chaque oiseau chante sa propre chanson.
     De   Jeder Vogel singt, wie ihm der Schnabel gewachsen ist.
     It   Ogni uccello canta il suo verso.
     El   Cada cual canta lo que sabe.
     Ru   Всякая птица свои песни поёт.

11   *En*   The master's eye maketh the horse fat.*
     Fr   L'œil du maître engraisse le cheval.
     De   Des Herrn Auge macht das Pferd fett.
     It   L'occhio del padrone fa ingrassare il cavallo.
     El   El ojo del amo engorda al caballo.
     Ru   От хозяйского глаза и конь добреет.

12   *En*   The master's footsteps fatten the soil.
     Fr   L'œil du fermier vaut fumier.
     De   Des Herrn Fuss düngt den Acker.
     It   Il piè del padrone ingrassa il campo.
     El   El pie del dueño estiércol es para la heredad.
     Ru   Где хозяин ходит, там земля родит.

13   *En*   The eye of the master will do more than both his hands.
     Fr   L'œil du maître fait plus que ses deux mains.
     De   Das Auge des Herrn schafft mehr als seine beiden Hände.
     It   Più vede un occhio del padrone che quattro del servo.
     El   Más labra el dueño mirando que diez yuntas arando.
     Ru   Хозяйский глаз–алмаз (–смотрок).

14 *En* Every miller draws water to his own mill.
   Fr Chacun tire l'eau à son moulin.
   De Jeder leitet das Wasser auf seine eigene Mühle.
   It Ognuno tira l'acqua al suo mulino.
   El Cada uno quiere llevar el agua a su molino.
   Ru Каждый льёт воду на свою собственную мельницу.

15 *En* Every man shall bear his own burden. *(B)*
   Fr Chacun portera son propre fardeau.
   De Ein jeglicher soll seine eigene Bürde tragen.
   It Ciascuno porterà il suo proprio peso.
   El Cada cual llevará su carga.
   Ru Каждый понесёт своё бремя. *(Б)*

29 **Rule–Power**
   Domination–Pouvoir
   Herrschaft–Macht
   Dominio–Potere
   Dominio–Poder
   Господство–Власть

1 *En* Divide and rule.*
   Fr Divise afin de régner.
   De Teile und herrsche.
   It Nemico diviso, mezzo vinto.
   El Divide y gobierna.
   Ru Разделяй и властвуй.

2 *En* Nothing that is violent is permanent.*
   Fr Chose violente n'est pas permanente.
   De Strenge Herren regieren nicht lange.
        Grosse Gewalt wird selten alt.
   It Violenza non dura a lungo.
   El Lo que es violento no puede durar.
   Ru На кнуте далеко не уедешь.

3 *En* Put not your trust in princes. *(B)*
   Fr Ne vous confiez pas aux grands.
   De Verlasset euch nicht auf Fürsten.
   It Non vi confidate in principi.
   El No confiéis en los príncipes.
   Ru Не надейтесь на князей. *(Б)*

4 *En* The pleasures of the mighty are the tears of the poor.*
   Fr De tout temps, les petits ont pâti des sottises des grands.

De Der Herren Sünde–der Bauern Busse.
It De' peccati de' signori fanno penitenza i poveri.
El Los griegos pagan las locuras de sus reyes.
Ru Бары дерутся, а у холопов чубы трещат.

5 *En* The king reigns, but does not govern.*
  Fr Le roi règne et ne gouverne pas.
  De Der König herrscht, aber er regiert nicht.
  It Il re regna, ma non governa.
  El El rey reina, mas no gobierna.
  Ru (Монарх царствует, но не правит.)

6 *En* Kings have long arms (hands).
  Fr Les rois ont les bras longs.
  De Könige haben lange Arme (Hände).
  It I principi hanno le braccia lunghe.
  El Los reyes han los brazos largos.
  Ru У царя руки долги.

7 *En* Like prince, like people.
  Fr Tel prince, tel peuple.
  De Wie der Herrscher, so das Volk.
  It Il popolo è simile al signore.
  El Cual es el rey, tal es el grey.
  Ru (Каков владыка, таков и народ.)

8 *En* Like master, like man.*
  Fr Tel maître, tel valet.
  De Wie der Herr, so der Knecht.
      Wie der Herr, so's Gescherr.
  It Tal padrone, tal servitore.
  El A tal señor, tal servidor.
  Ru Каков хозяин, таков и слуга.

9   *En*   Those that eat cherries with great persons shall have their
         eyes squirted out with the stones.

    Fr   Ne mangez point de cerises avec les grands, de crainte
         qu'ils ne vous jettent les noyaux au nez.

    De   Mit grossen Herren ist nicht gut Kirschen essen, sie
         werfen einem die Stengel ins Gesicht.

    It   Non è buono mangiar ciliege co' signori.

    El   Si con tu señor comes cerezas, tú apenas las probarás,
         y él quedará harto de ellas.

    Ru   С барином не ешь вишен: косточками закидает.

10 *En*   To rule with a rod of iron.
    Fr   Commander à la baguette.
    De   Mit dem Stock regieren.
    It   Comandare a bacchetta.
    El   Meter (Poner) en un puño.
    Ru   Управлять железной рукой.

11 *En*   So many servants, so many enemies.*
    Fr   Autant de valets, autant d'ennemis.
    De   Wieviel Knechte, soviel Feinde.
    It   Tanti servitori, tanti nemici.
    El   Quien ha criados, ha enemigos no excusados.
    Ru   Сколько рабов, столько врагов.

12 *En*   The great fish eat up the small.*
    Fr   Les gros poissons mangent les petits.
    De   Die grossen Fische fressen die kleinen.
    It   I pesci grossi mangiano i piccini.
    El   Los peces grandes se comen a los chicos.
    Ru   Большая рыба маленькую целиком глотает.

13 *En*   Woe to thee, O land, when thy king is a child! *(B)*
    Fr   Malheur à toi, pays dont le roi est un enfant!
    De   Wehe dir, Land, dessen König ein Kind ist!

157

It Guai a te, o paese, il cui re è fanciullo!

El ¡Ay de ti, tierra, cuando tu rey es muchacho!

Ru Горе тебе, земля, когда царь твой отрок! *(Б)*

30 Love and Beauty
Amour–Beauté
Liebe und Schönheit
Amore–Bellezza
Amor–Hermosura
Любовь–Красота

1 *En* Old love will not be forgotten.*
   Fr On revient toujours à ses premières amours.
   De Alte Liebe rostet nicht.
   It Il primo amore non si scorda mai.
   El Quien bien ama, tarde olvida.
   Ru Старая любовь не ржавеет (долго помнится).

2 *En* Love is blind.*
   Fr L'amour est aveugle.
   De Die Liebe ist blind.
   It L'amore è cieco.
   El El amor es ciego.
   Ru Любовь слепа.

3 *En* Love is full of trouble.*
   Fr Aimer n'est pas sans amer.
   De Wer liebt muss leiden.
         Keine Liebe ohne Leid.
   It Amore non è senza amaro.
   El Amor con dolor se paga.
         Donde hay amor, hay dolor.
   Ru Нет любви без горя.
         Полюбив, нагорюешься.

4 *En* Perfect love casteth out fear. *(B)*

Fr L'amour parfait bannit la crainte.
De Die völlige Liebe treibt die Furcht aus.
It La compiuta carità caccia fuori la paura.
El El perfecto amor echa fuera el temor.
Ru Совершенная любовь изгоняет страх. *(Б)*

5 *En* Love and a cough cannot be hid.*
Fr L'amour et la toux ne se peuvent cacher.
De Liebe und Husten lässt sich nicht verbergen.
It L'amore e la tosse presto si conosce.
El El amor y la tos no se pueden ocultar.
Ru Любви да кашля от людей не утаишь.

6 *En* Love cannot be compelled.
Fr L'amour ne se commande pas.
De Liebe lässt sich nicht erzwingen.
It Non si può dettar leggi al cuore.
    Cosa per forza non vale scorza.
El En el corazón no se manda.
Ru Насильно мил не будешь.

7 *En* Love is the reward of love.
Fr L'amour ne se paie qu'avec l'amour.
De Die Liebe ist der Liebe Preis.
It In premio d'amor, amor si rende.
El Amor con amor se paga.
Ru Ответная любовь–лучшая награда.

8 *En* Love will find out the way.*
Fr L'amour vainc tout.
De Liebe überwindet alles.
It Tutto vince amor.
El El amor todo lo vence.
Ru Любовь всё побеждает.

9   *En*   Love is strong as death. *(B)*
    Fr   L'amour est fort comme la mort.
    De   Liebe ist stark wie der Tod.
    It   L'amore è forte come la morte.
    El   Fuerte como la muerte es el amor.
    Ru   Крепка, как смерть, любовь. *(Б)*

10 *En*   Love makes all equal.
    Fr   L'amour égalise toutes les conditions.
    De   Gleichheit ist der Liebe Band.
    It   Ogni disuguaglianza amor agguaglia.
    El   Amor ni mira linaje, ni fe, ni pleito homenaje.
    Ru   Для любви нет различия.

11 *En*   Love is never without jealousy.
    Fr   Il n'y a pas d'amour sans jalousie.
    De   Wo keine Eifersucht, ist keine Liebe.
    It   Non è amore senza gelosia.
    El   No hay amor sin celos perfecto.
    Ru   Нет любви без ревности.

12 *En*   Jealousy is cruel as the grave. *(B)*
    Fr   La jalousie est inflexible comme le séjour des morts.
    De   Eifersucht ist hart wie das Totenreich.
    It   La gelosia è dura come l'inferno.
    El   Duro como el sepulcro es el celo.
    Ru   Люта, как преисподняя, ревность. *(Б)*

13 *En*   A cold hand and a warm heart.
    Fr   A main froide cœur chaud.
    De   Kalte Hände, warme Liebe.
    It   Mani fredde e cuore caldo.
    El   Manos frías, corazón caliente.
    Ru   Холодные руки, горячее сердце.

14 *En* Love covereth all sins. *(B)*
   Fr L'amour couvre toutes les fautes.
   De Die Liebe deckt alle Übertretungen zu.
   It La carità ricopre ogni misfatto.
   El La caridad cubrirá todas las faltas.
   Ru Любовь покрывает все грехи. *(Б)*

15 *En* Love does much, money does everything.
   Fr Amour peut beaucoup, argent peut tout.
   De Liebe kann viel, Geld kann alles.
   It Amor fa molto, il denaro tutto.
   El El amor hace mucho, el dinero hace todo.
       Gran poder tiene el amor, pero el dinero, mayor.
   Ru Сильна любовь, да деньги сильнее.

16 *En* Lovers' tiffs are harmless.
   Fr Les petits demêlés entretiennent l'amour.
   De Der Geliebten Zank ist süsser Klang.
       Was sich liebt, das neckt sich.
   It Chi ti berteggia, ti vagheggia.
   El Quien bien te quiera, te hará llorar.
   Ru Кого люблю, того и бью.

17 *En* The falling out of lovers is the renewing of love.*
       The quarrels of lovers are the renewal of love.
   Fr Fâcherie d'amoureux, renouveau d'amour.
       Querelles d'amants, renouvellement d'amour.
   De Liebeszorn ist neuer Liebeszunder.
   It Sdegno cresce amore.
   El Riñas de enamorados paran en besos y abrazos.
   Ru Милые бранятся–только тешатся.

18 *En* Lucky at cards, unlucky in love.
   Fr Heureux au jeu, malheureux en amour.
   De Glück im Spiel, Unglück in der Liebe.

It Fortuna al gioco, sfortuna in amore.

El Afortunado en el juego, desgraciado en amores.

Ru Счастлив в игре, несчастлив в любви.

19 *En* The heart's letter is read in the eye.*

   Fr Les yeux sont les messagers du cœur.

      L'œil est le conducteur de l'amour.

   De Die Augen sind der Liebe Boten.

   It Dov'è l'amore, là è l'occhio.

      L'occhio attira l'amore.

   El Do van antojos, van los ojos.

   Ru Где сердце лежит, туда и око бежит.

      Глаза–вестники любви.

20 *En* One love expels another.

   Fr Un nouvel amour en remplace un ancien.

   De Neue Liebe verdrängt die alte.

      Neue Liebe macht der alten vergessen.

   It Gli amori nuovi fanno dimenticare i vecchi.

   El Amores nuevos olvidan viejos.

   Ru Одна любовь вытесняет другую.

      Две любви в одном сердце не поместятся.

21 *En* Out of sight, out of mind.*

   Fr Loin des yeux, loin du cœur.

   De Aus den Augen, aus dem Sinn.

   It Lontano dagli occhi, lontano dal cuore.

   El Tan lejos de ojo, tan lejos de corazón.

   Ru С глаз долой–из сердца вон.

22 *En* Salt water and absence wash away love.

   Fr L'absence est l'ennemie de l'amour.

   De Abwesenheit ist eine Feindin der Liebe.

   It Assenza nemica d'amore, quanto lontan dall'occhio, tanto dal cuore.

El   Ausencia enemiga de amor, cuan lejos de ojos, tan lejos de corazón.

Cuanto más alejado, más olvidado.

Ru   Кто далеко, тот забывается легко.

Далеко из очей–далеко из сердца.

23 *En* When poverty comes in at doors, love leaps out at windows.

      Fr Quand la pauvreté frappe à la porte, l'amour s'en va par la fenêtre.

      De Kommt Armut durch die Tür ins Haus, fliegt Liebe gleich zum Fenster hinaus.

      It Quando la fame vien dentro la porte, l'amore se ne va dalla finestra.

      El Cuando el hambre entra por la puerta, el amor huye por la fenestra.

      Ru С деньгами мил, без денег постыл.

24 *En* A fair face is half a portion.*

      Fr Jolie fille porte sur son front sa dot.

      De Ein schönes Gesicht ist halbe Mitgift.

      It Bellezza è mezza dote.

      El Una cara hermosa lleva en sí secreta recomendación.

      Ru Не бери приданое, бери милу девицу.

25 *En* Fair is not fair, but that which pleaseth.

      Fr Tout ce qu'on aime paraît beau.

      De Liebes geht über Schönes.

Schön ist, was schön lässt.

      It Non è bello quelch'è bello, ma quel che piace.

      El Lo que me gusta, es lo hermoso.

El deseo hace hermoso lo feo.

      Ru Не славится красавица, а кому что нравится.

Не по хорошу мил, а по милу хорош.

26 *En* Beauty and honesty seldom agree.
   Fr Beauté et folie sont souvent en compagnie.
       Beau et bon ne sont pas souvent compagnons.
   De Schönheit und Verstand sind selten verwandt
   It Beltà e follia vanno spesso in compagnia.
   El Lo hermoso y lo bueno pocas veces son compañeros.
   Ru Красота разума не придаст.

27 *En* Beauty is but skin-deep.
   Fr La beauté est éphémère.
   De Schönheit ist vergänglich.
   It La bellezza è effimera.
   El Hermosura, al fin, basura.
   Ru Красота недолговечна.

28 *En* Favour is deceitful, and beauty is vain. *(B)*
   Fr La grâce est trompeuse, et la beauté est vaine.
   De Anmut besticht, und Schönheit vergeht.
   It La grazia è cosa fallace, e la bellezza è cosa vana.
   El Engañosa es la gracia, y vana la hermosura.
   Ru Миловидность обманчива, и красота суетна. *(Б)*

31 Man and Woman
   L'Homme et la Femme
   Mann und Weib
   Uomo e Donna
   Hombre y Mujer
   Муж и жена

1 *En* It is not good that the man should be alone. *(B)*
   Fr Il n'est pas bon que l'homme soit seul.
   De Es ist nicht gut, dass der Mensch allein sei.
   It Non è bene che l'uomo sia solo.
   El No es bueno que el hombre esté solo.
   Ru Не хорошо быть человеку одному. *(Б)*

2 *En* A man's best fortune or his worst is a wife.
   Fr Le plus grand malheur ou bonheur de l'homme est une femme.
   De Das Weib ist des Mannes grösstes Glück oder Unglück.
   It La maggior' sventura o ventura de l'uomo è la moglie.
   El La mayor dicha o desdicha del hombre es la mujer.
   Ru Одному с женою радость, другому горе.
         Добрая жена–веселье, а худая–злое зелье.

3 *En* Every Jack must have his Jill.
   Fr A chacun sa chacune.
   De Jeder Hans findet seine Grete.
   It Pari con pari ben sta e dura.
   El Tal para tal, María para Juan.
   Ru Всякая невеста для своего жениха родится.

4 *En* Marriages are made in heaven.*
   Fr Les mariages sont écrit au ciel.

De Ehen werden im Himmel geschlossen.

It   Vescovi e maritati sono dal ciel destinati.

El   Casamiento y mortaja del cielo baja.

Ru Смерть да жена–Богом суждена.

5   En The husband is the head of the wife. *(B)*

     Fr Le mari est le chef de la femme.

     De Der Mann ist des Weibes Haupt.

     It   Il marito sia capo della donna.

     El   El marido es cabeza de la mujer.

     Ru Муж есть глава жены. *(Б)*

6   En Wedlock is a padlock.

     Fr Le mariage est la saison des orages.

     De Ehestand–Wehestand.

     It   Lo stato coniugale è di ogni male.

     El   Casar, malo de sustentar.

     Ru Женишься раз, а плачешься век.

7   En Marry in haste, and repent at leisure.

     Fr Qui en hâte se marie, à loisir se repente.

     De Heiraten in Eile bereut man mit Weile.

     It   Chi si marita in fretta, stenta adagio.

     El   Antes que te cases, mira lo que haces.

     Ru Женился на скорую руку, да на долгую муку.

8   En A married man turns his staff into a stake.

     Fr L'homme marié est un oiseau en cage.

     De Männer, die ein Weib genommen, sind um ihre Freiheit gekommen.

     It   Uomo ammogliato, uccello in gabbia.

     El   Él que se casa, por todo pasa.

     Ru Женихом весел, а мужем нос повесил.

9 *En* Who marries does well, who marries not does better.

   Fr Celui qui se marie fait bien, celui qui ne se marie pas
        fait mieux.

   De Wer heiratet, tut wohl; wer ledig bleibt, tut besser.

   It Chi si marita fa bene, chi no, meglio.

   El Él que se casa hace bien, y él que no se casa hace mejor.

   Ru Жениться–хорошо, а не жениться–ещё лучше.

10 *En* It is a sad house where the hen crows louder than the
        cock.

   Fr La maison est misérable et méchante où la poule plus
        haut que le coq chante.

   De Kräht die Henn' und schweigt der Hahn, ist das Haus gar
        übel dran.

   It Trista è quella casa, dove le galline cantano e 'l gallo
        tace.

   El Casa perdida, donde calla el gallo y canta la gallina.

   Ru Мало мира в том доме, где курица поёт, а петух молчит.

11 *En* What God hath joined together, let not man put asunder.
        (B)

   Fr Ce que Dieu a uni, l'homme ne doit séparer.

   De Was Gott zusammengefügt hat, das soll der Mensch
        nicht scheiden.

   It Ciò che Iddio ha congiunto l'uomo nol separi.

   El Lo que Dios juntó, no lo aparte el hombre.

   Ru Что Бог сочетал, того человек да не разлучает. *(Б)*

12 *En* A woman's mind and winter wind change oft.

   Fr Femmes, vent, temps et fortune se changent comme la
        lune.

   De Weiber, Glück und Wind ändern sich geschwind.

   It Donna e luna, oggi serena e domani bruna.

   El Viento, mujer y fortuna, mudables como la luna.

   Ru Женские думы изменчивы.

13 *En* A woman, an ass, and a walnut tree, the more you beat them, the better they'll be.*

Fr Bon cheval, mauvais cheval veut l'éperon; bonne femme, mauvaise femme veut le bâton.

De Ein Weib, ein Esel und eine Nuss–diese drei man klopfen muss.

It Donne, asini e noci voglion le mani atroci.

El Asnos y mujeres, por la fuerza entienden.
El asno y la mujer, a palos se han de vencer.

Ru Люби жену, как душу, тряси её, как грушу.

14 *En* Three things drive a man out of his house –
smoke, rain, and a scolding wife.

Fr Fumée, pluie et femme sans raison chassent l'homme de sa maison.

De Drei Dinge treiben den Mann aus dem Haus: ein Rauch, ein übel Dach und ein böses Weib.

It Tre cose cacciano l'uomo di casa: fumo, goccia e femmina arrabbiata.

El Humo, gotera, y mujer parlera, echan al hombre de su casa fuera.

Ru От пожара, от потопа, от злой жены–Боже сохрани!

15 *En* Three women and a goose make a market.*

Fr Deux femmes font un plaid, trois un grand caquet, quatre un plein marché.

De Drei Weiber und eine Gans machen einen Jahrmarkt.

It Tre donne e un papero fanno un mercato.

El Tres mujeres y un ganso hacen un mercado.

Ru Гусь да баба–торг; два гуся, две бабы–ярмарка.

16 *En* Women laugh when they can, and weep when they will.

Fr Femme rit quand elle peut, et pleure quand elle veut.

De Die Weiber haben das Weinen und Lachen in einem Säckel.

(31) 16

It   Donna si lagna, donna si duole, donna s'ammala quando la vuole

El   Siempre que lo desea, la mujer llora y el perro mea.

Ru   У баб да у пьяных слёзы дёшевы.

32 Parents–Children
Parents et Enfants
Eltern und Kinder
Parenti e Figli
Padres e Hijos
Родители и дети

1   *En*   Like father, like son; like mother, like daughter.*
    Fr   Tel père, tel fils; telle mère, telle fille.
    De   Wie der Vater, so der Sohn; wie die Mutter, so die
          Tochter.
    It   Il figlio al padre s'assomiglia, alla madre la figlia.
    El   Cuales fueron los padres, los hijos serán.
    Ru   Каков отец, таков и сын; какова мать, такова и дочь.

2   *En*   Children when little make parents fool, when great, mad.
    Fr   Petits enfants, petits tourments; grands enfants, grands
          tourments.
    De   Kleine Kinder– kleine Sorgen; grosse Kinder–grosse
          Sorgen.
    It   Figliuoli piccoli, fastidi piccoli; figliuoli grandi, fastidi
          grandi.
    El   Hijos criados, duelos doblados.
    Ru   Малые детки–малые бедки, а большие детки–большие и
          бедки.

3   *En*   One father can support ten children; ten children cannot
          support one father.
    Fr   Un père nourrit sept enfants, mais ceux-ci non pas leur
          père.

De Eher ernährt ein Vater zehn Kinder als zehn Kinder einen Vater.

It Un padre governa cento figliuoli, e cento figliuoli non bastano a un padre.

El Hay un padre para cien hijos, y no hay cien hijos para un padre.

Ru Один отец прокормит девятерых детей, а девятеро детей не прокормят одного отца.

4 *En* After a thrifty father, a prodigal son.

Fr A père avare, fils prodigue.

De Der Vater ein Sparer, der Sohn ein Vergeuder.

It A padre avaro, figliuol prodigo.

El A padre guardador, hijo gastador.

Ru Отцы наживают, детки проживают.

Отец накопил, а сын раструсил.

5 *En* The father a saint, the son a devil.

Fr De père saintelot, enfant diablot.

De Der Vater ein Heiliger, der Sohn ein Teufel.

It Di padre santolotto, figlio diavolotto.

El De padre santo, hijo diablo.

Ru И от доброго отца родится бешеная овца.

6 *En* Marry your son when you will, your daughter when you can.

Fr Marie ton fils quand tu voudras et ta fille quand tu pourras.

De Söhne verheirate, wenn du willst–Töchter, wenn du kannst.

It Casa il figlio quando vuoi, e la figlia quando puoi.

El Casa el hijo cuando quisieres, y la hija cuando pudieres.

Ru Сына жени, когда хочешь, а дочь выдай замуж, когда можешь.

7   *En* A chip of the old block.
     Fr C'est bien le fils de son père.
     De Die Zweige arten nach dem Stamme.
          Der Apfel fällt nicht weit vom Stamm.
     It Il ramo somiglia al tronco.
          Il frutto cade non lontano dall'albero.
     El De tal palo, tal astilla.
     Ru Яблоко от яблони недалеко падает.

8   *En* Spare the rod and spoil the child.*
     Fr Qui aime bien châtie bien.
     De Je lieber das Kind, je schärfer die Rute.
     It Chi ben ama, ben castiga.
     El Quien te castiga, te ama.
     Ru Пожалеешь розгу, испортишь ребёнка.

9   *En* Better children weep than old men.*
     Fr Il vaut mieux que les enfants pleurent que les vieillards.
     De Besser das Kind weint jetzt als die Eltern künftig.
     It È meglio che gli fanciulli pianghino che gli vecchi.
     El Mejor es que los niños lloren que los viejos.
     Ru Кто детям потакает, тот сам плачет.

10 *En* Take heed of a stepmother: the very name of her
         sufficeth.
     Fr Qui a marâtre, a le diable en l'âtre.
     De Stiefmutter ist des Teufels Unterfutter.
     It Chi ha matrigna, di dietro si signa.
     El De madrastra, el nombre le basta.
     Ru Из дому гонит мачеха, а из лесу—медведь.

11 *En* The owl thinks her own young fairest.*
     Fr Chacun trouve beau ceux qu'il aime.
     De Es ist keine Eule, die nicht schwüre, sie hätte die
         schönsten Jungen.

It   All'orsa paion belli i suoi orsacchini.
El   Dijo el escarabajo a sus hijos: venid acá, mis flores.
Ru И сова своих детей хвалит.
      Всякой матери своё дитя мило.

12 *En* The crow thinks her own birds fairest.
    Fr Le corbeau pense que ses poussins sont les plus beaux.
    De Der Bärin scheinen ihre Jungen schön.
    It Il corvo pensa ch'i suoi pulcini sieno gli più belli.
    El El cuervo piensa que sus pollos son los más lindos.
    Ru И ворона воронят хвалит.
        Своё дитя и горбато, да мило.

13 *En* What children hear at home, doth soon fly abroad.
    Fr Ce que l'enfant écoute au foyer, est bientôt connu
        jusqu'au moutier.
    De Was die Kinder hören im Haus, plaudern sie auf der
        Gasse aus.
    It Quando il piccolo parla, il grande ha parlato.
    El Lo que el niño oyó en el hogar, eso dice en el portal.
    Ru Что говорит большой, слышит и малый.

14 *En* An evil crow, an evil egg.*
        Like crow, like egg.*
    Fr De mauvais corbeau mauvais œuf.
    De Wie der Vogel, so das Ei.
    It Il mal corvo fa mal uovo.
    El Cual el cuervo, tal su huevo.
    Ru По матке и детки.

15 *En* He that comes of a hen must scrape.
    Fr Qui naît de poule aime à gratter.
    De Was von der Henne kommt, das gackert.
    It Chi di gallina nasce, convien che raspi.

El   De casta le viene al galgo el ser rabilargo.
Ru   Отец рыбак, и дети в воду смотрят.

16 *En* Cat after kind, good mouse-hunt.
    Fr Qui naquit chat court après les souris.
    De Katzenkinder mausen gern.
    It Chi di gatta nasce, sorci piglia.
    El   El hijo de la gata ratones mata.
    Ru За что батька, за то и детки.

17 *En* Eagles do not breed doves.*
    Fr L'aigle n'engendre point la colombe.
    De Adler brüten keine Tauben.
    It D'aquila non nasce colomba.
    El De águila no nace paloma.
    Ru Орёл орла родит, а сова сову

33 **Young–Old–New**
Jeunesse–Vieillesse–Nouveauté
Jung–Alt–Neu
Gioventù–Vecchiezza–Novità
Mocedad–Vejez–Novedad
Молодость–Старость–Новизна

1 *En* Boys will be boys.
   Fr Jeunesse n'a pas de sagesse.
   De Jugend hat keine Tugend.
   It Gioventù non ha virtù.
   El Juventud no conoce virtud.
   Ru Всякая молодость резвости полна.

2 *En* Boys will be men.
   Fr Enfants deviennent gens.
   De Aus Kindern werden Leute.
   It I fanciulli diventano uomini.
   El Mozos fueron ante los que ahora son hombres.
   Ru Дети возмужают–батьку испугают.

3 *En* Youth will have its course (swing).*
   Fr Il faut que jeunesse se passe.
   De Jugend muss sich austoben.
   It Gioventù vuol fare il corso suo.
   El Locura tras locura la mocedad madura.
   Ru Молодо-зелено, погулять велено.

4 *En* What youth is used to, age remembers.
   Fr Ce que poulain prend en jeunesse, il le continue en
        vieillesse.

De Jung gewohnt, alt getan.

It Chi da giovane ha un vizio, in vecchiaia fa sempre quell'uffizio.

El Lo que en la leche se mama, en la mortaja se derrama.

Ru К чему смалу привык, тому под старость не учиться.

5 *En* He is scarcely out of the shell yet.

Fr Il ne fait que de sortir de la coque.

De Er ist hinter den Ohren noch nicht trocken.

It Ha ancora il latte alla bocca.

El Está con la leche en los labios.

Ru У него молоко на губах не обсохло.

6 *En* If youth knew what age would crave, it would both get and save.

Fr Si jeunesse savait, si vieillesse pouvait, jamais le monde ne faillirait.

De Wenn die Jugend wüsste, wenn das Alter könnte, würde die Welt nie schiefgehen.

It Se il giovane sapesse, se il vecchio potesse, non c'è cosa non si facesse.

El El viejo por no poder, y el mozo por no saber, dejan las cosas perder.

Ru Если б молодость знала, если б старость могла…

7 *En* As the old cook crows, so crows the young.

Fr Ce que chante la corneille, chantera le corneillon.

De Wie die Alten sungen, so zwitschern auch die Jungen.

It Come canta il gallo, canterà il galletto.

El Por donde salta la cabra, salta la chiva.

Ru Каковы дядьки, таковы и дитятки.

8 *En* Young men may die, but old must die.

Fr La mort assise à la porte des vieux, guette les jeunes.

De Der Junge kann sterben, der Alte muss sterben.

It   I giovani possono morir presto, ma i vecchi non possono campar molto.

El   El mozo puede morir, y el viejo non puede vivir.

Ru   Молодые по выбору мрут, а старые поголовно.

9   *En*   Keep something for him that rides on the white horse.

      Fr   On doit quérir en jeunesse dont on vive en la vieillesse.

      De   Jugendfleiss belohnt sich im Alter.

      It   In gioventù devi acquistare, quel che in vecchiaia ti può giovare.

      El   Guarda mozo, y hallarás viejo.

      Ru   Молод–кости гложи, стар–кашу ешь.

10   *En*   For age and want save while you may: no morning sun lasts a whole day.*

      Fr   Il faut travailler en jeunesse pour reposer en vieillesse.

      De   Schwere Arbeit in der Jugend ist sanfte Ruhe im Alter.

      It   Chi fatica in gioventù, gode in vecchiaia.

      El   A mocedad sin vicio y de buena pasada, larga vejez y descansada.

      Ru   Смолоду наживай, а под старость проживай.

11   *En*   It early pricks that will be a thorn.*

      Fr   L'épine en naissant va la pointe devant.

      De   Was ein Dörnchen werden will, spitzt sich beizeiten.

      It   Al nascer la spina porta la punta in cima.

      El   La espina cuando nace, la punta lleva delante.

      Ru   Какому быть в старости, молоды лета объявляют.

12   *En*   A ragged colt may make a good horse.

      Fr   Méchant poulain peut devenir bon cheval.

      De   Aus klattrigen Fohlen werden die schönsten Hengste.

      It   Di puledro scabioso talvolta hai cavallo prezioso.

      El   De potro sarnoso, caballo hermoso.

      Ru   И плохой жеребёнок превратится в хорошего коня.

13 *En* An old ox makes a straight furrow.
   Fr Vieux bœuf fait sillon droit.
   De Ein alter Ochs macht gerade Furchen.
   It Bue vecchio, solco diritto.
   El Buey viejo, surco derecho.
   Ru Старый конь борозды не портит.

14 *En* An old dog barks not in vain.
   Fr Un vieux chien n'aboie pas en vain.
   De Wenn alte Hunde bellen, sieh man hinaus!
   It Cane vecchio non abbaia invano.
   El El perro viejo, si ladra, da consejo.
   Ru Старая собака понапрасну не лает.

15 *En* It is hard to teach an old dog tricks.
   Fr Vieil chien est mal à mettre en lien.
   De Einem alten Köter kann man keine neuen Kunststücke beibringen.
   It Can vecchio mal s'avvezza a portar collare.
   El Caballo viejo no aprende trote nuevo.
   Ru Старого пса к цепи не приучишь.
       Старую лису хитростям не учат.

16 *En* If you wish good advice, consult an old man.*
   Fr En conseil écoute l'homme âgé.
   De Die Alten zum Rat, die Jungen zur Tat.
   It Fatti di giovani, e consigli di vecchi.
   El Consejo, tómalo del hombre viejo.
   Ru Молодой на службу, старый на совет.

17 *En* Remove an old tree, and it will wither to death.
   Fr Le vieil arbre transplanté meurt.
   De Alte Bäume soll man nicht verpflanzen.
   It Albero vecchio trapiantato mai di frutti è caricato.

El   Viejas plantas traspuestas, ni crecen ni medran.
Ru   Старое дерево пересадить трудно.

18   En   An idle youth, a needy age.*
  Fr   Jeunesse oiseuse, vieillesse disetteuse.
  De   Faule Jugend, lausiges Alter.
  It   Gioventù in olio, vecchiezza in duolo.
  El   A mocedad ociosa, vejez menesterosa.
  Ru   Гулять смолоду–помирать под старость с голоду.

19   En   Teach your grandmother to suck eggs.*
  Fr   Les oisons veulent mener les oies paître.
  De   Junge Gänse wollen die alten zur Tränke führen.
  It   I paperi vogliono menare a bere le oche.
  El   Los pollos no enseñan a los recoveros.
  Ru   Яйцо учит курицу.

20   En   If you want to be old long, be old young.*
  Fr   Il faut devenir vieux de bonne heure pour rester vieux longtemps.
  De   Werde jung alt, so bleibst du lange alt.
  It   Divieni tosto vecchio, se vuoi viver lungo tempo vecchio.
  El   Quien quisiere ser mucho tiempo viejo, comiéncelo presto.
  Ru   Хочешь быть долго старым–будь стар смолоду.

21   En   Every oak has been an acorn.
  Fr   D'un petit gland provient un grand chêne.
  De   Es ist kein Baum, der nicht zuvor ein Sträuchlein gewesen ist.
  It   La quercia cresce da piccola ghianda.
  El   De una bellota chica se hace una gran encina.
  Ru   От малого большое зарождается.

22   En   The priest forgets that he was clerk.
  Fr   Il est avis à vieille vache qu'elle ne fut jamais veau.

De Alte Kuh gar leicht vergisst, dass sie ein Kalb gewesen ist.
It La suocera non pensa mai che la fu nuora.
El No se acuerda la suegra que fué nuera.
Ru Забыл бык, когда телёнком был.

23 *En* Old men are twice children.*
   Fr Un vieillard est deux fois enfant.
   De Alte Leute sind zweimal Kinder.
   It L'uomo vecchio è due volte bambino.
   El Los viejos son dos veces niños.
   Ru Старый, что малый, а малый, что глупый.

24 *En* A man of the old stock.
   Fr Homme de vieille roche.
   De Ein Mann von altem Schrot und Korn.
   It Uomo di antico stampo.
   El Persona de viejo temple.
   Ru Человек старого закала.

25 *En* Age is a heavy burden.*
   Fr La vieillesse est un pesant fardeau.
   De Alter ist ein schweres Malter.
   It La vecchiaia è una grave soma.
   El La vida pasada hace la vejez pesada.
   Ru Старость–не радость.

26 *En* An old man is a bed full of bones.*
   Fr La vieillesse est elle-même une maladie.
   De Alter kommt mit allerlei.
   It La vecchiaia viene con ogni male.
   El Hombre viejo, saco de azares.
   Ru Старость–увечье, старость–неволя.

27 *En* A new broom sweeps clean.
   Fr Il n'est rien tel que balai neuf.

	De	Neue Besen kehren gut.
	It	Granata nuova spazza ben tre giorni.
	El	Escoba nueva barre bien.
	Ru	Новая метла хорошо метёт.

28 | *En* | Everything new is fine.* |
	New things are fair.*
Fr	Tout nouveau paraît beau.
De	Was neu ist, gefällt.
	Neukommen, willkommen.
It	Di novello, tutto è bello.
El	Todo lo nuevo agrada.
	Lo novel todo es bel.
Ru	Что ново, то и мило.

29 | *En* | Spick and span. |
Fr	Tiré à quatre épingles.
De	Geschniegelt und gebügelt.
It	Nuovo di zecca.
El	Prendido con cuarenta alfileres.
Ru	Одетый с иголочки.

34 Life–Death
Vie et Mort
Leben–Sterben
Vita e Morte
Vida y Muerte
Жизнь и смерть

1 *En* Life is a battle.*
   Fr La vie est un combat.
   De Unser Leben ist ein Kampf.
   It La vita è una continua battaglia.
   El La vida es una lucha.
   Ru Жизнь это вечная борьба.

2 *En* Life is but a span.
   Fr La vie est un sommeil (un songe).
   De Das Leben ist ein Traum.
   It La vita è un sogno.
   El La vida es sueño.
   Ru Жизнь (человека) коротка.

3 *En* Life is not a bed of roses.
   Fr La vie n'est pas "tout rose".
   De Im Leben ist nicht alles rosig.
   It La vita non è tutta rosa.
   El La vida no es senda de rosas.
   Ru Жизнь прожить–не поле перейти.

4 *En* Live and let live.
   Fr Il faut vivre et laisser vivre.
   De Leben und leben lassen!

It   Vivi e lascia vivere.
El   Vivir y dejar vivir.
Ru   Жить и жить давать другим.

5 *En*   Such a life, such a death.*
   Fr   De telle vie, telle fin.
   De   Wie gelebt, so gestorben.
   It   Come si vive, così si muore.
   El   Según es la vida, es la muerte.
   Ru   Кто как живёт, так и умирает.

6 *En*   Art is long, life is short.*
   Fr   L'art est long, la vie est courte.
   De   Das Leben ist kurz, die Kunst ist lang.
   It   La vita è breve e l'arte è lunga.
   El   El arte es largo y la vida breve.
   Ru   Искусство долговечно, а жизнь коротка.

7 *En*   A living dog is better than a dead lion. *(B)**
   Fr   Un chien vivant vaut mieux qu'un lion mort.
   De   Ein lebendiger Hund ist besser als ein toter Löwe.
   It   È meglio cane vivo che leon morte.
   El   Mejor es perro vivo que león muerto.
   Ru   Живой пёс лучше мёртвого льва. *(Б)*

8 *En*   All that lives must die. *(Sh)*
   Fr   Tout ce qui vit doit mourir.
   De   Was lebt, muss sterben.
   It   Tutti siamo nati per morire.
   El   Se nace para morir.
   Ru   Сколько ни живи, а умирать надо.

9 *En*   A man can die but once.
   Fr   On ne meurt qu'une fois.
   De   Einen Tod kann der Mensch nur sterben.

It   Si muore una volta sola.

El   Ninguno muere dos veces.

Ru   Двум смертям не бывать, а одной не миновать.

10   *En*   Say nothing of the dead but what is good.*

    Fr   Il ne faut pas dire du mal des morts.

    De   Von Toten soll man nichts Übles reden.

    It   Dei morti non si deve dire che bene.

    El   No hay que hablar mal de los muertos.

    Ru   Покойника не поминай лихом.

11   *En*   There is a time to be born, and a time to die. *(B)*

    Fr   Il y a un temps pour naître, et un temps pour mourir.

    De   Geborenwerden hat seine Zeit, und Sterben hat seine Zeit.

    It   Vi è tempo di nascere, e tempo di morire.

    El   Hay tiempos de nacer, y tiempos de morir.

    Ru   Есть время рождаться, и время умирать. *(Б)*

12   *En*   Man doth not live by bread only. *(B)*

    Fr   L'homme ne vit pas de pain seulement.

    De   Nicht vom Brot allein lebt der Mensch.

    It   L'uomo non vive di pan solo.

    El   El hombre no vivirá de solo pan.

    Ru   Не единым хлебом жив человек. *(Б)*

13   *En*   Death is the grand leveller.*

    Fr   La mort nous rend tous égaux.

    De   Der Tod macht uns alle gleich.

    It   La morte pareggia tutti.

    El   La muerte a todos nos iguala.

    Ru   Смерть всех поравняет.

14   *En*   Death makes equal the high and low.

    Fr   La mort n'épargne ni petit, ni grand.

    De   Arm und reich, der Tod macht alles gleich.

It   L'eccelse ed umil porte batte egualmente morte.
El   Muerte y enfermedades no distinguen linajes.
Ru   Смерть не разбирает чина.

15 *En*   Deaths foreseen come not.
    Fr   La mort vient, mais on ne sait l'heure.
    De   Der Tod kommt nicht, wenn wir wollen.
    It   La morte viene quando meno s'aspetta.
    El   La muerte, a quien más la desea, no le viene.
    Ru   Смерть берёт расплохом.

16 *En*   Death keeps no calender.
    Fr   La mort ne connaît ni âge, ni jour.
    De   Der Tod hat keinen Kalender.
    It   La morte non guarda calendario.
    El   La muerte no respeta edades ni dignidades.
    Ru   На смерть и родины нет годины.

17 *En*   There is a remedy for all things but death.*
    Fr   On trouve remède à tout, excepté à la mort.
    De   Gegen den Tod ist kein Kraut gewachsen.
    It   A ogni cosa è rimedio fuorchè alla morte.
    El   Todo tiene remedio menos la muerte.
    Ru   От всего вылечишься, кроме смерти.

18 *En*   Death defies the doctor.
    Fr   Contre la mort il n'y a nul ressort.
    De   Kein Harnisch schützt wider den Tod.
    It   Contro la morte non v'è cosa forte.
    El   En mal de muerte no hay médico que acierte.
    Ru   От смерти нет зелья (лекарства).

19 *En*   Death is deaf and will hear no denial.*
    Fr   Contre la mort il n'y a pas d'appel.
    De   Gegen den Tod gibt es keinen Dispens vor Rom.

It La morte non riceve alcuna scusa.

El A la muerte no hay casa fuerte.

Ru Смерть не спросит, придёт да скосит.

20 *En* Better a glorious death than a shameful life.

Fr Mieux vaut mourir avec honneur que vivre avec honte.

De Besser ehrlich gestorben als schändlich verdorben.

It Meglio è morte onorata che vita svergognata.

El Más vale con honra morir que deshonrado vivir.

Ru Лучше славная смерть, чем позорная жизнь.

21 *En* Dead men do not harm.

Fr Homme mort ne fait pas la guerre.

De Toter Mann macht keinen Krieg.

It Uomo morto non fa più guerra.

El Hombre muerto no hace guerra.

Ru Умерший никому не помеха.

22 *En* Dead dogs bite not.*

Fr Chien mort ne mord pas.

De Tote Hunde beissen nicht.

It Cane morto non morde.

El Muerto el perro, muerta la rabia.

Ru Мёртвая собака не кусает.

23 *En* A cat has nine lives.

Fr Les chats ont neuf vies.

De Eine Katze hat neun Leben.

It Gatti hanno nove vite.

El Gatos tienen nueve vidas.

Ru Кошку девятая смерть донимает.

24 *En* He that died half a year ago is as dead as Adam.

Fr Les morts sont bientôt oubliés.

De Wer tot ist, ist bald vergessen.

It   I morti e gli andati presto sono dimenticati.

El   A muertos y idos, no hay más amigos.

Ru Схоронили–позабыли.

25 *En* Let the dead bury their dead. *(B)*

     Fr Laisse les morts ensevelir leurs morts.

     De Lass die Toten ihre Toten begraben.

     It   Lascia i morti seppellire i loro morti.

     El Deja que los muertos entierren a sus muertos.

     Ru Предоставь мёртвым погребать своих мертвецов. *(Б)*

26 *En* A ground sweat cures all disorders.*

     Fr La mort nous guérit de tous nos maux.

     De Der Tod macht Ende aller Not.

     It   Chi muore, esce d'affani.

     El No hay mal tan fuerte, que no lo cure la muerte.

     Ru Горя много, да смерть одна.

         Умрётся, так всё минётся.

27 *En* All are of the dust, and all turn to dust again. *(B)*

     Fr Tout a été fait de la poussière, et tout retourne à la poussière.

     De Alles ist aus dem Staube geworden, und alles kehrt auch wieder zum Staub zurück.

     It   Tutti sono stati fatti di polvere, e tutti ritornano in polvere.

     El Todo es hecho del polvo, y todo se tornará en el mismo polvo.

     Ru Всё произошло из праха, и всё возвратится в прах. *(Б)*

28 *En* To have one foot in the grave.

     Fr Avoir un pied dans la tombe.

     De Mit einem Fuss im Grabe stehen.

     It   Essere con un piede nella tomba.

El   Estar con un pie en la sepultura.

Ru   Стоять одной ногой в могиле.

29 *En*   To be or not to be: that is the question. *(Sh)*

    Fr   Être ou ne pas être, voilà la question.

    De   Sein oder Nichtsein, das ist hier die Frage.

    It   Essere o non essere, questa è la questione.

    El   Ser o no ser–esa es la cuestión.

    Ru   Быть или не быть–вот в чём вопрос. *(Ш)*

35 Health–Illness
  Santé–Maladie
  Gesundheit–Krankheit
  Sanità–Infermità
  Salud–Enfermedad
  Здоровье–Болезнь

1   *En* A sound mind in a sound body.*
    Fr Âme saine dans un corps sain.
    De Gesunder Sinn in gesundem Leib.
    It Mente sana in corpo sano.
    El Alma sana en un cuerpo sano.
    Ru В здравом теле здравый дух.

2   *En* Health is better than wealth.*
    Fr Santé passe richesse.
    De Gesundheit ist der grösste Reichtum.
    It La maggior ricchezza che sia, è la sanità.
    El Primero es la salud que el dinero.
    Ru Здоровье дороже всякого богатства.

3   *En* Health is not valued till sickness comes.
    Fr Demandez à un malade s'il veut santé.
    De Gesundheit schätzt man erst, wenn man krank wird.
    It Nell'infermità si conosce la sanità.
    El ¿Quién querria la salud más bien que el enfermo?
    Ru Тот здоровья не знает, кто болен не бывает.

4   *En* Diseases come on horseback, but go away on foot.*
    Fr La maladie vient à cheval et s'en retourne à pied.
    De Krankheit kommt zu Pferde und geht zu Fusse weg.

190

It   Il male viene a cavallo e se ne va a piedi.
El   Los males entran por arrobas y salen por adarmes.
Ru Болезнь к нам верхом, а от нас пешком.

5   *En* Bitter pills may have blessed effects.*
     Fr Ce qui est amer à la bouche, est doux à l'estomac.
     De Was bitter ist dem Mund, ist innerlich gesund.
     It   Amaro, tienlo caro.
     El   En lo amargo está lo sano.
     Ru Горьким лечат, а сладким калечат.

6   *En* Prevention is better than cure.
     Fr Mieux vaut prévenir que guérir.
     De Vorbeugen ist besser denn heilen.
     It   Meglio prevedere che provvedere.
     El   Más vale prevenir que curar.
     Ru Предупреждение лучше лечения.

7   *En* Like cures like.*
     Fr Les semblables guérissent les semblables.
     De Gleiches durch Gleiches (heilen).
     It   I simili si curano coi simili.
     El   Los semejantes se curan por los semejantes.
     Ru Подобное излечивается подобным.

8   *En* The remedy is worse than the disease.*
     Fr Le remède est souvent pire que le mal.
     De Die Arznei ist ärger als die Krankheit.
     It   Il rimedio è peggiore che il male.
     El   Es peor el remedio que la enfermedad.
     Ru Лекарство хуже болезни.

9   *En* The tongue ever turns to the aching tooth.
     Fr La langue va où le dent fait mal.
     De Wo es schmerzt, da greift man hin.

It La lingua batte, dove il dente duole.

El Allá va la lengua, do duele la muela.

Ru Что у кого болит, тот о том и говорит.

10 *En* Better to have one eye than be blind altogether.

Fr Mieux vaut être borgne qu'aveugle.

De Besser einäugig als gar blind.

It È meglio esser losco che cieco in tutto.

El Más vale ser tuerto que ciego.

Ru Лучше кривой, чем слепой.

11 *En* A hair of the dog that bit you.

Fr Reprendre du poil de la bête.

De Hundbiss heilt Hundshaar.

It Con la pelle del cane si sana la morditura.

El La mordedura del perro cúrase con sus pelos.

Ru Чем ушибся, тем и лечись.

12 *En* Physician, heal thyself. *(B)* *

Fr Médecin, guéris-toi toi-même!

De Arzt, hilf dir selber!

It Medico, cura te stesso.

El Médico, cúrate a ti mismo.

Ru Врачу, исцелися сам! *(Б)*

13 *En* The healthful man can give counsel to the sick.

Fr Il est bien aise aux sains de consoler le malade.

De Der Gesunde kann dem Kranken gut Rat geben.

It Il sano consiglia bene l'ammalato.

El El sano al doliente su regla le mete.

Ru Здоровый больному советов не жалеет.

14 *En* When the head acheth, all the body is the worse.*

Fr A qui la tête fait mal, souffre par tout le corps.

De Wenn das Haupt krank ist, trauern alle Glieder.

It Quando il capo non sta bene, ogni membro se ne sente.

El Cuando la cabeza duele, los pies mal sostienen.

Ru Голова болит–всё тело скорбит.

15 *En* The best physicians are Dr. Diet, Dr. Quiet, and Dr. Merryman.

    Fr Les meilleurs médecins sont le Dr. Gai, le Dr. Diète et le Dr. Tranquille.

    De Freude, Mässigkeit und Ruh' schliesst dem Arzt die Türe zu.

    It Dottor Acqua, Dottor Dieta e Dottor Quiete sono i migliori medici.

    El Los mejores médicos son: el Dr. Alegría, el Dr. Dieta y el Dr. Tranquilidad.

    Ru Умеренность–мать здоровья, смех–силе брат.

16 *En* They that be whole need not a physician, but they that are sick. *(B)*

    Fr Ce ne sont pas les sains qui ont besoin de médecin, mais les malades.

    De Die Gesunden bedürfen des Arztes nicht, sondern die Kranken.

    It Coloro che stanno bene non han bisogno di medico, ma i malati.

    El Los que están sanos no tienen necesidad de médico, sino los enfermos.

    Ru Не здоровые нуждаются во враче, но больные. *(Б)*

17 *En* Desperate diseases must have desperate cures.*

    Fr Aux grands maux les grands remèdes.

    De Ein verzweifeltes Übel will eine verwegene Arznei.

    It A mali estremi, estremi rimedi.

    El A grandes males, remedios tales.

    Ru Сильную болезнь врачуют сильно действующим средством.

36 Certainty–Uncertainty
   Certitude–Incertitude
   Gewissheit–Ungewissheit
   Certezza–Incertezza
   Certeza–Incertidumbre
   Надёжность–Ненадёжность

1   *En*   Words are but wind, the written letter remains.*
    Fr   Les paroles s'envolent, les écrits demeurent.
    De   Die Rede verfliegt, das Geschriebene bleibt.
    It   Le parole volano, quel ch'è scritto rimane.
    El   Lo que se habla, se va; lo que se escribe, quedará.
    Ru   Написано пером–не вырубишь и топором.

2   *En*   Great men's favours are uncertain.
           A king's favour is no inheritance.
    Fr   Amitié de seigneur n'est pas héritage.
    De   Herrengunst währt nicht lange (vererbt sich nicht).
    It   Amicizia di signore non è retaggio.
    El   Sirve a señor, y sabrás de dolor.
    Ru   Боярская ласка–до порога.

3   *En*   Praise the sea, but keep on land.*
    Fr   Loue la mer et tiens-toi à la terre.
    De   Lobe die See, aber bleibe auf dem Lande.
    It   Loda il mar e tienti alla terra.
    El   Hablar de la mar, pero en tierra estar.
    Ru   Хорошо море с берегу.

4   *En*   Try before you trust.*
    Fr   Bien fou qui s'y fie.

194

De Trau-schau-wem!
It Bada di chi ti fidi!
El A todo espíritu no es de creer.
Ru Доверяй, да знай кому!

5 *En* Measure twice, cut but once.
   Fr Regardez à deux fois avant de sauter.
   De Besser zweimal messen als einmal vergessen.
   It Misura tre, e taglia una.
   El Contar muchas veces, y pagar una.
   Ru Семь раз отмерь, один раз отрежь.

6 *En* One eye-witness is better than two hear-so's.
   Fr Un seul témoin oculaire en vaut dix qui ont entendu.
   De Ein Augenzeuge gilt mehr denn zehn Ohrenzeugen.
   It Val più un testimonio di vista che diece d'udita.
   El Más vale testigo de vista que testigo de oídas.
   Ru Не верь ушам, а верь глазам.

7 *En* You will catch more flies with a spoonful of honey than
        with a gallon of vinegar.
   Fr On prend plus de mouches avec du miel qu'avec du
        vinaigre.
   De Mit einem Löffel Honig fängt man mehr Fliegen als mit
        einem Fass voll Essig.
   It Si pigliano più mosche in una gocciola di miele che in un
        barile d'aceto.
   El Se cazan más moscas con una gota de miel que no con un
        barril de vinagre.
   Ru Мёдом больше мух наловишь, чем уксусом.

8 *En* So many men, so many minds.*
   Fr Autant de têtes, autant d'avis.
   De Soviel Köpfe, soviel Sinne.
   It Tante teste, tante sentenze.

El   Tantos hombres, tantos pareceres.
Ru Сколько голов, столько умов.

9   En Four eyes see more than two.*
     Fr Quatre yeux voient plus que deux.
     De Vier Augen sehen mehr als zwei.
     It   Vedono più quattr'occhi che due.
     El   Más ven cuatro ojos que dos.
     Ru Один ум хорошо, а два лучше.

10 En Second thoughts are best.*
     Fr Les secondes pensées sont les meilleures.
     De Die letzten Gedanken sind die besten.
     It   I secondi pensieri sono i migliori.
     El   El pensamiento postrero es más sabio que el primero.
     Ru Сперва думай, а вздумал, так делай.

11 En Distrust is the mother of safety.
     Fr Méfiance est mère de sûreté.
     De Vorsicht ist die Mutter der Weisheit.
     It   La diffidenza è la madre della sicurtà.
     El   La desconfianza aparta el engaño.
     Ru Недоверчивость–мать безопасности.

12 En A threefold cord is not quickly broken. *(B)*
     Fr La corde à trois fils ne se rompt pas facilement.
     De Eine dreifache Schnur wird nicht so bald zerrissen.
     It   Il cordone a tre fili non si rompe prestamente.
     El   Cordón de tres dobleces no presto se rompe.
     Ru И нитка, втрое скрученная, не скоро порвётся. *(Б)*

13 En Never quit certainty for hope.*
     Fr Ne préfère pas l'inconnu au connu.
     De Gewiss geht vor Ungewiss.

It Non lassar il certo per l'incerto.

El Quien por lo dudoso deja lo cierto, tiene poco seso.

Ru Лучше телёнка в хлеву, нежели корову за горой.

14 *En* As sure as eggs is eggs.

   Fr Aussi sûr que deux et deux font quatre.

   De So gewiss, wie zweimal zwei vier ist.

   It Così sicuro, come è certo che le uova sono uova.

   El Tan cierto como dos y dos son cuatro.

   Ru Верно, как дважды два—четыре.

15 *En* Slow and (but) sure.*

   Fr Lentement mais sûrement.

   De Langsam, aber sicher.

   It Chi va piano, va sano.

   El El que anda despacio, anda con seguridad.

   Ru Не скоро, да здорово.

16 *En* It is a good horse that never stumbles.*

   Fr Il n'est si bon cheval qui ne bronche.

   De Auch der beste Gaul stolpert einmal.

   It E cade anche un cavallo che ha quattro gambe.

   El No hay caballo tan bueno que no tropiece.

   Ru Конь о четырёх ногах, да и то спотыкается.

17 *En* Ye know not what shall be on the tomorrow. *(B)*

   Fr Vous ne savez pas ce qui arrivera demain.

   De Ihr wisst nicht, was morgen sein wird.

   It Non sapete ciò che sarà domani.

   El No sabéis lo que será mañana.

   Ru Вы не знаете, что случится завтра. *(Б)*

18 *En* Between two stools one falls to the ground.

   Fr Demeurer entre deux selles le cul à terre.

   De Wer auf zwei Stühlen sitzt, fällt oft mitten durch.

It   Chi in due scanni vuol sedere, darà in terra del messere.
El   Quien se acuesta en dos sillas, da de costillas.
Ru   Тот, кто сидит на двух стульях, легко может упасть.

19   *En*   Seeing is believing.*
      Fr   Voir c'est croire.
      De   Was man sieht, das glaubt man.
      It   Chi non l'occhio vede, col cuor crede.
      El   Ver es creer.
      Ru   Когда увижу, тогда и поверю.

20   *En*   Into a shut mouth flies fly not.
      Fr   Dans une bouche close, il n'entre point de mouche.
      De   Halt's Maul, so fliegt dir keine Mücke hinein.
      It   In bocca chiusa non entrò mai mosca.
      El   En bocca cerrada, ni moscas ni nada.
      Ru   В закрытый рот муха не влетит.

21   *En*   To have two strings to one's bow.
      Fr   Avoir deux cordes à son arc.
      De   Doppelt genäht hält besser.
      It   Corda doppia regge di più.
      El   Cuerda triplicada difícil de romper.
      Ru   Раз хорошо, а два лучше.

22   *En*   Do not say, I'll never drink of this water.*
      Fr   Il ne faut pas dire: Fontaine, je ne boirai pas de ton eau.
      De   Niemand kann sagen: Von diesem Wasser werde ich nicht trinken.
      It   Non serve dire: Di tal acqua non beverò.
      El   No hay que decir: De esa agua no beberé.
      Ru   Не плюй в колодец: пригодится воды напиться.

23   *En*   Do not count your chickens before they are hatched.
      Fr   Il ne faut pas compter l'œuf dans le cul de la poule.

De Zähle erst, wenn du das Geld in der Tasche hast.

It Non vendere la pelle dell'orso prima di averlo ucciso.

El No hay mujer tan ladina, que cuente los huevos en el culo de la gallina.

Ru Не считай утят, пока не вылупились.

24 *En* Between the cup and the lip a morsel may slip.

Fr De la main à la bouche se perd souvent la soupe.

De Von der Hand zum Mund verschüttet mancher die Suppe.

It Dalla mano alla bocca spesso si perde la zuppa.

El De la mano a la boca se pierde la sopa.

Ru Не суженый кус изо рту валится.

По усам потекло, а в рот не попало.

25 *En* He that seeketh findeth. *(B)**

Fr Celui qui cherche trouve.

De Wer da sucht, der findet.

It Chi cerca, trova.

El El que busca, halla.

Ru Тот и сыщет, кто ищет. *(Б)*

26 *En* He that leaves the highway to cut short, commonly goes about.

Fr Mieux vaut la vieille voie que le nouveau sentier.

De Besser ist die alte Strasse als der neue Pfad.

It Chi lascia la via vecchia per la nuova, spesse volte ingannato si trova.

El No dejar los caminos viejos por los senderos nuevos.

Ru Кто прямой дороги ищет, дома не ночует.

27 *En* A tree is known by its fruit. *(B)*

Fr On connaît l'arbre par le fruit.

De An der Frucht erkennt man den Baum.

It Dal frutto si conosce l'albero.

El Por el fruto es conocido el árbol.

Ru Дерево познаётся по плоду. *(Б)*

28 *En* To stumble at a straw and leap over a block.

    Fr Broncher contre une paille et sauter pas dessus un poutre.

    De Viele stolpern über einen Strohhalm, die über einen Balken gesprungen.

    It Inciampar contro una paglia e balzar di sopra un tronco.

    El Tropezar contra una paja, y saltar sobre un tronco.

    Ru Собаку съел, только хвостом подавился.

29 *En* Quick believers need broad shoulders.*

    Fr Croire de léger n'est pas sûr.

    De Wer leicht glaubt, wird leicht betrogen.

    It Chi troppo si fida, spesso grida.

    El No fíate, no serás engañado.

    Ru Кто легко верит, тот легко и погибает.

30 *En* First catch your hare, then cook him.

    Fr C'est viande mal prête que lièvre en buisson.

    De Ungefangene Fische sind nicht gut zu Tische.

    It Mal si mangia la lepre, se prima non si piglia.

    El No hay que contar con el huevo antes de poner la gallina.

    Ru Нечего жарить непойманного зайца.

31 *En* Never fry a fish till it's caught.

    Fr Pour faire un civet, prenez un lièvre.

    De Man soll nicht rufen: Holt Fische!, ehe man sie hat.

    It Non gridar pesci prima di avergli presi.

    El No le llames grano hasta que esté encerrado.

    Ru Не убив медведя, шкуры не продавай.

32 *En* A bird in the hand is worth two in the bush.*

    Fr Moineau à la main vaut mieux que grue qui vole.

    De Besser ein Sperling in der Hand als eine Taube auf dem Dach.

It È meglio un uccello in gabbia che cento fuori.

El Más vale un pájaro en mano que ciento volando.

Ru Птица в руках стоит двух в кустах.

33 *En* One "Take it" is more worth than two "Thou shalt have it".

Fr Mieux vaut un "tiens" que deux "tu l'auras".

De Ein "haben" ist besser als zwei "kriegen".

It È meglio un "ti dò" che cento "ti prometto".

El Más vale un "toma" que dos "te daré".

Ru Лучше синицу в руки, чем журавля в небе.

34 *En* Better spare at brim than at bottom.

Fr Il vaut mieux épargner au bord qu'au fond.

De Spare in der Zeit, dann hast du in der Not.

It Meglio è sparagnar all'orlo ch'al fondo.

El Más vale ahorrar al borde que no al hondo.

Ru Поздно беречь вино, когда бочка пуста.

35 *En* Better to have than wish.

Fr Mieux vaut tenir que courir.

De Besser haben als hoffen.

It È meglio posseder che desiare.

El Mejor es poseer que desear.

Ru Лучше иметь, чем желать.

36 *En* Better an egg today than a hen tomorrow.

Fr Mieux vaut maintenant un œuf que dans le temps un bœuf.

De Besser heut' ein Ei als morgen ein Küchlein.

It È meglio oggi l'uovo che domani la gallina.

El Mejor es huevo hoy que pollo mañana.

Ru Лучше суп сегодня, чем каша завтра.

37 *En* One today is worth two tomorrows.

   Fr Mieux vaut un présent que deux futurs.

   De Ein Heut' ist besser denn zehn Morgen.

   Il È meglio un presente che due futuri.

   El Más vale un presente que dos después, y decir atiende.

   Ru Одно "нынче" лучше двух "завтра".

37 Hope–Patience
Espoir–Patience
Hoffnung–Geduld
Speranza–Pazienza
Esperanza–Paciencia
Надежда–Терпение

1 *En* While there is life there is hope.*
   Fr Tant qu'il y a de la vie, il y a de l'espoir.
   De Es hofft der Mensch, solang er lebt.
   It Finchè c'è vita, c'è speranza.
   El Mientras hay vida, hay esperanza.
   Ru Где жизнь, там и надежда.
         Век живи, век надейся!

2 *En* He that lives in hope danceth without music.
   Fr Qui vit en espérance, danse sans tambourin.
   De Wer von Hoffnung lebt, der tanzt ohne Musik.
   It Chi vive a speranza, fa la fresca danza.
   El Quien vive de esperanza, baila sin música.
   Ru С надеждой легко живётся.

3 *En* Hope is the poor man's bread.*
   Fr L'espérance est le pain des misérables.
   De Hoffnung macht den Bettler reich.
         In Hoffnung schweben macht süsses Leben.
   It La speranza è il pan de' poveri.
   El La esperanza es el pan de los míseros.
   Ru Без одежды, но не без надежды.

4 *En* Hope maketh not ashamed. *(B)*
   Fr L'espérance ne trompe point.

De Hoffnung lässt nicht zuschanden werden.
It La speranza non confonde.
El La esperanza no avergüenza.
Ru Надежда не постыжает. *(Б)*

5 En Too much hope deceiveth.*
      Hope often deludes the foolish man.*
   Fr On est souvent dupé par l'espoir.
      L'espoir est souvent une chimère.
   De Hoffen und Harren macht manchen zum Narren.
   It La speranza molte volte inganna.
   El Esperanza luenga, esperando desespera.
   Ru Надеяться и ждать–одураченным стать.

6 En Who lives by hope will die by hunger.
   Fr Qui vit d'espoir, mourra à jeun.
   De Wer von Hoffnung lebt, stirbt an Fasten.
   It Chi pasce di speranza, muore di fame.
   El Quien espera en la esfera, muere en la rueda.
   Ru Много надежды впереди, а смерть на носу.

7 En All is not lost that is delayed.*
   Fr Ce qui est différé n'est pas perdu.
   De Aufgeschoben ist nicht aufgehoben.
   It Quello che è differito non è perduto.
      Lo allungare non leva via la cosa.
   El Lo que se difiere, no se pierde.
   Ru Отложить не значит отменить.
      Отложено–не уничтожоно.

8 En Our day will come.
   Fr Notre jour viendra.
   De Auch unser Weizen wird einmal blühen!
   It Verrà anche il nostro giorno.

El ¡También nos llegará nuestra hora de alegría!
Ru Будет и на нашей улице праздник.

9 *En* Everything comes to him who waits.
   Fr Tout vient à point, qui peut attendre.
   De Wer's abwarten kann, kommt endlich dran.
   It Chi aspettar puole, ha ciò che vuole.
   El Quien sabe esperar, llega a lograr.
   Ru Всё приходит вовремя для того, кто умеет ждать.

10 *En* Wait and see.
   Fr Qui vivra verra.
   De Abwarten und Tee trinken!
   It Chi vivrà, vedrà.
   El El que viva, verá.
   Ru Поживём–увидим.

11 *En* Patient men win the day.*
   Fr La patience vient à bout de tout.
   De Geduld überwindet alles.
   It Colla pazienza si vince tutto.
   El Con la paciencia todo se alcanza.
   Ru Терпение и труд всё перетрут.

12 *En* Patience is a plaster for all sores.*
   Fr La patience est un remède à tous les maux.
   De Geduld ist die beste Arznei im Unglück.
   It D'ogni dolor rimedio è la pazienza.
   El No hay tal ciencia como tener paciencia.
   Ru Терпение принесёт спасение.

13 *En* There is a limit to one's patience.
   Fr La patience a des limites.
   De Geduld hat Grenzen.

It   Anche la pazienza ha un limite.

El   La paciencia tiene su fin.

Ru   Всякому терпению бывает конец.

14   *En*   Beware the fury of a patient man.

     Fr   La patience poussée à bout se tourne en fureur.

     De   Verletzte Geduld wird zur Wut.

     It   Pazienza spinta all'estremo, furia diventa.

     El   Injuriada la paciencia, a veces, en ira quiebra.

     Ru   Тут и у святого терпение лопнет!

38 Eating and Drinking
Boire et Manger
Essen und Trinken
Bere e Mangiare
Comer y Beber
Еда и питьё

1 *En* Appetite comes with eating.
   Fr L'appétit vient en mangeant.
   De Der Appetit kommt mit dem Essen.
   It L'appetito vien mangiando.
   El Al apetito, comiendo se llama.
   Ru Аппетит приходит во время еды.

2 *En* Live not to eat, but eat to live.*
   Fr Il faut manger pour vivre, et non pas vivre pour manger.
   De Wir leben nicht, um zu essen–wir essen, um zu leben.
   It Si deve mangiar per vivere, non vivere per mangiare.
   El No hay que vivir para comer, sino comer para vivir.
   Ru Живи не для того, чтобы есть, но ешь для того, чтобы жить.

3 *En* A belly full of gluttony will never study willingly.*
   Fr Le ventre plein rend le cerveau paresseux.
   De Ein voller Bauch studiert nicht gern.
   It A buzzo pieno mal si lavora.
   El A panza llena no le gusta estudiar.
   Ru Сытое брюхо к учению глухо.

4 *En* A fat belly, a lean brain.
   Fr Estomac plein, cerveau vide.
   De Voll macht faul.

It   Il ventre pieno fa la testa vuota.
El   Estómago lleno, cerebro vacío.
Ru   Живот толстой, да лоб пустой.

5   *En*   The eye is bigger than the belly.
    Fr   Les yeux sont plus grands que le ventre.
    De   Die Augen sind grösser als der Magen.
    It   Aver gli occhi più grandi del ventre.
    El   Tener los ojos más grandes que el estómago.
    Ru   Глаза шире брюха.

6   *En*   Gluttony kills more than the sword.
    Fr   La gourmandise tue plus de gens que l'épée.
    De   Mehr sterben vom Frass als vom Schwert.
    It   Più ne uccide la gola che la spada.
    El   Más mató la cena que sanó Avicena.
    Ru   Не с поста, а с обжорства мрут люди.

7   *En*   Too many cooks spoil the broth.
    Fr   Trop de cuisiniers gâtent le potage.
           Quand il y a plusieurs cuisiniers, la soupe est trop salée
    De   Viele Köche verderben den Brei.
    It   I troppi cuochi guastano la cucina.
    El   Muchos componedores descomponen la olla.
    Ru   Десять поваров только щи пересаливают.

8   *En*   Back may trust, but belly won't.
    Fr   Mieux vaut bon repas que bel habit.
    De   Erst der Magen, dann der Kragen.
    It   Meglio buon desinare che una bella giubba.
    El   Pan y vino anda camino, que no mozo garrido.
    Ru   Хлеб греет, не шуба.

9   *En*   The sauce is better than the fish.
    Fr   La sauce vaut mieux que le poisson.

De Oft kommt die Brühe teurer als das Fleisch.

It È più la giunta della carne.

El Más vale la salsa que los caracoles.
    Más vale la envoltura que la criatura.

Ru Приправа лучше кушанья.

10 *En* Fish mars water, flesh mends it.

    Fr Chair fait chair et poisson poison.

    De Fleisch macht wieder Fleisch, Fisch macht nisch.

    It Carne fa carne, pesce fa vesce.

    El Carne carne cría, y peces agua fría.

    Ru Рыба не мясо, ею сыт не будешь.

11 *En* They have most bread who have least teeth.

    Fr Tel a du pain qui n'a point de dents.

    De Mancher hat Brot, wenn er keine Zähne mehr hat.

    It Chi ha denti non ha pane, e chi ha pane non ha denti.

    El Da Dios almendras (higos) a quien no tiene muelas.

    Ru Когда зубов не стало, тогда и орехов принесли.

12 *En* Who depends upon another man's table often dines late.

    Fr Qui s'attend à l'écuelle d'autrui, a souvent mal dîné.

    De Wer sich auf anderer Leute Schüssel verlässt, geht
        hungrig zu Bett.

    It Chi per le man d'altri s'imbocca, tardi si satolla.

    El Quien espera a mano ajena, mal yanta y peor cena.

    Ru Кто надеется на соседа, тот останется без обеда.
        Не надейся, дед, на чужой обед!

13 *En* When the mouse has had enough, the meal is bitter.*

    Fr A pigeon soûl cerises sont amères.

    De Wenn die Maus satt ist, schmeckt das Mehl bitter.

    It Colombo pasciuto, ciliegia amara.

    El Al hombre harto las cerezas le amargan.

    Ru Мышь сыта, и мука горька.

14 *En* Eaten bread is soon forgotten.
   Fr Morceau avalé n'a plus de goût.
   De Gegessenes Brot ist bald vergessen.
   It Il pan mangiato presto è dimenticato.
   El El pan comido, presto se echa en olvido.
   Ru Брюхо–злодей: старого добра не помнит.

15 *En* After dinner sit a while, after supper walk a mile.*
   Fr Après dîner repose un peu, après souper promène une mille.
   De Nach dem Essen soll man ruh'n oder tausend Schritte tun.
   It Dopo pranzo riposar un poco, dopo cena passeggiar un miglio.
   El Después de yantar reposad un poco, después de cenar pasead una milla.
   Ru После обеда полежи, после ужина походи.

16 *En* He that will eat the kernel must crack the nut.*
   Fr Pour avoir l'amande il faut casser le noyau.
   De Wer den Kern essen will, muss die Nuss knacken.
   It Bisogna rompere la noce, se si vuol mangiare il nocciuolo.
   El Quien peces quiere, tiene que mojarse.
   Ru Не разгрызёшь ореха, так не съешь и ядра.

17 *En* Who goes to bed supperless, all night tumbles and tosses.
   Fr Qui s'en va coucher sans souper ne cesse la nuit de se démener.
   De Wer ohne Essen zu Bett geht, der wird leicht am Schlaf verhindert.
   It Chi va a letto senza cena, tutta notte si dimena.
   El Quien se echa sin cena, toda la noche devanea.
   Ru Без ужина подушка в головах вертится.

18 *En* Every time the sheep bleats it loses a mouthful.
   Fr Brebis qui bêle perd sa goulée.

De Wenn die Schafe blocken, fällt ihnen das Futter aus dem Maul.

It Pecora che bela, perde il boccone.

El Oveja que bala, bocado pierde.

Ru Кто за обедом много болтает, тот голодный бывает.

19 En The belly hates a long sermon.

Fr Court sermon et long dîner.

De Kurze Predigt, lange Bratwurst.

It Messa corta e lunga tavola.

El Oración larga, más que mueve, cansa.

Ru Голодному животу и молебен не в утеху.

20 En When wine is in, wit is out.*

Fr Quand le vin entre, la raison sort.

De Wein ein, Witz aus.

It Vino dentro, senno fuori.

El Do entra beber, sale saber.
    El mucho vino saca al hombre de tino.

Ru Вино входит–ум выходит.

21 En What soberness conceals, drunkenness reveals.

Fr Ce que le sobre tient au cœur, est sur la langue du buveur.

De Trunkener Mund verrät des Herzens Grund.

It Bocca ubriaca scopre il fondo del cuore.

El Cuando el vino entra, el secreto se sale afuera.

Ru Что у трезвого на уме, то у пьяного на языке.

22 En A sleeping man is not hungry.

Fr Qui dort dîne.

De Wer schläft, den hungert nicht.

It Chi dorme, non sente la fame.

El Quien duerme, engorda.

Ru Сонный хлеба не просит.

23 *En* Hungry bellies have no ears.*
    Fr Ventre affamé n'a point d'oreilles.
    De Ein hungriger Bauch hat keine Ohren.
    It Ventre digiuno non ode nessuno.
    El El vientre ayuno non oye a ninguno.
    Ru Голодное брюхо к словам глухо.

24 *En* Hunger fetches the wolf out of the woods.*
    Fr La faim fait sortir le loup du bois.
    De Der Hunger treibt den Wolf aus dem Walde.
    It La fame caccia il lupo dal bosco.
    El La hambre echa el lobo del monte.
    Ru Голод и волка из лесу гонит.

25 *En* Hunger finds no fault with the cookery.*
    Fr Ventre affamé prend tout en gré.
    De Hunger ist der beste Koch.
          Dem hungrigen Bauch schmeckt alles wohl.
    It A buona fame non vi è cattivo pane.
          A chi è affamato, ogni cibo è grato.
    El Para el hambre no hay pan duro.
    Ru Голод–лучший повар.

26 *En* Hunger is the best sauce.
    Fr Il n'est sauce que d'appétit.
          La faim assaisonne tout.
    De Hunger ist die beste Würze.
    It Buon appetito non vuol salsa.
    El A buen hambre no hay falta salsa.
    Ru Голодному Федоту и репа в охоту.

27 *En* Hunger makes hard beans sweet.
    Fr Qui a faim mange tout pain.
    De Hunger macht saure Bohnen süss.

It La fame muta le fave in mandorle.

El A quien tiene hambre, todo a rosquillas le sabe.

Ru Голодному и вода, что с яйца, вкусна.

28 *En* Hungry flies bite sore.

Fr De maigre poil aigre morsure.

De Hungrige Fliegen stechen scharf.

It Mosche e pulci magre son le più affamate.

El Pulga flaca de gran picada.

Ru Голодная муха больнее кусает.

29 *En* A hungry man, an angry man.

Fr Vilain affamé est demi-enragé.

De Hungern und Harren macht das Haupt närrisch.

It Villano affamato è mezzo arrabbiato.

El Campesinos hambrientos, perros con rabia.

Ru Никого так не бойся, как голодного человека.

30 *En* While the grass grows the horse starves.*

Fr Pendant que l'herbe pousse, le cheval meurt.
       Ne meurs, cheval, l'herbe te vient!

De Stirb nicht, lieber Hengst, es kommt die Zeit, wo Gras
       wächst.

It Caval non stare a morire, che l'erba ha da venire.

El Mientras la yerba crece, el caballo muere.

Ru Пока солнце взойдёт, роса очи выест.
       Пока трава растёт, хилая лощадь околеет с голоду.

213

39 Friendship–Enmity
Ami et Ennemi
Freundschaft–Feindschaft
Amico e Nemico
Amigo y Enemigo
Дружба–Вражда

1   *En*   A friend in need is a friend indeed.*
     Fr   On connaît le véritable ami dans le besoin.
     De   Freunde in der Not gehen hundert auf ein Lot.
         Freunde erkennt man in der Not.
     It   A'bisogni si conoscono gli amici.
         Nei pericoli si vede, chi d'amico ha vera fede.
     El   En el peligro se conoce al amigo.
         En la adversidad se prueba la amistad.
     Ru   Друг в нужде–истинный друг.
         Друзья познаются в беде.

2   *En*   A good friend is my nearest relation.
     Fr   Un bon ami vaut mieux que cent parents.
     De   Ein guter Freund ist mehr wert als hundert Verwandte.
     It   Val più un buon amico che cento parenti.
     El   Más vale buen amigo que pariente o primo.
     Ru   Добрый друг лучше ста родственников.

3   *En*   Even reckoning makes long friends.*
     Fr   Les bons comptes font les bons amis.
     De   Kurze Rechnung–lange Freundschaft.
     It   Conti spessi, amicizia lunga.
     El   Buenas cuentas, buenos amigos.
     Ru   Короткий счёт–длинная дружба.
         Счёт дружбе не помеха.

4 *En* Old friends and old wine are best.
   Fr Ami et vin vieux sont bons en tous lieux.
   De Alte Freunde und alter Wein sind am besten.
   It Amico e vino vogliono esser vecchi.
   El Amigo viejo, y vino añejo.
   Ru Нет лучше старого друга и старого вина.
         Старый друг лучше новых двух.

5 *En* Small gifts keep friendship alive.
   Fr Les petits cadeaux entretiennent l'amitié.
   De Kleine Geschenke erhalten die Freundschaft.
   It Piccoli regali mantengono l'amicizia.
   El Pequeños regalos conservan la amistad.
   Ru Не дорог подарок, дорога любовь.

6 *En* The friends of my friends are also my friends.
   Fr Les amis de nos amis sont nos amis.
   De Die Freunde meiner Freunde sind auch meine Freunde.
   It Gli amici dei miei amici sono miei amici.
   El Los amigos de nuestros amigos son nuestros amigos.
   Ru Друзья наших друзей–наши друзья.

7 *En* A friend in the market is better than money in the chest.
   Fr Mieux vaut ami en voie que denier en courroie.
   De Freunde sind gut am Wege.
   It Gli amici son buoni in ogni piazza.
   El Más valen amigos en la plaza que dineros en el arca.
   Ru Не имей сто рублей, а имей сто друзей.

8 *En* A friend to everybody is a friend to nobody.*
   Fr L'ami de tout le monde n'est l'ami de personne.
   De Jedermanns Freund ist niemandes Freund.
   It Amico d'ognuno, amico di nessuno.
   El Quien de todos es amigo, de ninguno es amigo.
   Ru Тот, кто дружит со всеми, не дружит ни с кем.

9   *En*   Love me, love my dog.*

     Fr   Qui aime Martin, aime son chien.

     De Wer mich liebt, der liebt auch meinen Hund.

     It   Chi ama me, ama il mio cane.

     El   Quien quiere a Beltrán, quiere a su can.

     Ru Любишь меня, так люби и собачку мою.

10 *En*   A broken friendship may be soldered, but will never be sound.*

          Take heed of reconciled enemies.*

     Fr   Amitié rompue n'est jamais bien soudée.

          Ne te fie jamais à l'ami reconcilié.

     De Geflickte Freundschaft wird nimmer wieder ganz.

     It   Amicizia riconciliata è come piaga mal saldata.

     El   Amistad quebrada, soldada, mas nunca sana.

     Ru Замиренный друг ненадёжен.

11 *En*   In time of prosperity friends will be plenty; in time of adversity, not one amongst twenty.*

     Fr   Tant que tu seras heureux, tu compteras beaucoup d'amis.

     De Bei Reichtum wirst du viele Freunde finden, bei Armut werden sie dir alle schwinden.

     It   Amici molti avrai finchè ricco sarai.

          Chi cade in povertà, perde ogni amico.

     El   Quien tuvo dineros, tuvo compañeros; mas si los dineros perdió, sin compañeros se quedó.

     Ru При пире, при бражке–все дружки; при горе, кручине-нет никого

12 *En*   When good cheer is lacking, our friends will be packing.

     Fr   Ami de table est bien variable.

          Amis de bouche ne valent pas une mouche.

     De Siedet der Topf, so blüht die Freundschaft.

     It   Amico di buon tempo mutasi col vento.

          Mangiato il fico, perso l'amico.

El Comido el pan y alzada la mesa, la compañía deshecha.
Amigo del buen tiempo múdase con el viento.

Ru Скатерть со стола–и дружба сплыла.
Хлеба нет–друзей и не бывало.

13 *En* Before you make a friend eat a bushel of salt with him.
Fr On ne connaît son ami qu'après avoir mangé avec lui beaucoup de sel.
De Um den Freund zu erkennen, musst du erst einen Scheffel Salz mit ihm gegessen haben.
It Prima di scegliere l'amico bisogna averci mangiato il sale sett'anni.
El En tu amigo confiarás, cuando hayas comido con él media fanega de sal.
Ru Чтоб узнать друга, надо с ним пуд соли съесть.

14 *En* Better an open enemy than a false friend.
Fr L'ennemi couvert est le pire.
De Besser ein offener Feind als ein falscher Freund.
It Peggio l'invidia dell'amico che l'insidia del nemico.
El El peor enemigo es el escondido.
Ru Лучше явный враг, чем лживый друг.

15 *En* Gifts from enemies are dangerous.*
Fr Don d'ennemi, don funeste.
De Geschenk vom Feind ist nicht gut gemeint.
It Doni di nemici non sono doni.
El Un presente griego.
Ru Недруг дарит–зло мыслит.

16 *En* There is no little enemy.*
Fr Il n'est nuls petits ennemis.
De Auch den kleinsten Feind verachte nicht.
It Il più piccolo nemico può darti briga assai.

El   No hay enemigo pequeño.

No menosprecies al enemigo menor.

Ru И слабого врага надо остерегаться.

17 En Man is to man a wolf.*

Fr L'homme est un loup pour l'homme.

De Ein Mensch ist des andern Wolf.

It L'uomo è lupo all'uomo.

El El hombre es el lobo del hombre.

Ru Человек человеку–волк.

18 En God defend me from my friends; from my enemies I can (will) defend myself.*

Fr Dieu me garde de mes amis! Je me garderai de mes ennemis.

De Behüte mich Gott vor meinen Freunden, mit den Feinden will ich schon fertig werden.

It Dagli amici mi guardi Dio; che dai nemici mi guardo io.

El De quien me fío, Dios me guarde; de quien no me fío, me guardaré yo.

Ru Избавь меня, Боже, от друзей, а от врагов я сам избавлюсь.

40 Neighbours–Guests
Voisinage–Hospitalité
Nachbarn–Gäste
Vicino–Ospite
Vecino–Huésped
Соседи–Гости

1 *En* Better is a neighbour that is near than a brother far off. *(B)*
   Fr Mieux vaut un voisin proche qu'un frère éloigné.
   De Ein Nachbar in der Nähe ist besser als ein Bruder in der Ferne.
   It Meglio vale un vicino presso, che un fratello lontano.
   El Mejor es el vecino cerca que el hermano lejano.
   Ru Лучше сосед вблизи, нежели брат вдали. *(Б)*

2 *En* A good neighbour, a good morrow.*
   Fr Qui a bon voisin a bon matin.
   De Wer gute Nachbarn hat, schläft ruhig.
   It Chi ha il buon vicino, ha il buon mattutino.
   El Quien ha buen vecino, ha buen amigo.
   Ru Не купи двора, купи соседа.

3 *En* Love your neighbour, yet pull not down your hedge.
       A hedge between keeps friendship green.
   Fr Aimez votre voisin, mais n'abattez pas la haie.
   De Zwischen Nachbars Garten ist ein Zaun gut.
   It Vicinanza senza siepe porta nimicizia in casa.
   El Ama tu vecino, pero no deshagas tu seto.
       Por conservar amistad, pared en medio.
   Ru С соседом дружись, а забор городи.

219

4   *En* Look to thyself when the neighbour's house is on fire.
     Fr Il s'agit de toi, si la maison de ton voisin brûle.
     De Wenn des Nachbars Haus brennt, so gilt dir's auch.
     It Quando egli arde in vicinanza, porta l'acqua a casa tua.
     El Cuando vieres la barba de tu vecino pelar, echa la tuya a remojar.
     Ru (Если у соседа пожар, то и тебе опасность грозит).

5   *En* A great lord is a bad neighbour.*
     Fr Un grand seigneur, un mauvais voisin.
     De Grosser Fluss und grosser Herr sind schlechte Nachbarn.
     It Nè mulo, nè mulino, nè signore per vicino.
     El Peligrosa es la vecindad de los poderosos.
     Ru От соседа-богача не жди добра.

6   *En* An unbidden guest knoweth not where to sit.*
     Fr Qui va à noce sans prier s'en revient sans dîner.
     De Ungebetener Gast findet keinen Stuhl.
     It Chi va alla festa e non è invitato, ben gli sta se n'è scacciato.
     El A boda ni a bautismo no vayas sin ser llamado.
     Ru На незваного гостя не припасена и ложка.
        Незваные гости с пиру долой.

7   *En* A constant guest is never welcome.
     Fr L'hôte et la pluie, après trois jours ennuient.
     De Ein seltner Gast fällt nie zur Last.
     It Ospite raro, ospite caro.
     El A casa de tu tía, mas no cada día.
        Visita rara, convidado amable.
     Ru Хорош гость, коли редко ходит.
        Редкое свидание–приятный гость.

8   *En* Fresh fish and new-come guests smell in three days.*
     Fr L'hôte et le poisson après trois jours puent.

De Gast und Fisch sind nach drei Tagen nicht mehr frisch.
It L'ospite e il pesce dopo tre giorni ti rincresce.
El El huésped y el pez a tres días hiede.
Ru Гость–до трёх дней.
    Пора гостям и честь знать.

9 *En* They are welcome that bring.
   Fr Bienvenu qui apporte.
   De Wer bringt, ist überall willkommen.
   It Chi porta, è sempre il benvenuto.
   El Los dones cautivan hasta a los dioses.
   Ru Идёшь в гости, неси подарок в горсти.

10 *En* As welcome as flowers in May.
   Fr Aussi bienvenu comme fleurs en mai.
   De So willkommen wie die Blumen im Mai.
   It Tanto benvenuto come fiori in maggio.
   El Tan bienvenido como flores en mayo.
   Ru Желанный гость, как цветы в мае.

41 Concord–Discord
Concorde–Discorde
Eintracht–Zwietracht
Concordia–Discordia
Acuerdo–Discordia
Согласие–Раздор

1 *En* Union is strength.
Fr L'union fait la force.
De Eintracht hat grosse Macht.
Einigkeit macht stark.
It L'unione fa la forza.
El La unión hace la fuerza.
Ru В единении сила.

2 *En* United we stand, divided we fall.*
Fr Concorde construit, discorde détruit.
De Eintracht ernährt, Zwietracht verzehrt.
It L'ordine è pane, il disordine è fame.
El No bastan en una nación las fuerzas sin la unión.
Ru Дружба созидает, вражда разрушает.

3 *En* A lean compromise is better than a fat law-suit.
Fr Un mauvais accommodement vaut mieux qu'un bon
procès.
De Ein magerer Vergleich ist besser als ein fetter Prozess.
It Meglio un magro accordo che una grassa sentenza.
El Más vale mala avenencia que buena sentencia.
Ru Худой мир лучше доброй ссоры.

4 *En* Injuries don't use to be written on ice.
Fr Les injures s'écrivent sur l'airain.

De Böses schreibt man in Stein, Gutes in Sand.

It Le offese si scrivono nel marmo.

Chi offende, scrive sulla rena; chi è offeso, nel marmo.

El Hombre agraviado, nunca desmemoriado.

Ru Лихое долго помнится.

5 *En* Not even Hercules could contend against two.*

Fr Contre deux Hercule ne peut.

De Roland auch, der kühne Mann, nahm es nicht mit zweinen an.

It Contro due non la potrebbe Orlando.

El Ni Hércules contre dos.

Ru Много и того, как два на одного.

Двое одному рать.

6 *En* Between two brothers two witnesses and a notary.*

Fr Courroux de frères, courroux de diables d'enfer.

Entre deux frères, deux témoins et un notaire.

De Bruderzwist–gar heftig ist.

It Ira di fratelli, ira di diavoli.

El Entre dos hermanos, dos testigos y un notario.

Ira de hermanos, ira de diablos.

Ru Брат на брата–пуще супостата.

7 *En* Hatred stirreth up strife. *(B)*

Fr La haine excite des querelles.

De Hass erregt Hader.

It L'odio muove contese.

El El odio despierta rencillas.

Ru Ненависть возбуждает раздоры. *(Б)*

8 *En* It takes two to make a quarrel.

Fr Il faut être deux pour se quereller.

De Zum Streiten gehören zwei.

It Bisogna essere in due per fare una lite.
El Cuando uno no quiere, dos no contienden.
Ru Для ссоры нужны двое.

9 *En* The offender never pardons.
    Fr L'offenseur ne pardonne jamais.
    De Der Beleidiger verzeihet nie.
    It Chi offende non perdona.
    El Después que te erré, nunca bien te quise.
    Ru Кто кого обидит, тот того и ненавидит.

10 *En* Two dogs over one bone seldom agree.*
    Fr Deux chiens ne s'accordent point à un os.
    De Zwei Hunde an einem Bein kommen selten überein.
    It Due cani, che un sol osso hanno, difficilmente in pace
       stanno.
    El Habiendo un hueso entre ellos, no son amigos dos
       perros.
    Ru Двум собакам одной кости не поделить.

11 *En* Quarrelling dogs come halting home.
    Fr Chien hargneux a toujours l'oreille déchirée.
    De Böser Hund–zerrissenes Fell.
    It Can ringhioso e non forzoso guai alla sua pelle.
    El Gente discutidora siempre recibe algún arañazo.
    Ru На задорном буяне вся шкура в изъяне.

12 *En* Two dogs strive for a bone, and a third runs away with it.*
    Fr Quand les chiens s'entre-pillent, le loup fait ses affaires.
    De Wenn zwei sich zanken, lacht der Dritte in Gedanken.
    It Tra due litiganti il terzo gode.
    El Cuando dos pleitean un tercero se aprovecha.
    Ru Пастухи за чубы, а волки за овец.
       Орлы бьются, а молодцам перья достаются.

13   *En*   To agree like cats and dogs.
     Fr   S'entendre comme chien et chat.
     De   Sich vertragen wie Hund und Katze.
     It   Stare come cani i gatti.
     El   Vivir como perros y gatos.
     Ru   Дружат, как кошка с собакой.

14   *En*   To rise on the wrong side.
     Fr   Se lever du pied gauche.
     De   Mit dem linken Bein aufstehen.
     It   Levarsi di cattivo umore.
     El   Levantarse con el pie izquierdo.
     Ru   Встать с левой ноги.

15   *En*   Anger is a short madness.*
     Fr   La colère est une courte folie.
     De   Zorn ist kurze Unsinnigkeit.
     It   L'ira acceca la ragione.
     El   La ira es una locura corta.
     Ru   Гнев–недолгое безумие.

16   *En*   Anger cannot stand without a strong hand.*
     Fr   Courroux est vain sans forte main.
     De   Zorn ohne Macht wird verlacht.
     It   L'ira senza forza non vale una scorza.
     El   Enojo sin poder es flojo.
     Ru   Сердит, да не силён–сам себе враг.

42 **War and Peace**
    Guerre et Paix
    Krieg und Frieden
    La guerra e la pace
    Guerra y Paz
    Война и мир

1   *En* Better an egg in peace than an ox in war.
    Fr Mieux vaut en paix un œuf qu'en guerre un bœuf.
    De Besser ein Ei im Frieden als ein Ochs im Kriege.
    It Più vale un pan con amore che un cappone con dolore.
    El Más vale en paz un huevo que en guerra un gallinero.
    Ru Лучше хлеб с водой, чем пирог с бедой.

2   *En* To smoke the pipe of peace.
    Fr Fumer le calumet de paix avec quelqu'un.
    De Mit jemandem eine Friedenspfeife rauchen.
    It Fumare la pipa di pace.
    El Fumar la pipa de paz.
    Ru Выкурить с кем-нибудь трубку мира.

3   *En* All they that take the sword shall perish with the sword. *(B)*
    Fr Tous ceux qui prendront l'épée périront par l'épée.
    De Wer das Schwert nimmt, der soll durchs Schwert umkommen.
    It Tutti coloro che avran presa la spada, periranno per la spada.
    El Todos los que tomaren espada, a espada perecerán.
    Ru Поднявшие меч от меча и погибнут. *(Б)*

226

4   *En* For a flying enemy make a golden bridge.
     Fr Il faut faire un pont d'or à l'ennemi qui fuit.
     De Dem fliehenden Feind baue goldene Brücken.
     It Al nemico che fugge, ponti d'oro.
     El Al enemigo que huye, puente de plata.
     Ru Отступающему врагу–скатертью дорога.

5   *En* Too light winning makes the prize light.
     Fr A vaincre sans péril on triomphe sans gloire.
     De Gefahrlos siegen ist ruhmlos triumphieren.
     It Dove non è pericolo, non è gloria.
     El El que sin peligro vence, no consigue la gloria.
     Ru Побеждать без риска–побеждать без славы.

6   *En* If you wish for peace, be prepared for war.*
     Fr Que celui qui veut la paix prépare la guerre.
     De Wer Frieden haben will, muss zum Kriege rüsten.
     It Chi vuol la pace, guerra apparecchi.
     El Si quieres la paz, prepárate para la guerra.
     Ru Хочешь мира–готовься к войне.

7   *En* Where drums beat laws are silent.*
     Fr Au milieu des armes, les lois sont silencieuses.
     De Im Kriege schweigt das Recht.
     It Dove parlano i tamburi, taccion le leggi.
     El Cuando los tambores hablan, las leyes callan.
     Ru Где сила владеет, там закон уступает.

8   *En* They shall beat their swords into ploughshares. *(B)*
     Fr De leurs glaives ils forgeront des hoyaux.
     De Sie werden ihre Schwerter zu Pflugscharen verschmieden.
     It Ed essi delle loro spade fabbricheranno zappe.
     El Y volverán sus espadas en rejas de arado.
     Ru И перекуют мечи свои на орала. *(Б)*

9   *En*   Obedience is the first duty of a soldier.

     Fr   L'obéissance est le premier devoir du soldat.

     De Gehorsam ist die erste Soldatenpflicht.

     It   L'obbedienza è il primo dovere del soldato.

     El   La obediencia es el primer deber del soldado.

     Ru Приказ свят: без дисциплины солдат не солдат.

10 *En*   Armed to the teeth.

     Fr   Armé de pied en cap.

     De Bis auf die Zähne bewaffnet.

     It   Armato fino ai denti.

     El   Armado de punta en blanco.

     Ru Вооружённый до зубов.

11 *En*   War to the knife.

     Fr   Guerre à outrance.

     De Krieg bis aufs Messer.

     It   Guerra di sterminio.

     El   Guerra al cuchillo.

     Ru Борьба не на жизнь, а на смерть.

43 Solidarity–Reciprocation
Solidarité–Réciprocité
Solidarität–Erwiderung
Solidarietà–Reciprocità
Solidaridad–Reciprocidad
Солидарность–Взаимность

1   *En*   One hand washeth the other.*
      Fr   Une main lave l'autre.
      De   Eine Hand wäscht die andere.
      It   Una mano lava l'altra.
      El   Una mano lava a la otra.
      Ru   Рука руку моет.

2   *En*   Claw me, and I'll claw thee.
      Fr   Gratte-moi l'épaule et je t'en ferai autant.
      De   Wie du mir, so ich dir.
      It   Grattami e ti gratterò.
      El   Donde las dan, las toman.
      Ru   Услуга за услугу.

3   *En*   Roll my log, and I'll roll yours.
      Fr   Passez-moi la rhubarbe, je vous passerai le séné.
      De   Brätst du mir die Wurst, so lösch ich dir den Durst.
      It   Tienmi il sacco oggi, e domani lo terrò io a te.
      El   Hazme la barba, hacerte he el copete.
      Ru   Послужи на меня, а я на тебя.

4   *En*   One good turn deserves another.
      Fr   Un service en vaut un autre.
      De   Eine Gefälligkeit ist der andern wert.

It Un servizio per altro.
     A buon rendere.
El Un favor se paga con otro.
Ru За добро добром и платят.
     Долг платежом красен.

5 *En* Good finds good.
    Fr Qui fera bien, bien trouvera.
    De Wer Gutes tut, wird Gutes finden.
    It Chi fa bene, ha bene.
    El A quien bien hace, otro bien le nace.
    Ru Делай добро, и тебе будет добро.

6 *En* One must howl with the wolves.*
    Fr Il faut hurler avec les loups.
    De Mit den Wölfen muss man heulen.
    It Chi pratica col lupo, impara a urlare.
    El Quien con lobos anda, a aullar aprende.
    Ru С волками жить–по-волчьи выть.

7 *En* When at Rome do as the Romans do.*
    Fr Quand tu seras à Rome, agis comme les Romains.
    De In Rom tue, wie Rom tut.
    It Quando a Roma vai, fa come vedrai.
    El Cuando a Roma fueres, haz como vieres.
    Ru В какой народ попадёшь, такую и шапку наденешь.

8 *En* Like will to like.*
    Fr Chacun cherche son semblable.
    De Gleich und gleich gesellt sich gern.
    It Ogni simile ama il suo simile.
    El Cada cual con su igual.
    Ru Свой своего ищет.

9   *En*   Birds of a feather flock together.*
     Fr   Les oiseaux de même plumage volent en troupe.
     De   Vögel von einerlei Federn fliegen gern beisammen.
     It   Gli uccelli si appaiano co' loro pari.
     El   Todas las aves con sus pares.
     Ru   Кто на кого похож, тот с тем и схож.

10   *En*   One sheep follows another.
     Fr   Sauter comme les moutons de Panurge.
     De   Wo ein Schaf vorgeht, folgen die anderen auch.
     It   Far come le pecore: ove va uno, andar tutti.
     El   Por donde una oveja echa, todas detrás hacen senda.
     Ru   Куда стадо, туда и овца.

11   *En*   One ass doth scrub another.*
     Fr   Un âne gratte l'autre.
     De   Ein Esel kraut den andern.
     It   Un asino gratta l'altro.
     El   Los asnos se rascan uno a otro.
     Ru   Дурак дураку и рад.

12   *En*   Hand and glove.
     Fr   Etre comme cul et chemise.
         Deux têtes dans un bonnet.
     De   Ein Herz und eine Seele sein.
     It   Sono due anime in un nocciolo.
     El   Ser uña y carne.
         Dos cuerpos y un alma.
     Ru   Жить душа в душу.

13   *En*   Both of a hair.
     Fr   Les deux font la paire.
     De   Zwei Hosen eines Tuchs.
     It   Una coppia e un paio.

El   Son tal para cual.

Ru   Два сапога-пара.

      Одного поля ягода.

14 En   They are finger and thumb.

    Fr   Ils sont liés comme les doigts de la main.

    De   Sie sind wie Zwillingsbrüder.

    It   Essi sono legati come le dita della mano.

    El   Son dos patas de un mismo banco.

    Ru   Словно их чёрт верёвочкой связал.

15 En   They agree like pickpockets in a fair.*

    Fr   Ils s'entendent comme larrons en foire.

    De   Sie verstehen einander wie Diebe beim Jahrmarkt.

    It   Intendersi come i tiraborse alla fiera.

    El   Entenderse como lobos de la misma camada.

    Ru   Злой с лукавым знаются, друг на друга ссылаются.

16 En   Crows will not pick out crows' eyes.*

    Fr   Les corbeaux entre eux ne se crèvent pas les yeux.

    De   Eine Krähe hackt der andern die Augen nicht aus.

    It   Corvi con corvi non si cavano gli occhi.

    El   Dos leznas no se pinchan.

    Ru   Ворон ворону глаза не выклюет.

17 En   Dog does not eat dog.

    Fr   Les chiens ne se mangent pas entre eux.

    De   Ein Wolf frisst nicht den andern.

    It   Cane non mangia cane.

    El   Un lobo a otro no se muerde.

    Ru   Собака собаку не ест.

18 En   One nail drives out another.*

    Fr   Un clou chasse l'autre.

    De   Ein Keil treibt den andern aus.

It Un chiodo caccia l'altro.

El Un clavo saca otro.

Ru Клин клином вышибают.

19 *En* Measure for measure.

   Fr Mesure pour mesure.

   De Mass für Mass.

   It La pena del taglione.

   El Medida por medida.

   Ru Мера за меру.

20 *En* Eye for eye, tooth for tooth. *(B)*

   Fr Oeil pour œil, dent pour dent.

   De Auge um Auge, Zahn um Zahn.

   It Occhio per occhio, dente per dente.

   El Ojo por ojo, diente por diente.

   Ru Глаз за глаз, зуб за зуб. *(Б)*

21 *En* Tit for tat.*

   Fr Quitte à quitte.

   De Wurst wider Wurst.

   It Colpo per colpo.

   El Cuerda a cuerda.

   Ru Корень за корень.

22 *En* A crabbed knot must have a crabbed wedge.*

   Fr A bois noueux hache affilée.

   De Auf einen groben Klotz gehört ein grober Keil.

   It A duro ceppo dura accetta.

   El A mal nudo mal cuño.
       Tal tronco, tal hacha.

   Ru На крепкий сук–острый топор.

23 *En* Diamond cut diamond.

Fr   Fin contre fin.

      A bon chat, bon rat.

De   List gegen List.

It   Duro con duro.

El   A un pícaro, otro mayor.

Ru   Нашла коса на камень.

      Алмаз алмазом рушится.

24 En To pay one in his own coin.

    Fr Payer quelqu'un de la même monnaie.

    De Jemand mit gleicher Münze zahlen.

    It Pagarlo della stessa moneta.

    El Pagar en la misma moneda.

    Ru Платить кому-нибудь той же монетой.

25 En He loves me well that makes by belly swell.

    Fr Il est mon oncle, qui le ventre me comble.

    De Wer mir Brot gibt, den nenn' ich Vater.

    It Colui è mio zio, che vuole il ben mio.

    El Aquel loar debemos de cuyo pan comemos.

        Quien bien me hace, ése es mi compadre.

    Ru Чей хлеб ем, того и песенку пою.

26 En He is my friend that grindeth at my mill.

    Fr Je suis du parti de celui qui me fait vivre.

    De Wes Brot ich esse, des Lied ich singe.

    It Canto di colui che mi dà pane.

    El Ese es mi amigo qui muele en mi molinillo.

    Ru На чьём возу сижу, того и песенку пою.

44 World and Home
   Le Monde et le Chez-soi
   Welt und Heim
   Mondo e Casa
   Mundo y Casa
   Свет и дом

1   *En*   The world is a wide parish (place).
    Fr   Il y a assez de place pour tous sous le soleil.
    De   Platz für alle hat die Erde.
    It   C'è per tutti posto sotto il sole.
    El   Bajo el sol hay bastante lugar para todos.
    Ru   Белый свет не клином сошёлся.
           Всем хватит места под солнцем.

2   *En*   All the world's a stage, and all the men and women
           merely players. *(Sh)**
    Fr   Le monde entier est une scène, hommes et femmes,
           tous, n'y sont que des acteurs.
    De   Die ganze Welt ist Bühne, und alle Frau'n und Männer
           blosse Spieler.
    It   Teatro è il mondo, e l'uomo è marionetta.
    El   Todo es farsa en este mundo, hasta llegar al segundo.
    Ru   Весь мир–театр, а женщины, мужчины, все–актёры. *(Ш)*

3   *En*   The world is a ladder for some to go up and some down.
    Fr   Le monde est fait comme un degré: l'un le monte, l'autre
           le descend.
    De   Also geht es in der Welt: der eine steigt, der andre fällt.
    It   Il mondo è fatto a scale, chi le scende e chi le sale.

El   Este mundo es golfo redondo, quien no sabe nadar, vase al hondo.

Ru   В миру, как на большом пиру: кто скачет, а кто плачет.

4   *En*   Behind the mountains there are people to be found.
      Fr   Au delà du mont il y a du monde.
      De   Hinter dem Berge wohnen auch Leute.
      It   Al di là del monte c'è gente anche.
      El   Detrás del monte hay gente también.
      Ru   И за горами люди живут.

5   *En*   The sun shines everywhere.
      Fr   Le soleil brille partout.
      De   Die Sonne scheint allenthalben.
      It   Tutto il mondo è paese.
      El   En todo el mundo se cuecen habas.
      Ru   Солнце светит повсюду.

6   *En*   The sun shines upon all alike.
      Fr   Le soleil luit pour tout le monde.
      De   Die Sonne scheint für jedermann.
      It   Il sole splende per tutti.
      El   Para todos sale el sol.
      Ru   Солнце сияет на благие и злые.

7   *En*   There is no new thing under the sun. *(B)**
      Fr   Il n'y a rien de nouveau sous le soleil.
      De   Es gibt nichts Neues unter der Sonne.
      It   Non vi è nulla di nuovo sotto il sole.
      El   Nada hay nuevo debajo del sol.
      Ru   Нет ничего нового под солнцем. *(Б)*

8   *En*   So many countries, so many customs.*
      Fr   Autres pays, autres mœurs.
      De   Andere Länder, andere Sitten.

It   Tanti paesi, tanti costumi.

El   En cada tierra su uso.

Ru   Что город, то норов.

9   *En*   Who loves the roam may lose his home.

    Fr   Qui va à la chasse perd sa place.

    De   Wer seinen Platz verlässt, verliert sein Recht darauf.

    It   Chi va all'osto, perde il posto.

    El   Quien se ausentó, su sitio dejó.

    Ru   Кто место своё покидает, тот его теряет.

10   *En*   Where is well with me there is my country.*

    Fr   Là où l'on est bien, là est la patrie.

    De   Wo es mir wholergeht, da ist mein Vaterland.

    It   La patria è dove si sta bene.

    El   Esa es mi patria donde todo me sobra y nada me falta.

    Ru   Там отечество, где хлеба довольно.

11   *En*   One generation passeth away, and another generation cometh: but the earth abideth for ever. *(B)*

    Fr   Une génération s'en va, une autre vient, et la terre subsiste toujours.

    De   Ein Geschlecht geht, das andre kommt; die Erde aber bleibt ewiglich.

    It   Una età va via, e un'altra età viene; e la terra resta in perpetuo.

    El   Generación va, y generación viene: mas la tierra siempre permanece.

    Ru   Род проходит, и род приходит, а земля пребывает во веки. *(Б)*

12   *En*   Every bird likes his own nest best.*

    Fr   A chaque oiseau son nid paraît beau.

    De   Einem jeden Vogel gefällt sein Nest.

It   Ad ogni uccello suo nido è bello.

El   A cada pájaro le gusta su nido.

Ru   Всякая птица своё гнездо любит.

Всяк кулик своё болото хвалит.

13 *En* A little bird is content with a little nest.

Fr   Tel oiseau, tel nid.

De Kleine Vöglein, kleine Nestlein.

It   Quale uccello, tale il nido.

El   A chico pajarillo, chico nidillo.

Ru   Малые птички свивают малые гнёзда.

14 *En* It is an ill bird that fouls its own nest.

Fr   Vilain oiseau que celui qui salit son nid.

De Ein schlechter Vogel, der sein eigenes Nest beschmutzt.

It   Cattivo quell'uccello che sporca il suo nido.

El   Aquella ave es mala, que en su nido caga.

Ru   Худая та птица, которая своё гнездо марает.

15 *En* The hare always returns to her form.

Fr   Le lièvre retourne toujours au lancer.

De Wo der Hase geworfen wird, will er bleiben.

It   La lepre sta volentieri dove è nata.

El   Quien nace en el muladar, allí se querría quedar.

Ru   Где выросла сосна, там она и красна.

16 *En* East or west, home is best.*

Fr   On n'est bien que chez soi.

De Ost und West, daheim am best.

It   Dove se nasce, ogni erba pasce.

El   Mi casa y mi hogar cien doblas val.

Ru   В гостях хорошо, а дома лучше.

17 *En* There is no place like home.*

Fr   Rien n'est si chaud ou si froid que l'âtre.

De Eigener Herd ist Goldes wert.

It Casa propria non c'è oro che la paghi.

El Tranquila y propia casa, con ningún dinero es bien pagada.

Ru Свой уголок всего краше.

Своя хатка–родная матка.

18 *En* A man's house is his castle.*

Fr Charbonnier est maître chez lui.

De Jeder ist Herr in seinem Hause.

It Ognuno è padrone a casa sua.

El Mientras en mi casa me estoy, rey me soy.

Ru Всяк хозяин в своём доме.

45 **Chance–Destiny**
   Hasard–Destin
   Zufall–Schicksal
   Casualità–Destino
   Casualidad–Destino
   Случайность–Судьба

1   *En*   Friends may meet, but mountains never greet.*
    Fr   Les montagnes ne se rencontrent pas, mais les hommes.
    De   Berg und Tal kommen nicht zusammen, wohl aber
          Menschen.
    It   Si rincontrano gli uomini e non le montagne.
    El   Tópanse los hombres, y no los montes.
    Ru   Гора с горой не сходится, а человек с человеком сойдётся.

2   *En*   A blind man may perchance hit the mark.*
    Fr   Une poule aveugle peut quelquefois trouver son grain.
    De   Eine blinde Henne findet wohl auch ein Korn.
          Es findet wohl auch ein Blinder ein Hufeisen.
    It   Talvolta una gallina cieca trova un granello.
    El   Pollo ciego halla los granos a tiento.
    Ru   И слепая курица найдёт порой зёрнышко.

3   *En*   He that is born to be hanged shall never be drowned.*
    Fr   Qui est né pour le gibet ne se noyera jamais.
    De   Wer hängen soll, ertrinkt nicht.
          Wer zu Galgen geboren ist, ersäuft nicht.
    It   Chi ha da morir di forca, può ballar sul fiume.
    El   Quien es nacido para la horca, no se anega.
    Ru   Кому быть повешенным, тот не утонет.

240

4   *En*   It is the unexpected that always happens.*
    Fr   L'imprévu est moins rare qu'on ne pense.
           L'imprévu arrive souvent.
    De   Unverhofft kommt oft.
    It   Vien più presto quel che non si spera.
    El   Lo menos esperado, más pronto llegado.
    Ru   Чего не чаешь, то получаешь.

5   *En*   Where we least think there goes the hare away.
    Fr   De là où l'homme ne pense pas sort le lièvre.
    De   Wenn man's am wenigsten denkt, liegt ein Fisch in den
           Reusen.
    It   Di dove men si pensa, si leva la lepre.
    El   Donde menos se piensa, salta la liebra.
    Ru   Чего не чаешь, то скорее сбудется.

6   *En*   Like a bolt from the blue.
    Fr   Comme un coup de foudre.
    De   Wie ein Blitz aus blauem Himmel.
    It   Come fulmine a ciel sereno.
    El   Como llovido del cielo.
    Ru   Как гром среди ясного неба.

7   *En*   I today, you tomorrow.*
           Today me, tomorrow thee.*
    Fr   Aujourd'hui à moi, demain à toi.
    De   Heute mir, morgen dir.
    It   Oggi a me, domani a te.
    El   Hoy por mí, mañana por ti.
    Ru   Сегодня мне, завтра тебе.

8   *En*   Stuff today and starve tomorrow.
    Fr   Après grand banquet, petit pain.
    De   Heute in Putz, morgen in Schmutz.

It   Oggi fave, domani fame.

El   Día de mucho, víspera de nada.

Ru   Сегодня густо, а завтра пусто.

9   *En*   Here today and gone tomorrow.

          Today gold, tomorrow dust.

     Fr   Aujourd'hui en fleurs, demain en vers.

          Aujourd'hui en chère, demain en bière.

     De   Heute rot, morgen tot.

     It   Oggi in figura, domani in sepoltura.

     El   Hoy en figura, y mañana en sepultura.

     Ru   Сегодня в порфире, а завтра в могиле.

          Сегодня живой, а завтра святой.

10 *En*   Today a man, tomorrow none.

     Fr   Aujourd'hui chevalier, demain vacher.

     De   Heute Kaufmann, morgen Bettelmann.

     It   Oggi mercante, domani viandante.

          Oggi è Caifasso chi ieri fu Giovanni.

     El   Hoy en palco, y mañana en catafalco.

     Ru   Сегодня пан, а завтра пропал.

          Сегодня в латах, завтра в заплатах.

11 *En*   What must be must be.

     Fr   Ce qui doit être, ne peut manquer.

     De   Was sein soll, das schickt sich wohl.

          Was geschehen soll, das geschieht.

     It   Quel ch'è disposto in cielo, convien che sia.

     El   Siempre fué lo que había de ser.

     Ru   Чему быть, того не миновать.

12 *En*   No flying from fate.*

     Fr   Nul ne peut éviter sa destinée.

     De   Seinem Schicksal kann niemand entgehen.

It   Nessuno può sfuggire al proprio destino.
El   Nadie puede evitar su destino.
Ru   От судьбы не уйдёшь.

13 *En*   No man is content with his lot.*
    Fr   Nul n'est content de sa fortune.
    De   Niemand ist mit seinem Schicksal zufrieden.
    It   Non è un per cento di sua sorte contento.
    El   Nadie está contento con su suerte.
    Ru   Никто своей судьбой недоволен.

14 *En*   Good swimmers at length are drowned.
    Fr   Bons nageurs sont à la fin noyés.
    De   Die besten Schwimmer ertrinken.
    It   I buoni nuotatori alfin si affogano.
    El   Quien mejor nada, muere en el agua.
        El mejor nadador es del agua.
    Ru   И лучший пловец в конце утонет.

15 *En*   The die is cast.*
    Fr   Le dé en est jeté.
    De   Der Würfel ist gefallen.
    It   Il dado è tratto.
    El   La suerte está echada.
    Ru   Жребий брошен.

46 Contrasts
  Contrastes
  Gegensätze
  Contrasti
  Contrastes
  Противоположность

1   *En* Dreams go by contraries.
    Fr Tous songes sont mensonges.
    De Träume sind Schäume.
    It Non bisogna fidarsi nei sogni.
    El Y los sueños, sueños son.
    Ru Страшен сон, да милостив Бог.

2   *En* Better be first in a village than second at Rome.*
    Fr Mieux vaut être le premier au village que le second à Rome.
    De Lieber der Erste im Dorfe als der Letzte in der Stadt.
    It Meglio essere il primo a casa sua che il secondo a casa d'altri.
    El Más vale ser el primero en su aldea que el segundo en Roma.
    Ru Лучше быть первым в деревне, чем последним в городе.

3   *En* Better be the head of a dog than the tail of a lion.
    Fr Mieux vaut être tête de chat que queue de lion.
    De Besser ein kleiner Herr als ein grosser Knecht.
    It Meglio essere capo di gatto che coda di leone.
    El Antes cabeza de ratón que cola de león.
    Ru Лучше быть головой собаки, чем хвостом льва.

244

4   *En* It is more blessed to give than to receive. *(B)*

     Fr Il y a plus de bonheur à donner qu'à recevoir.

     De Geben ist seliger als nehmen.

     It Più felice cosa è il dare che il ricevere.

     El Más bienaventurada cosa es dar que recibir.

     Ru Блаженнее давать, нежели принимать. *(Б)*

5   *En* Fire and water are good servants, but bad masters.

     Fr Le feu et l'eau sont bons serviteurs, mais mauvais maîtres.

     De Feuer und Wasser sind gute Diener, aber schlimme Herren.

     It Il fuoco e l'acqua son buoni servitori, ma cattivi padroni.

     El El fuego y el agua son buenos servidores, mas ruines amos.

     Ru Огонь и вода–хорошие слуги человека, но им нельзя давать воли.

6   *En* The higher standing, the lower fall.

     Fr Bien bas choit qui trop haut monte.

         De grande montée grande chute.

     De Wer hoch steht, kann tief fallen.

     It A cader và, chi troppo in alto sale.

     El A gran salto, gran quebranto.

         Después de una gran subida, una gran caída.

     Ru Высоко летаешь, да низко садишься.

7   *En* The letter killeth, but the spirit giveth life. *(B)*

     Fr La lettre tue, mais l'esprit vivifie.

     De Der Buchstabe tötet, aber der Geist macht lebendig.

     It La lettera uccida, ma lo spirito vivifichi.

     El La letra mata, mas el espíritu vivifica.

     Ru Буква убивает, а дух животворит. *(Б)*

8   *En* The mountain has brought forth a mouse.*

     Fr La montagne a accouché d'une souris.

De Der kreissende Berg hat ein Mäuslein geboren.
It La montagna ha partorito un topolino.
    Partoriscono i monti, e nasce un topolino.
El Parieron los montes, y nació un ratoncito.
Ru Гора родила мышь.

9 *En* He is not fit to hold a candle to him.
   Fr Il ne lui vient pas à la cheville (ceinture).
   De Er kann ihm das Wasser nicht reichen.
   It Non è degno di lustrargli le scarpe.
   El No le sirve ni para suela de zapatos.
   Ru Он ему в подмётки не годится.

10 *En* One beats the bush, and another catches the birds.
    Fr Il a battu les buissons, et un autre a pris les oisillons.
    De Der eine klopft auf den Busch, der andre fängt den Vogel.
    It Uno scuote il cespuglio, e un altro acchiappa l'uccello.
    El Uno levanta la caza, y otro la mata.
        Yo acoto el matorral, y otro toma los pájaros.
    Ru Медведь пляшет, а цыган деньги берёт.

11 *En* Every medal hath its reverse.
    Fr Chaque médaille a son revers.
    De Jedes Ding hat zwei Seiten.
        Das ist die Kehrseite der Medaille.
    It Ogni medaglia ha il suo rovescio.
    El Toda medalla tiene su reverso.
    Ru У всякой медали есть оборотная сторона.

12 *En* He that is not with me is against me. *(B)*
    Fr Celui qui n'est pas avec moi est contre moi.
    De Wer nicht mit mir ist, der ist wider mich.
    It Chi non è meco, è contro a me.
    El El que no es conmigo, contra mí es.
    Ru Кто не со мною, тот против меня. *(Б)*

13 *En* Man or mouse.*
    Fr Roi ou rien.
    De Bischof oder Bader.
    It O Cesare, o niente.
    El O Cesar, o nada.
    Ru Либо пан, либо пропал.

14 *En* The worst wheel of a cart makes most noise.*
    Fr C'est la plus mauvaise roue du chariot qui fait le plus de bruit.
    De Das schlimmste Rad am Wagen knarrt am lautesten.
    It La più cattiva ruota del carro sempre più cigola.
    El La peor rueda de la carreta chirria lo más.
    Ru Худое колесо пуще скрипит.

15 *En* Empty vessels make the greatest sound.*
    Fr Ce sont les tonneaux vides qui font le plus de bruit.
    De Leere Tonnen geben grossen Schall.
    It Sono le botti vuote quelle che cantano.
    El Cosa hueca, mucho suena.
    Ru Пустая бочка звонче гремит.

16 *En* A little body often harbours a great soul.
    Fr Dans les petites boîtes sont les bons onguents.
    De Kleine Leute haben oft mehr Geist als grosse.
          In den kleinsten Töpfchen sind die besten Sälblein.
    It Le spezierie migliori stanno nei sacchi piccoli.
          Poca mole, gran valore.
    El La buena esencia se vende en frascos pequeños.
          En los barriles está el buen vino.
    Ru Мал золотник, да дорог.

17 *En* To strain at a gnat and swallow a camel. *(B)*
    Fr Couler le moucheron et avaler le chameau.
    De Mücken seien und Kamele verschlucken.

It   Colare la zanzara, e inghiottire il cammello.

El   Colar el mosquito, y tragar el camello.

Ru   Отцеживать комара и проглотить верблюда. *(Б)*

18   *En*   The higher the mountain, the lower the vale.*

      Fr   Après grande montagne, grande vallée.

          A grande montée, grande descente.

      De   Je höher der Berg, desto tiefer das Tal.

      It   Quanto più alto il monte, tanto più profonda la valle.

          A gran salita, gran discesa.

      El   Cuanto mayor es la subida, tanto mayor es la descendida.

          A gran subida, gran descendida.

      Ru   Всякий подъём имеет и свой спуск.

19   *En*   One man's meat is another man's poison.*

      Fr   Ce qui guérit l'un, tue l'autre.

          L'un meurt dont l'autre vit.

      De   Des einen Tod, des andern Brot.

          Des einen Glück, des andern Unglück.

      It   Non è mai mal per uno che non sia ben per un altro.

          Morte tua, vita mia.

      El   Con lo que Pedro adolece, Sancho sana.

          Lo que uno pierde, otro lo gana.

      Ru   Что полезно одному, то другому вредно.

20   *En*   None worse shod than the shoemaker's wife.

      Fr   Les cordonniers sont les plus mal chaussés.

      De   Der Schuster trägt die schlechtesten Schuhe.

      It   In casa di calzolaio non si hanno scarpe.

      El   No hay sastro bien vestido, ni zapatero bien calzado.

      Ru   Портной без порток, сапожник без сапог.

21   *En*   Great cry and little wool.*

      Fr   Grand bruit, petite toison.

      De   Viel Geschrei und wenig Wolle.

It   Molto rumore e poca lana.

El   Más es el ruido que las nueces.

Ru   Визгу много, а шерсти нет.

22 *En*   Much bran and little meal.

    Fr   Beaucoup de paille, peu de grains.

    De   Viel Stroh, wenig Korn.

    It   Molto paglia, poco grano.

    El   Mucha paja y poco grano.

    Ru   Много соломы, мало зерна.

23 *En*   Many go out for wool and come home shorn.

    Fr   Tel qui cherche de la laine s'en retourne tondu.

    De   Mancher geht nach Wolle aus und kommt geschoren nach Haus.

    It   Andar per lana e tornarsene tosi.

    El   Muchos van por lana y vuelven trasquilados.

    Ru   Пошёл по шерсть, а воротился стриженый.

24 *En*   It becomes him as well as a cow doth a cart-saddle.

    Fr   Cela lui va comme un tablier à une vache.

    De   Es passt wie dem Ochsen ein Sattel.

    It   Gli sta come la sella all'asino.

    El   Pega como a un santo un par de pistolas.

    Ru   Это ему пристало, как корове седло.

25 *En*   Extremes meet.*

    Fr   Les extrêmes se touchent.

    De   Gegensätze berühren sich.

    It   Gli estremi si toccano.

    El   Los extremos se tocan.

    Ru   Крайности сходятся.

26 *En*   A bull in a china-shop.

    Fr   C'est l'éléphant dans les porcelaines.

De   Der Elefant im Porzellanladen.
It   Fortunato come un cane in chiesa.
El   Como los perros en misa.
Ru Слон в посудной лавке.

27 *En* Chalk and cheese.
     Fr   C'est le jour et la nuit.
     De Ein Unterschied wie Tag und Nacht.
     It   Ci corre come tra il giorno e la notte.
     El Como día y noche.
     Ru Как небо от земли.
         Похож, как вилка на бутылку.

28 *En* A storm in a tea-cup.
     Fr   Une tempête dans une verre d'eau.
     De Ein Sturm im Glase Wasser.
     It   Tempesta in un bicchier d'acqua.
     El Tempestad en un vaso de agua.
     Ru Буря в стакане воды.

47 Ethics–Practical Philosophy
Éthique–Philosophie pratique
Sittenlehre–Lebensweisheit
Etica–Filosofia pratica
Ética–Mundología
Этика–Житейская мудрость

1   *En*   Tell me with whom thou goest, and I'll tell thee what
         thou doest.
    Fr   Dis-moi qui tu hantes, et je te dirai qui tu es.
    De   Sage mir, mit wem du umgehst, und ich sage dir, wer
         du bist.
    It   Dimmi con chi vai, e ti dirò chi sei.
    El   Dime con quién andas, te diré quién eres.
    Ru   Скажи, с кем ты знаком, и я скажу, кто ты таков.

2   *En*   Do as you would be done by.*
    Fr   Ne faites pas à autrui ce que vous ne voulez pas qu'on
         vous fasse.
    De   Was du nicht willst, dass man dir tu', das füg' auch
         keinem andern zu.
    It   Non fare agli altri ciò che non vorresti fosse fatto a te.
    El   Lo que no quieres para ti, no lo quieras para otro.
    Ru   Чего себе не хочешь, того и другому не делай.

3   *En*   Come not to counsel uncalled.*
    Fr   Ne donnez jamais conseil avant qu'on vous le demande.
    De   Rate niemandem ungebeten.
    It   Non dare consigli a chi non li chiede.
    El   A quien no pide consejo, darlo es de necios.
    Ru   На чужой совет без зову не ходи.

4 *En* Scald not your lips in another man's pottage.
   Fr Ne fourrez pas votre nez dans les soupes d'autrui.
   De Was dich nicht brennt, das blase nicht.
   It Ciò che non ti scotta, non vi soffiare sopra.
   El Lo que no has de comer, déjalo bien cocer.
   Ru Не суй свой нос не в свой вопрос.

5 *En* Sweep before your own door.
   Fr Que chacun balaie devant sa porte.
   De Jeder fege vor seiner Tür!
   It Non ficchi il naso negli affari altrui.
   El Sopla tu sopa y no la mía.
   Ru Мети всяк перед своими воротами.

6 *En* People who live in glass houses shouldn't throw stones.
   Fr Quand on habite une maison de verre, il ne faut pas
        lancer des pierres.
   De Wer im Glashaus sitzt, soll nicht mit Steinen werfen.
   It Chi ha tegoli di vetro, non tiri sassi al vicino.
   El El que tiene tejado de vidrio, no tire piedras al de su
        vecino.
   Ru Других не суди, на себя погляди.
        Не суди других за то, в чём сам не без греха.

7 *En* Name not a rope in the house of him that was hanged.*
   Fr Il ne faut pas parler de corde dans la maison d'un pendu.
   De Im Hause des Gehängten soll man nicht vom Strick
        sprechen.
   It Non nominar la fune in casa dell'impiccato.
   El No hay que mentar la soga en casa del ahorcado.
   Ru В доме повешенного не говорят о верёвке.

8 *En* Look not a gift horse in the mouth.*
   Fr A cheval donné on ne regarde pas à la bouche.
   De Einem geschenkten Gaul sieht man nicht ins Maul.

It A caval donato non si guarda in bocca.

El A caballo regalado no hay que mirarle el diente.

Ru Дарёному коню в зубы не смотрят.

9 *En* Put not thy hand between the bark and the tree.

    Fr Entre l'enclume et le marteau il ne faut pas mettre le doigt.

    De Zwischen Tür und Wand lege niemand seine Hand.

    It Tra l'incudine ed il martello man non metta chi ha cervello.

    El Entre dos muelas molares nunca metas tus pulgares.

    Ru Свои собаки грызутся, чужая не приставай.

10 *En* Do not wash your dirty linen in public.

    Fr Il faut laver son linge sale en famille.

    De Schmutzige Wäsche soll man zuhause waschen.

    It I panni sporchi si lavano in casa.

    El Los trapos sucios se lavan en casa.

    Ru Не выноси сора из избы.

11 *En* Listeners hear no good of themselves.

    Fr Qui écoute aux portes entend souvent sa propre honte.

    De Der Horcher an der Wand hört seine eigne Schand.

    It Chi sta alle scolte, sente le sue colpe.

    El Quien escucha por el horado, oye de su daño.

    Ru Подслушал, да подзатыльника скушал.

12 *En* He that praiseth himself, spattereth himself.*

    Fr Qui se loue, s'emboue.

    De Eigenlob stinkt, Eigenruhm hinkt.

    It Chi si loda, s'imbroda.

    El La alabanza propia siente mal.

    Ru Хвастливое слово гнило.

13 *En* Honour the tree that gives you shelter.*

    Fr Un arbre qui t'abrite, salue-le, il le mérite.

De Verachte den Busch nicht, der dich schirmt.
Der Baum, der kühlen Schatten gibt, sei hochgeachtet und geliebt.

It Bisogna rispettare l'albero per la sua ombra.

El Quien a buen árbol se arrima, buena sombra le cobija.

Ru Как куст ни мал, а тень даёт.
Каков ни будь пень, а всё за ним тень.

14 *En* Hide nothing from thy minister, physician, and lawyer.

Fr Au confesseur, au médecin et à l'avocat la vérité ne cèle de ton cas.

De Dem Beichtvater, Arzt und Advokaten darf man nichts verschweigen.

It Al confessore, medico e avvocato non tenere il ver celato.

El Al médico, confesor, y letrado no le trayas engañado.

Ru От духовника да от лекаря не таись.

15 *En* Give a thing and take again, and you shall ride in hell's wain.

Fr Chose donnée ne se doit pas redemander.

De Was gegeben ist, das darf man nicht wiedernehmen.

It Chi dà e ritoglie, il diavolo lo raccoglie.

El A quien da y quita lo dado, lléveselo el diablo.

Ru Лучше не давай, да не отнимай.

16 *En* Leave a jest when it pleases you best.*

Fr Pendant que le jeu est beau, il fait bon le laisser.

De Wenn der Scherz am besten ist, soll man aufhören.

It Ogni bel gioco dura un poco.
Scherzo lungo non fu mai buono.

El A la burla dejarla cuando más agrada.

Ru Умей пошутить, умей и перестать.

17 *En* Good jests bite like lambs, not like dogs.

Fr Jeu où il y a dommage ne vaut rien.
La plaisanterie doit mordre comme une brebis, et non comme un chien.

De Scherz soll Schafs- nicht Hundezähne haben.

It Lo scherzo deve mordere come la pecora, non come il cane.

El A las burlas, así ve a ellas, que no te salgan a veras.

Ru Не шути над тем, что дорого другому.

18 *En* If you make a jest, you must take a jest.*

Fr Qui en jeu entre, jeu consente.

De Wer scherzen will, soll auch Scherz aufnehmen.

It Chi scherza con altrui, non si sdegni se altri scherza con lui.

El El que por gusto navega, no debe temer al agua.

Ru Любил шутить над Фомой, так люби и над собой.

19 *En* Look not too high, lest something fall into thy eye.

Fr Ne mires trop haut, de peur que quelque chose ne te tombe en l'œil.

De Wer zu hoch langt, verrenkt sich den Arm.

It Non mirar troppo alto, de paura che qualche cosa non ti caschi nell'occhio.

El No mires muy alto de miedo que algo no te caiga en el ojo.

Ru Не гляди высоко, запорошишь око.

20 *En* Never too late to mend.

Fr Il n'est jamais trop tard pour bien faire.

De Zur Besserung ist es nie zu spät.

It Non è mai troppo tardi per ravvedersi.

El Nunca es tarde para hacer el bien.

Ru Исправиться никогда не поздно.

21 *En* Pride goeth before destruction. *(B)*

Fr L'orgueil précède la chute.

De Hochmut kommt vor dem Fall.

It La superbia viene davanti alla ruina.

El Antes del quebrantamiento es la soberbia.

Ru Погибели предшествует гордость. *(Б)*

Кто высоко заносится, тому не миновать упасть.

22 *En* We never know the worth of water till the well is dry.

Fr Quand le puits est à sec, on connaît la valeur de l'eau.

De Wenn der Brunnen trocken ist, schätzt man erst das Wasser.

It Pozzo secco, acqua stimata.

Non si conosce il bene, se non quando s'è perso.

El Cuando se seca el pozo, se sabe lo que vale el agua.

El bien no es conocido, hasta que es perdido.

Ru Что имеем, не храним, потерявши-плачем.

23 *En* None so blind as those who won't see.

Fr Il n'est pire aveugle que celui qui ne veut pas voir.

De Keiner ist so blind, als wer nicht sehen will.

It Non c'è maggior cieco di quello che non vuol vedere.

El No hay peor ciego que él que no quiere ver.

Ru Нет более слепого, чем тот, кто не желает видеть.

24 *En* None so deaf as those who won't hear.*

Fr Il n'est pire sourd que celui qui ne veut pas entendre.

De Niemand ist so taub, wie wer nicht hören will.

It Gran sordo è quello che non vuol udire.

El No hay peor sordo que él que no quiere oír.

Ru Нет более глухого, чем тот, кто не желает слышать.

25 *En* Take things as they come.*

Fr Il faut prendre le temps comme il vient.

De Man muss sich nach der Zeit richten.

It Bisogna pigliare il mondo come viene.

El Toma las cosas como vienen.

Ru Надо жить, как набежит.

26 *En* Take things as you find them.

Fr Il faut laisser aller le monde comme il va.

De Man muss sich in die Welt schicken.

It Bisogna accomodarsi ai tempi.

El Toma el tiempo según que viene.

Buen tiento es vivir conforme al tiempo.

Ru Как живётся, так и живи.

Что миром положено, тому быть так.

27 *En* Render unto Caesar the things which are Caesar's. *(B)*

Fr Rendez à César ce qui est à César.

De Gebet dem Kaiser, was des Kaisers ist.

It Rendete a Cesare le cose che appartengono a Cesare.

El Pagad a Cesar lo que es de Cesar.

Ru Отдавайте кесарево кесарю. *(Б)*

28 *En* To stand still is to move back.*

Fr Quand on n'avance pas, on recule.

De Stillstand ist Rückgang.

It Chi se ferma è perduto.

El Si adelante no vas, atrasarás.

Quien adelante no mira, atrás se queda.

Ru На месте застрял–от жизни отстал.

29 *En* To err is human.*

Fr Tout homme est faillible.

De Irren ist menschlich.

It Errare è cosa umana.

El Errar es humano.

Ru Ошибаться–человеческое дело.

30 *En* To fall into sin is human, to remain in sin is devilish.

Fr Se tromper est humain, persister dans son erreur est diabolique.

De Irren ist menschlich, im Irrtum verharren ist teuflisch.

It Il peccare è da uomini, l'ostinarsi è da bestia.

El De hombres es errar, de bestias perseverar en el error.

Ru Ошибаться–человеческое дело, а не сознаваться–дьявольское.

31 *En* Three may keep counsel if two be away.

Fr Secret de deux, secret de Dieu; secret de trois, secret de tous.

De Was dreie wissen, erfahren bald dreissig.
    Was kommt in den dritten Mund, wird aller Welt kund.

It Secreto di due, secreto di Dio; secreto di tre, secreto d'ognuno.

El Lo que saben tres, sabe toda res.
    Secreto de dos, sábelo Dios; secreto de tres, toda res.

Ru Один–тайна, два–полтайны, три–нет тайны.

32 *En* Habit is a second nature.*

Fr L'habitude est une seconde nature.

De Gewohnheit wird zur zweiten Natur.

It L'abitudine è una seconda natura.

El La costumbre es segunda naturaleza.

Ru Привычка–вторая натура.

33 *En* The command of custom is great.

Fr Accoutumance est loi bien dure.
    La pire tyrannie est celle de l'habitude.

De Gross ist die Macht der Gewohnheit.

It Grande è la forza dell'abitudine.

El La costumbre tiene más fuerza que diez toros.

Ru Привычку не переделаешь.

34 *En* A merry companion is a waggon in the way.*

Fr Compagnon bien parlant vaut en chemin chariot branlant.

De Auf der Reise ein guter Gefährt ist so gut wie ein Pferd.

It Compagno allegro per cammino ti serve per ronzino.

El Charlando y andando, sin sentir se va caminando.
Alivia el trabajo del camino el compañero elocuente.

Ru Умный товарищ–половина дороги.
Беседа коротает дорогу.

35 *En* It is ill to waken sleeping dogs.*

Fr Il ne faut pas réveiller le chien qui dort.
Ne réveillez pas le chat qui dort.

De Schlafende Hunde soll man nicht wecken.

It Non svegliar il cane che dorme.

El Al léon que duerme, que no lo despierten.

Ru Сонного пса не буди.
Не буди лиха, пока лихо спит.

36 *En* Every one knows best where the shoe pinches him.
No one but the wearer knows where the shoe pinches.

Fr Chacun sait le mieux où son soulier le blesse.

De Jeder weiss am besten, wo ihn der Schuh drückt.

It Ognuno sà, dove la scarpa lo stringe.

El Cada uno sabe, done le aprieta el zapato.

Ru Только тот, на чьей ноге башмак, знает, где он жмёт.

37 *En* He gives twice who gives quickly.*

Fr Qui donne vite donne deux fois.

De Doppelt gibt, wer schnell gibt.

It Chi dà presto, dà due volte.

El Quien presto da, dos veces da.

Ru Дважды даёт, кто скоро даёт.

38 *En* Let not the cobbler go beyond his last.*

Fr Cordonnier, borne-toi à la chaussure!
Chacun son métier, les vaches seront bien gardées.
De Schuster, bleib bei deinem Leisten!
It Ciabattiere, parla del tuo mestiere.
El ¡Zapatero, a tus zapatos!
Ru Знай сверчок свой шесток.

39 *En* The world's coin is ingratitude.*
Ingratitude is the way of the world.
Fr Le monde paie d'ingratitude.
Qui oblige, fait des ingrats.
De Undank ist der Welt Lohn.
It Il mondo paga d'ingratitudine.
El De los ingratos, el mundo lleno.
Ru За добро не жди добра.
Одолжать–неблагодарность умножать.

40 *En* Virtue is her own reward.
Fr La vertu trouve sa récompense en elle-même.
De Die Tugend ist sich selbst ihr Preis.
It La virtù è premio a se stessa.
El El precio de la virtud es ella misma.
Ru Добродетель не нуждается в награде.

41 *En* The devil take the hindmost.
Fr Le dernier, le loup le mange.
De Den Letzten beissen die Hunde.
It All'ultimo tocca il peggio.
El Al postrero muerde el perro.
Ru Последнего и собаки рвут.
Отставшего собаки заедят.

48 Miscellanea
Miscellanées
Allerlei
Varia
Miscelánea
Разное

1   *En*   A staff is quickly found to beat a dog.
    Fr   Qui veut frapper un chien, facilement trouve un bâton.
    De   Wenn man den Hund schlagen will, findet man bald einen Stock.
    It   Tosto si trova il bastone per dare al cane.
    El   Presto hay un bastón para dar al perro.
    Ru   Кто захочет собаку ударить, тот найдёт и палку.

2   *En*   Give a dog an ill name and hang him.
    Fr   Qui veut noyer son chien, l'accuse de la rage.
    De   Wer seinen Hund los sein will, dichtet ihm Tollwut an.
    It   Chi vuol ammazzare il suo cane, basta che dica ch'è arrabbiato.
    El   Quien a su perro ha de matar, rabia le ha de levantar.
    Ru   Была бы собака, а камень найдётся.

3   *En*   Walls have ears.
    Fr   Les murs ont des oreilles.
    De   Die Wände haben Ohren.
    It   I muri hanno orecchi.
    El   Las paredes oyen.
    Ru   У стен есть уши.

4   *En*   The voice of the people, the voice of God.*

Fr La voix du peuple est la voix de Dieu.
De Volkes Stimme–Gottes Stimme.
It Voce di popolo voce di Dio.
El La voz del pueblo es voz de Dios.
Ru Глас народа–глас божий.

5 *En* Eagles catch no flies.*
   Fr L'aigle ne chasse point aux mouches.
   De Adler fangen keine Fliegen.
   It L'aquila non piglia mosche.
   El El águila no se entretiene en cazar moscas.
   Ru Орёл мух не ловит.

6 *En* Blood is thicker than water.*
   Fr C'est la voix du sang.
   De Blut ist dicker als Wasser.
         Es ist die Stimme des Blutes.
   It Il sangue non è acqua.
         È la voce del sangue.
   El La sangre es más espesa que el océano.
         La voz de la sangre.
   Ru Кровь не вода.

7 *En* Liberty is better than gold.*
   Fr Liberté et pain cuit.
   De Freiheit geht über Silber und Gold.
   It Meglio un'oncia di libertà che dieci libbre d'oro.
   El No hay cosa que a la libertad es comparada.
   Ru Пташке ветка дороже золотой клетки.

8 *En* No man loveth his fetters, be they made of gold.
   Fr Personne n'aime les ceps quoiqu'ils soient d'or.
   De Jede Kette drückt, und wären ihre Glieder von Gold.
   It Nessuno ama ceppi ancor'che sieno d'oro.

El Nadie quiere grillos, aunque sean de oro.

Ru Оковы всегда в тягость, будь они хоть из золота.

9 *En* The cow knows not what her tail is worth till she hath lost it.

    Fr L'âne ne sait ce que vaut la queue, qu'après l'avoir perdu.

    De Wenn die Kuh den Schwanz verloren hat, merkt sie erst, wozu er gut war.

    It L'asino non conosce la coda, se non quando non l'ha più.

    El El asno conoce la cola cuando le falta.

    Ru Цену вещи узнаешь, как потеряешь.

10 *En* Comparisons are odious.*

    Fr Comparaison n'est pas raison.

    De Jeder Vergleich hinkt.

    It I confronti sono odiosi.

    El Toda comparación es odiosa.

    Ru Сравнения не всегда уместны.

11 *En* The mouse that hath but one hole is quickly taken.*

    Fr Souris qui n'a qu'un trou est bientôt prise.

    De Das ist eine arme Maus, die nur weiss zu einem Loch hinaus.

    It Tristo è quel topo che ha un buco solo.

    El Ratón que no sabe más de un agujero, cázale el gato presto.

    Ru Худа та мышь, которая одну только лазейку знает.

12 *En* A common servant is no man's servant.

    Fr Qui sert au commun ne sert pas un.

    De Wer vielen dient, der dient niemandem.

    It Chi serve al comune, non serve a nessuno.

    El Quien sirve al común, sirve a ningún.

    Ru На двух господ служить–ни одному не угодить.

13 *En* There is a measure in all things.*
   Fr Il y a une mesure en toutes choses.
   De Alles hat sein Mass und Ziel.
   It Ogni cosa vuol misura.
   El Hay en todas las cosas una medida.
   Ru Всему есть своя мера.

14 *En* Nature draws more than ten oxen.*
   Fr Plus tire nature que cent chevaux.
   De Natur zieht stärker denn sieben Pferde.
   It Natura tira più che cento cavalli.
   El Más tira moza que soga.
   Ru Природа берёт своё.
      Гони природу в дверь, она влетит в окно.

15 *En* What is bred in the bone will not out of the flesh.*
   Fr Chassez le naturel il revient au galop.
   De Die Natur lässt sich nicht überwinden.
   It Ciò che si ha per natura, sino alla fossa dura.
   El Natural y figura hasta la sepultura.
   Ru Что засело в костях, того из мяса не выколотишь.

16 *En* It is enough to make a cat laugh.
   Fr C'est à dérider un mort.
   De Da lachen ja die Hühner.
   It È da far ridere i polli.
   El Es para morirse de risa.
   Ru Это курам на смех.

17 *En* To make a mountain out of a molehill.*
   Fr Faire d'une mouche un éléphant.
   De Aus einer Mücke einen Elefanten machen.
   It Fare d'una mosca un elefante.
   El Hacer de una pulga un elefante.
   Ru Делать из мухи слона.

18   *En*   A cat may look at a king.
      Fr   Un chien regarde bien un évêque.
      De   Sieht doch die Katz' den Kaiser an!
      It   Anche un gatto può guardare un re!
      El   Un perro puede mirar al rey.
      Ru   Собака и на владыку лает.

19   *En*   Even a fly hath its spleen.*
      Fr   La fourmi a sa colère.
      De   Ameisen haben auch Galle.
      It   Anche la mosca ha la sua collera.
      El   Cada hormiga tiene su ira.
      Ru   И у курицы сердце есть.

20   *En*   You look for the horse you ride on.
      Fr   Il cherche son âne, il est dessus.
      De   Er sucht den Esel und sitzt darauf.
      It   Fare come colui che cercava l'asino e c'era sopra.
      El   Buscaba el necio su asno, y lo llevaba debajo.
      Ru   На коне сидит, а коня ищет.

21   *En*   Wherever an ass falleth, there will he never fall again.
      Fr   Un âne ne trébuche pas deux fois contre la même pierre.
      De   Den Esel führt man nur einmal aufs Eis.
      It   Dove l'asino casca una volta, non ci casca più.
      El   Jumento declarado, quien tropieza dos veces en un mismo canto.
      Ru   Раз козу на лёд свести можно.

22   *En*   Where your will is ready, your feet are light.
      Fr   Besogne qui plaît est à demi faite.
      De   Williges Herz macht leichte Füsse.
      It   Dove la voglia è pronta, le gambe sono leggiere.
      El   Quien tiene el amor en el pecho, tiene los pies alados.
      Ru   К милому и семь вёрст не околица.

23 *En*   When all men say you are an ass, it is time to bray.
   Fr   Si tous disent que tu es un âne: brais.
   De   Wenn alle dir sagen, du seist betrunken, geh schlafen.
   It   Quando tutti ti dicono briaco, va a dormire.
   El   Cuando todos dicen que eres asno, rebuzna.
   Ru   Коли двое скажут, что пьян–иди, ложись спать.

24 *En*   When Adam delved and Eve span who was then a gentleman?*
   Fr   Lorsque Adam maniait le hoyau, et Eve le fuseau, où étaient les hobereaux?
   De   Als Adam hackt' und Eva spann, wer war da ein Edelmann?
   It   Quando Adamo zappava ed Eva filava, dov'era il primo nobile?
   El   Cuando Adán cavaba y Eva hilaba, la hidalguía, ¿donde estaba?
   Ru   Когда Адам пахал и пряла Ева, где родословное стояло древо?

25 *En*   What the eye sees not, the heart craves not.*
   Fr   Le cœur ne peut douloir ce que l'œil ne peut voir.
   De   Was das Auge nicht sieht, bekümmert das Herz nicht.
   It   Se l'occhio non mira, il cuor non sospira.
   El   Ojos que non ven, corazón que no duele.
   Ru   Чего глаза не видят, того сердце не бредит.

26 *En*   What is sauce for the goose is sauce for the gander.
   Fr   Ce qui est bon pour l'un l'est aussi pour l'autre.
   De   Was dem einen recht ist, ist dem andern billig.
   It   Non si deve avere due pesi e due misure.
   El   No tengas dos medidas métricas.
   Ru   Что подходит одному, должно подходить и другому.

27 *En*   We soon believe what we desire.*

Fr Chacun croit aisément ce qu'il désire.

De Was man wünscht, das glaubt man gern.

It Quel che si vuol, presto si crede.

El El afligido cree con más facilidad lo que desea.

Ru Чего хочется, тому верится.

28 *En* We may give advice, but we cannot give conduct.

   Fr Il est plus facile de conseiller que de faire.

   De Raten ist leichter als helfen.

   It È più facile consigliare che fare.

   El Aconsejar es más fácil que ejecutar.

   Ru Советчиков много, да помощников нет.

29 *En* To rob Peter to pay Paul.*

   Fr Dépouiller Saint-Pierre pour habiller Saint-Paul.

   De Einen Altar entblössen, um den andern zu decken.

       Dem Peter nehmen und dem Paul geben.

   It Scoprire un altare per ricoprirne un altro.

   El Devestir un santo para vestir un otro.

   Ru Церковь грабит, да колокольню кроет.

30 *En* Thoughts be free from toll.*

   Fr Les pensées ne paient point de douane.

   De Gedanken sind zollfrei.

   It I pensieri non pagano gabelle.

   El El pensamiento no tiene barrera.

   Ru Мысли пошлинами не облагаются.

31 *En* The wolf eats often the sheep that have been told.*

   Fr Brebis comptées, le loup les mange.

   De Der Wolf frisst auch die gezählten Schafe.

   It Pecore contate, il lupo se le mangia.

   El De lo contado come el lobo.

   Ru Крадёт волк и считанную овцу.

32 *En* All good things go by threes.*
     Fr Toutes les bonnes choses vont par trois.
     De Aller guten Dinge sind drei.
     It Tutte le cose favorevoli sono in numero di tre.
     El La tercera es buena y verdadera.
     Ru Бог Троицу любит.

33 *En* The third time's lucky.
     Fr Le troisième coup fait mouche.
     De Die Drei ist eine heilige Zahl.
     It Ogni trino è perfetto.
     El A las tres va la vencida.
     Ru По третьему разу всегда вырубишь огня.

34 *En* The lion is known by his claws.*
     Fr A l'ongle on connaît le lion.
     De An den Klauen erkennt man den Löwen.
     It Dall'unghia si conosce il leone.
     El Por las uñas se descubre al león.
     Ru Знать зверя по когтям.

35 *En* The bird is known by his note.
     Fr Au chant on connaît l'oiseau.
     De Am Gesang erkennt man den Vogel.
     It Dal canto si conosce l'uccello.
     El Por el canto se conoce el pájaro.
     Ru Видна птица по полёту.

36 *En* The eye is the mirror of the soul*
     Fr Les yeux sont le miroir de l'âme.
     De Das Auge ist der Seele Spiegel.
     It L'occhio è lo specchio dell'anima.
     El Los ojos son el espejo del alma.
     Ru Глаза–зеркало души.

37 *En* Soon ripe, soon rotten.*
   Fr Ce qui croît soudain, périt le lendemain.
   De Was bald reif wird, wird bald faul.
   It Quel che presto matura, poco dura.
   El Sol que mucho madruga, poco dura.
   Ru Что быстро созревает, то скоро погибает.

38 *En* Much of a muchness.
   Fr C'est chou vert et vert chou.
   De Das ist Jacke wie Hose.
   It La stessa cosa, press'a poco.
       Esser zuppa o pan molle.
   El Olivo y aceituno, todo es uno.
   Ru Что в лоб, что по лбу.

39 *En* It is as broad as it is long.
   Fr C'est bonnet blanc et blanc bonnet.
   De Das ist gehupft wie gesprungen.
   It È lungo quanto largo.
   El Lo mismo es negro que tiznado.
   Ru Не мытьём, так катаньем.
       Всё одно, что дерево, что бревно.

40 *En* Six of one and half a dozen of the other.
   Fr C'est jus vert et verjus.
   De Das ist hin wie her.
   It Se non è zuppa, è pan bagnato.
   El Lo misma da atrás que a las espaldas.
   Ru Всё равно, что восемнадцать, что без двух двадцать.

41 *En* Put that in your pipe and smoke it.
   Fr Mettez ça dans votre pipe!
       Mettez-vous bien cela dans la tête.
   De Schreib dir das hinter die Ohren!

It Prendi e metti in tasca.
Tenetelo bene in mente.

El ¡No los eches en saco roto!

Ru Заруби это себе на носу.

42 *En* Like the gardener's dog that neither eats cabbage himself
nor lets anybody else.

Fr Le chien du jardinier ne mange pas de chou et n'en veut
pas laisser manger aux autres.

De Des Gärtners Hund isst keinen Kohl und will nicht, dass
andere davon essen.

It Can dell'ortolano non mangia la lattuga en non lascia
mangiar agli altri.

El El perro del hortelano, ni come las berzas, ni las deja
comer al extraño.

Ru Собака на сене лежит: и сама не ест, и другим не даёт.

43 *En* In the place where the tree falleth, there it shall be. *(B)*
As a tree falls, so shall it lie.

Fr Si un arbre tombe, il reste à la place où il est tombé.

De Nach welchem Ort der Baum fällt, da bleibt er liegen.

It Quando l'albero cade, ove egli cade quivi resta.

El Al lugar que el árbol cayere, allí quedará.

Ru Куда упадёт дерево, там оно и останется. *(Б)*

44 *En* Ignorance is the mother of impudence.*

Fr L'orgueil est frère de l'ignorance.

De Dummheit und Stolz wachsen auf einem Holz.

It La presunzione è figlia della ignoranza.

El El orgullo depende de la ignorancia.

Ru Глупость и чванство неразлучны.

45 *En* Neither fish nor flesh.*

Fr Ni chair, ni poisson.

De Weder Fisch noch Fleisch.

It Nè carne nè pesce.

El Ni carne ni pescado.

Ru Ни рыба, ни мясо.

46 *En* Honours nourish arts.*

   Fr Les honneurs nourrissent les arts.

   De Ehre mehrt Kunst.

       Kunst bringt Gunst.

   It L'onore nutrisce le arti.

   El El honor sostiene las artes.

   Ru Награда побуждает искусство.

47 *En* Honours change manners.*

   Fr Les honneurs changent les mœurs.

   De Würden ändern die Sitten.

   It Gli onori cambiano i costumi.

   El Con las glorias se olvidan las memorias.

   Ru Слава меняет людей.

48 *En* History repeats itself.

   Fr L'histoire se répète.

   De Die Geschichte wiederholt sich.

   It La storia si ripete.

   El La historia se repite.

   Ru История повторяется.

49 *En* The end justifies the means.*

   Fr La fin justifie les moyens.

   De Der Zweck heiligt die Mittel.

   It Il fine giustifica i mezzi.

   El El fin justifica los medios.

   Ru Цель оправдывает средства.

50 *En* Every grain has its bran.

   Fr Chaque grain a sa paille.

De Kein Korn ohne Spreu.
   Jedes Mehl hat seine Kleie.
It Ogni farina ha crusca.
El No hay grano sin paja.
Ru Во всяком хлебе есть мякина.

51 *En* Grass grows not upon the highway.
   Fr A chemin battu, il ne croît point d'herbe.
   De Auf dem Fahrweg wächst kein Gras.
   It L'erba non cresce sulla strada maestra.
   El Calle pasajera no cría hierba.
   Ru На битой дороге трава не растёт.

52 *En* Familiarity breeds contempt.*
   Fr La familiarité engendre le mépris.
   De Vertraulichkeit erzeugt Verachtung.
      Allzu gemein macht dich klein.
   It Confidenza toglie riverenza.
   El La familiaridad es causa de menosprecio.
   Ru Фамильярность порождает презрение.

53 *En* After us the deluge.
   Fr Après nous, le déluge!
   De Nach uns, die Sintflut!
   It Morto io, vada il mondo in carbonata.
   El Detrás de mí, el diluvio.
   Ru После нас хоть потоп!

54 *En* To dance to a person's pipe.
   Fr Marcher sous la houlette de quelqu'un.
   De Nach jemands Pfeife tanzen.
   It Ballare secondo il suono di qualcuno.
   El Bailar al son que le tocan.
   Ru Плясать под чью-нибудь дудку.

55 *En* Better be envied than pitied.*
   Fr Mieux vaut faire envie que pitié.
   De Besser beneidet als bemitleidet.
   It È meglio esser invidiato che compassionato.
   El Mejor es ser envidiado que apiadado.
   Ru Лучше жить в зависти, чем в жалости.

56 *En* To be on pins and needles.
   Fr Etre sur des épines.
   De Wie auf Nadeln sitzen.
   It Stare sulle spine.
   El Estar sobre espinas (agujas).
   Ru Сидеть как на иголках.

arms (hands) (29) 6

art, arts (7) 7; (18) 14; (25) 22; (34) 6; (48) 46

ashamed (37) 4

ask (11) 13; (24) 14

asleep (19) 9

a-sorrowing (27) 1

ass (11) 17; (15) 8, 10, 12, 25; (31) 13; (43) 11; (48) 21, 23

asunder s. put

Athens (15) 32

attend (6) 23

aught (24) 18

authority (2) 17

Avarice s. Covetousness

away s. be, pass, run, wash

awhile (38) 15

axe (13) 1

B (10) 18

back *(part of body)* (3) 8; (22) 5; (38) 8

back *(away from the front)* (47) 28

bad (3) 13; (6) 14; (13) 26; (16) 12, 15; (17) 13; (18) 16; (40) 5; (46) 5

bag (24) 16

bargain (7) 10

bark, barking (4) 9; (15) 11; (33) 14

bark (of tree) (47) 9

barn (9) 29

battle (34) 1

bauble (11) 27

be (away, down, in, out, over) (10) 20, 21; (19) 16; (33) 5; (34) 29; (38) 20; (45) 11; (47) 31; (48) 43

beans (38) 27

bear *(animal)* (15) 21

bear *(carry, endure)* (19) 17; (28) 15

beard (4) 7

beat (4) 17; (31) 13; (42) 7, 8; (46) 10; (48) 1

Beauty s. Love

beauty (30) 26–28

become *(be suitable for)* (46) 24

bed (12) 4; (27) 8; (33) 26;(34) 3; (38) 17

before (10) 24; (14) 11; (15) 21; (17) 7; (20) 7; (36) 4, 23; (39) 13; (47) 5, 21

beg (7) 9

beget (25) 12

beggar, beggars (25) 24; (26) 4

beggary (6) 20

Beginning–End (10)

begin, begun (10) 3, 11; (28) 3

beginning, beginnings (10) 1, 2, 5, 6, 10

behind (23) 1; (44) 4

believe, believed, believing (2) 14; (25) 26; (36) 19; (48) 27

believers (36) 29

bells (22) 14

belly, bellies (1) 29; (3) 8; (15) 14; (18) 14; (24) 3; (25) 26; (38) 3–5, 8, 19, 23; (43) 25

bend, bent (12) 2; (18) 9

best (3) 1; (8) 14; (9) 7; (10) 17; (11) 27; (16) 3, 8; (20) 6; (28) 9; (31) 2; (35) 15; (36) 10; (38) 26; (39) 4; (44) 12, 16; (47) 16, 36

better (1) 25; (3) 2, 6, 22; (9) 11; (10) 10, 11; (16) 4, 15; (18) 9, 11; (24) 18–21; (27) 2, 8; (31) 9, 13; (32) 9; (34) 7, 20; (35) 2, 6, 10; (36) 6, 34–36; (38) 9; (39) 7, 14; (40) 1, 3; (42) 1; (46) 2, 3; (48) 7, 55

between (18) 15; (36) 18, 24; (40) 3; (41) 6; (47) 9

beware (5) 5, 9; (37) 14

beyond (11) 3; (47) 38

bigger (38) 5

bill *(beak)* (5) 7

bird, birds (1) 27; (6) 9; (13) 32; (14) 16; (28) 10; (32) 12; (36) 32; (43) 9; (44) 12–14; (46) 10; (48) 35

bitch (19) 8

bite, bit (3) 23; (4) 9; (5) 7; (34) 22; (35) 11; (38) 28; (47) 17

biter (3) 23

bitter (13) 32; (20) 12; (35) 5; (38) 13

black (13) 33; (16) 17; (23) 3

blame, blamed (2) 3, 20

bleat (38) 18

blessed (35) 5; (46) 4

blind (13) 2, 8; (15) 4, 5; (19) 3; (30) 2; (35) 10; (45) 2; (47) 23

block (32) 7; (36) 28

blood (48) 6

blow (4) 5; (18) 10

blue (45) 6

blush (2) 21

body (35) 1, 14; (46) 16

bold (21) 5, 11

bolt (45) 6

bone, bones (33) 26; (41) 10, 12; (48) 15

books (8) 7

born (11) 16; (14) 11; (34) 11; (45) 3

Borrowing–Debts (27)

borrower (27) 3, 4

borrowing s. a-borrowing

bosom (5) 3

both (13) 2; (15) 12; (28) 13; (33) 6; (43) 13

bottom (36) 34

bound (12) 25; (14) 2

bow (12) 2; (18) 9; (36) 21

boys (33) 1, 2

brain (6) 18; (38) 4

bran (23) 6; (46) 22; (48) 50

bray, braying (15) 10; (48) 23

bread (7) 9; (24) 21; (25) 30; (34) 12; (37) 3; (38) 11, 14

break, breaking (6) 26; (13) 11; (15) 28; (18) 9; (24) 16; s. broken

breakfast (20) 7

breast (5) 1

breed, bred (32) 17; (48) 15, 52

brew (12) 12

bridge (9) 16; (14) 12; (42) 4

brim (36) 34

bring (forth, in) (1) 21; (9) 28, 29; (16) 23; (17) 17; (19) 8; (40) 9; (46) 8; s. brought

broad (36) 29; (48) 39

broken (12) 19; (36) 12; (39) 10

broom (33) 27

broth (7) 5; (38) 7

brother, brothers (40) 1; (41) 6

brought (up) (5) 4; (10) 23

build, built (9) 13; (13) 17; (14) 12; (15) 27

bull (46) 26

burden, burdens (13) 23; (22) 5; (28) 1, 4, 15; (33) 25

burnt (21) 10

bury (34) 25

bush (7) 2; (36) 32; (46) 10

bushel (39) 13

Business and Trade (7)

business (7) 1; (18) 16

butter (1) 30

butterfly (15) 28

buy (7) 12, 14

cabbage (48) 42

cackle (4) 14

Caesar (47) 27

calendar (34) 16

call, called (13) 20, 33; (19) 10; (22) 14; (24) 27

calm (9) 26

camel (46) 17

can, cannot, could (2) 3; (4) 17; (6) 23; (9) 5; (10) 18; (11) 13; (13) 5; (14) 1, 4–6, 13–16, 19; (15) 5; (16) 23; (18) 2, 7; (22) 12, 18; (23) 4; (24) 10, 25; (25) 27; (30) 5, 6; (31) 16; (32) 3, 6; (34) 9; (35) 13; (39) 18; (41) 5, 16; (48) 28

candle (15) 18; (23) 8; (46) 9

cap (13) 4

capon (18) 8

carcase (12) 13

cards (30) 18

care (20) 11; (25) 1, 15

carrion kite (14) 7

carry (15) 32, 33; (28) 4

cart (46) 14

cart-saddle (46) 24

cask (12) 10

cast (out) (15) 26, 34; (30) 4; (45) 15

castle, castles (15) 27; (44) 18

cat, cats (6) 15, 24, 27; (12) 7; (13) 13; (20) 11; (21) 10; (32) 16; (34) 23; (41) 13; (48) 16, 18

catch (3) 12; (6) 9, 15, 16; (13) 3; (14) 16; (15) 6, 13; (18) 1; (36) 7, 30; (46) 10; (48) 5

caught (15) 21; (36) 31

Cause and Effect (12)

cellar (9) 29

Certainty–Uncertainty (36)

certainty (36) 13

chaff (14) 16

chalk (46) 27

Chance–Destiny (45)

change (7) 12; (9) 8; (31) 12; (48) 47

charity (28) 3

Charybdis (19) 27

cheap (7) 11

cheer (39) 12

cheese (46) 27

cherries (29) 9

chest (39) 7

chestnuts (6) 27

cheverel (3) 21

chickens (36) 23

Children s. Parents

child, children (2) 6; (4) 18; (21) 10; (29) 13; (32) 2, 3, 8, 9, 13; (33) 23

china-shop (46) 26

chipping, chips (12) 6; (32) 7

choice (28) 1

choose, chosen (16) 9; (24) 27

Christmas (9) 28

church (4) 6; (22) 14, 15

clad (4) 12

claw, claws (43) 2; (48) 34

clean (33) 27

clerk (33) 22

climbers (12) 24

cloth (25) 33

clothing (5) 6

cloud (13) 27

coach (15) 3

coals (15) 33

coat (25) 33; (28) 2

cobbler (47) 38

cock (21) 11; (31) 10; (33) 7

coin (25) 1; (43) 24; (47) 39

cold (21) 10; (30) 13

colours (15) 5

colt (33) 12

come (in) (3) 15; (9) 23, 24, 26; (10) 26; (11) 17; (14) 17; (16) 10, 12, 22; (17) 16; (18) 18; (19) 9, 23–25; (20) 2; (21) 6, 7; (23) 4; (24) 24; (30) 23; (32) 15; (35) 3, 4; (37) 8,

(20) 5; (33) 10; (37) 8, 11; (40) 8

dead (15) 22; (34) 7, 10, 21, 22, 24,25

deaf (34) 19; (47) 24

dear (7) 11; (25) 30

Death s. Life

death (15) 2; (26) 4; (30) 9; (33) 17; (34) 5, 13–20

Debts s. Borrowing

debt (27) 5, 8, 9, 11

debtors (27) 2, 6

deceit, deceitful (4) 1; (12) 23; (30) 28

deceive (1) 7; (37) 5

Deeds s. Words

deed, deeds (1) 4, 6, 7; (16) 1

deem (17) 14

deemers (3) 14

deep (4) 8

defend (39) 18

defiled (12) 3

defy (34) 18

delayed (37) 7

delude (37) 5

deluge (48) 53

delve (48) 24

denial (34) 19

depend (38) 12

deprive (22) 9

desert *(go away)* (21) 15

deserve (43) 4

desire (48) 27

desperate (35) 17

Destiny s. Chance

destroy (19) 19

destruction (23) 9; (47) 21

Devil–Hell (23)

devil (1) 32; (3) 8; (5) 1; (6) 18; (23) 1–8; (32) 5; (47) 41

devilish (47) 30

devour (12) 27

diamond (43) 23

die (14) 11; (19) 10; (26) 3; (33) 8; (34) 8, 9, 11, 24; (37) 6

die *(dice)* (45) 15

diet (35) 15

differ (13) 29

difficult, difficulty (10) 6, 7

dig (12) 17

dine (38) 12

dinner (38) 15

dirty (47) 10

Discord s. Concord

discover (11) 21

discretion (19) 11

disease, diseases (35) 4, 8, 17

dish (24) 20

Dishonesty s. Honesty

dispose (22) 1

dispute (15) 25

distress (19) 20

distrust (36) 11

ditch (13) 2

divide, divided (11) 25; (29) 1; (41) 2

do, doing (1) 3; (3) 5; (4) 15; (6) 17, 22, 23; (14) 2; (15) 15; (18) 2; (25) 5; (26) 3; (28) 13; (30) 15; (31) 9; (34) 21; (43) 7; (47) 1, 2; s. done, doers

doctor (15) 2; (34) 18; (35) 15

dog, dogs (4) 9; (12) 5; (15) 11, 19; (16) 6; (33) 14, 15; (34) 7, 22; (35) 11; (39) 9; (41) 10–13; (43) 17; (46) 3; (47) 17, 35; (48) 1, 2, 42

done (1) 1; (6) 10, 11, 22; (10) 3, 26; (14) 1; (47) 2

door, doors (3) 10; (4) 10; (10) 8; (25) 7, 9; (30) 23; (47) 5; s. stable-door

doubt (8) 11

doves (32) 17

down (19) 16; (44) 3; s. go, pull

dozen (48) 40

draw (15) 23; (25) 13; (28) 14; (48) 14

dread (21) 10

dreaders (3) 14

dreams (46) 1

dress up (4) 16

drink (12) 12; (14) 6, 14; (36) 22

Drinking s. Eating

drive (out) (31) 14; (43) 18

drop, drops, dropping (12) 15, 18; (24) 4, 22

drown, drowned, drowning (18) 1; (19) 15; (45) 3, 14

drumming (15) 13

drums (42) 7

drunkenness (38) 21

dry (9) 29; (47) 22

due (17) 18; (23) 7

dunghill (21) 11

dust (34) 27; (45) 9

duty (42) 9

each, each other (20) 3; (28) 10

eagle, eagles (12) 13; (32) 17; (48) 5

ear, ears (14) 15; (15) 17; (27) 5; (38) 23; (48) 3

early (6) 9; (33) 11

earth (21) 8; (44) 11

ease (14) 10

east (44) 16

Easter (9) 28

easy (11) 7; (28) 8

Eating and Drinking (38)

eat (up), eaten, eating (6) 21; 24; (11) 14; (12) 21, 28; (29) 9, 12; (38) 1, 2, 14, 16; (39) 13; (43) 17; (48) 31, 42

echo (13) 20

Effect s. Cause

effects (35) 5

egg, eggs (3) 17; (4) 14; (6) 26; (26) 12; (32) 14; (33) 19; (36) 14, 36; (42) 1

either... or... (13) 17

ell (26) 13

embrace (19) 18

embroidery (3) 6

Emergency s. Necessity

empty (24) 20; (46) 15

End s. Beginning

end, ending (9) 17; (10) 2, 5, 10–15, 27, 30; (48) 49

endure, endured (10) 27; (18) 7; (20) 12

enemy, enemies (16) 8; (29) 11; (39) 10, 14–16, 18; (42) 4

Enmity s. Friendship

enough (11) 4; (24) 15, 17; (25) 28; (38) 13; (48) 16

enter (22) 14

envy, envied (16) 18; (48) 55

equal (17) 1; (30) 10; (34) 14

ere (6) 3

err (47) 29

escape (3) 18

Ethics–Practical Philosophy (47)

Eve (48) 24

even (41) 5; (48) 19

even *(regular)* (39) 3

event (11) 7

ever (2) 1; (3) 16; (35) 8; (44) 11

every (7) 4, 5; (9) 18; (11) 27, 28; (13) 27, 28, 36; (16) 17; (17) 5; (19) 1, 17; (20) 10; (22) 10; (25) 3, 7; (28) 9, 14, 15; (31) 3; (33) 21); (38) 18; (44) 12; (46) 11; (48) 50

everybody (14) 11; (39) 8

every one (11) 11; (13) 1; (47) 36
everything (9) 1; (10) 1, 15, 16; (30) 15; (33) 28; (37) 9
everywhere (7) 7; (44) 5
Evil s. Good
evil, evils (6) 19; (16) 9, 16, 23; (26) 1, 8; (32) 14
evil-gotten (3) 7
example (16) 3, 4
exception (13) 34, 35
excuse (12) 11; (17) 2
expect (11) 26
expel (30) 20
Experience s. Knowledge
experience (8) 5
extreme (17) 10; (46) 25
eye, eyes (5) 4; (17) 1; (28) 11, 13; (29) 9; (30) 19; (35) 10; (36) 8; (38) 5; (43) 16, 20; (47) 19; (48) 25, 36
eye-witness (36) 6

face (12) 22; (18) 16; (30) 24
fair, fairer, fairest (1) 6, 29; (4) 3; (9) 19; (12) 26; (30) 24, 25; (32) 11, 12; (33) 28
fair *(market)* (43) 15
Faith s. God
faith (22) 18, 19
fall, falls (12) 24; (46) 6
fall (in) (6) 25; (12) 17, 22; (13) 2, 3; (36) 18; (41) 2; (47) 19, 30; (48) 21, 43
fall(ing) out (3) 15; (30) 17
fallen (13) 1
Falsehood–Hypocrisy (5)
false (5) 5; (39) 14
fame (2) 20
familiarity (48) 52
far (off) (8) 9; (9) 19; (40) 1

farther, farthest (3) 24; (22) 15
fast (16) 14
fasting (25) 26
fat (20) 6; (28) 11; (38) 4; (41) 3
fate (45) 10
father (32) 1, 3–5
fatten (28) 12
fault, faults (13) 36; (17) 8; (38) 25 28; (36) 2
favour, favours (19) 7; (21) 5; (30) 28; (36) 2
Fear s. Will
fear (21) 10, 12, 13; (30) 4
feasts (11) 14
feather (43) 9
feed (18) 8
feet, s. foot
felled (10) 25
fellowship (25) 23
felt (28) 1
fetch (38) 24
fetters (48) 8
few (10) 9; (24) 27
fiddle (15) 9
fifth (15) 3
fight (15) 30
fill (1) 29; (9) 29; (12) 10; (15) 14; (24) 3
filth (13) 14
find (out), found (2) 8; (14) 10; (30) 8; (36) 25; (38) 25; (43) 5; (44) 4; (47) 26; (48) 1
fine (1) 30; (33) 28
finger (43) 14
finish (10) 9
fire (6) 27; (11) 19; (12) 1, 8; (19) 26; (21) 10; (40) 4; (46) 5
fire (6) 27; (11) 19; (12) 1, 8; (19) 26; (21) 10; (40) 4; (46) 5
first (1) 12; (8) 13; (9) 24; (10) 7;

(12) 10; (19) 19; (22) 9; (36) 30;
(42) 9; (46) 2

fish (3) 26; (6) 24; (15) 20; (24) 20;
(29) 12; (36) 31; (38) 9, 10; (40) 8;
(48) 45

fit (13) 4; (46) 9

fitly (1) 15

fleas (12) 5

flesh (38) 10; (48) 15, 45

flies s. fly

flock (12) 14; (16) 17; (43) 9

flog (15) 22

flow, flowing (19) 12; (24) 4

flower, flowers (24) 6; (40) 10

fly, flies (12) 27; (19) 14; (36) 20;
(38) 28; (48) 5, 19

fly, flying (9) 3; (32) 13; (36) 7, 20;
(42) 4; (45) 10

foes (2) 8

follow (2) 10; (43) 10

folly (11) 21

fool, fools (1) 7; (2) 6; (11) 5, 11–16,
18, 22–27, 29; (19) 7; (32) 2

foolish (37) 5

Foolishness s. Wisdom

foot, feet (1) 25; (6) 24; (11) 30; (13)
31; (22) 3; (34) 28; (35) 4; (48) 22

footsteps (28) 12

forbidden (3) 25

ford (10) 20

forearmed (13) 21

forelock (19) 13

foreseen (34) 15

forewarned (13) 21

forget, forgotten (8) 12; (30) 1; (33)
22; (38) 14

form (44) 15

fortune (19) 1–7, 11, 19; (21) 5; (31)
2

foul, fouler (1) 6; (4) 3; (12) 26;

(44) 14

found s. find

fountains (24) 4

four (36) 9

fox (3) 24; (5) 9; (6) 16; (10) 23;
(13 5

free (28) 7; (48) 30

fresh (40) 8

Friday (20) 8

Friendship–Enmity (39)

friend, friends (25) 14, 16, 23; (27) 7;
(39) 1–4, 6–8, 11–14, 18; (43) 26;
(45) 1

friendship (39) 5, 10; (40) 3

fruit (3) 25; (16) 23; (36) 27

fry (36) 31

frying-pan (19) 26

full (23) 9; (25) 26; (30) 3; (33) 26;
(38) 3

furrier (10) 23

furrow (33) 13

fury (37) 14

gained (25) 17, 18

gains (3) 7; (6) 4

gall (1) 31

gallon (36) 7

game (15) 18

gamesters (13) 37

gander (48) 26

gardener (48) 42

garland (24) 6

garment (4) 11

gather, gathered (12) 13; (13) 14, 18

geese s. goose

general *(not special)* (13) 34

generation (44) 11

gentleman (48) 24

get, got (1) 23, 24; (3) 8; (24) 26;
(33) 6

gift, gifts (12) 25; (13) 15; (39) 5, 15;
(47) 8
give (1) 18, 23; (11) 12; (18) 11;
(21) 13; (23) 7; (26) 13; (46) 4, 7;
(47) 13, 15, 37; (48) 2, 28
give in (11) 6
given (13) 15
gladness (20) 3
glass (19) 4; (47) 6
glitter (4) 2
glorious (34) 20
glove, gloves (6) 15; (43) 12
gluttony (38) 3, 6
gnashing (19) 29
gnat (46) 17
go, going (about, away, down, out,
up) (1) 22; (2) 18; (3) 6; (4) 6;
(9) 19; (10) 3; (11) 17; (12) 19;
(18) 18; (19) 14, 25; (22) 11, 17;
(27) 1, 8; (34) 4; (36) 26; (38) 17;
(44) 5; (46) 1, 23; (47) 13; (45)
21, 38; (48) 32; s. gone
God–Faith (22)
God (19) 8; (22) 1–10, 12‘ 15; (31)
11; (39) 18; (48) 4
gold, golden (1) 14; (4) 2; (6) 8; (7)
6; (15) 14; (25) 3, 4, 7, 8; (26) 12,
14; (42) 4; (45) 9; (48) 7, 8
gone (45) 9
Good–Evil (16)
good (1) 7; (2) 12; (3) 2, 3; (7) 2, 3,
10, 11; (9) 9; (10) 2, 4, 20; (13) 26;
(14) 7, 8; (15) 15; (16) 1–3, 5, 8,
16, 23; (17) 4, 13; (18) 16; (19) 9,
11; (23) 10; (24) 15; (27) 3; (28) 6;
(31) 1; (32) 16; (33) 12, 16; (34)
10; (36) 16; (39) 2, 12; (40) 2;
(43) 4, 5; (45) 14; (46) 5; (47) 11,
17; (48) 32
good(s) (3) 7; (25) 21; (28) 7

goose, geese (5) 9; (26) 12; (31) 15
(48) 26
Gordian (10) 28
got s. get
govern (29) 5
grain (24) 3; (48) 50
grand (34) 13
grandmother (33) 19
grasp (26) 11
grass (5) 2; (38) 30; (48) 51
grave (30) 12; (34) 28
grease (13) 22
great, greatest (1) 4, 5; (2) 13; (3) 18,
19; (10) 8; (11) 10, 15; (11) 10, 15;
(12) 1; (13) 23, 25; (19) 22; (29) 9,
12; (32) 2; (36) 2; (40) 5; (46) 15,
16; 21; (47) 33
green (9) 28; (40) 3
greet (45) 1
grey (13) 13
griefs (9) 6
grind (22) 7; (43) 26
ground (34) 26; (36) 18
grow (16) 14; (20) 6; (38) 30; (48) 51
Guests s. Neighbours
guest, guests (40) 6–8
guilty (3) 4

habit (47) 32
had s. have
hair (11) 20; (35) 11; (43) 13
half (3) 11; (10) 3, 4; (17) 8; (23) 6;
(24) 21; (30) 24; (34) 24; (48) 40
halloo (10) 21
halting (41) 11
hammer (18) 15
hand, hands (5) 8; (6) 5, 23; (22) 3;
(25) 25; (28) 13; (29) 6; (30) 13;
(36) 32; (41) 16; (43) 1, 12; (47) 9
handful (7) 6

handsome (4) 15

hang, hanged (3) 18, 19; (4) 10; (45) 3; (47) 7; (48) 2

happen (9) 12; (45) 4

Happiness–Misfortune (19)

happy (19) 10

harbour (46) 16

hard (10) 6; (14) 9, 20; (18) 3; (33) 15; (38) 27

hare, hares (5) 10; (15) 6, 13; (24) 13; (36) 30; (44) 15; (45) 5

harm, harms (1) 17; (11) 5; (16) 9; (34) 21

harmless (30) 16

haste (9) 20–22; (31) 7

hasty (12) 24

hatched (36) 23

hate, hated (16) 21; (38) 19

hateful (25) 21

hatred (41) 7

have, had (3) 5; (21) 2, 9; (23) 5; (24) 14, 25; (26) 9; (29) 6; (31) 3; (33) 3; (34) 28; (35) 10, 17; (36) 21, 33, 35; (38) 11, 13, 23; (43) 22; (48) 3, 19

hawk (14) 7

hay (6) 7; (9) 29

haystack (14) 18

head (11) 6, 30; (15) 12, 24; (19) 21; (27) 5; (31) 5; (35) 14; (46) 3

heal, healer (9) 7; (35) 12

Health–Illness (35)

health, healthful (35) 2, 3; (35) 13

hear, heard (1) 11, 13; (11) 8; (25) 27; (28) 10; (32) 13; (34) 19; (47) 11, 24

hear-so (36) 6

heart (1) 10, 31; (5) 1; (20) 10; (21) 3; (25) 24; (30) 13, 19; (48) 25

heaven (3) 6; (12) 22; (15) 10; (22)

11, 13; (31) 4

heavy (33) 25

hedge (13) 12; (40) 3

heed (15) 11; (32) 10; (39) 10

heels (2) 10; (20) 4

Hell s. Devil

hell (3) 6; (23) 9, 10; (47) 15

help, helped (6) 23; (13) 22; (14) 13; (22) 2, 8

hen (24) 3; (31) 10; (32) 15; (36) 36

hence (9) 25

Hercules (41) 5

here (45) 9

hide, hid (2) 16; (26) 5; (30) 5; (47) 14

high, higher, highest (13) 17; (22) 8; (34) 14; (46) 6, 17; (47) 19

highway (36) 26; (48) 51

hindmost (47) 41

hinges (4) 10

hired (27) 12

history (48) 48

hit (45) 2

hold (16) 19; (23) 8; (25) 8; (46) 9

hole (48) 11

Home s. World

home (3) 24; (11) 17; (16) 22; (28) 3; (32) 13; (41) 11; (44) 9, 16; 17; (46) 23

Honesty–Dishonesty (3)

honest, honesty (3) 1, 15; (30) 26

honey (1) 31; (12) 27; (15) 8; (19) 12; (36) 7

honour, honours (13) 23, 24; (17) 18; (47) 13; (48) 46; 47

Hope–Patience (37)

hope (36) 13; (37) 1–6

horn, horns (1) 26; (4) 5

horse, horses (4) 17; (11) 17; (12) 20; (14) 14; (15) 22; (16)5; (18) 12;

kingdom (13) 8; (25) 29

kiss (4) 18; (5) 8

knave, knaves (3) 16; (11) 25; (25) 16

knife (42) 11

knot (10) 28; (43) 22

know, known, knew (1) 27; (3) 22; (6) 12; (8) 2, 7, 9, 11; (11) 15; (18) 5; (33) 6; (36) 17, 27; (40) 6; (47) 22, 36; (48) 9, 34, 35

Knowledge–Experience (8)

knowledge (8) 1, 5

labour (15) 12

lacking (39) 12

ladder (44) 3

laid up (24) 2

lamb, lambs (22) 6; (47) 17

lame (1) 24; (17) 16

land (19) 12; (29) 13; (36) 3

large (24) 4; (28) 5

larks (6) 25; (13) 3

last, at last (10) 17; (12) 2, 19

last *(go on)* (33) 10

last *(block)* (13) 31; (47) 38

late (8) 4; (9) 11, 23; (10) 26; (15) 7; (38) 12; (47) 20

lather (10) 4

Latin (11) 15

laugh, laughing (10) 17; (20) 6, 7, 9, 14; (31) 16; (48) 16

laughter (11) 21; (20) 6

Law–Justice (17)

law, laws (17) 1, 2, 4–6, 9, 17; (18) 5; (42) 7

law-breakers (17) 3

lawfully (17) 4

law-makers (17) 3

law-suit (41) 3; s. suit

lawyer (47) 14

lay (4) 14; (26) 12

lazy (27) 3

lead *(conduct)* (10) 22; (13) 2

leaden (22) 3

lean *(thin)* (19) 14; (38) 4; (41) 3

leap (out, over) (10) 24; (13) 12; (30) 23; (36) 28

learn (6) 17; (8) 3, 4, 8, 10, 12; (11) 5; (22) 17; (28) 6

least (1) 5; (16) 9; (38) 11; (45) 5

leather (28) 5

leave *(let)* (16) 20; (36) 26; (47) 16

leaves *(pl of leaf)* (21) 6

legs (2) 11; (25) 32

leisure (31) 7

lend, lender (27) 4, 7

length, at length (10) 23; (45) 14

less (9) 22; (19) 20

let (16) 20; (34) 4; (48) 42

letter (30) 19; (36) 1; (46) 7

leveller (34) 13

liar, liars (2) 12–14

liberty (48) 7

Lie s. Truth

lie, lies (2) 11, 15, 17; s. lying

lie *(down, be flat)* (12) 4, 5; (25) 19; (48) 43

Life–Death (34)

life, lives (10) 30; (34) 1–3, 5, 6, 20, 23; (37) 1; (46) 7

light, lightly (6) 5; (25) 18; (42) 5; (48) 22

like *(be fond of)* (1) 11; (11) 27; (28) 9; (44) 12

like *(similar)* (35) 7; (43) 8; (45) 6

like… like… (22) 16; **(29)** 7, 8; (32) 1, 14

limit (10) 16; (37) 13

linen (47) 10

lining (13) 27

lion (13) 5; (34) 7; (46) 3; (48) 34

lip, lips (36) 24; (47) 4

lip-honour (1) 21

listeners (47) 11

Little s. Much

little (1) 13, 21; (3) 18, 19; (11) 30; (12) 1; (13) 16; (24) 1, 4, 14; (32) 2; (39) 16; (44) 13; (46) 16, 21–23

live (8) 3; (22) 19; (25) 25; (34) 4, 8, 12; (37) 2, 6; (38) 2; (47) 6

living (34) 7

loaf (24) 21

lock (25) 8

lodge (9) 23

log (43) 3

long, longest (1) 22; (4) 10; (9) 17; (11) 20; (12) 2; (13) 9, 15; (23) 5; (29) 6; (33) 20; (34) 6; (38) 19; (39) 3; (48) 39

look (at, for, to) (9) 10; (10) 12, 24; (14) 18; (15) 19; (40) 4; (47) 8, 19; (48) 18, 20

looking-glass (15) 4

loophole (17) 5

lord, lords (17) 6; (25) 24; (40) 5

lose (9) 10; (15) 12; (16) 7; (24) 26; (26) 10, 11; (27) 7; (38) 18; (44) 9

losers (19) 18

loss (13) 25; (19) 18

lost (9) 5; (12) 20; (16) 1; (25) 18; (37) 7; (48) 9

lot *(destiny)* (45) 13

louder (1) 2; (31) 10

louse (26) 5

Love and Beauty (30)

love (16) 21; (19) 8; (26) 1; (28) 10; (30) 1–11, 14, 15, 17, 18, 20, 22, 23; (39) 9; (40) 3; (43) 25; (44) 9; (48) 8

lovers (30) 16, 17

low, lower, lowest (13) 12, 17; (34) 14; (46) 6, 18

lucky (30) 18; (48) 33

lurk (23) 1

lying (2) 18

mad, madness (11) 28; (19) 19; (32) 2; (41) 15

made (6) 26; (14) 19; (31) 4; (48) 8

Mahomet (18) 18

main (21) 7

make (2) 8, 15; (3) 9; (4) 4, 7, 11; (6) 5, 7; (7) 3; (8) 6; (9) 20, 21; (10) 2, 11; (11) 2, 14, 22, 30; (12) 4, 27; 88; (14) 7, 14, 15, 20; (18) 6, 17; (19) 19, 20; (24) 1, 4, 5; (28) 11; (30) 10; (31) 15; (32) 2, 12, 13; (34) 14; (37) 4; (38) 27; (39) 3, 13; (41) 8; (42) 4, 5; (43) 25; (46) 14, 15; (47) 18; (48) 16, 17; s. made

mammon (22) 12

Man and Woman (31)

man, men (1) 23, 26, 27; (2) 19; (3) 11, 15; (4) 11, 13; (7) 9; (8) 13; (9) 4; (10) 20; (11) 2, 5, 9, 12–14, 28; (13) 8, 12, 28, 31, 36; (14) 3, 4, 6; (15) 4, 5, 15; (17) 1, 2, 4, 15, 17; (18) 1; (19) 1, 10, 15; (20) 9; (21) 2; (22) 1, 10; (25) 27, 31; (26) 2, 3; (27) 6; (28) 5, 7–9, 15; (29) 8; (31) 1, 2, 8, 11, 14; (32) 9; (33) 2, 8, 16, 23, 24, 26; (34) 9, 12, 21; (35) 13; (36) 2, 8; (37) 3, 5, 11, 14; (38) 12, 22, 29; (39) 17; (44) 2, 18; (45) 2, 10, 13; (46) 13, 19; (47) 4; (48) 8, 12, 23

manners (9) 14; (16) 16; (48) 47

many (2) 2, 4, 15; (4) 18; (5) 8; (6) 5; (7) 9; (10) 9; (13) 17; (16) 10; (24) 1, 2, 4, 13, 27; (25) 14; (29)

move back (47) 28

mow (6) 2

Much–Little–Nothing (24)

much (1) 9, 13, 21; (8) 9; (9) 16, 29; (11) 21, 30; (24) 9, 15, 16; (25) 1; (26) 9; (30) 15; (37) 5; (46) 22

much of a muchness (48) 38

murder (2) 16

music (37) 2

musk (15) 19

must, must not (7) 12; (9) 17; (10) 1; (12) 4, 5; (15) 20; (16) 6; (18) 7, 10, 18; (21) 6, 7; (31) 3; (32) 15; (33) 8; (34) 8; (35) 17; (38) 16; (43) 6, 22; (45) 11; (47) 18

mustard (15) 1

nail (12) 20; (43) 18

naked (14) 3

name (3) 2; (32) 10; (47) 7; (48) 2

nature (16) 7; (47) 32; (48) 14

naught (24) 18; s. nought

near, nearer, nearest (2) 10; (22) 15; (28) 2; (39) 2; (40) 1

Necessity–Emergency (18)

necessity (18) 3–5, 17

neck (19) 24

need, needy (2) 2, 12; (3) 4; (7) 2; (15) 4; (18) 6; (22) 8; (33) 18; (35) 16; (36) 29; (39) 1

needle, needles (7) 4; (14) 18; (48) 56

Neighbours–Guests (40)

neighbour, neighbours (12) 16; (40) 1–5

neither (... nor...) (15) 6; (25) 16; (48) 42, 45

nest (44) 12, 13, 14

never (3) 7; (4) 14; (6) 11; (8) 4; (9) 11; (10) 11; (11) 15, 16; (14) 7, 10; (16) 1, 7; (19) 6, 21, 23; (21) 7, 8; (23) 9; (27) 10, 12; (30) 11; (36) 13, 16, 22, 31; (38) 3; (39) 10; (40) 7; (41) 9; (45) 1, 3; (47) 20, 22; (48) 21

New s. Young

new (17) 6; (33) 27; 28; (44) 7

Newcastle (15) 33

new-come (40) 8

news (16) 11, 12

nighest (22) 8

night (9) 15; (10) 30; (13) 13; (38) 17

nine (13) 19; (34) 23

nobody (39) 8

noise (46) 14 6

none, no one (2) 8; (14) 2; (24) 12, 19; (45) 10; (46) 20; (47) 23, 24, 36

notary (41)

note (1) 27) (48) 35

Nothing s. Much

nothing (1) 9, 24; (2) 7; (6) 17; (8) 10, 11; (13) 26; (17) 7; (21) 3, 9; (24) 9, 15, 24, 25; (25) 24, 28; (26) 3; (29) 2; (34) 10; (47) 14

nought (14) 17; (24) 26; s. naught

nourish (48) 46

nurse (4) 18

nut (38) 16

oak (10) 25; (33) 21

oats (27) 6

obedience (42) 9

obedient (25) 6

occasion (19) 13

ocean (14) 12; (24) 22

odious (48) 10

offender (41) 9

oft, often (4) 14; (7) 12; (8) 14; (12) 17, 19; (16) 11; (31) 12; (37) 5; (38) 12; (46) 16; (48) 31

oil (2) 1

Old s. Young

(21) 8; (29) 3; (31) 11; (47) 9; (48) 41

quarrel, quarrels, quarrelling (6) 14; (30) 17; (41) 8, 11

question, questions (8) 10; (11) 13; (34) 29

quick, quickly (7) 3; (14) 8; (25) 18; (36) 12, 29; (47) 37; (48) 1, 11

quiet (35) 15

quit (36) 13

ragged (33) 12

rags (3) 6

rain (31) 14

rats (21) 15

raven (13) 32

reach (15) 10

read (30) 19

ready (48) 22

reap (6) 3; (12) 9

reason (22) 9

recalling (1) 19

receive (46) 4

receiver *(of stolen goods)* (3) 13

Reciprocation s. Solidarity

reckon, reckoning (12) 26; (15) 31; (39) 3

reconciled (39) 10

redressed (17) 8

reign (29) 5

relation (39) 2

Relativity s. Conditioned

remain (36) 1; (47) 30

remedy (34) 17; (35) 8

remember (20) 12; (33) 4

remove (22) 18; (33) 17

render (47) 27

renewal, renewing (30) 17

repeat (48) 48

repent (1) 16; (17) 14; (31) 7

repose (6) 10

reveal (38) 21

reverse (46) 11

reward (30) 7; (47) 40

rich (9) 27; (25) 14, 28

riches (3) 2; (26) 2

ride (18) 12; (33) 9; (47) 15; (48) 20

rifled (14) 3

right (3) 5; (17) 10, 11

ripe (48) 37

rise (up) (12) 5; (22) 13; (27) 8; (41) 14

roads (10) 22

roadside (13) 17

roam (44) 9

roasted (6) 25

rob (3) 20; (48) 29

robbery (7) 12

rod (29) 10; (32) 8

roll, rolling (13) 18; (25) 2; (43) 3

Romans (43) 7

Rome (9) 13; (10) 22; (43) 7; (46) 2

root (6) 19; (26) 1, 8

rope (47) 7

rose, roses (20) 13; (34) 3

rose-water (15) 15

rotten (12) 16; (48) 37

round (25) 2

ruin (22) 9

Rule–Power (29)

rule (13) 34; 35; (17) 9; (29) 1, 10

run, running (away) (4) 8; (5) 10; (9) 16; (13) 1; (15) 6, 24; (19) 27; (26) 4; (41) 12

rush (upon (19) 27

rust (12) 21

sack (14) 17

sad (31) 10

saddle (4) 17; s. cart-saddle

sadness (20) 3
safety (36) 11
said (1) 1; (13) 32
sail (18) 10; (21) 7
saint, saints (3) 10; (4) 6; (32) 5
salt (30) 22; (39) 13
same (14) 6
sauce (38) 9, 26; (48) 26
save, saved (10) 27; (13) 19; (25) 17;
   (33) 6, 10
savour (12) 10
say, saying (1) 3, 11; (2) 19; (10) 18;
   (34) 10; (36) 22; (48) 23; s. said
scabbed (12) 14
scald, scalded (21) 10; (47) 4
scarlet (4) 12
scarsely (33) 5
scolding (31) 14
scot (24) 26
scrape (32) 15
scrub (43) 11
Scylla (19) 27
sea (15) 15, 34; (21) 7; (22) 17; (36) 3
second (36) 10; (46) 2; (47) 32
sedan (22) 11
see, seeing, seen (13) 7, 37; (24) 10;
   (36) 9, 19; (37) 10; (47) 23; (48) 25
seek (36) 25; s. sought after
seldom (1) 17; (2) 20; (4) 9; (14) 8;
   (16) 5; (30) 26; (41) 10
sell (7) 12; (15) 21; s. sold
send (11) 26; (23) 4; (26) 5
sermon (16) 3; (38) 19
servant, servants (27) 4; (29) 11; (46)
   5; (48) 12
serve, served (9) 24; (14) 4; (22) 12;
   (26) 2
set (3) 12; (11) 19; (15) 29; (18) 10
seven (9) 12; (11) 13
Shadow and Substance (4)

shadow (15) 25; (21) 14
shame, shameful (2) 3; (19) 18; (34)
   20; s. ashamed
shape (22) 5
shave (10) 4
sheep (5) 6; (12) 14, 28; (15) 29;
   (16) 17; (18) 11; (38) 18; (43) 10;
   (48) 31
shell (33) 5
shelter (47) 13
shine (6) 7; (13) 7; (44) 5, 6
ship (21) 15
shirt (28) 2
shod (46) 20
shoe (12) 20; (47) 36
shoemaker (46) 20
shoot (16) 18
shop (6) 18; (10) 29
shorn (22) 6; (46) 23
short (2) 11; (11) 20; (16) 6; (22) 13;
   (34) 6; (36) 26; (41) 15
shoulders (36) 29
show (6) 13; (9) 9
shower (24) 4
shut (up) (10) 29; (15) 7; (36) 20
sick, sickness (23) 2; (35) 3, 13, 16
side (41) 14
sieve (15) 23
sight (30) 21
silence (1) 14, 16–18, 20
silent (1) 15, 33; (19) 22; (25) 3;
   (42) 7
silk (4) 12; (14) 15
silver, silvern (1) 14; (13) 27
sin, sins (17) 15; (25) 20; (30) 14;
   (47) 30
since then (9) 16
sinews (25) 10
sing (20) 8; (28) 10
sink, sinking (18) 13; (21) 15

sit (38) 15; (40) 6

six (48) 40

skin (3) 21; (13) 5; (15) 21; (26) 5; (28) 2

skin-deep (30) 27

sky (13) 3

sleeping (6) 16; (38) 22; (47) 35

sleeve (11) 11

slip (1) 25; (36) 24

slow, slowly (9) 20; (22) 7; (36) 15

small (13) 25; (19) 22; (24) 20; (29) 12; (39) 5

smart (13) 6

smell (25) 11; (40) 8

smoke (12) 8; (31) 14; (42) 2; (48) 41

snake (5) 2, 3

snow (9) 27

soap (15) 12

soberness (38) 21

soft, softly (3) 3; (9) 19

soften (9) 6

soil (28) 12

sold (13) 15

soldered (39) 10

soldier (42) 9

Solidarity–Reciprocation (43)

some (11) 28; (13) 25, 34; (19) 9; (24) 19; (44) 3

something (11) 8; (13) 26; (33) 9; (47) 19

son (32) 1, 4–6

soon, sooner (1) 1; (11) 18; (13) 16; (17) 14; (24) 13; (32) 13; (38) 14; (48) 27, 37

sore, sores (24) 7; (37) 12; (38) 28

Sorrow s. Joy

sorrow, sorrows (19) 20, 22; (20) 4, 5

sorrowing s. a-sorrowing

sought after (14) 3

soul (46) 16; (48) 36

sound (35) 1; (39) 10

sound *(noise)* (46) 15

sow (6) 2, 3; (12) 9; (14) 15; (15) 9

space (1) 4

Spain (15) 27

span (34) 2; s. spick

span *(spun)* (48) 24

spare (24) 17; (32) 8; (36) 34

spark (12) 1

spatter (47) 12

speak (1) 2, 10, 12, 13, 15, 33; (2) 6, 14; (19) 22; (25) 3; s. spoken

speech (1) 14, 16

speed (9) 22

spending (25) 19

spent (3) 8

spick and span (33) 29

spirit (46) 7

spit (12) 22

spleen (48) 19

spoil, spoiling (24) 23; (32) 8; (38) 7

spoken (2) 4; s. speak

spoon, spoonful (23) 5; (36) 7

spurred (16) 5

squirted out (29) 9

stable-door (15) 7

staff (18) 12; (31) 8; (48) 1

stage (44) 2

stake (31) 8

stand, standing (13) 14; (41) 2, 16; (46) 6; (47) 28

standers-by (13) 37

starling (13) 32

starve (38) 30; (45) 8

steal (3) 17; s. stolen

steed (15) 7

step (10) 7, 8

stepmother (32) 10

stew (19) 28

stick (4) 16

295

still *(without movement)* (4) 8; (47) 28

stir up (41) 7

stitch (13) 19

stock (33) 24

stolen (15) 7; s. steal

stone, stones (12) 18; (13) 18; (14) 20; (15) 24; (29) 9; (47) 6

stools (36) 18

stopped (19) 6

store (24) 7

storm (9) 26; (46) 28

straight (14) 19; (33) 13

strain (46) 17

stranger (13) 6

straw (13) 9; (18) 1; (36) 28

streams (24) 4

strength (11) 3; (41) 1

stretch (25) 32

stricken (4) 13

strife (41) 7

strike (6) 6

strings (36) 21

strive (41) 12

stroke (10) 25

strong (30) 9; (41) 16

study (38) 3

stuff (45) 8

stumble (36) 16, 28

Substance s. Shadow

succeed (20) 3

such... such... (1) 23; (10) 5; (34) 5

suck (33) 19

sudden (12) 24

suffice (32) 10

suit (17) 17; s. law-suit

summer (24) 5

sun (6) 7; (13) 7; (33) 10; (44) 5–7

Sunday (7) 9; (9) 18; (20) 8

sup (23) 5

supper, supperless (20) 7; (27) 8; (38) 15, 17

support (32) 3

sure (1) 32; (22) 7; (36) 14, 15

surety (13) 6

swallow (24) 5

swallow *(eat up)* (46) 17

sweat (34) 26

sweept (33) 27; (47) 5

sweet (3) 25; (6) 10; (20) 12; (38) 27

swell (43) 25

swim (15) 20; (18) 13

swimmers (45) 14

swine (15) 26

swing (33) 3

Swiss (24) 28

sword (1) 28; (38) 6; (42) 3, 8

table (38) 12

tail (46) 3; (48) 9

take, taken (1) 26; (6) 27; (12) 25; (14) 14; (19) 13; (21) 12; (26) 13; (27) 6; (32) 10; (36) 33; (39) 10; (41) 8; (42) 3; (47) 15, 18, 25, 26, 41; (48) 11

tale (25) 27

talk (1) 32; (25) 4

talkers (1) 5; (2) 13

taste, tastes (13) 28–30

tat s. tit

teach, teaching (8) 8; (15) 20; (18) 14; (33) 15, 19

teachers (8) 14

tea-cup (19) 15; (46) 28

tears (29) 4

teeth s. tooth

tell (47) 1; s. told

temper *(soften, modify)* (22) 6

tempt (3) 10

ten (32) 3; (48) 14

Thames (11) 19

thicker (48) 6

thief, thieves (3) 9, 12, 13, 15, 18–20

thieving (2) 18

Thine s. Mine

thing, things (1) 3, 8; (6) 22; (10) 9, 10, 26; (14) 1; (19) 9; (21) 4; (24) 15; (25) 6; (28) 9; (31) 14; (33) 28; (34) 17; (44) 7; (47) 15, 25–27; (48) 13, 32

think (1) 12; (6) 25; (32) 11, 12; (45) 5

third (41) 12; (48) 33

thongs (28) 5

thorn (20) 13; (33) 11

though (4) 12; (26) 7

thoughts (36) 10; (48) 30

thread (13) 11

threathened (4) 13

three (31) 14, 15; (40) 8; (47) 31; (48) 32

threefold (36) 12

thrifty (32) 4

throw (15) 15; (47) 6

thumb (43) 14

tide (9) 4

tied (16) 6

tiffs (30) 16

tilt (15) 30

Time–Weather (9)

time, times (1) 33; (9) 1–10, 14; (11) 9; (13) 19; (14) 6; (17) 7; (19) 13; (20) 14; (34) 11; (38) 18; (39) 11; (48) 23, 33

tinkers (13) 10

tired (27) 12

tit for tat (43) 21

today (6) 11; (36) 36, 37; (45) 7–10

together (2) 18; (12) 13; (31) 11; (43) 9

told (2) 9

told *(counted)* (48) 31

toll (48) 30

tomorrow (6) 11; (36) 17, 36, 37; (45) 7–10

tongue (1) 24–26, 31; (25) 3; (35) 9

tools (6) 14

tooth, teeth (2) 10; (16) 7; (19) 29; (35) 9; (38) 11; (42) 10; (43) 20

toss (38) 17

touch (12) 3

Trade s. Business

trade, trades (7) 6, 8, 9; (13) 10

traitor (16) 21, 22

travel, travelling (8) 9; (11) 17

traveller (2) 17

treachery (16) 22

tread (20) 4

treason (16) 21

tree, trees (13) 1; (16) 23; (24) 10; (31) 13; (33) 17; (36) 27; (47) 9, 13; (48) 43

tricks (33) 15

trot (18) 6

trouble (30) 3

troubled (3) 26

true (2) 4, 19; (16) 11

trust, trusted (3) 22; (12) 23; (22) 4; (29) 3; (36) 4; (38) 8

Truth–Lie (2)

truth, truths (2) 1–3, 5–10, 14

try (36) 4

tumble (38) 17

tun (12) 15

turn (31) 8; (34) 27; (35) 9; (43) 4

twenty (39) 11

twice (33) 23; (36) 5; (47) 37

two (14) 4, 5; (15) 6; (16) 9; (19) 20; (20) 5; (36) 6, 9, 18, 21, 32, 33, 37; (41) 5, 6, 8, 10, 12; (47) 31

297

unbidden (40) 6
uncalled (47) 3
uncertain (36) 2
Uncertainty s. Certainty
undo, undone (14) 1; (20) 9
unexpected (45) 4
unfortunate (19) 15
union (41) 1
united (41) 2
unlucky (30) 18
up s. go, shut
urinal (17) 17
use, used (17) 4; (33) 4; (41) 4
Uselessness (15)

vain (30) 28; (33) 14
vale (46) 18
value (35) 3
variant (19) 5
varlet (4) 12
venture (21) 9
very *(just, even)* (32) 10
vessels (46) 15
village (46) 2
vinegar (36) 7
violent (29) 2
viper (5) 3
virtue (18) 17; (47) 40
voice (15) 16; (48) 4

waggon (47) 34
wain (47) 15
wait, waited (9) 4; (13) 15; (37) 9, 10
waken (47) 35
walk (38) 15
wall, walls (11) 29; (14) 20; (15) 24; (48) 3
walnut (31) 13
want (6) 22; (7) 12; (25) 28; (33) 20

want *(lack)* (12) 20; (26) 6; (33) 10
War and Peace (42)
war (25) 10; (42) 1, 6, 11
ware (7) 3
warm (30) 13
wash (away) (15) 12; (30) 22; (41) 1; (47) 10
waste (9) 21
water, waters (3) 26; (4) 8; (9) 16; (12) 19; (14) 14; (15) 23, 34; (21) 10; (28) 14; (30) 22; (36) 22; (46) 5; (47) 22; (48) 6
wax (12) 2; (16) 13
way (1) 22; (15) 13; (21) 1, 2; (30) 8; (47) 34, 39
wayside (13) 17
weak, weakest (12) 2; (13) 11
Wealth–Poverty (25)
wealth (26) 7; (35) 2
wear, wearer (12) 18; (13) 4; (47) 36
Weather s. Time
wedding (24) 23
wedge (43) 22
wedlock (31) 6
weeds (16) 13, 14
weep, weeping (19) 29; (20) 8, 14; (31) 16; (32) 9
weigh (13) 9
welcome (40) 7, 9, 10
well (3) 5; (6) 22; (10) 3, 14; (16) 13, 19; (31) 9; (43) 25; (44) 10; (46) 24
well *(spring, fountain)* (12) 19; (47) 22
west (44) 16
wet (6) 24; (9) 29
wheel, wheels (13) 22; (15) 3, 28; (19) 6; (46) 14
while (6) 6, 7; (33) 10; (37) 1; (38) 30
whirlwind (12) 9
whistle (14) 6

white (9) 28; (11) 29; (33) 9

whole (12) 14, 15; (33) 10

whole *(well)* (35) 16

wide (44) 1

wife (18) 6; (31) 2, 5, 14; (46) 20

wilderness (15) 16

wilful (21) 2

Will–Courage–Fear (21)

will (21) 1; (31) 16; (32) 6; (43) 8; (48) 22

willing, willingly (21) 3; (38) 3

win, winning (37) 11; (42) 5; s. won

wind (12) 9; (18) 10; (22) 6; (31) 12; (36) 1

windmills (15) 30

window, windows (10) 29; (30) 23

wine (2) 5; (7) 2; (12) 15; (20) 9; (38) 20; (39) 4

wings (5) 7; (16) 12; (21) 13

winter (31) 12

Wisdom–Foolishness (11)

wisdom (1) 20; (11) 3

wise, wiser, wisely (1) 7, 15; (11) 1, 2, 4–9, 12–14

wish (5) 8; (19) 19; (33) 16; (36) 35; (42) 6

wit, wits (11) 10, 20, 30; (38) 20

with... against... (46) 12

wither (33) 17

within (4) 3

without *(outside)* (4) 3

witness, witnesses (41) 6; s. eye-witness

woe (29) 12

wolf, wolves (5) 6; (12) 28; (15) 29; (16) 7; (38) 24; (39) 17; (43) 6; (48) 31

Woman s. Man

woman, women (20) 9; (31) 12, 13, 15, 16; (44) 2

won (9) 5

wood (10) 21; (21) 6; (24) 10; (38) 24

wool (18) 11; (46) 21, 23

Words and Deeds (1)

word, words (1) 2, 4, 6, 7, 19, 22, 27–30; (2) 2, 4; (11) 4; (36) 1

Work–Industry–Idleness (6)

work (6) 1, 5, 10, 12, 13, 21; (10) 13, 30

workman (6) 12–14

World and Home (44)

world (11) 25; (44) 1–3; (47) 39

worm (6) 9

worry (24) 13

worse, worst (25) 24; (31) 2; (35) 8, 14; (46) 14, 20

worth (15) 18; (19) 11; (20) 5; (36) 32, 33, 37; (47) 22; (48) 9

wound (16) 18

written (36) 1; (41) 4

wrong (17) 10, 12; (19) 18; (41) 14

year, years (8) 7; (9) 12, 25; 27, 30; (11) 13; (34) 24

you s. I...

Young–Old–New

young (8) 12; (32) 11; (33) 7, 8, 20

youth (33) 3, 4, 6, 18

Yule, Yuleday (9) 18; (28) 8

Français

A (10) 18
abattre (s') (10) 25; (40) 3
abbaye (24) 23
abîme (23) 9
aboiement, aboiements (15) 11
abondance (1) 10; (24) 8
aboyer (4) 9; (33) 14
abriter (47) 13
absence (30) 22
absent, absents (12) 7; (17) 12
accablé (24) 13
accommodement (41) 3
accompagné (16) 15
accorder (s') (41) 10
accoucher (46) 8
accoutumance (47) 33
accrocher (s') (18) 1
accuser (s') (12) 11; (48) 2
acheter (7) 12; (14
achever (10) 9, 11
acquis (3) 7
Actes v. Paroles
acteur, acteurs (44) 2
Adam (11) 25; (48) 24
advenir (3) 5; (9) 12
affaire, affaires (7) 1; (41) 12
affamé (38) 23, 25, 29
affilé, affilée (43) 22
afin de (29) 1
âge (8) 3; (11) 1; (34) 16
âgé (33) 16
agir (s') (40) 4; (43) 7
agneau (5) 6
agréer (14) 10

aider (s') (22) 2
aigle, aigles (12) 13; (32) 17; (48) 5
aigre (38) 28
aiguille, aiguilles (7) 4; (15) 25
aile, ailes (16) 12; (21) 13
aimer (6) 24; (16) 21; (22) 3; (28) 1,
    9; (30) 3, 25; (32) 8, 11, 15; (39) 9;
    (40) 3; (48) 8
air *(aspect, vue)* (4) 16
airain (41) 4
aise, aisément (20) 4; (35) 13; (48) 27
aller (s'en) (3) 1; (4) 6; (9) 19; (11)
    17; (12) 19; (13) 22; (18) 18; (19)
    14; (21) 6, 7; (22) 17; (23) 4;
    (25) 18; (28) 4; (30) 23; (33) 11;
    (35) 9; (38) 17; (40) 6; (44) 9, 11;
    (46) 24; (47) 26; (48) 32
alouette, alouettes (6) 25; (13) 3
amande (38) 16
amant, amants (30) 17
amasser (13) 18
âme (35) 1; (48) 36
amende (19) 18
amener (19) 24
amer (30) 3; (35) 5; (38) 13
Ami et Ennemi (39)
ami, amis (6) 8; (25) 14, 16; (27) 7;
    (39) 1–4, 6–8, 10–13, 18
amitié (36) 2; (39) 5, 10
Amour–Beauté (30)
amour, amours (4) 18; (26) 1; (30) 1,
    2, 4–11, 14–20, 22, 23
amoureux (30) 17
an, ans (9) 12, 25, 29

FRANÇAIS

avril (9) 29, 30

B (10) 18
baguette (29) 10
baiser (4) 18; (5) 8
balai (33) 27
balayer (47) 5
balcon (9) 28
bannir (30) 4
banquet (45) 8
barbe (4) 5; (10) 4
barbeau, barbeaux (24) 20
baron (4) 16
barque (22) 8
bas, basse (13) 12, 17; (46) 6
bataille (21) 4
bâtir (9) 13; (24) 2
bâton (4) 16; (15) 22; (31) 13; (48) 1
battre (se) (3) 15; (4) 17; (6) 6; (15)
    22; (46) 10
battu, battus (19) 18; (48) 51
béat (5) 1
beau, belle (1) 6, 7, 21, 30; (4) 3, 15;
    (9) 26; (10) 30; (11) 23; (12) 26;
    (15) 14; (19) 8; (30) 25, 26; (32)
    11, 12; (33) 28; (38) 8; (44) 12;
    (47) 16; v. avoir beau
Beaucoup–Peu–Rien (24)
beaucoup (1) 13; (12) 15; (24) 1, 9,
    14, 27; (30) 15; (39) 11, 13; (46) 22
Beauté v. Amour
beauté (4) 15; (30) 26–28
bêler (4) 14; (38) 18
belle v. beau
berceau (8) 12
besogne (6) 10; (48) 22
Besoin v. Nécessité
besoin (16) 5; (18) 6; (35) 16; (39) 1
bête, bêtes (1) 26; (11) 17; (35) 11
Bien et Mal (16)

bien *(bon, utile)* (1) 2; (4) 15; (6) 22;
    (10) 3, 4, 14, 17; (11) 12; (13) 15,
    26; (14) 3, 8; (16) 8, 19, 20; (19) 2;
    (20) 5; (28) 3; (31) 9; (32) 8; (43)
    5; (44) 10; (47) 20, 38
bien *(beaucoup, très)* (9) 16; (21) 11;
    (47) 34
bien, biens (3) 7; (6) 4; (19) 4; (24)
    8; (25) 13; (28) 7
bienfait (15) 15; (16) 1
bientôt (11) 18; (13) 16; (32) 13;
    (34) 24; (48) 11; v. tôt
bienvenu (40) 9, 10
bière *(cercueil)* (45) 9
blanc, blanche (3) 22; (11) 29; (14)
    15; (48) 39
blancher (20) 11
blé (6) 7
blesser (47) 36
bœuf (3) 17; (18) 12; (19) 8; (33) 13;
    (36) 36; (42) 1
Boire v. Manger
boire (10) 19; (12) 12; (14) 14; (36)
    22
bois (21) 6; (38) 24; (43) 22
boîte, boîtes (46) 16
boiter (17) 16
bon, bonne (1) 22, 27; (2) 9, 12; (3)
    2, 3, 24; (6) 14; (7) 2, 3; (10) 2;
    (11) 30; (13) 25, 27; (14) 20; (16)
    2, 5, 16, 23; (17) 4, 13; (18) 16;
    (21) 1; (23) 10; (26) 3; (27) 3, 10;
    (28) 7; (30) 26; (31) 1, 13; (33) 12;
    (36) 16; (38) 8; (39) 2–4; (40) 2;
    (41) 3; (43) 23; (45) 14; (46) 5, 16;
    (47) 16; (48) 26, 32
bon marché (7) 10, 11
bon sens (22) 9
bon temps (20) 3
(de) bonne heure (14) 11; (20) 11;

(33) 20

Bonheur–Malheur (19)

bonheur (31) 2; (46) 4

bonnet (43) 12; (48) 39

bonté (4) 15

bord (36) 34

borgne, borgnes (13) 8; (35) 10

borner (se) (47) 38

botte (14) 18

bouche (1) 10; (14) 12; (25) 33; (35) 5; (36) 20, 24; (39) 12; (47) 8

bouiller (1) 30

bourse (7) 10; (12) 26; (25) 33; (27) 10

bout (37) 11, 14

boutique (10) 29

braire (48) 23

braise (19) 26

bran (23) 6

branche, branches (13) 1

branlant (47) 34

bras (26) 13; (29) 6

brave, braves (21) 5

brebis (4) 14; (12) 14, 28; (15) 29; (16) 17; (22) 6; (38) 18; (47) 17; (48) 31

brève (22) 13

briller (44) 5

brin (18) 1

briser (se) (2) 10; (12) 19

broncher (36) 16, 28

bruit (24) 9; (46) 14, 15, 21

brûler (23) 8; (40) 4

buisson, buissons (36) 30; (46) 10

buse (14) 7

buveur (38) 21

cacher (5) 2; (30) 5

cadavre (12) 13

cadeau, cadeaux (39) 5

cage (15) 14; (31) 8

calumet (42) 2

cap (42) 10

caque (12) 10

caquet (31) 15

carrosse (15) 3

cas (47) 14

casser (6) 26; (38) 16

Cause et Effet (12)

cause (9) 22

cautionner (13) 6

ceinture (46) 9

cela, ça (46) 24; (48) 41

celer (47) 14

censé (17) 2

cent (9) 12; (11) 22; (12) 16; (13) 19; (39) 2; (48) 14

ceps *(fers)* (48) 8

cerise, cerises (29) 9; (38) 13

Certitude–Incertitude (36)

cerveau, cervelle (1) 27; (11) 20; (38) 3, 4

César (47) 27

cesse v. sans cesse

cesser (38) 17

chacun, chacune (7) 4, 5; (11) 7, 11, 28; (13) 1, 28, 36; (13) 1, 28, 36; (19) 1, 17; (20) 10; (22) 10; (28) 4, 9, 14, 15; (31) 3; (32) 11; (43) 8; (47) 5, 36, 38; (48) 27

Chagrin v. Joie

chair (38) 10; (48) 45

chameau (46) 17

chandelle (15) 18; (23) 8

change (7) 13

changer (se) (9) 8; (31) 12; (48) 47

chanson (28) 10

chant (1) 27; (48) 35

chanter (10) 20; (14) 12; (19) 2; (24) 29; (28) 10; (31) 10; (33) 7

chapelain (22) 16
chapon (18) 8
chaque (9) 1; (11) 27; (16) 17; (21) 8;
   (28) 10; (44) 12; (46) 11; (48) 50
charbon (14) 15
charbonnier (44) 18
chariot (13) 22; (46) 14; (47) 34
charité (28) 3
charretée (19) 25
Charybde (19) 27
chasse (44) 9
chasser (17) 17; (31) 14; (43) 18;
   (48) 5, 15
chasseur, chasseurs (4) 5
chat, chats (5) 1; (6) 15, 24, 27; (7)
   14; (12) 7; (13) 13; (21) 10; (32)
   16; (34) 23; (41) 13; (43) 23; (46)
   3; (47) 35
château, châteaux (15) 27
châtier (22) 9; (32) 8
chaud (6) 6; (30) 13; (44) 17
chaudron (13) 33
chaussé, chaussés (46) 20
chaussure (47) 38
chef (31) 5
chemin, chemins (10) 22; (12) 24;
   (13) 9; (47) 34; (48) 51
chemise (28) 2; (43) 12
chêne (10) 25; (33) 21
cher (7) 11
chercher (14) 18; (25) 13; (36) 25;
   (43) 8; (46) 23; (48) 20
chère *(mets)* (45) 9
cheval, chevaux (4) 17; (15) 7; (16)
   5; (19) 14; (27) 12; (28) 11; (31)
   13; (33) 12; (35) 4; (36) 16; (38)
   30 (47) 8; (48) 14
chevalier (4) 18; (45) 10
cheveux (11) 20; (19) 13; (20) 11
cheville (46) 9

Chez-soi v. Monde
chez soi, chez lui (44) 16, 18
chiche (26) 7
chien, chiens (4) 9; (10) 21; (12) 5;
   (15) 11; (16) 6; (19) 16; (33) 14,
   15; (34) 7, 22; (39) 9; (41) 10–13;
   (43) 17; (47) 17, 35; (48) 1, 2, 18,
   42
chimère (37) 5
choir *(tomber)* (46) 6
choisir (16) 9
chômer (24) 23
chose, choses (9) 1; (10) 9, 10; (13)
   25, 27; (14) 1, 10; (25) 24; (27) 11;
   (29) 2; (47) 15, 19; (48) 13, 32
chou (48) 38, 42
chouette, chouettes (15) 32
chute (46) 6; (47) 21
ciel, cieux (12) 22; (13) 3; (22) 2, 11,
   13; (31) 4
cinquième (15) 3
civet (36) 31
clef (25) 7
cloche (22) 14
close (36) 20
clou (43) 18
cochon (26) 3
cœur (1) 10, 31; (21) 3; (30) 13, 19,
   21; (38) 21; (48) 25
coffre (3) 10
colère (41) 15; (48) 19
colombe (32) 17
combat (34) 1
combler (43) 25
commander (se) (29) 10; (30) 6
Commencement–Fin (10)
commencement (10) 1, 2, 5, 6, 10
commencer (10) 3, 9, 11; (28) 3
Commerce–Métier (7)
commun (15) 9; (48) 12

compagnie, compagnies (16) 16; (19) 20; (30) 26

compagnon, compagnons (30) 26; (47) 34

comparaison (48) 10

comptant (25) 4, 6

compte, comptes (39) 3

compter (15) 31; (36) 23; (39) 11; (48) 31

Concorde–Discorde (41)

concorde (41) 2

condition, conditions (3) 14; (30) 10

Conditionnellement–Relativité (13)

conducteur (30) 19

conduire (13) 2

confesseur (47) 14

confiance (12) 23

confier (se) (29) 3

confirmer (13) 35

confort (19) 20

connaître (6) 12; (8) 2; (25) 16; (34) 16; (34) 16; (36) 27; (39) 1, 13; (47) 22; (48) 34, 35

connu (3) 22; (32) 13; (36) 13

conscience (3) 3, 21

conseil (9) 9, 15; (10) 26; (14) 13; (33) 16; (47) 3

conseiller (48) 28

consentir (1) 18; (47) 18

considerer (10) 12

consoler (35) 13

construire (41) 2

content (25) 28; (45) 13

contentement (25) 29

contenter (14) 9

continuer (33) 4

Contrastes (46)

contre (41) 5; (46) 12

convoiter (26) 10

coq (21) 11; (31) 10

coque (33) 5

coquin (3) 16

cor (4) 5

corbeau, corbeaux (5) 4; (32) 12, 14; (43) 16

corde, cordes (36) 12, 21; (47) 7

cordelier (3) 21

cordonnier, cordonniers (46) 20; (47) 38

corne, cornes (1) 26

corneille, corneillon (33) 7

corps (35) 1, 14

corriger (17) 15

corrompre (16) 16

côté (13) 11, 27

coucher (se) (12) 4, 5; (27) 8; (38) 17

coudre (13) 5

couler (21) 15; (46) 17

couleur, couleurs (15) 5

coup (1) 28; (10) 25; (45) 6; (48) 33

coupé (5) 8

Courage v. Volonté

courbé (14) 19

courir (3) 18; (13) 1, 14; (14) 6; (32) 16; (36) 35

couronner (10) 13

courroie (28) 5; (39) 7

courroux (41) 6, 16

court, courte (2) 11; (11) 20; (16) 6; (34) 6; (38) 19; (41) 15

coûter (1) 21; (7) 11; (10) 7

coutume (24) 11

couvercle (24) 16

couvert (39) 14

couvrir (30) 14

crachat (19) 15

cracher (12) 22

craindre (21) 7, 10

crainte (29) 9; (30) 4

creuser (12) 17, 18

Diable–Enfer (23)

diable, diables (3) 8; (6) 18; (23) 1–8; (32) 10; (41) 6

diablot (32) 5

diabolique (47) 30

diète (35) 15

Dieu–la Foi (22)

Dieu (22) 1, 3–10, 12, 15; (31) 11; (39) 18; (47) 31; (48) 4

différent (13) 29

différer (6) 11; (37) 7

difficile (10) 6

dimanche (20) 8

dîner (15) 1; (23) 5; (38) 12, 15, 19, 22; (40) 6

dire, dit (1) 1–4, 11, 18; (2) 4, 6, 9, 14, 19; (10) 18; (19) 10; (34) 10; (36) 22; (47) 1; (48) 23

Discorde v. Concorde

discorde (41) 2

disetteuse (33) 18

diseur, diseurs (1) 5

disposer (22) 1

disputer (13) 30; (15) 25

diviser (29) 1

dix (36) 6

docteur (35) 15

doigt, doigts (12) 3; (26) 13; (43) 14; (47) 9

Domination–Pouvoir (29)

dommage (11) 2, 5, 7; (47) 17

don (39) 15

donner (11) 14; (13) 15; (15) 24, 29; (21) 13; (23) 7; (24) 25; (26) 13; (46) 4; (47) 3, 8, 15, 37

donneur (1) 9

dormir (4) 8; (13) 14; (19) 9; (38) 22; (47) 35; v. endormi

dot (30) 24

douane (48) 30

doucement (9) 19

douleur, douleurs (9) 6; (19) 22

douloir (48) 25

douter (8) 11

doux (3) 3, 25; (6) 10; (20) 12; (35) 5

douze (7) 9

drap, draps (25) 32, 33

Droit–Justice (17)

droit, droits (17) 11; (24) 26

droit *(direct)* (33) 13

dû, due (23) 7; (27) 11

dupé (37) 5

dur, dure (14) 20; (18) 3; (25) 30; (47) 33

durer (4) 10; (8) 12

eau, eaux (3) 26; (4) 8; (5) 10; (9) 16; (12) 19; (13) 14; (15) 22, 23, 34; (21) 10; (24) 22; (28) 14; (36) 22; (46) 5, 28; (47) 22

échaudé (21) 10

échauffé (13) 16

écho (13) 20

éclipsé, éclipsée (2) 3

économiser (25) 15

écorcher (26) 5

écouter (1) 13; (2) 14; (11) 8; (15) 10; (25) 27; (32) 13; (33) 16; (47) 11

écrire (s') (41) 4

écrit, écrits (31) 4; (36) 1

écuelle (38) 12

écuyer (4) 18

édifier (13) 17

Effet v. Cause

égal, égaux (9) 25; (17) 1; (34) 13

égaliser (30) 10

église (4) 6; (22) 14, 15

éléphant (46) 26; (48) 17

éloigné (40) 1

éloquant (25) 4
élu, élus (24) 27
éluder (17) 5
embonpoint (16) 18
embouer (s') (47) 12
embrasser (18) 7; (26) 11
emmitouflé (6) 15
empêcher (24) 10
emporter (25) 6
Emprunt–Dette (27)
emprunter (27) 1, 4, 12
emprunteur (27) 2, 3
enclume (18) 15; (47) 9
endormi (6) 16
Enfants v. Parents
enfant, enfants (2) 6; (29) 13; (32) 2, 3, 5, 9, 13; (33) 2, 23
Enfer v. Diable
enfer (23) 10; (41) 6
engendrer (2) 8; (12) 1; (32) 17; (48) 51
engraisser (28) 11
Ennemi v. Ami
ennemi, ennemis (4) 13; (16) 8; (27) 7; (29) 11; (30) 22; (39) 14–16, 18; (42) 4
ennuyer (40) 7
enragé v. demi-enragé
enrichir (s') (25) 16; (27) 9
enseigne (7) 2
enseigner (8) 8; (15) 20
ensemble (14) 8
ensevelir (34) 25
entendre (s') (11) 4, 8; (36) 6; (41) 13; (43) 15; (47) 11, 24
entier (44) 2
entraîner (2) 15
entre (18) 15; (36) 18; (47) 9
entrée (22) 11
entre-piller (s') (41) 12

entrer (15) 17; (22) 14; (36) 20; (38) 20; (47) 18
entretenir (20) 9; (30) 16; (39) 5
envie (16) 18; (48) 55
envieux (16) 18
envoler (s') (36) 1
envoyer (11) 26
épargne (25) 17
épargner (13) 19; (17) 13; (34) 14; (36) 34
épaule (43) 2
épée (38) 6; (42) 3
éperon (16) 5; (31) 13
épervier (14) 7
éphémère (30) 27
épine, épines (20) 13; (33) 11; (48) 56
épingle (14) 18; (33) 29
ermite (23) 2
erreur (47) 30
esclave (27) 4
Espagne (15) 27
espérance (37) 2–4
Espoir–Patience (37)
espoir (37) 1, 5, 6
esprit, esprits (11) 10; (46) 7
estimé (1) 20
estomac (35) 5; (38) 4
étable (15) 7
établir (17) 3
éteint, éteinte (2) 3
étendre (25) 32
Éthique–Philosophie pratique (47)
étincelle (12) 1
être (14) 5, 17; (16) 15; (33) 22; (34) 29; (35) 10; (41) 8; (43) 7, 12; (44) 10; (45) 11; (46) 2, 3, 12, 16; (47) 1, 27; (48) 56
étreindre (26) 11
étuvé, étuvée (10) 4
Ève (48) 24

évêque (48) 18
éviter (18) 7; (45) 12
excepté (34) 17
exception (13) 34, 35
excès (24) 15
exciter (41) 7
excuser (s') (12) 11
exemple (16) 3, 4
Expérience v. Science
expérience (8) 5
extrême, extrêmes (17) 10; (46) 25

fâcherie (30) 17
facile, facilement (36) 12; (48) 1, 28
faculté (21) 1
faillible (47) 29
faillir (33) 6
faim (38) 24, 26, 27
faire (1) 2, 3; (3) 5; (4) 15; (6) 11, 17,
  23, 26; (8) 14; (9) 30; (10) 12;
  (11) 13, 22; (12) 4, 12; (13) 7, 17;
  (14) 7, 20; (15) 27; (17) 4, 9; (18)
  2, 16, 17; (19) 20; (21) 8; (23) 3;
  (24) 1, 4–6; (25) 5, 19; (28) 13;
  (31) 9, 15; (33) 13; (34) 21; (36)
  31; (39) 3; (41) 1, 12; (42) 4; (43)
  2, 5, 13; (46) 14, 15; (47) 2, 20,
  39; (48) 17, 28, 33, 55
faire (se) (5) 6; (12) 27, 28; (22) 11;
  (23) 2; (27) 7
faiseur, faiseurs (1) 5
fait, faite (1) 1, 4, 6; (6) 10; (10) 3;
  (13) 19; (14) 1; (15) 8; (34) 27;
  (44) 3; (48) 22
falloir (1) 12; (2) 12, 19; (6) 3, 6;
  (7) 2; (10) 19–21; (11) 30; (13) 22,
  30; (16) 3, 9, 19; (18) 2, 7, 10, 13,
  14; (19) 13; (21) 1; (23) 5, 7; (25)
  32, 33; (33) 3, 10, 20; (34) 4, 10;
  (36) 22, 23; (38) 2, 16; (41) 8;

(42) 4; (43) 6; (47) 6, 7, 9, 10, 25,
  26, 35
familiarité (48) 52
famille (47) 10
fardeau (28) 1, 15; (33) 25
farine (14) 15; (23) 6
fatigue (25) 21
Fausseté–Hypocrisie (5)
faute, fautes (8) 14; (12) 12; (17) 8;
  (30) 14
faute de (12) 20; (18) 8, 12; (24) 19,
  20, 23
faux (5) 5
fêlé (4) 10
(la) Femme v. (l')Homme
femme, femmes (20) 9; (31) 2, 5,
  12–16; (44) 2
fenêtre (30) 23
fer (6) 6; (12) 21
fermer (10) 29; (15) 7
fermier (28) 12
fertil (9) 29
fesse, fesses (19) 16
fête (9) 18
feu (6) 27; (12) 1, 8; (46) 5
feuille, feuilles (21) 6
fiel (1) 31; (12) 15
fier (se) (36) 4; (39) 10
fil, fils (36) 12
fille (30) 24; (32) 1, 6
fils (32) 1, 4, 6, 7
Fin v. Commencement
fin (10) 2, 5, 10, 12, 13, 15, 23, 27;
  (12) 19; (34) 5; (45) 14; (48) 49
fin *(délicat)* (22) 7
fin *(rusé, malin)* (43) 23
finalement (24) 13
finir (2) 16; (10) 14; (20) 2
flambeau (15) 33
fleur, fleurs (5) 2; (24) 6; (40) 10;

(45) 9
flûte (25) 18
(la) Foi v. Dieu
foi (22) 18, 19
foin (14) 18; (27) 6
foire (43) 15
fois (1) 12; (3) 16; (10) 24; (14) 5, 6;
  (24) 11; (33) 23; (34) 9; (36) 5;
  (47) 37; (48) 21
fol (11) 18
folie (10) 11; (11) 9; (30) 26; (41) 15
Fond v. Apparence
fond (7) 6; (36) 34
fontaine (36) 22
force (1) 21; (11) 3; (17) 9, 11; (41) 1
forêt (24) 10
forger (42) 8
fort, forte (21) 11; (30) 9; (41) 16
fortifier (2) 20
fortune (19) 1–9, 11, 19; (21) 5; (31)
  12; (45) 13
fosse (12) 17; (13) 2
fou, fous (2) 6; (11) 5, 11–14, 16,
  22, 24–27; (15) 10; (19) 19; (36) 4;
  v. fol
foudre (45) 6
four (14) 5
fourmi (48) 19
fourrer (47) 4
foyer (32) 13
frapper (30) 23; (48) 1
frère, frères (6) 20; (40) 1; (41) 6;
  (48) 44
froid, froide (21) 10; (30) 13; (44) 17
front (30) 24
fructueuse (9) 27
fruit, fruits (3) 25; (16) 23; (36) 27
fuir (9) 3; (42) 4
fumée (12) 8; (31) 14
fumer (42) 2

fumier (21) 11; (28) 12
funeste (39) 15
fureur (37) 14
fuseau (48) 25
futur, futurs (36) 37

gagner (1) 24; (21) 4, 9
gai (9) 29; (35) 15
gain (6) 9
galeux (12) 14; (13) 4; (16) 17
galop, galoper (26) 4; (48) 15
garde (21) 8
garder (se) (5) 5, 7; (15) 29; (17) 3;
  (39) 18; (47) 38
gare (5) 9
gâter (12) 14–16; (38) 7
gauche (41) 14
génération (44) 11
gens (5) 7; (33) 2; (38) 6
Georges (24) 29
gésir (12) 29
gibet (45) 3
gît v. gésir
glaive, glaives (42) 8
gland (33) 21
glisser (1) 25
gloire (42) 5
gordien (10) 28
goulée (38) 18
gourmandise (38) 6
goût, goûts (13) 28–30; (38) 14
goutte, gouttes (12) 18; (24) 3, 22
gouverner (25) 33; (29) 5
grâce (30) 28
grain, grains (45) 2; (46) 22; (48) 50
graisser (13) 22
grand, grands (1) 4, 5, 9; (2) 13;
  (3) 2, 18; (9) 22, 25; (11) 10; (12)
  1; (13) 17; (19) 22; (24) 4; (25)
  17;

(29) 3, 4, 9; (31) 2, 15; (32) 2; (33) 21; (34) 14; (35) 17; (38) 5; (40) 5; (45) 8; (46) 6, 18, 21

gratter (se) (13) 4; (32) 15; (43) 2, 11

gré (38) 25

grief (20) 12

grincement, grincements (19) 29

gris (13) 13

grive, grives (24) 19

gros (3) 19; (29) 12

grossir (21) 12

grue (36) 32

guérir (se) (9) 6; (11) 16; (34) 26; (35) 6, 7, 12; (46) 19

Guerre et Paix (42)

guerre (25) 10; (34) 21; (42) 1, 6, 11

guetter (33) 8

gueule (6) 16

gueux (26) 4

guirlande (24) 6

habiller (4) 16; (48) 29

habit (4) 4, 11; (5) 1; (38) 8

habiter (47) 6

habitude (47) 32, 33

hache (43) 22

haie (13) 12; (40) 3

haine (2) 8; (41) 7

hanter (47) 1

hareng (12) 10

hargneux (41) 11

Hasard–Destin (45)

hâte (9) 22; (31) 7

hâter (se) (9) 20; (12) 24

hâtif (17) 13

haut, haute (13) 17; (14) 12; (31) 10; (46) 6; (47) 19

herbe (16) 13, 14; (38) 30; (48) 51

Hercule (41) 5

héritage (36) 2

heure (6) 9; (20) 5; (34) 15; v. (de) bonne heure

heureux (19) 10; (30) 18; (39) 11

hirondelle (24) 5

histoire (48) 48

hobereau, hobereaux (48) 24

(l')Homme et la Femme (31)

homme, hommes (1) 26; (4) 11; (13) 21; (17) 1, 15, 17; (19) 15; (22) 1; (24) 12; (25) 21, 31; (26) 6; (31) 1, 2, 8, 11, 14; (33) 16, 24; (34) 12, 21; (39) 17; (44) 2; (45) 1, 5; (47) 29

Honnêteté–Malhonnêteté (3)

honnêteté (3) 1

honneur, honneurs (3) 6; (13) 23; (17) 18; (34) 20; (48) 46, 47

honte (34) 20; (47) 11

hôpital (17) 17

Hospitalité v. Voisinage

hôte (15) 31; (40) 7, 8

hôtesse (12) 26

houlette (48) 54

hoyau, hoyaux (42) 8; (48) 24

huile (2) 1

humain (47) 30

humilier (25) 21

Hypocrisie v. Fausseté

ignorance (48) 44

ignorant (11) 15

ignorer (17) 2

Impossibilité (14)

impossible (14) 2; (21) 3

imprévu (45) 4

impur, impure (13) 14

Incertitude v. Certitude

inconnu (36) 13

inflexible (30) 12

ingrat, ingratitude (15) 15; (47) 39

injure, injures (41) 4
injuste (3) 6
injustice (17) 10
insatiable, insatiables (23) 9
instruire (s') (8) 3, 9
intention, intentions (23) 10
Inutilité (15)
inventer (11) 19
invention (18) 4

jalousie (30) 11, 12
jamais (1) 16, 19; (3) 7; (6) 14, 15, 22, 23; (8) 4; (9) 5, 11; (11) 16; (13) 10; (16) 1; (19) 23; (21) 8; (24) 7; (26) 6; (33) 6, 22; (39) 10; (41) 9; (45) 3; (47) 3, 20
jambe, jambes (2) 11; (11) 30
jardinier (48) 42
jeter (15) 26; (29) 9; (45) 15
jeu (1) 7; (15) 18; (18) 16; (30) 18; (47) 16–18
jeun (37) 6
jeune, jeunes (1) 7; (33) 8
Jeunesse–Vieillesse–Nouveauté (33)
jeunesse (33) 1, 3, 4, 6, 9, 10, 18
Joie–Chagrin (20)
joie (20) 1
joli, jolie (9) 20; (30) 24
jouet (28) 7
joueur, joueurs (13) 37
jour, jours (9) 9, 12, 13, 17, 18; (10) 30; (25) 25; (34) 16; (37) 8; (40) 7, 8; (46) 27
juge, juger (15) 5; (17) 7, 14
jus (19) 28; (48) 40
juste (3) 10; (22) 19
Justice v. Droit
justice (17) 10; (22) 3
justifier (48) 49

là (44) 10; (45) 5
labourer (18) 12
lâcher (1) 19; (12) 2
laine (15) 19; (18) 11; (46) 23
laisser (3) 18; (34,) 25; (47) 16, 26; (48) 42
lait (4) 14; (19) 12
lance (1) 28
lancer (47) 6
lancer *(mise-bas)* (44) 15
langue (1) 12, 25, 28, 31; (25) 3; (35) 9; (38) 21
larcin (3) 15
larder (19) 16
large (3) 21; (28) 5
larron, larrons (3) 9, 14, 15, 19, 20; (43) 15
laver (15) 12; (43) 1; (47) 10
léger (36) 29
légitime (17) 4
lendemain (6) 11; (48) 37
lentement (9) 20; (22) 7; (36) 15
lessive (15) 12
lettre (46) 7
lever (se) (12) 5; (14) 11; (27) 8; (41) 14
liberté (48) 7
lié, liés (43) 14
lien (16) 6; (33) 15
lieu, lieux (1) 22; (12) 13; (22) 4; (39) 4
lièvre, lièvres (12) 29; (15) 6, 13; (36) 30, 31; (44) 15; (45) 5
limite, limites (10) 16; (37) 13
linge (47) 10
lion (13) 5; (34) 7; (46) 3; (48) 34
lit (12) 4
livre, livres (8) 7
livre *(poids)* (19) 11
loger (9) 23

loi, lois (17) 1–6, 9; (18) 3, 5; (42) 7;
  (47) 33
loin (2) 17; (3) 1; (9) 19; (22) 15;
  (30) 21
loisir (31) 7
long, longue (9) 17; (11) 20; (13) 9;
  (23) 5; (26) 13; (29) 6; (34) 6;
  (38) 19
longtemps (4) 10; (33) 20
louer (se) (7) 5; (10) 30; (36) 3; (47)
  12
louis (25) 15
loup, loups (1) 32; (3) 22; (5) 6;
  (12) 28; (15) 29; (16) 7; (18) 16;
  (25) 31; (38) 24; (39) 17; (41) 12;
  (43) 6; (47) 41; (48) 31
luire (13) 7; (44) 6
lune (13) 7; (15) 11; (19) 4; (31) 12
lyre (15) 9

Mahomet (18) 18
mai (9) 29, 30; (40) 10
maigre (19) 14; (38) 28
maigrir (16) 18
main, mains (6) 5; (16) 2; (28) 13;
  (30) 13; (36) 24, 32; (41) 16; (43)
  1, 14
maintenant (36) 36
mais (13) 10
maison (13) 17; (20) 10; (24) 2; (31)
  10, 14; (40) 4; (47) 6, 7
maître, maîtres (7) 7; (8) 6; (14) 4;
  (28) 11, 13; (29) 8; (44) 18; (46) 5
majorité (11) 25
Mal v. Bien
mal (1) 15; (3) 7; (6) 17; (9) 23;
  (12) 23, 26; (13) 6, 26; (16) 15;
  (19) 21, 25; (20) 4; (26) 11; (33)
  15; (34) 10; (35) 8, 9, 14; (36) 30;
  (38) 12; (46) 20; v. maux

malade, malades (35) 3, 13, 16
Maladie v. Santé
maladie (33) 26; (35) 4
Malheur v. Bonheur
malheur, malheurs (7) 9; (13) 25;
  (19) 23, 24; (29) 13; (31) 2
malheureux (19) 15, 18, 20; (20) 5;
  (30) 18
Malhonnêteté v. Honnêteté
malin (3) 11
Mammon (22) 12
manche (3) 21; (11) 11
mander (23) 4
Manger et Boire (38)
manger (3) 24; (6) 21; (11) 14; (12)
  27, 28; (24) 19, 20; (28) 8; (29) 9,
  12; (38) 1, 2, 27; (39) 13; (43) 17;
  (47) 41; (48) 31, 42
manier (48) 24
manquer (45) 11
marâtre (32) 10
marchandise (7) 3
marché (31) 15; v. bon marché
marcher (48) 54
marée (9) 4
mari (31) 5
mariage, mariages (31) 4, 6
marier (se) (31) 7–9; (32) 6
marmite (1) 30
marotte (11) 27, 28
marron, marrons (6) 27
mars (9) 29
marteau (18) 15; (47) 9
Martin (12) 20; (39) 9
matin (6) 9; (20) 7; (40) 2
mauvais, mauvaise (1) 6, 7; (6) 14;
  (16) 11–14, 16, 23; (18) 16; (27)
  3, 6; (31) 13; (32) 14; (40) 5; (41)
  3; (46) 5, 14
maux (16) 9; (26) 1; (34) 26; (35) 17;

(32) 12; v. mal

méchant, méchante (16) 6; (17) 13; (31) 10; (33) 12

médaille (46) 11

médecin, médecins (9) 7; (15) 2; (35) 12, 15, 16; (47) 14

méfiance (36) 11

meilleur, meilleurs (9) 7; (27) 2; (28) 8; (35) 15; (36) 10

mélange (20) 1

membre (17) 15

même (2) 14; (3) 10; (6) 22; (7) 3; (8) 2; (12) 17; (28) 3; (35) 12; (43) 9, 24; (48) 21

mémoire (2) 12; (27) 2

menacer (4) 13

mendiant (6) 20

mener (10) 22; (33) 19

Mensonge v. Vérité

mensonge, mensonges (2) 11, 15; (46) 1

menteur, menteurs (2) 12–14, 18

mentir (2) 17

mépris (48) 52

mer (15) 34; (21) 7; (22) 17; (24) 22; (36) 3

mercier (7) 4; (28) 4

mère (6) 19; (8) 5; (12) 23; (18) 4; (23) 4; (25) 22; (26) 8; (32) 1; (36) 1

mériter (47) 13

merle, merles (24) 19

messager, messagers (30) 19

mesure, mesurer (13) 31; (22) 6; (43) 19; (48) 13

Métier v. Commerce

métier, métiers (7) 6–9; (47) 38

mettre (se) (5) 9; (33) 15; (47) 9; (48) 41

meule (22) 7

miel (1) 31; (12) 15, 27; (15) 8; (19) 12; (36) 7

(le) Mien et le Tien (28)

mieux (16) 8; (27) 12; (31) 9; (47) 36

mieux vaut... (1) 15, 25; (3) 2, 6, 13; (9) 11; (10) 10; (11) 3; (16) 4, 15; (18) 9, 11; (19) 11; (24) 18, 21; (27) 8; (32) 9; (34) 7, 20; (35) 6, 10; (36) 26, 32–37; (38) 8, 9; (39) 2, 7; (40) 1; (41) 3; (42) 1; (46) 2, 3; (48) 55

milieu (42) 7

mille (9) 25

mille *(mille pas)* (38) 15

mine (18) 16

Minerve (15) 32

mirer (47) 19

miroir (15) 4; (48) 36

Miscellanées (48)

misérable, misérables (31) 10; (37) 3

mœurs (9) 14; (16) 16; (17) 9; (44) 8; (48) 47

moi (45) 7; (46) 12

moindre (16) 9

moine (4) 4; (24) 23

moineau, moineaux (14) 16; (15) 28; (36) 32

moins (4) 14

moissonner (6) 2

moitié (10) 3

mondain, mondains (20) 2

(le) Monde et le Chez-soi (44)

monde (19) 17; (33) 6; (44) 2–4; (47) 26, 39; v. tout le monde

monnaie (43) 24

mont (44) 4

montagne, montagnes (18) 18; (22) 18; (45) 1; (46) 8, 18

montée (46) 6, 18

monter (44) 3; (46) 6

montrer (15) 33

monture (26) 4

moquer (se) (10) 21; (13) 33

morceau (38) 14

mordre (4) 9; (34) 22; (47) 17

morsure (38) 28

Mort v. Vie et Mort

mort (10) 30; (15) 2; (26) 3; (30) 9; (33) 8, 13–19, 26

mort, morts (23) 9; (30) 12; (34) 7, 10, 21, 24, 25; (48) 16

mot (1) 18; v. demi-mot

mouche, mouches (12) 27; (19) 14; (36) 7, 20; (39) 12; (48) 5, 17, 33

moucheron (46) 17

moudre (22) 7

mouiller (6) 24

moulin, moulins (14) 5; (15) 30; (28) 4, 14

mourir (16) 13; (19) 10; (20) 9; (33) 17; (34) 8, 9, 11, 20; (37) 6; (38) 30; (46) 19

mousse (13) 18

moutarde (15) 1

moutier (32) 13

mouton, moutons (18) 11; (43) 10

mouvant (19) 5

moyen, moyens (48) 49

muette, muettes (19) 22

munir (se) 23) 5

mur, murs (14) 20; (15) 24; (48) 3

mûr (6) 7

muraille (11) 29

Muses (6) 8

nager (5) 10; (15) 20

nageur, nageurs (45) 14

naître (8) 13; (11) 16; (32) 15, 16; (33) 11; (34) 11; v. né

nature (11) 21; (47) 32; (48) 14

naturel (16) 7; (48) 15

navire (21) 15

né (45) 3

néant (14) 13

Nécessité–Besoin (18)

nécessité (18) 3–5, 17

neigeuse (9) 27

nerf (25) 10

neuf (33) 27; (34) 23

nez (29) 9; (47) 4

ni... ni... (48) 45

nid (44) 12–14

noble (25) 24

noce (40) 6

Noël (9) 28

nœud (10) 28

noir (23) 3

nombre (24) 13

nombreux (25) 14

notaire (41) 6

notre (37) 8

noueux (43) 22

nourrir (5) 3, 4; (15) 14; (32) 3; (48) 46

nous (48) 53

Nouveauté v. Jeunesse

nouveau (17) 6; (30) 20; (33) 28; (36) 26; (44) 7

nouvelle, nouvelles (16) 11, 12

noyau, noyaux (29) 9; (38) 16

noyé, noyés (18) 1; (45) 14

noyer (se) (19) 15; (45) 3; (48) 2

nu (14) 3

nuage (21) 8

nuire (9) 21; (17) 13; (24) 8

nuit (9) 15, 17; (13) 13; (38) 17; (46) 27

nul, nuls (6) 4; (13) 24; (14) 2, 4; (17) 2; (19) 10; (24) 12, 25; (34) 18; (39) 16; (45) 12, 13

Paroles et Actes (1)
parole, paroles (1) 6, 7, 14, 19, 21, 22, 26, 29, 30; (2) 2; (25) 27; (36) 1
parti (10) 26; (43) 26
partout (7) 7; (44) 5
pas *(marche)* (10) 7, 8
passer (se) (9) 16; (13) 12; (19) 4; (25) 29; (33) 3; (35) 2; (43) 3
passion (20) 10
Patience v. Espoir
patience (37) 11–14
pâtir (29) 4
patrie (44) 10
patte (5) 7; (6) 24, 27
pauvre (3) 6; (25) 27
Pauvreté v. Richesse
pauvreté (20) 9; (25) 20–23; (30) 23
pavé (23) 10
payer (se) (19) 18; (27) 9; (30) 7; (43) 24; (47) 39; (48) 30
payeur (27) 3, 10
pays (13) 24; (29) 13; (44) 8
peau (13) 5; (15) 21; (26) 5; (28) 2
péché (16) 10
pécher (3) 10; (17) 15
pêcher (3) 26
pécheur (3) 4
paine (6) 4; (25) 21
pelletier (10) 23
pencher (13) 11
pendant (6) 6; (38) 30; (47) 16
pendre (3) 18, 19
pendu (47) 7
pénétrer (22) 13
pensée, pensées (36) 10; (48) 30
penser (3) 14; (12) 23; (32) 12; (45, 4, 5)
perdre (se) (9) 10; (12) 20; (15) 12 15; (16) 7; (18) 11; (19) 19; (24) 26; (26) 10; (36) 24; (38) 18; (44) 9

perdu (9) 5; (16) 1; (37) 6; (48) 9
père (14) 9; (32) 1, 3–5, 7
perfidie (16) 22
péril (42) 5
périlleux (17) 14
périr (18) 13; (42) 3; (48) 37
perle, perles (15) 26
permanent, permanente (29) 2
persévérer (10) 27
persister (47) 30
personne (9) 4; (39) 8; (48) 8
pesant (28) 1; (33) 25
peser (13) 9, 23
petit, petits (1) 9; (3) 18, 19; (9) 25; (12) 1; (13) 16; (24) 4; (29) 4, 12; (30) 16; (32) 2; (33) 21; (34) 14; (39) 5, 16; (45) 8; (46) 16, 21
Peu v. Beaucoup
peu; (1) 13, 20, 21 (10) 9; (12) 15; (24) 1, 14, 18, 27; (25) 24; (38) 15; (46) 22
peuple (29) 7; (48) 4
Peur v. Volonté
peur (3) 4; (21) 6, 12–14; (47) 19
philosophe (4) 7
Philosophie pratique v. Éthique
pied, pieds (1) 25; (5) 8; (22) 3; (25) 32; (34) 28; (35) 4; (41) 14; (42) 10
pierre, pierres (12) 18; (13) 18; (47) 6; (48) 21
pigeon (38) 13
piller v. entre-piller
pipe (48) 41
pire (1) 28; (4) 8; (11) 24; (13) 14; (35) 8; (39) 14; (47) 23, 24, 33
pitié (48) 55
place (13) 17; (44) 1, 9; (48) 43
plaid (31) 15
plaire (1) 11; (11) 27; (14) 9, 11; (48) 22

primer (17) 11
prince (4) 12; (29) 7
printemps (24) 5
pris, prise (10) 26; (13) 3; (19) 16;
  (48) 11
priser (7) 4
procès (17) 17; (41) 3
proche (28) 2; (40) 1
prodigue (32) 4
profiter (3) 7
profond, profonde (14) 10
promener (38) 15
prometteur (1) 9
promettre (1) 8
promis, promise (27) 11
prophète (5) 5; (13) 24
proposer (22) 1
propre (27) 12; (28) 4, 10, 15; (47) 11
provenir (33) 21
prudent (28) 6
public (2) 20
puce, puces (12) 5
puer (40) 8
puiser (15) 23
puits (47) 22
punition (17) 16

quarante (14) 3
quatorze (7) 9
quatre (31) 15; (33) 29; (36) 8, 14
quelque (12) 13; (13) 25; (22) 9; (47)
  19
quelquefois (11) 9; (45) 2
querelle, querelles (9) 6; (30) 17;
  (41) 7
quereller (se) (41) 8
quérir (33) 9
question, questions (11) 13; (34) 29
queue (1) 32; (46) 3; (48) 9
quitte (43) 21

quitter (21) 15

race, races (9) 25
racine (26) 1
raconter (20) 12
rage (48) 2
raison, raisons (11) 13; (31) 14; (38)
  20; (48) 10
rare, rarement (14) 8; (45) 4
rasé, rasée (10) 4
rassasier (se) (1) 29; (25) 26
rat, rats (21) 15; (43) 23
receleur (3) 13
recevoir (46) 4
Réciprocité v. Solidarité
récolter (6) 7; (12) 9
recommander (se) (7) 3
récompense (47) 40
reconcilié (39) 10
recueillir (6) 3
reculer (47) 28
redemander (47) 15
redresser (se) (14) 19
regarder (10) 24; (36) 5; (47) 8; (48)
  18
règle (13) 34, 35
régner (29) 1, 5
Relativité v. Conditionnellement
reluire (4) 2
remède, remèdes (14) 1; (34) 17;
  (35) 8, 17; (37) 12
remercier (15) 4
remplacer (30) 20
remplir (24) 3
renard, renards (3) 24; (5) 9; (6) 16;
  (10) 23; (13) 5
rencontrer (se) (11) 10; (45) 1
rendre (se) (8) 6; (11) 2; (12) 25;
  (19) 19; (34) 13; (38) 3; (47) 27
renommée (3) 2

subsister (44) 11
Suisse (24) 28
suivre (se) (20) 4
sujet (12) 25
supporter (20) 12
sûr, sûrement (22) 4; (36) 14, 15, 29
sûreté (36) 11
surplus (24) 16

table (28) 8; (39) 12
tablier (46) 24
tâcher (23) 4
tailler (25) 33
taire (se) (1) 2, 3, 15–17, 33; (11) 6;
    (25) 3
talonner (2) 10
tambour (25) 18
tambourin (15) 13; (37) 2
tant (que) (12) 19; (24) 9; (37) 1;
    (39) 11
tard (9) 11, 23; (47) 20
taverne (17) 17
tel, telle (1) 23; (5) 8; (6) 1; (10) 5;
    (11) 17; (12) 17; (13) 20; (17) 15;
    (20) 7, 8; (22) 16; (29) 7, 8; (32) 1;
    (34) 5; (38) 11; (44) 13; (46) 23
témoin, témoins (36) 6; (41) 6
tempête (12) 9; (46) 28
Temps (9)
temps (1) 33; (9) 1–8, 10, 14, 26;
    (13) 19; (15) 7; (17) 7; (20) 14;
    (29) 4; (31) 12; (34) 11; (36) 36;
    (47) 25; v. bon temps
tenace tenaces (21) 4
tendre, tendu (12) 2; (18) 10
tenir (se) (1) 8, 22; (14) 2; (16) 19;
    (18) 13; (23) 1; (36) 3, 33, 35;
    (38) 21
terre (19) 12; (36) 3, 18; (44) 11
tête, têtes (6) 18; (11) 30; (12) 22;

(15) 12, 24; (27) 5; (35) 14; (36) 8;
    (43) 12; (46) 3; (48) 41
(le) Tien v. le Mien
tirer (6) 27; (7) 10; (10) 19; (15) 28;
    (28) 14; (33) 29; (48) 14
tison (9) 28
toi (40) 4; (45) 7
toison (46) 21
tombe, tombeau (8) 12; (34) 28
tomber (6) 16, 25; (12) 17, 18, 22;
    (13) 1–3, 11; (19) 26, 27; (47) 19;
    (48) 43
tondu, tondue (22) 6; (46) 23
tonneau, tonneaux (46) 15
tort (17) 12; (19) 18
tôt (12) 2, 23; v. bientôt
toucher (se) (12) 3; (16) 20; (46) 25
toujours (3) 4, 16; (4) 12; (12) 10;
    (13) 11; (16) 11; (17) 5, 12; (19) 6,
    18; (20) 5; (25) 30; (30) 1; (41) 11;
    (44) 11, 15
tourment, tourments (32) 2
tourner (se) (1) 12; (37) 14
tous (3) 14; (4) 5, 6; (6) 19; (9) 18;
    (13) 2, 10, 13; (17) 1; (19) 16; (22)
    10; (25) 8; (26) 1, 8; (34) 13, 26;
    (39) 4; (42) 3; (44) 1, 2; (46) 1;
    (47) 31; (48) 23
tout, toute (1) 11, 17; (2) 9, 16, 21;
    (4) 2; (6) 25; (7) 7; (8) 3; (10) 1, 8,
    12, 14–16; (12) 14; (13) 27; (17)
    18; (18) 14; (22) 4; (24) 15, 21;
    (25) 3, 5, 7, 9; (26) 10; (29) 4;
    (30) 8, 10, 14, 15, 25; (33) 28;
    (34) 8, 17, 27; (37) 9, 11; (38)
    25–27; (47) 29; (48) 13, 32
tout le monde (2) 19; (13) 12; (14)
    9–11; (39) 8; (44) 6
tout rose (34) 3
toux (30) 5

322

verre (46) 28; (47) 6
verrou, verroux (25) 8
vert (48) 38, 40
vertu (18) 17; (47) 40
vêtu, vêtus (14) 3
viande (36) 30
vice, vices (6) 19; (25) 20; (26) 8
victoire (10) 20
vide, vides (38) 4; (46) 15
Vie et Mort (34)
vie, vies (10) 30; (20) 6; (34) 1–3, 5,
   6, 23; (37) 1
vieil (33) 15, 17
vieillard, vieillards (32) 9; (33) 23
vieille (18) 6; (33) 22, 24; (36) 26
Vieillesse v. Jeunesse
vieillesse (33) 4, 6, 9, 10, 18, 25, 26
vieux (1) 7; (8) 4; (11) 24; (14) 16;
   (23) 2; (33) 8, 13, 14, 20; (39) 4
vilain (25) 16; (38) 29; (44) 14
village (10) 21; (46) 2
vin (2) 5; (7) 2; (10) 19; (38) 20;
   (39) 4
vinaigre (36) 7
violent, violente (29) 2
vite (14) 8; (16) 14; (47) 37
vivant (34) 7
vivifier (46) 7

vivre (3) 6; (7) 7; (22) 19; (25) 25;
   (33) 9; (34) 4, 8, 12, 20; (37) 2, 6,
   10; (38) 2; (43) 26; (46) 19
voie (36) 26; (39) 7
voilà (34) 29
voile (18) 10
voir (1) 32; (13) 37; (24) 10; (36) 8,
   19; (37) 10; (47) 23; (48) 25
voisin (3) 24; (40) 1–5
Voisinage–Hospitalité (40)
voix (13) 20; (15) 16; (48) 4, 6
vol *(fraude)* (7) 13
voler (36) 32; (43) 9
voler *(dérober)* (3) 17
voleur, voleurs (2) 18; (3) 12, 13, 18
Volonté–Courage–Peur (21)
volonté (21) 1
vouloir (1) 11, 24; (4) 13; (5) 8; (6)
   21; (7) 12; (14) 11, 13; (18) 2;
   (19) 19; (21) 2; (22) 5, 9, 17; (31)
   13, 16; (32) 6; (33) 19; (35) 3;
   (42) 6; (47) 2, 23, 24; (48) 1, 2, 42
voyage (21) 8
voyager (8) 9
vrai (2) 19; (16) 11

yeux v. œil

zèle (22) 11

Deutsch

A (10) 18
Aas (12) 13
Abend (9) 17; (10) 30
Abendbrot (27) 8
abends (20) 7
aber (13) 10
abgehauen (5) 8
Abgrund (23) 9
abwarten (37) 9, 10
Abwesende (17) 12
Abwesenheit (30) 22
Achsel (5) 10
achten (12) 20
Acker (28) 12
Adam (48) 24
Adel (4) 15; (25) 24
Adler (12) 13; (32) 17; (48) 5
Advokat (47) 14
Affe (4) 12
alle (3) 14; (4) 5, 6; (6) 19; (9) 6, 18;
  (10) 22, 23; (11) 7, 25; (13) 3, 13;
  (14) 9–11; (17) 1; (18) 14; (19) 16;
  (22) 10; (25) 7, 9, 22; (26) 1, 8;
  (30) 14; (34) 13, 26; (35) 14; (39)
  11; (44) 1, 2; (47) 31; (48) 23, 32
allein (16) 15; (19) 23, (31) 1; (34) 12
allenthalben (44) 5
aller *(jeder)* (10) 6
Allerlei (48)
allerlei (33) 26
alles (1) 11; (4) 2; (9) 25; (10) 14–16;
  (21) 2, 4; (25) 5; (26) 10; (30) 8,
  15; (34) 3, 14, 27; (37) 11; (38) 25;
  (48) 13

allgemach (9) 19
allgemein (2) 20
allzu, allzuviel (24) 15, 16; (48) 52
also *(so)* (44) 3
Alt s. Jung
alt, Alte (8) 4; (14) 16; (18) 6; (23)
  4; (29) 2; (30) 1, 20; (33) 4, 7, 13,–
  17, 19, 20, 22–24; (36) 26; (39) 4
Altar (48) 29
Alter (11) 24; (33) 6, 9, 10, 18, 25, 26
Amboss (18) 15
Ameise (48) 19
anbefehlen (15) 29
anbellen (15) 11
anbinden (16) 6
Andacht (22) 13
ander(e) (2) 15; (6) 23; (9) 14; (11)
  23; (12) 16, 17; (13) 2, 32; (15) 17;
  (19) 24; (25) 4; (28) 6–8; (38) 12;
  (39) 17; (43) 1, 4, 10, 11, 16–18;
  (44) 3, 8, 11; (46) 10, 19; (47)2
  (48) 26, 29, 42
ändern (sich) (9) 8; (16) 7; (18) 7;
  (31) 12; (48) 47
anderthalb (3) 11
andichten (48) 2
Anfang–Ende (10)
Anfang (6) 19; (10) 1, 2, 5, 6, 10
anfangen (10) 3, 9
angreifen (12) 3
Angst s. Wille
anklagen (sich) (12) 11
Anmut (30) 28
annähen (13) 5

325

behüten (39) 18

beibringen (33) 15

Beichtvater (47) 14

beide (5) 10; (13) 2; (28) 13

Bein, Beine (2) 11; (11) 30; (21) 13; (41) 10, 14

beisammen (14) 8; (43) 9

Beispiel (16) 3, 4

beissen (4) 9; (34) 22; (47) 41

beizeiten (33) 11

bekannt (3) 22; (17) 8

bekommen (3) 15; (18) 8

bekümmern (48) 25

Beleidiger (41) 9

bellen (4) 9; (33) 14

belohnen (sich) (33) 9

bemitleidet (48) 55

bemühen (6) 23

benaschen (12) 27

beneidet (48) 55

bereuen (31) 7

Berg (9) 16; (18) 18; (22) 18; (44) 4; (45) 1; (46) 8, 18

berufen (24) 27

berühren (sich) (46) 25

Bescheid (2) 2

beschmieren (11) 29

beschmutzen (44) 14

beschweren (sich) (13) 10

Besen (33) 27

besorgen (6) 11

besser (24) 8; (31) 9; (36) 21

besser... als (denn)... (1) 15, 21, 25; (3) 2, 6, 13; (9) 11; (10) 10, 11; (11) 3; (16) 15; (18) 11; (19) 11; (24) 18, 20, 21; (27) 8; (32) 9; (34) 7, 20; (35) 6, 10; (36) 5, 26, 32, 33, 35–37; (39) 14; (40) 1; (41) 3; (42) 1; (46) 3; (48) 55

Besseres, besseres (16) 8; (27) 2

Besserung (47) 20

bestätigen (13) 35

beste, am besten (8) 5; (9) 7; (10) 17; (16) 3; (36) 10, 16; (37) 12; (38) 25, 26; (39) 4; (44) 16; (45) 14; (46) 16; (47) 16, 36

bestechen (30) 28

besudeln (sich) (12) 3

beten (22) 17

betrogen (3) 23; (12) 23; (36) 29

Betrüger (3) 23

betrunken (48) 23

Bett (12) 5; (27) 8; (38) 17

Bettelmann (7) 9; (45) 10

betten (sich) (12) 4

Bettler (26) 4; (37) 3

Beutel (7) 10; (25) 33; (28) 7

bevor (10) 20, 21; (15) 21

bewaffnet (42) 10

bezahlen (27) 9

biegen (18) 9

billig, billigste (7) 11

billig *(recht)* (48) 26

binden (12) 25

Bischof (46) 13

bitter (2) 7; (12) 15; (35) 5; (38) 13

blasen (4) 5; (14) 6; (47) 4

blass (16) 18

blau (45) 6

bleiben (3) 16; (4) 12; (11) 16, 17; (16) 1, 7; (21) 6, 8; (31) 9; (33) 20; (36) 1, 3; (44) 11, 15; (47) 38; (48) 43

blind, Blinder (13) 2, 8; (15) 4, 5; (19) 3; (30) 2; (35) 10; (45) 2; (47) 23

Blitz (45) 6

blöcken (38) 18

blühen (37) 8; (39) 12

Blume (24) 6; (40) 10

Blut (48) 6
Bock (15) 29
Boden (7) 6; (9) 29
Bogen (12) 2
Bohne (38) 27
Bohnenstroh (27) 6
Borgen–Schulden (27)
borgen, Borgen (27) 1, 4
Borger (27) 3
böse, Böse (3) 8; (13) 26; (16) 6, 12, 14, 15; (17) 13; (18) 16; (27) 6; (31) 14; (41) 11
Böses s. Gutes
Böses (19) 25; (41) 4
Bote (30) 19
Botschaft (16) 12
braten (43) 3
Bratwurst (38) 19
brauchen (7) 3; (15) 2; (17) 4; (18) 12
brechen (12) 19, 24; (18) 9; (19) 4, 15; (25) 8
Brei (12) 15; (38) 7
breit (3) 21
brennen (40) 4; (47) 4
bringen (2) 8, 16; (9) 12; (14) 14; (16) 12, 23; (40) 9; (48) 46
Brot (6) 9; (18) 8; (24) 21; (25) 30; (34) 12; (38) 11, 14; (43) 25, 26; (46) 19
Brücke (42) 4
Bruder (40) 1
Bruderzwist (41) 6
Brühe (38) 9
Brunnen (12) 19; (15) 7; (47) 22
brüten (32) 17
Bube (16) 10
Buch (8) 7
Buchstabe (46) 7
Bude (10) 29

Bühne (44) 2
bullern (13) 20
bunt (3) 22
Bürde (13) 23; (22) 5; (28) 15
bürgen (13) 6
Busch (46) 10; (47) 13
Busen (5) 3
Busse (29) 4

Charybdis (19) 27

Dach (31) 14; (36) 32
daheim (44) 16
dahinfahren (3) 8
Dank (13) 15
Decke (25) 32
decken (48) 29
Dein s. (das) Mein
denken (1) 17; (22) 1; (45) 5
dicker (48) 6
Dieb (3) 9, 14–16, 18–20; (43) 15
dienen (14) 4; (22) 12; (48) 12
Diener (46) 5
Dienst (16) 1
Ding (9) 1; (10) 1; (31) 14; (46) 11; (48) 32
dir (40) 4; (43) 2, 3; (47) 2; (48) 23
Dispens (34) 19
doppelt (36) 21; (47) 37
Dorf (46) 2
Dorn (20) 13
Dörnchen (33) 11
dort (14) 5; (19) 29
drankommen (37) 9
drei(e) (31) 13–15; (40) 8; (47) 31; (48) 32, 33
dreifach (36) 12
dreissig (47) 31
dreschen (15) 22
drinnen (14) 17

dritter, Dritter (41) 12; (47) 31

drohen (4) 13

drücken (47) 36; (48) 8

dumm, Dummheit (19) 7; (48) 44

düngen (28) 12

dünn (13) 11

durchfallen (36) 18

dürfen (19) 18; (21) 7; (27) 12; (47) 14, 15

Durst (43) 3

Ebbe (9) 4

Edelmann (48) 24

ehe, eher (1) 12; (32) 3; (36) 31

Ehe, Ehestand (31) 4, 6

Ehre (3) 6; (17) 18; (48) 46

ehren (25) 15

ehrlich (3) 1, 15; (34) 20

Ehrlichkeit–Unehrlichkeit (3)

Ei (4) 14; (6) 26; (19) 8; (26) 12; (32) 14; (36) 36; (42) 1

Eiche (10) 25

Eierkuchen (6) 26

Eifersucht (30) 11, 12

eigen (12) 22; (13) 31; (16) 22; (19) 28; (21) 14; (28) 1, 14, 15; (44) 14, 17; (47) 11

Eigenlob, Eigenruhm (47) 12

Eile, Eilesehr (12) 24; (31) 7

eilen (9) 20–22

ein (9) 13; (10) 25; (12) 15; (15) 1, 17; (16) 10; (24) 5, 6, 12, 23; (31) 15, 16; (32) 3; (34) 9, 28; (36) 33, 37; (41) 10; (43) 1, 4, 12, 13, 16–18; (44) 3; (46) 10, 19; (48) 26, 29

ein... aus (38) 20

einander (43) 15

einäugig, Einäugiger (13) 8; (35) 10

einbrocken (10) 19; (12) 12

einer *(jemand)* (17) 15; (22) 9

einerlei (43) 9

einfangen (1) 19

Einigkeit (41) 1

einmal (2) 14; (3) 16; (10) 15; (24) 11; (36) 5, 16; (37) 8; (48) 21

eins (9) 25

Einsatz (15) 18

einschlagen (6) 26

einstürzen (13) 3

Eintracht–Zwietracht (41)

Eintracht (41) 1, 2

Eis (48) 21

Eisen (6) 6; (12) 21

eisern (25) 8

Elefant (46) 26; (48) 17

Elle (26) 13

Eltern–Kinder (32)

Eltern (32) 9

empfangen (11) 26

Ende s. Anfang

Ende (6) 5; (10) 2, 5, 13–15, 27; (34) 26

endlich (37) 9

entblössen (48) 29

entgehen (45) 12

entschuldigen (sich) (12) 11

Erde (44) 1, 11

erfahren (47) 31

Erfahrung s. Wissen

Erfahrung (8) 5

erfinden (11) 19

erfinderisch (18) 4

erfochten (10) 20

erhalten (13) 19; (20) 6; (39) 5

erkennen (1) 27; (6) 12; (8) 2; (11) 21; (36) 27; (39) 1, 13; (48) 34, 35

erlegen (15) 21

ernähren (32) 3; (41) 2

Ernte, ernten (6) 2, 3; (12) 9

erregen (41) 7

ersäufen (45) 3

erspart (25) 17

erst (3) 17; (10) 24; (26) 3; (35) 3; (36) 23; (38) 8; (39) 13; (47) 22; (48) 9

erste, erster (10) 7; (12) 10; (42) 9; (46) 2

ertrinken (45) 3, 14

Ertrinkender (18) 1

Erwiderung s. Solidarität

erwiegen (21) 8

erzeugen (48) 52

erziehen (5) 4

erzwingen (30) 6

es geht (44) 3

es gibt (44) 7

Esel (4) 17; (11) 17; (13) 32; (14) 7, 15; (15) 8, 9, 19; (18) 12; (31) 13; (43) 11; (48) 20, 21

Eselskopf (15) 12

Essen und Trinken (38)

essen, Essen (6) 21; (11) 14; (12) 12; (23) 5; (29) 9; (38) 1, 2, 15–17; (39) 13; (43) 26; (48) 42; s. gegessen

Essig (36) 7

etwas (1) 9; (13) 26; (24) 18

Eule (15) 32; (32) 11

Eva (48) 24

ewig, ewiglich (21) 8; (44) 11

Faden (13) 11

fahren (13) 22

Fahrweg (48) 51

Fall (47) 22

fallen (8) 13; (10) 25; (12) 22; (13) 1, 2, 20; (15) 7; (19) 16, 26; (32) 7; (38) 18; (40) 7; (44) 3; (45) 15; (46) 6; (48) 43

fallenlassen (26) 11

falsch (5) 5; (39) 14

Falschheit–Heuchelei (5)

fangen (1) 7; (3) 12; (6) 15, 16; (14) 16; (15) 6, 13; (36) 7; (46) 10; (48) 5; s. gefangen

Farbe (15) 5

Fass (12) 10; (36) 7

fassen (1) 26; (19) 13; (26) 11

Fasten (37) 6

faul (1) 6; (12) 16; (33) 18; (33) 18; (38) 4; (48) 37

Faulheit s. Arbeit

Faulheit (6) 20

Feder, Federn (43) 9

fegen (47) 5

fehlen (9) 10

Fehler (8) 14; (13) 36

feilhaben (17) 14

fein (14) 15

Feind, Feindin (16) 8; (29) 11; (30) 22; (39) 14–16, 18; (42) 4

Feindschaft s. Freundschaft

Feindschaft (27) 7

Fell (41) 11

Fenster (30) 23

Ferne (2) 17; (40) 1

Ferse, Fersen (19) 24

fertig werden (39) 18

fett, Fett (1) 30; (19) 28; (26) 3; (28) 11; (41) 3

Feuer (6) 27; (12) 1, 8; (19) 26; (21) 10; (46) 5

finden (sich) (1) 22; (6) 14; (13) 26; (16) 17; (17) 5; (31) 3; (36) 25; (39) 11; (40) 6; (43) 5; (45) 2; (48) 1

Finger (19) 15

Fisch, Fische (6) 24; (15) 20; (24) 20; (29) 12; (36) 30, 31; (38) 10; (40) 8; (45) 5; (48) 45

fischen (3) 26

fix (4) 3

Fleisch (18) 8; (38) 9, 10; (48) 45

Fleiss s. Arbeit

Fleiss (6) 4

Fliege, Fliegen (12) 15, 27; (19) 14; (24) 19; (36) 7; (38) 28; (48) 5

fliegen (6) 25; (43) 9

fliehend (42) 4

fliessen (9) 16; (19) 12

Flöhe (12) 5

Flügel (9) 3

Fluss (40) 5

Flut (9) 4

Fohlen (33) 12

folgen (20) 2; (43) 10

fordern (24) 14

fortsein (12) 7

Frage, fragen (1) 23; (8) 10; (11) 13; (13) 7; (34) 29

Franziskanerärmel (3) 21

Frass (38) 6

Frauen (44) 2

Freiheit (31) 8; (48) 7

fremd, Fremder (13) 6; (19) 21; (25) 30; (28) 5

fressen (6) 24; (12) 21, 28; (18) 13; (24) 19; (29) 12; (43) 17; (48) 31

Freude–Sorge (20)

Freude (9) 25; (20) 1, 3, 4; (35) 15

Freund (11) 18; (25) 14; (39) 1, 2, 4, 6–8, 11, 13, 14, 18

Freundschaft–Feindschaft (39)

Freundschaft (27) 7; (39) 3, 5, 10, 12

Frieden s. Krieg

Frieden (42) 1, 6

Friedenspfeife (42) 2

frisch (40) 8

fröhlich (20) 6

Fromme (17) 13

Frucht (3) 25; (16) 23; (36) 27

früh (20) 7

Fuchs (3) 12, 24; (5) 9; (6) 16; (10) 23

Fuchsbalg (13) 5

Fuder (14) 18

führen (10) 22; (13) 2; (17) 17; (33) 19; (48) 21

Fülle (24) 17

füllen (9) 29

fünftes (15) 3

fünfzehn (7) 9

fünfzig (9) 25

Funken (12) 1

Furche (33) 13

Furcht (21) 12, 13; (30) 4

fürchten (sich) (21) 6, 7, 10, 14

Fürsten (29) 3

Fuss (1) 25; (28) 12; (34) 28; (35) 4; (48) 22

Futter (38) 18

Gabe (1) 21; (13) 15

gackern (4) 14; (32) 15

Galgen (45) 3

Galle (1) 31; (12) 15; (48) 19

Gans (5) 9; (31) 15; (33) 19

ganz (9) 30; (12) 14, 15; (26) 13; (39) 10; (44) 2

gar (24) 20, 21; (31) 10; (33) 22; (35) 10; (41) 6

Garten (40) 3

Gärtner (15) 29; (48) 42

Gasse (32) 13

Gast (28) 8; (40) 6–8

Gäste s. Nachbarn

Gasterei (11) 14

Gaul (36) 16; (47) 8

gebären, geboren (45) 3; (46) 8

geben (2) 2; (14) 15; (17) 3; (18) 11; (19) 9; (22) 5, 6; (23) 7; (24) 25;

(26) 13; (35) 13; (43) 25; (46) 4,
15; (47) 13, 15, 27, 37; (48) 29;
s. es gibt

Gebet (22) 13

Geblüt (4) 15

Geborenwerden (34) 11

Gebot (18) 5

gebrannt (21) 10

gebraten (6) 25

gebrüht (21) 10

gebügelt (33) 29

gebühren (17) 18

gebüst (17) 8

Gedächtnis (2) 12; (27) 2

Gedanke, Gedanken (36) 10; (41)
12; (48) 30

gedeihen (3) 7

gedenken (20) 12

Geduld s. Hoffnung

Geduld (37) 11-14

geduldig (2) 21; (27) 10

Gefahr, Gefährde (21) 7, 8

gefahrlos (42) 5

Gefährt (47) 34

gefallen (11) 27; (14) 11; (28) 9;
(33) 28; (44) 12

Gefälligkeit (43) 4

gefangen (13) 3

geflickt (39) 10

gegen (34) 17, 19; (43) 23

Gegensätze (46)

Gegensätze (46) 25

gegessen (38) 14

Gehängter (47) 7

gehen (4) 6, 10; (12) 5, 19; (15) 10;
(17) 11; (19) 21, 25; (27) 8; (30) 25;
(36) 13; (38) 12, 17; (39) 1; (44) 11;
(48) 23; s. es geht

gehören (41) 8; (43) 22

Gehorsam (42) 9

gehupft (48) 39

Geige (2) 10

Geiz s. Habsucht

Geiz (26) 6-8

Geizhals, Geiziger (26) 2, 3

Geld (9) 2; (11) 18; (24) 29; (25) 1-6,
9-13, 24, 31; (26) 2; (30) 15; (36)
23

Geldgier (26) 1

Gelegenheit (3) 9

gelehrter (11) 15

Gelehrter (11) 4

Gelenk, Gelenke (12) 25

geliebt (47) 13

Geliebte (30) 16

gelten (11) 23; (13) 24; (25) 4, 24;
(36) 6; (40) 4

Gemein, gemein (16) 15; (48) 52

gemeint (2) 4; (39) 15

Gemüt (4) 15

genäht (36) 21

genug (24) 17; (25) 28

genügen (25) 28

gepflastert (23) 10

gerade, gerademachen (14) 19; (33)
13

Gerät (6) 14

geraten (19) 27

Gerechter (22) 19

Gerechtigkeit s. Recht

gerettet (10) 27; (13) 21

gern (2) 17; (6) 24; (20) 7, 12; (25)
2; (32) 16; (43) 8, 9; (48) 27; s.
nicht gern

gesagt (1) 1; (2) 4

Gesang (48) 35

Geschäft (7) 1

geschehen, Geschehenes (14) 1; (45)
11

gescheit (11) 23

grösste, grösster (10) 8; (17) 10; (22)
    8; (25) 29; (26) 7; (31) 2; (35) 2
Grube (12) 17; (13) 2
grün (9) 28
Grund (26) 6; (38) 21
gründen (4) 8
grundlos (2) 20
Gulden (7) 8
Gunst (48) 46
gut (1) 7, 21, 22; (2) 12; (3) 2, 3;
    (4) 5; (6) 10, 14, 22; (7) 2, 3; (9)
    15, 27; (10) 2, 4, 14; (13) 22; (14)
    8, 11; (16) 1–3, 16, 19, 23; (17) 4;
    (18) 16; (22) 4; (23) 10; (27) 3;
    (28) 5–8; (33) 27; (35) 13; (39)
    2, 7; (40) 2, 3; (46) 5; (47) 34;
    (48) 32; s. nicht gut
Gut, Güter (3) 7; (15) 15; (27) 9
Gutes–Böses (16)
Gutes (13) 26, 27; (16) 8; (41) 4;
    (43) 5
guttun (9) 21

Haar (11) 20; (16) 7
haben (11) 30; (18) 12; (19) 15, 18;
    (23) 5; (24) 14, 25; (26) 9, 10; (31)
    16; (32) 11; (36) 23, 31, 33–35; (38)
    11; (42) 6
Habsucht–Geiz (26)
 hacken (48) 24
Hader (41) 7
Hahn (19) 8; (21) 11; (31) 10
halb (10) 3, 4; (13) 21; (17) 8; (19)
    20; (24) 21; (30) 24
Hals (12) 24
halten (1) 8, 9; (4) 10; (36) 20, 21
Hammer (18) 15; (25) 8
Hand (5) 8; (6) 5; (25) 25; (28) 13;
    (29) 6; (30) 13; (36) 24, 32; (43) 1;
    (47) 9

Handbreit (26) 13
Handel und Gewerbe (7)
Handschuh (6) 15
Handwerk (7) 6–10
hängen (3) 18, 19; (11) 8; (45) 3
Hans (31) 3
Harnisch (34) 18
harren, Harren (24) 23; (37) 5; (38)
    29
hart (14) 20; (18) 3; (30) 12
Hase (12) 29; (15) 6, 13; (24) 13;
    (44) 15
Hass (2) 8; (41) 7
hassen (16) 21
hauen (12) 6
Haufen (24) 3
Haupt (31) 5; (35) 14; (38) 29
Haus (30) 23; (31) 10, 14; (32) 13;
    (40) 4; (44) 18; (46) 23; (47) 7
Häuschen (20) 10
heftig (41) 6
Hehler (3) 13
heilen (9) 6; (35) 6, 7, 11
heilig, Heiliger (3) 10; (4) 6; (5) 1;
    (32) 5; (48) 33
heiligen (48) 49
Heim s. Welt
heimkommen (9) 22
heiraten (31) 7, 9
heiss (6) 6
helfen (sich) (1) 24; (14) 13; (22) 2;
    (35) 12; (48) 28
Hemd (28) 2
Hengst (33) 12; (38) 30
Henne (26) 12; (31) 10; (32) 15;
    (45) 2
heraus (15) 17
herausnehmen (14) 17
herb (25) 30
Herd (44) 17

innen (4) 3
innerlich (35) 5
irren, Irren (47) 29, 30
Irrtum (47) 30

Jacke (48) 38
jagen (15) 6; (26) 4
Jäger (4) 5
Jahr, Jahre (8) 7; (9) 12, 25, 27, 30;
  (20) 5
Jahrmarkt (31) 15; (43) 15
je... desto... (11) 15; (24) 8; (46) 18
je... je... (12) 26; (22) 15; (26) 9;
  (32) 8
jeder (4) 7; (7) 4, 5; (9) 1; (10) 1;
  (11) 27, 28; (13) 1, 12, 28 (16) 17;
  (19) 1, 17; (20) 10; (22) 10; (28)
  3, 4, 9, 10, 14; (31) 3; (44) 12, 18;
  (46) 11; (47) 5, 36; (48) 8, 10, 50
jedermann (11) 11; (39) 8; (44) 6
jeglicher (7) 7; (28) 15
jemand (42) 2; (43) 24; (48) 54
jetzt (32) 9
Juch! (10) 21
jucken (13) 4
Jugend (8) 12; (33) 1, 3, 6, 10, 18
Jugendfleiss (33) 9
Jung–Alt–Neu (33)
jung (33) 4, 19, 20
Junge (32) 11, 12; (33) 7, 8, 16

Käfig (15) 14
Kaiser (15) 25; (24) 26; (47) 27; (48)
  18
Kalb (3) 17; (26) 14; (33) 22
kälbern (19) 8
Kalender (34) 16
kalt (21) 10; (30) 13
Kamele (46) 17
Kampf (34) 1

kämpfen (15) 30
Kanonen (15) 28
Kappe (11) 27
Karren (4) 10
Kastanien (6) 27
Katze (5) 1, 7; (6) 15, 24; (7) 14;
  (12) 7; (13) 13; (20) 11; (21) 10;
  (34) 23; (41) 13; (48) 18
Katzengebet (15) 10
Katzenkinder (32) 16
Katzenpfoten (6) 27
kaufen (7) 12, 14
Kaufmann (45) 10
kehren (33) 27
Kehrseite (46) 11
Keil (43) 18, 22
kein(er) (15) 6; (24) 5, 6, 12, 21, 28;
  (47) 23
keinmal (24) 11
Keller (9) 29
kennen (18) 5; (25) 16
Kern (38) 16
Kerze (23) 8
Kessel (13) 33
Kette (48) 8
Kinder s. Eltern
Kind, Kinder (2) 6; (4) 18; (15) 7;
  (21) 10; (29) 13; (32) 2, 3, 8, 9, 13;
  (33) 2, 23
Kirche (4) 6; (22) 14, 15
Kirchweih (28) 8
Kirschen (29) 9
Kissen (22) 11
klammern (sich) (18) 1
Klang (30) 16
klattrig (33) 12
Klauen (5) 1; (48) 34
Kleid, Kleider (4) 11; (13) 19; (14)
  15
kleiden (4) 12

Kleie (23) 6; (48) 50

klein, kleiner (3) 18, 19; (21) 1; (13) 16; (14) 20; (16) 9; (24) 4, 20; (29) 12; (32) 2; (39) 5, 16; (44) 13; (46) 3, 16

kleinmachen (48) 52

klopfen (31) 13; (46) 10

Klotz (43) 22

klug (2) 9; (8) 10; (11) 1, 2, 7 9

Klügere(r) (11) 6

knacken (38) 16

knarren, knarrig (4) 10; (46) 14

Knecht (27) 4; (29) 8, 11; (46) 3

Knoten (10) 28

Koch (38) 7, 25

kochen (28) 6

Kohl (1) 30; (48) 42

kommen (1) 32; (7) 8; (9) 9, 15, 19, 23, 24, 26; (11) 17; (15) 1; (18) 18; (19) 23, 25, 26; (20) 3; (22) 3; (25) 13; (30) 23; (32) 15; (33) 26; (34) 15; (35) 4; (38) 1, 30; (44) 11; (45) 4; (46) 23; (47) 21, 31

kommen (um etwas) (31) 8

König (13) 8; (29) 5, 6, 13

können (6) 11, 23; (7) 9; (11) 12, 13; (14) 1–6, 9, 10, 17, 19; (16) 23; (18) 2, 7; (20) 8; (22) 12, 17, 18; (24) 25; (30) 15; (32) 6; (33) 6, 8, 15; (34) 9, 13; (36) 22; (37) 9; (45) 12; (46) 6, 9

Kopf (2) 10; (11) 30; (15) 24; (36) 8

Korn, Körner (24) 3; (45) 2; (46) 22; (48) 50

Köter (33) 15

Kragen (38) 8

Krähe (43) 16

krähen (31) 10

Krämer (7) 4

krank, Kranker (23) 2; (35) 3, 13, 14, 16

kränken (1) 17

Krankheit s. Gesundheit

Krankheit (35) 4, 8

Kranz (7) 2; (24) 6

kratzen (sich) (5) 7; (13) 4

krauen (43) 11

Kraut (16) 14; (34) 17

kreissend (46) 8

Kreuz, Kreuzchen (19) 17; (20) 10; (23) 1

Kreuzer (24) 28

Krieg und Frieden (42)

Krieg (25) 10; (34) 21; (42) 1, 6 7, 11

kriegen *(erhalten)* (36) 33

krönen (10) 13

Krug (12) 19

krumm (14) 19

Küche (28) 6

Küchlein (36) 36

Kuh (3) 17; (17) 17; (33) 22; (48) 9

kühl (9) 29; (47) 13

kühn, Kühner (21) 3, 5, 11; (41) 5

kümmern (15) 11

kundwerden (47) 31

künftig (32) 9

Kunst (1) 20; (14) 10; (18) 14; (25) 22; (34) 6; (48) 46

Kunststück (33) 15

Kürschner (10) 23

kurz (2) 2, 11; (11) 20; (16) 6; (22) 13; (34) 6; (38) 19; (39) 3; (41) 15

küssen (4) 18; (5) 8

Kutte (4) 4

lachen, Lachen (10) 17; (11) 21; (20) 2, 7, 8, 14; (31) 16; (41) 12; (48) 16

laden *(einladen)* (28) 8

Lager (3) 24

Lamm (12) 28

loben (6) 13; (7) 4, 5; (10) 30; (36) 3

Loch (17) 5; (48) 11

Löffel (23) 5; (36) 7

Lohn (6) 1; (47) 39

lohnen (15) 18

los sein (48) 2

löschen *(stillen)* (43) 3

Lot (39) 1

Löwe (34) 7; (48) 34

Löwenhaut (13) 5

Luftschlösser (15) 27

Lüge s. Wahrheit

Lüge (2) 11, 15

lügen (2) 13, 14, 17, 18

Lügner (2) 12

lustig (27) 10

machen (1) 30; (3) 9; (4) 4, 11; (6) 5, 7; (8) 6, 9; (11) 14, 22; (12) 15; (13) 1; (14))1, 9; (15) 31; (16) 10; (18) 4, 16, 17; (19; (20) 11; (21) 13; (24) 1–6; (25) 5; (27) 1, 7, 11; (28) 11; (30) 20; (31) 15; (33) 13; (34) 13, 14, 21, 26; (37) 3, 5; (38) 4, 10, 27, 29; (41) 1; (46) 7; (48) 17, 22

machen (sich) (12) 27, 28

Macht s. Herrschaft

Macht (8) 1; (41) 1, 16; (47) 33

Magen (38) 5, 8

mager (19) 14; (41) 3

mahlen (9) 24; (14) 20; (22) 7

Mahnen (27) 7

Mai (9) 29, 30; (40) 10

mal (16) 17

malen (23) 3

Malter (33) 25

Mammon (22) 12

mancher (3) 21; (36) 24; (37) 5; (38) 11; (46) 23

Mann und Weib (31)

Mann (1) 26, 27; (17) 7; (13) 21; (24) 12; (25) 31; (31) 2, 5, 8, 14; (33) 24; (34) 21; (41) 5; (44) 2

März (9) 29

Mass (43) 19; (48) 13

Mässigkeit (35) 15

Massstab (13) 31

Maul (1) 15, 24; (6) 25; (36) 20; (38) 18; (47) 8

Maus (6) 15; (12) 7; (38) 13; (48) 11

mausen (32) 16

Mäuslein (46) 8

Medaille (46) 11

Meer (15) 34; (21) 7; (24) 22

Mehl (23) 6; (38) 13; (48) 50

mehr (8) 7; (11) 13; (13) 37; (16) 4, 10; (24) 8, 14, 17; (26) 9; (28) 13; (36) 6, 7, 9; (38) 6; (39) 2; (46) 16

mehren (48) 46

(das) Mein und Dein (28)

mein, meine (39) 6, 9

meinen (3) 14; (4) 17; s. gemeint

meist (19) 7

Meister (6) 12, 13; (8) 6, 13; (13) 17; (25) 22

Mensch (20) 9; (22) 1; (31) 1, 11; (34) 9, 12; (37) 1; (39) 17; (45) 1

menschlich (47) 29, 30

merken (48) 9

messen (13) 31; (36) 5

Messer (42) 11

Miene (18) 16

Mietsgaul (27) 12

Milch (19) 12

mir (43) 2, 3; (45) 7; (46) 12

Mist (21) 11

mitbringen (9) 17

Mitgift (30) 24

Mittel (48) 49

DEUTSCH

mitten (36) 18
mögen (9) 12; (14) 7
möglich (21) 2
Mönch (4) 4; (23) 2
Mond (15) 11
Moos (13) 18
morgen (6) 11; (20) 8; (36) 17, 36,
  37; (45) 7–10
Morgenrot (6) 9
Morgenstunde (6) 8
Mücke (36) 20; (46) 17; (48) 17
müde (27) 12
Mühle (22) 7; (28) 4, 14
Mund (1) 10; (6) 8; (15) 8; (25) 25;
  (35) 5; (36) 24; (38) 21; (47) 31
munkeln (2) 19
Münze (43) 24
Musik (37) 2
Muss (18) 3
müssen (2) 12; (3) 12; (6) 6, 7, 26;
  (10) 18, 19; (11) 30; (12) 12; (13)
  5; (16) 6, 9; (17) 3; (18) 2, 7, 8,
  10, 18; (19) 13; (23) 5; (24) 14; (25)
  32, 33; (30) 3; (31) 13; (33) 3, 8;
  (34) 8; (38) 16; (39) 13; (42) 6;
  (43) 6; (47) 25, 26
Müssiggang (6) 18, 19
Mut s. Wille
Mutter (4) 18; (32) 1; (36) 11

nach uns (48) 53
Nachbarn–Gäste (40)
Nachbar, Nachbarn (40) 1–5
nachgeben (11) 6
Nachrichten (16) 11
Nachsehen haben (9) 23
nächste, Nächste (22) 8; (28) 3
Nacht (9) 15; (13) 13; (46) 27
Nackter (14) 3
Nadeln (48) 56

Nagel (12) 20
Nähe (40) 1
näher (22) 15; (18) 2
nähren (5) 3; (7) 7; (15) 14
Name (3) 2
Narr (2) 6; (11) 5, 11–14, 16, 18,
  21–23, 25–27; (19) 19; (24) 23;
  (37) 5
Narrenhände (11) 29
närrisch (38) 29
nass (9) 29
Natur (47) 31; (48) 14, 15
necken (sich) (30) 16
nehmen (22) 9; (26) 13; (27) 6; (31)
  8; (42) 3; (46) 4; (48) 29
Neid (16) 18
nennen (1) 32; (43) 25
Nessel (11) 9
Nest, Nestlein (44) 12–14
Neu s. Jung
neu, Neues (17) 6; (30) 17,20; (33)
  15, 27, 28; (36) 26; (44) 7
neukommen (33) 28
neun (34) 23
nicht gern (38) 3
nicht gut (3) 20; (29) 9; (31) 1; (36)
  30; (39) 15
nicht lange (29) 2; (36) 2
Nichts s. Viel
nichts, Nichts (2) 19; (13) 24, 26;
  (14) 17; (17) 7; (21) 3; (24) 9, 18,
  20, 24–26; (25) 19; (26) 10; (34)
  10; (44) 7; (47) 14
Nichtsein (34) 29
Nichtstun (6) 17
niedrig (13) 12
nie(mals) (1) 16; (2) 3; (6) 14, 23;
  (9) 5, 11; (33) 6; (40) 7; (41) 9;
  (47) 20
niemand (1) 17; (3) 5; (8) 4; (9) 4;

340

reden (1) 3, 5, 13, 14, 16, 33; (2) 13; (25) 3, 4; (34) 10

Regel (13) 34, 35

Regen (9) 26; (19) 26

regieren (25) 6; (29) 2, 5, 10

reich, Reicher (3) 6; (25) 14, 16; (34) 14; (37) 3

reichen (13) 5; (46) 9

Reichtum–Armut (25)

Reichtum (25) 29; (35) 2; (39) 11

reif (48) 37

Reise (8) 9; (47) 34

reissen (13) 11

Reitpferd (14) 7

Relativität s. Bedingtheit

rennen (1) 32; (15) 24

Reue (17) 14

Reuse(n) (45) 5

richten (sich) (17) 7; (47) 25

riechen (12) 10

Riemen (28) 5

Ritt (19) 25

Ritter (26) 4

Rock (4) 16; (28) 2

Roland (41) 5

rollen, rollend (13) 18; (25) 2

Rom (9) 13; (10) 22; (11) 17; (34) 19; (43) 7

Rose (20) 13

rosig (34) 3

Rost, rosten (12) 21; (30) 1

rot (45) 9

rücken (16) 19

Rückgang (47) 28

Ruf (2) 20

rufen (10) 21; (22) 14; (36) 31

Ruhe (33) 10; (35) 15

Ruhebank (6) 18

Ruhekissen (3) 3

ruhen (6) 10; (38) 15

ruhig (40) 2

ruhmlos (42) 5

rund (25) 2

rüsten (42) 6

Rute (32) 8

rutschen (22) 11

Saat (6) 2

Sache (10) 10; (14) 19; (16) 20

Sack (4) 17; (7) 14; (14) 17; (24) 16; (28) 4

Säckel (31) 16

säen (6) 3; (12) 9

sagen (1) 11; (2) 6, 9; (10) 18; (36) 22; (47) 1; (48) 23; s. gesagt

Sälblein (46) 16

Salz (39) 13

sammeln (sich) (12) 13

Sammet (4) 12

Sand (41) 4

sanft (3) 3; (33) 10

satt, Satter (1) 29; (25) 26; (38) 13

Sattel (46) 24

sauer (38) 27

schaden (1) 16; (17) 13; (24) 7

Schaden (11) 2; (13) 25; (19) 18

Schaf, Schafe (12) 14; (15) 29; (16) 17; (18) 11; (22) 6; (38) 18; (43) 10; (48) 31

schaffen (6) 9; (28) 13

Schafspelz (5) 6

Schafszähne (47) 17

Schall (46) 15

Schande (3) 6; (47) 11

schändlich (34) 20

scharf, schärfer (1) 28; (32) 7; (38) 28

Schatten (21) 14; (47) 13

Schatz (25) 19

schätzen (35) 3; (47) 22

Schwanz (48) 9

schwarz (16) 17; (23) 3

schweben (37) 3

schweigen (1) 14–18, 20, 24, 33; (25) 3; (31) 10; (42) 7

Schwein (15) 26; (26) 3

Schweizer (24) 28

Schwelle (10) 8

schwer (10) 6, 7; (12) 26; (28) 1; (33) 10, 25

Schwert (1) 28; (38) 6; (42) 3, 8

schwimmen (15) 20

Schwimmer (45) 14

schwinden (39) 11

schwören (32) 11

sechs (24) 23

See (36) 3

Seele (43) 12; (48) 36

Segel (18) 10

sehen (5) 8; (13) 37; (24) 10; (36) 9, 19; (47) 8, 23; (48) 25

sehr (9) 22

seihen (46) 17

sein, Sein (14) 5; (16) 7; (24) 26; (25) 12; (31) 1; (33) 21–23; (34) 29; (36) 17; (43) 12; (45) 11; (46) 12; (47) 1

Seine (7) 5; (19) 9; (28) 9

seitdem (9) 16

Seiten (46) 11

selber (16) 18; (35) 12

selbst (3) 4; (6) 22, 23; (8) 2; (12) 17; (17) 3; (22) 2, 14; (23) 7; (28) 3; (47) 40

selig, seliger (20) 5; (46) 4

selten, seltener (1) 9; (2) 20; (14) 8, 20; (19) 23; (29) 2; (30) 26; (40) 7; (41) 10

setzen (sich) (15) 29; (19) 14

sich, für sich (22) 10; (28) 3

sicher (22) 7; (36) 15

Sieb (14) 15; (15) 23

sieben (11) 13; (24) 23; (48) 14

sieden (39) 12

Sieg, siegen (10) 20; (42) 5

Silber (1) 14; (3) 2; (48) 7

singen (10) 20; (28) 10; (33) 7; (43) 26

sinkend (21) 15

Sinn (30) 21; (35) 1; (36) 8

Sintflut (48) 53

Sitte, Sitten (9) 14; (16) 16; (44) 8; (48) 47

Sittenlehre–Lebensweisheit (47)

sitzen (4) 15; (16) 19; (36) 18; (47) 6; (48) 20, 56

Sohn (32) 1, 4–6

solange (6) 6; (8) 3; (37) 1

Soldatenpflicht (42) 9

Solidarität–Erwiderung (43)

sollen (15) 4, 5, 8, 9; (16) 5; (19) 15; (24) 23; (26) 10; (28) 15; (31) 11; (33) 17; (34) 10; (36) 31; (38) 15; (42) 3; (45) 3, 11; (47) 6, 7, 10, 16–18, 35

Sommer (24) 5

Sonne (2) 16; (6) 7; (13) 7; (44) 5–7

Sonnenschein (9) 26

Sonntag (9) 18

Sorge s. Freude

Sorge (20) 11; (25) 1; (27) 1; (32) 2

sorgen (14) 12; (19) 18

soviel (29) 11; (36) 8

Späne (12) 6

sparen (36) 34

Sparer (32) 4

spät (9) 11, 23; (15) 1; (47) 20

Spatz (14) 16; (15) 28

Speichel (12) 22

speien (12) 22

Sperling (36) 32

Spiegel (15) 4; (48) 36

Spiel (15) 18; (18) 16; (30) 18

Spieler (13) 37; (44) 2

spinnen (48) 24

spitzen (sich) (33) 11

Splitter (11) 28

Spott (19) 18

sprechen (1) 12, 19; (2) 14; (47) 7

sprengen (12) 2

Spreu (14) 16; (48) 50

springen (36) 28

Stadt (46) 2

Stamm (32) 7

stark (30) 9; (41) 1

Stärke (11) 3; (25) 10

stärker (1) 2; (48) 14

Staub (34) 27

stechen (38) 28

stecken (27) 5

Stecknadel (14) 18

stehen, stehend (13) 14; (34) 28; (46) 6

stehlen (2) 18; (3) 14, 16, 17, 20

Stehler (3) 13

steigen (44) 3

Stein (12) 18; (13) 18; (14) 20; (41) 4; (47) 6

Stengel (29) 9

Sterben s. Leben

sterben, Sterben (18) 13; (33) 8; (34) 5, 8, 9, 11, 20; (37) 6; (38) 6, 30

Stern (13) 7

steter (12) 18

Stich (13) 19

Stiefmutter (32) 10

still (4) 8

Stimme (15) 16; (48) 4, 6

stinken (13) 14; (25) 11; (47) 12

Stock (4) 16; (29) 10; (48) 1

stolpern (36) 16, 28

Stolz (48) 44

Strafe, strafen (17) 2, 15, 16; (22) 9

Strasse (36) 26

Sträuchlein (33) 21

strecken (sich) (25) 32

Streich (10) 25

streiten, Streiten (13) 30; (15) 25; (41) 8

streng, strengste (17) 10; (29) 2

Strick (47) 7

Stroh (15) 22; (46) 22

Strohhalm (18) 1; (36) 28

Strom (24) 4

studieren (38) 3

Stuhl (36) 18; (40) 6

stumm (19) 22

Stunde (20) 5

Sturm (12) 9; (46) 28

suchen (14) 18; (15) 19; (36) 25; (48) 20

Sünde (17) 16; (25) 20; (29) 4

sündigen (17) 15

Suppe (10) 19;)(36) 24

süss (3) 25; (30) 16; (37) 3; (38) 27

Szylla (19) 27

Tag, Tage (2) 1, 16; (9) 12, 13, 17, 18; (10) 30; (40) 8; (46) 27

Tal (45) 1; (46) 18

Taler (24) 2; (25) 15

tanzen (12) 7; (19) 2; (37) 2; (48) 54

Tasche (36) 23

Tat s. Wort

Tat (1) 6; (10) 24, 26; (11) 7; (33) 16

Tatsache (1) 2

taub (47) 24

Taube (6) 25; (32) 17; (36) 32

Tausch (7) 13

tausend (7) 8; (21) 12; (38) 15

Tee (37) 10

teilen (29) 1; s. geteilt

teuer, teuerste (7) 11; (38) 9

Teufel–Hölle (23)

Teufel (6) 18; (23) 1–8; (24) 19; (32) 5, 10

teuflisch (47) 30

tief, tiefer (4) 8; (22) 13; (46) 6, 18

Tisch (11) 29; (24) 20; (36) 30

Tochter (32) 1, 6

Tod (2) 3; (15) 2; (19) 10; (24) 13; (26) 3, 4; (34) 9, 13–19, 26; (46) 19

Tollwut (48) 2

Tonne (46) 15

Topf (4) 10; (13) 16; (39) 12

Töpfchen (46) 16

Tor *(Narr)* (11) 26

Tor *(grosse Tür)* (25) 7, 8

Torheit s. Weisheit

Torheit (11) 24

tot, Toter (34) 7, 10, 21, 22, 24, 25; (45) 9

töten (20) 11; (46) 7

Totenreich (30) 12

totmachen (4) 13

traben (18) 6

tragen (4) 7; (5) 10; (13) 9, 26; (15) 32–34; (19) 17; (28) 4, 15; (46) 20

Tränke (33) 19

trau-schau-wem! (36) 4

trauern (35) 14

Traufe (19) 26

Traum (34) 2; (46) 1

treffen (sich) (11) 10

treiben (31) 14; (38) 24

treten (19) 24

Trinken s. Essen

trinken (14) 14; (36) 22; (37) 10

triumphieren (42) 5

trocken (9) 29; (33) 5; (47) 22

Trommel (15) 12

Tropfen (12) 18; (24) 22

trüb (3) 26

trügen (4) 1

trunken (38) 21

Tuch (14) 15; (43) 13

Tugend (18) 17; (33) 1; (47) 40

tun (1) 3, 5; (3) 5; (6) 17, 23; (10) 12; (15) 15; (16) 4, 18; (31) 9; (38) 15; (43) 5, 7; (47) 2; s. getan

Tür (3) 10; (25) 9; (30) 23; (35) 15; (47) 5, 9

übel, Übel (13) 6; (15) 13; (16) 9; (26) 1, 8; (31) 10, 14; (35) 17; s. Übles

überall (40) 9

übereinkommen (41) 10

übergehen (1) 10

überkochen (13) 16

überlegen (1) 12

überspannen (12) 2

überspringen (13) 12

überstanden (20) 12

Übertretung (30) 14

überwinden (21) 4; (30) 8; (37) 11; (48) 15

Übles (6) 17; (34) 10

Übung (8) 6

umgehen (19) 6; (47) 1

umkommen (42) 3

umsonst (15) 12

unbegonnen (10) 11

Undank (47) 39

Undankbarer (15) 15

Unehrlichkeit s. Ehrlichkeit

Unfall (11) 5

ungebeten (40) 6; (47) 3

unbefangen (36) 30

ungeschehen (14) 1

ungesund (24) 15

ungewiss (36) 13
Ungewissheit s. Gewissheit
Unglück s. Glück
Unglück (7) 9; (13) 26, 27; (19) 15,
 23, 24; (30) 18; (31) 2; (37) 12;
 (46) 19
Unkenntnis (17) 2
Unkraut (16) 13
unmöglich (21) 3
Unmögliches (14)
Unmögliches (14) 2
Unnötiges (7) 12
unrecht, Unrecht (3) 7; (17) 10, 12
unser (34) 1; (37) 8
Unsinnigkeit (41) 15
Unterfutter (32) 10
Unterschied (46) 27
Untreue (16) 22
unverhofft (45) 4
unverloren (16) 1
unvollendet (10) 11
Ursache und Wirkung (12)
Urteil, urteilen (15) 5; (17) 14

Vater (32) 1, 3–5; (43) 25
Vaterland (13) 24; (44) 10
verachten (39) 16; (47) 13
Verachtung (48) 52
verbergen (30) 5
verborgen (25) 19
verbessern (27) 9
verboten (3) 25
verbrannt (1) 15
verderben (12) 15; (16) 13, 16; (20)
 9; (34) 20; (38) 7
verdient (25) 17
verdrängen (30) 20
vererben (sich) (36) 2
verfliegen (36) 1
verführen (3) 10

vergänglich (30) 27
vergehen (30) 28
vergessen (30) 20; (33) 22; (34) 24;
 (36) 5; (38) 14
Vergeuder (32) 4
Vergleich (48) 10
Vergleich *(Kompromiss)* (41) 3
verharren (47) 30
verheiraten (32) 6
verhindert (38) 17
verkaufen (7) 12; (15) 21
verkehrter (11) 15
verlacht (41) 16
verlangen (14) 2
verlassen (sich) (21) 15; (29) 3; (38)
 12; (44) 9
verletzt (37) 14
verlieren (12) 20; (13) 15; (24) 26;
 (44) 9; (48) 9
verloren (9) 5; (15) 15
vernichten (19) 19
verpflanzen (33) 17
Verrat (16) 21
verraten (sich) (3) 4; (38) 21
Verräter (16) 21
verrenken (47) 19
verschieben (6) 11
verschieden (13) 29
verschlucken (46) 17
verschmieden (42) 8
verschütten (36) 24
verschweigen (47) 14
versetzen (22) 18
versprechen, Versprechen (1) 8, 9;
 (27) 11
Verstand (11) 20; (22) 9; (30) 26
verstecken (sich) (23) 1
verstehen (43) 15
vertragen (sich) (41) 13
vertrauen (22) 4

Vertraulichkeit (48) 52
verwandt (30) 26
Verwandte (25) 16, 23; (39) 2
verwegen (35) 17
verzehren (41) 2
verzeihen (41) 9
verzweifelt (35) 17
Viel–Wenig–Nichts (24)
viel (1) 5, 9, 13; (2) 13; (4) 14; (9) 16;
   (10) 9; (11) 21; (12) 15; (20) 9;
   (24) 1, 9, 14; (25) 1, 14; (26) 11;
   (30) 15; (46) 21, 22
viele (5) 8; (6) 5; (7) 9; (13) 17; (16)
   4; (24) 2, 3, 13, 27; (36) 28; (38)
   7; (39) 11; (48) 12
vier (36) 9, 14
vierzehn (7) 9
Viktoria (10) 20
Vogel (13) 3; (15) 14; (28) 10; (32)
   14; (43) 9; (44) 12, 14; (46) 10;
   (48) 35
Vöglein (44) 13
Volk (29) 7; (48) 4
voll (1) 10; (23) 9; (36) 7; (38) 3, 4
völlig (30) 4
vorbeugen (35) 6
vorgehen (43) 10
vorne (5) 7
Vorrat (24) 7
Vorsatz (23) 10
Vorsicht (36) 11

wachsen (8) 11; (13) 18; (14) 12;
   (16) 14; (28) 10; (34) 17; (38) 30;
   (48) 44, 51
wagen (10) 24; (21) 9
Wagen (15) 3; (46) 14
wägen (10) 24
wählen (16) 9
wahr (16) 11

währen (3) 1; (36) 2
während (6) 7
Wahrheit–Lüge (2)
Wahrheit (2) 1–3, 5–10, 14
Wald (15) 33; (21) 6; (24) 10; (38) 24
Wand (11) 29; (15) 24; (47) 9, 11;
   (48) 3
wankelmütig (19) 5
Ware (7) 3, 4, 10
warm (30) 13
Warnung (11) 5
warten (9) 4, 10; s. abwarten
Wäsche (47) 10
waschen (43) 1; (47) 10
Wasser (4) 8; (6) 24; (9) 16; (13) 14;
   (14) 14; (15) 23, 34; (21) 10; (28)
   10; (28) 14; (36) 22; (46) 5, 9, 28;
   (47) 22; (48) 6
wecken (47) 36
Wedel (14) 15
weder... noch... (48) 45
Weg (1) 4; (10) 22; (13) 17; (21) 1;
   (23) 10; (39) 7
weggehen (35) 4
weh tun (25) 21
wehe (29) 13
Wehestand (31) 6
Wehmutstropfen (20) 4
Weib s. Mann
Weib (18) 6; (20) 9; (23) 4; (31) 2, 5,
   8, 12–16
Weihnacht (9) 28
Weile (9) 20; (31) 7
Wein (2) 5; (7) 2; (12) 10; (20) 9;
   (38) 20; (39) 4
weinen, Weinen (20) 2, 7, 8, 14; (31)
   16; (32) 9
weise, Weise (8) 9; (11) 5, 12–14
Weisheit–Torheit (11)
Weisheit (11) 3; (19) 11; (36) 11

Italiano

Amico e Nemico (39)

amico (25) 14; (27) 7; (39) 1, 2, 4, 6–8, 11–14, 18

ammaestrare (8) 8

ammalarsi (31) 16

ammalato (35) 13

ammazzare (4) 13; (48) 2

ammogliato (31) 8

Amore–Bellezza (30)

amore (30) 1–3, 5, 7–11, 15, 17–20, 22, 23; (42) 1

anche, anco (3) 4, 10; (4) 12; (11) 12; (13) 9; (18) 1; (36) 16; (37) 8, 13; (44) 4; (48) 18, 19

ancora (33) 5; (48) 8

andare (4) 6; (9) 19; (11) 17; (12) 5, 19; (15) 23; (16) 22; (18) 18; (19) 13, 15, 25; (21) 6; (22) 11, 17; (23) 6; (25) 13; (27) 8; (28) 4; (30) 26; (36) 15; (38) 17; (40) 6; (43) 7, 10; (44) 9, 11; (46) 6, 23; (47) 1; (48) 23, 53

andarsene (30) 23; (35) 4

andato (34) 24

anima (43) 12, 36

annata (3) 8

annestare (27) 1

anno (8) 7; (9) 12, 25, 27, 29, 30; (11) 1; (20) 5; (39) 13

antico (33) 24

aperto (3) 10

appaiarsi (43) 9

apparecchiare (42) 6

Apparenza e Realtà (4)

apparenza (4) 1

appartenere (47) 27

appetito (38) 1, 26

appiccare (3) 18; v. impiccare

aprile (9) 29, 30

aprire (25) 7–9

aquila (12) 13; (32) 17; (48) 5

arco (12) 2

ardere (40) 4

ardito (21) 11

argento (1) 14

aria (15) 27

armato (42) 10

arrabbiato (31) 14; (38) 29; (48) 2

arricchire (3) 7

arrivare (9) 12, 23, 24; (15) 1; (16) 12; (17) 16

arte (7) 7; (18) 14; (25) 22; (34) 6; (48) 46

artefice (19) 1

ascoltare (1) 13; (25) 27

asino (11) 23; (13) 32; (14) 14, 15; (15) 8–10, 12, 19, 25; (31) 13; (43) 11; (46) 24; (48) 9, 20, 21

aspettar, aspettarsi (6) 23; (9) 4, 10; (11) 26; (24) 23; (34) 15; (37) 9

aspettato (13) 15

assai (1) 13; (16) 21; (18) 2; (24) 1, 14; (25) 15, 28; (39) 16

assente (17) 12

assenza (30) 22

assenzio (12) 15

Assiduità v. Lavoro

assomigliar, assomigliarsi (11) 10; (32) 1

Atene (15) 32

atroce (31) 13

attaccare (13) 5; (18) 1

attenere (1) 9

attirare (30) 19

audace (21) 5

aurora (6) 8

avanti (19) 10

Avarizia v. Avidità

avarizia (26) 1, 7, 8

avaro (26) 2, 3, 6; (32) 4

aventura (31) 2

avere (9) 1, 10; (10) 1, 15, 21; (11) 11, 28, 30; (13) 29; (17) 12; (18) 8; (21) 14; (23) 5; (24) 25, 29; (26) 5, 9; (27) 2, 5; (34) 23; (38) 5; (39) 11; (41) 10; (43) 5; (46) 20; (48) 3, 9, 11, 15, 19, 26

Avidità–Avarizia (26)

avventurarsi (21) 9

avvezzarsi (33) 15

avvisato (13) 21

avvocato (47) 14

B (10) 18

bacchetta (29) 10

baciare (4) 18; (5) 8

badare (36) 4

bagnato (10) 4; (48) 40

ballare (12) 7; (19) 2; (28) 8; (45) 3; (48) 54

ballata (13) 20

balzare (36) 28

bambino (33) 23

barba (4) 7; (10) 4

barile (36) 7

basso (13) 12, 17

bastare (13) 5; (32) 3; (48) 2

bastone (48) 1

battaglia (34) 1

batter, battersi (4) 17; (6) 6; (15) 24, 30; (34) 14; (35) 9

beccare (6) 9

beffa (19) 18

belare (38) 18

Bellezza v. Amore

bellezza (30) 24, 27, 28

bello (1) 6, 7, 17; (4) 3, 15; (10) 30; (11) 23; (12) 26; (28) 9; (30) 25; (32) 11, 12; (33) 28; (38) 8; (44) 12; (47) 16

beltà (30) 26

Bene e Male (16)

bene (2) 12; (3) 15; (7) 5; (9) 27; (10) 3, 14, 17; (13) 27; (14) 8; (15) 15; (16) 3, 8, 19; (19) 2, 9; (22) 4; (24) 8; (28) 8; (31) 1, 3; (32) 8; (33) 27; (34) 10; (35) 13, 14, 16; (40) 6; (43) 5, 25; (44) 10; (46) 19; (47) 22; (48) 41

beneficato (27) 7

beni (3) 7, 15

benvenuto (40) 9, 10

Bere e Mangiare (38)

bere (10) 19; (12) 12; (14) 6, 14; (18) 8, 13; (24) 19; (33) 19; (36) 22

berteggiare (30) 16

bestia (11) 17; (47) 30

bettonica (3) 22

bianco (9) 28; (11) 24, 29

biasimare (18) 7

bicchiere (46) 28

bisogna (2) 19; (6) 7; (10) 18; (13) 5; (16) 9; (18) 10; (23) 5; (25) 32, 33; (38) 16; (39) 13; (41) 8; (46) 1; (47) 13, 25, 26

Bisogno v. Necessità

bisogno (7) 2; (16) 5; (18) 6; (22) 8; (35) 16; (39) 1

bizzeffe (24) 17

bocca (1) 10, 32; (6) 8, 25; (33) 5; (36) 20, 24; (38) 21; (47) 8

boccone (38) 18

borsa (7) 10

bosco (21) 6; (24) 10; (38) 24

botte (46) 15

bove (13) 32

braccio (29) 6

brace (19) 26

branco (12) 14

breve (34) 6

castello (15) 27

castigare (17) 15; (22) 9; (32) 8

Casualità–Destino (45)

cattivo (1) 6, 7, 28; (6) 14; (13) 26; (16) 6, 12, 14, 16, 23; (18) 16; (21) 3; (25) 21; (27) 6; (38) 25; (41) 14; (44) 14; (46) 5, 14

Causa ed Effetto (12)

cavallo (4) 17; (12) 20; (14) 7; (16) 5; (19) 14; (27) 12; (28) 11; (33) 12; (35) 4; (36) 16; (38) 30; (47) 8; (48) 14

cavare (5) 4; (6) 27; (43) 16

cedere (11) 6

celato (47) 14

cena (27) 8; (38) 15, 17

cento (2) 15; (9) 25; (11) 22; (12) 16; (14) 3; (20) 5; (21) 12; (32) 3; (36) 32, 33; (39) 2; (45) 13; (48) 14

ceppo (43) 22; (48) 8

cercare (14) 18; (15) 19; (36) 25; (48) 20

certamente (13) 6

Certezza–Incertezza (36)

certo (36) 13, 14

cervello (1) 27; (11) 20, 24, 30; (22) 9; (47) 9

Cesare (46) 13; (47) 27

cespuglio (46) 10

chiamare (13) 32; (19) 10; (22) 14

chiamati (24) 27

chiave (6) 20; (9) 30; (25) 7, 8

chiedere (1) 24; (47) 3

chiesa (4) 6; (22) 14, 15; (46) 26

chiodo (12) 20; (43) 18

chiudere (15) 7

chiuso (36) 20

ciabattiere (47) 38

ciascuno (13) 28; (28) 9, 15

cibo (38) 25

cieco (13) 2, 8; (15) 4, 5; (18) 3; (24) 28; (30) 2; (35) 10; (45) 2; (47) 23

cielo (13) 3; (15) 10; (22) 13; (31) 4; (45) 6, 11

cigolare (46) 14

ciliegia (29) 9; (38) 13

cima (33) 11

coda (14) 15; (46) 3; (48) 9

colare (46) 17

collare (33) 15

collera (48) 19

colomba, colombo (32) 17; (38) 13

colonna (4) 16

colore (15) 5

colpa (16) 10; (47) 11

colpo (10) 25; (43) 21

comandare (29) 10

come... cosí (12) 4; (34) 5

cominciare (10) 3, 11; (28) 3

Commercio–Mestiere (7)

compagnia (25) 21; (30) 26

compagno (47) 34

compassionato (48) 55

compiuto (30) 4

comprare (7) 12, 14

comune (19) 20; (48) 12

Concordia–Discordia (41)

Condizionatezza–Relatività (13)

condizione (3) 14

condurre (10) 22

confermare (13) 35

confessato (17) 8

confessore (47) 14

confidarsi (29) 3

confidenza (48) 52

confondere (37) 4

confortare (19) 21

confronto (48) 10

congiungere (31) 11

coniugale (31) 6

conoscere (6) 12; (8) 2; (11) 21;
(18) 5; (25) 16; (30) 5; (35) 2; (36)
27; (39) 1; (47) 22; (48) 9, 34, 35

conosciuto (3) 22

consigliare (14) 13; (35) 13; (48) 28

consiglio (9) 9, 15; (10) 26; (16) 2;
(33) 16; (47) 3

contante (25) 4

contare (16) 4; (48) 31

contentarsi (25) 29

contento (20) 3, 5; (45) 13

contesa (41) 7

continuo (34) 1

conto (12) 26; (15) 31; (39) 3; v.
tener conto

contrario (6) 14

contrastare (3) 15

Contrasti (46)

contro (15) 24, 28; (34) 18; (36) 28;
(41) 5; (46) 12

conversazione (16) 16

conviene (3) 12; (10) 20; (32) 15;
(45) 11

coperchio (24) 16

coppia (43) 13

Coraggio v. Volontà

corda (36) 21

cordone (36) 12

corno (1) 26; (4) 5

cornuto (13) 32

coronare (10) 13

corpo (1) 30; (25) 26; (35) 1

correre (13) 1; (16) 5, 20; (46) 27

corrompere (16) 16

corso (33) 3

corto (2) 11; (11) 20; (16) 6; (22) 13;
(27) 12; (38) 19

corvo (5) 4; (32) 12, 14; (43) 16

cosa (1) 3; (2) 20; (9) 1; (10) 1, 10,

16; (13) 26; (14) 19; (18) 3; (30) 6,
28; (31) 14; (33) 6; (34) 17, 18; (37;
7) (46) 4; (47) 27, 29; (48) 13, 32,
38; v. qualche cosa

coscienza (3) 3, 21

costare (1) 21

costume (9) 14; (16) 16; (44) 8; (48)
47

credere (2) 14; (22) 4; (25) 26; (36)
19; (48) 27

credito, creditor (27) 2, 9

crescere (16) 14; (30) 17; (33) 21;
(48) 51

croce (19) 17; (23) 1

crogiolare (19) 27

crusca (23) 6; (48) 50

cucchiaio (23) 5

cucina (38) 7

cuoco (38) 7

cuoio (28) 5

cuore (1) 10, 31; (21) 3; (30) 6, 13,
21, 22; (36) 19; (38) 21; (48) 25

curar, curarsi (13) 7; (15) 11; (35) 7,
12

dado (20) 9; (45) 15

dagli (19) 16

danno (3) 24; (11) 2; (19) 18; (26) 4

danza (37) 2

dappertutto (7) 6

dare (7) 8; (9) 9; (11) 1; (15) 29; (23)
7; (24) 25; (26) 13; (36) 18, 33;
(39) 16; (43) 26; (46) 4; (47) 3, 15,
37; (48) 1

davanti (5) 7; (17) 1; (47) 21

Debito v. Prestito

debito, debitor (27) 2, 5, 6, 8-11.

debole (13) 11

degno (46) 9

denaro (9) 2; (11) 18; (24) 29; (25)

2, 4, 9–11; (30) 15

dente (2) 10; (19) 29; (35) 9; (38) 11; (42) 10; (43) 20

dentro (4) 3; (12) 17; (30) 23; (38) 20

deserto (15) 16

desiare (36) 35

desiderare (26) 9

desinare (38) 8

destinato (31) 4

Destino v. Casualità

destino (45) 12

dettare (30) 6

detto (1) 1, 2, 4, 19

Diavolo–Inferno (23)

diavolo (6) 18; (22) 1–8; (41) 6; (47) 15

diavolotto (32) 5

dichiarato (27) 7

dieci (36) 6

dieta (35) 15

dietro (5) 7; (23) 1; (32) 10

difetto (13) 36

differire (37) 7

difficile (10) 6–8

difficilmente (41) 10

diffidenza (36) 11

digià (7) 7

digiuno (25) 26; (38) 23

dimenarsi (38) 17

dimenticare (8) 12; (30) 20; (34) 24; (38) 14

dinanzi (15) 26

Dio (5) 7; (15) 15; (22) 1, 3–10, 12, 15; (39) 18; (47) 31; (48) 4; v. Iddio

dipingere (23) 3

dire (1) 3, 11; (2) 4, 6, 9, 17, 19, 20; (10) 11, 18, 21; (11) 12; (13) 33; (34) 10; (36) 22; (47) 1; (48) 2, 23; v. detto

diritto (33) 13

dirizzare (14) 19

disagio (6) 4

discesa (46) 18

Discordia v. Concordia

disdetta (9) 22

disfare (14) 1

Disgrazia v. Felicità

disordine (41) 2

disporre (22) 1

disposto (45) 11

disputare (13) 30; (15) 25

disuguaglianza (30) 10

dito (26) 13; (43) 14

diventare (2) 21; (7) 11; (14) 7; (33) 2, 20; (37) 14

diviso (29) 1

dolce (6) 10; (20) 4, 12

doler, dolersi (31) 16; (35) 9

dolore (19) 22; (37) 12; (42) 1

domandare (8) 10; (11) 13; (24) 14

domani (6) 11; (31) 12; (36) 17, 36; (43) 3; (45) 7–10

domenica (20) 8

Dominio–Potere (29)

donato (13) 15; (47) 8

donna (4) 16; (20) 9; (31) 5, 12, 13, 15, 16

Donna v. Uomo

dono (12) 25; (13) 15; (39) 15

dopo (6) 10; (9) 26; (10) 26; (11) 7; (15) 2; (20) 3, 4; (26) 3; (38) 15; (40) 8

doppia (36) 21

dormire (6) 16; (16) 4; (18) 12; (19) 9; (38) 22; (47) 35; (48) 23

dote (30) 24

dottor (35) 15

dovere (3) 5; (17) 3; (24) 23; (33) 9; (34) 10; (38) 2; (42) 9; (47) 17;

(48) 26

dovuto (17) 18

dubbio (8) 11

due (14) 4, 5; (15) 6; (16) 9; (25) 17; (27) 3; (33) 23; (36) 9, 18, 37; (41) 5, 8, 10, 12; (43) 12; (47) 31, 37; (48) 26

duolo (33) 18

durare (3) 8; (4) 10; (21) 4; (29) 2; (31) 3; (47) 16; (48) 15, 37

duro (14) 20; (18) 3; (20) 12; (30) 12; (43) 22, 23

eccelso (34) 14

eccezione (13) 34, 35

Effetto v. Causa

effimero (30) 27

eguale (17) 1

egualmente (34) 14

elefante (48) 17

eletti (24) 27

eloquente (25) 4

empi(e)r, empi(e)rsi (1) 30; (24) 3

entrare (15) 10, 17; (22) 14; (23) 4; (36) 20

erba (5) 2; (16) 13, 14; (38) 30; (44) 16; (48) 51

errare (47) 29

esempio (16) 4

esercizio (8) 6

Esperienza v. Scienza

esperienza (8) 5

essere (13) 10; (14) 5, 17; (19) 16; (31) 1, 5; (33) 22; (34) 28, 29; (36) 17; (39) 4; (41) 8; (43) 12; (45) 11; (46) 2, 3, 19; (47) 1; (48) 20; 24

esso (10) 10; (42) 8; (43) 14

estremo (24) 15; (35) 17; (37) 14; (46) 25

età (44) 11

Etica–Filosofia pratica (47)

Eva (48) 24

fabbricare (42) 8

faccia (28) 9

facile (19) 21; (48) 28

facoltà (21) 1

fallace (30) 28

Falsità–Ipocrisia (5)

falso (5) 5

fame (18) 14; (30) 23; (36) 6; (38) 22, 24, 25, 27; (41) 2; (45) 8

fanciullo (2) 6; (4) 18; (19) 7; (29) 13; (32) 9; (33) 2

fardello (28) 1

fare (1) 3; (2) 15; (3) 5; (4) 4, 7, 11, 15; (6) 11, 17, 22, 23, 26; (8) 7; (9) 22; (10) 7; (11) 2, 22; (12) 4, 12; (13) 7; (14) 10, 12, 15; (15) 15, 27; (31) (17) 3, 9; (18) 2, 16, 17; (21) 13; (24) 1, 4–6; (25) 5, 12, 19, 33; (28) 5; (30) 15; (31) 9; (38) 10; (41) 1; (43) 5, 7, 10; (47) 2; (48) 17, 20, 28; v. fatto

farina (23) 6; (48) 50

farla finita (10) 29

farsi (in là) (12) 27, 28; (13) 33; (23) 2; (24) 2, 3

fastidio (32) 2

faticare (33) 10

fato (20) 9

Fatti v. Parole

fatto (1) 1, 2, 4, 6, 7; (9) 13; (10) 4, 26; (11) 7; (14) 1; (15) 8; (16) 1; (17) 5; (33) 16; (34) 27; (44) 3

fava (38) 27; (45) 8

favilla (12) 1

favorevole (48) 32

favorire (19) 19

feccia (10) 19

Fede v. Iddio
fede (22) 18, 19; (39) 1
felice (19) 10; (28) 6; (46) 4
Felicità–Disgrazia (19)
femmina (31) 14
fermarsi (47) 28
ferro (6) 6; (12) 20, 21
festa (11) 14; (40) 6
ficcare (47) 5
fico (39) 12
fidar, fidarsi (12) 23; (36) 4, 29; (46) 1
fiele (1) 31
fieno (14) 18
fiera (43) 15
Figli v. Parenti
figlia (32) 1, 6; (48) 44
figlio (32) 1, 5, 6
figliuolo (32) 2–4
figura (45) 9
filare (48) 24
filo (13) 11; (18) 1; (36) 12
Filosofia pratica v. Etica
filosofo (4) 7
finchè (37) 1; (39) 11
Fine v. Principio
fine (5) 4; (6) 7; (10) 2, 5, 10, 12, 13, 15, 23, 27; (20) 2; (48) 49; v. alfine
finestra (30) 23
finire (10) 9, 11, 14
fiore (5) 2; (24) 6; (40) 10
fiorino (24) 2
fischiare (14) 6
fiume (24) 4; (45) 3
foglia (21) 6
follia (30) 26
fondo (36) 34; (38) 21
forca (45) 3
forfante (3) 16
forte (21) 3; (30) 9; (34) 18

fortuna (19) 1–8, 11, 13, 19; (21) 5; (30) 18
fortunato (46) 26
forza (2) 12; (11) 3; (14) 14; (17) 11; (30) 6; (41) 1, 16; (47) 33
forzoso (41) 11
fossa (12) 17; (13) 2; (48) 15
frasca (7) 2
frate (23) 2
fratello (40) 1; (41) 6
freddo (21) 10; (30) 13
frequentare (8) 10
fresco (37) 2
fretta (9) 20–22; (12) 24; (22) 3; (31) 7
frittata (6) 26
frullare (13) 22
frutto (3) 25; (16) 23; (32) 7; (33) 17; (36) 27
fruttuoso (9) 29
fuggire (9) 3; (15) 7; (20) 9; (42) 4
fulmine (45) 6
fumare (42) 2
fumo (12) 8; (31) 14
fune (47) 7
fuoco (12) 1, 8; (21) 10; (46) 5
fuorchè (34) 17
fuori (30) 4; (36) 32; (38) 20
furbo (3) 11
furia (37) 14
furto (7) 13
futuro (36) 37

gabbia (15) 14; (31) 8; (36) 32
gabella (48) 30
galla, a galla (2) 16
galletto (33) 7
gallina (4) 14; (5) 9; (26) 12; (31) 10; (32) 15; (36) 36; (45) 2
gallo (21) 11; (31) 10; (33) 7

gamba (2) 11; (11) 30; (14) 12; (36) 16; (48) 22

gatta, gatto (5) 1, 7; (6) 15, 24, 27; (7) 14; (12) 7; (13) 13; (21) 10; (32) 16; (34) 23; (41) 13; (46) 3; (48) 18

gaudio (19) 20

gelosia (30) 11, 12

generare (2) 8

gente (4) 13; (44) 4

gettare (15) 26

ghianda (33) 21

ghirlanda (24) 6

giacere (5) 2; (12) 29

giammai (23) 9

giocatore (13) 37

gioco (18) 16; (30) 18; (47) 16

Gioia–Tristezza (20)

gioia (20) 1

giornata (25) 25

giorno (9) 13, 17, 18; (10) 30; (25) 25; (33) 27; (37) 8; (40) 8; (46) 27

giovane (33) 4, 6, 8, 16

Giovanni (45) 10

giovare (15) 4; (33) 9

Gioventù–Vecchiezza–Novità (33)

gioventù (8) 12; (33) 1, 3, 9, 10, 18

giubba (38) 8

giudicare (15) 5; (17) 7, 14

giunta (38) 9

giustificare (48) 49

Giustizia v. Legge

giustizia (17) 10

giusto (3) 10; (22) 19

gloria (42) 5

goccia (12) 15, 18; (24) 22; (31) 14

gocciola (12) 6; (36) 7

godere (11) 14; (33) 10; (41) 12

gola (38) 6

gonnella (28) 2

gordiano (10) 28

governare (25) 6; (29) 5; (32) 3

graffiare (5) 7

granata (33) 27

gran(de) (1) 4; (2) 13; (3) 19; (9) 6; (11) 10; (12) 1; (13) 19; (17) 10; (19) 22; (24) 4; (25) 1; (32) 2, 13; (38) 5; (46) 16, 18; (47) 24, 33

granello, grano (24) 3; (45) 2; (46) 22

grasso (41) 3

grato (38) 25

grattare (13) 4; (43) 2, 11

grave (33) 25

grazia (30) 28

gregge (16) 17; (22) 16

gridare (12 23; (15) 16; (19) 16; (36) 29, 31

groppa (1) 32

grosso (29) 12

guadagnare (1) 15; (25) 17

guadagno (25) 19

guai (29) 13; (41) 11

guanciale (3) 3

guardar, guardarsi (5) 5, 7, 9; (21) 8; (34) 16; (39) 18; (47) 8; (48) 18

guardia (15) 29

guarire (11) 16

guastare (12) 14–16; (38) 7

Guerra e Pace (42)

guerra (25) 10; (34) 21; (42) 6, 11

guidare (13) 2

gusto (13) 29 30

Iddio–Fede (22)

Iddio (22) 2; (31) 11; v. Dio

ieri (45) 10

ignoranza (17) 2; (48) 44

imboccare (38) 12

imbrattare (12) 3

imbrodarsi (47) 12
imparare (6) 17; (8) 3, 4, 9, 12, 14;
    (11) 5; (28) 6; (43) 6
impiccare (3) 19; v. appicare
impiccato (47) 7
impossibile (14) 2
Impossibilità (14)
Improbità v. Probità
incavare (12) 18
Incertezza v. Certezza
incerto (36) 13
inciampare (36) 28
incudine (18) 15; (47) 9
indietro (1) 19; (19) 15
indugiare (9) 20
Infermità v. Sanità
infermità (35) 3
Inferno v. Diavolo
inferno (23) 10; (30) 12
infortunio (7) 9
ingannare (1) 7; (4) 1; (36) 26; (37) 5
ingannatore (16) 22
inganno (16) 22
inghiottire (46) 17
ingrassare (28) 11, 12
ingratitudine (47) 39
ingrato (15) 15
inguantato (6) 15
inizio (10) 1
innanzi (10) 30; (17) 7
insaziabile (26) 6
insegnare (8) 8; (15) 20; (18) 14;
    (25) 22
insidia (39) 14
insieme (14) 8
intender, intendersi (8) 1; (43) 15
intenditor (11) 3
intenzione (23) 10
intraprendere (10) 9
inutile (15) 7

Inutilità (15)
invano (33) 14
inventare (11) 19
invenzione (18) 4
invidia, invidiato (16) 18; (39) 14;
    (48) 55
invitato (40) 6
io (39) 18; (43) 3; (48) 53
Ipocrisia v. Falsità
ira (41) 6, 15, 16
istupidire (19) 19

là (30) 19; (44) 4
ladro, ladrone (2) 18; **(3) 4, 9,** 13–15,
    18–20; (14) 3
ladroncello (3) 18
lagnarsi (31) 16
lana (15) 19; (18) 11; (46) 21, 23
languire (2) 3
largo (28) 5; (48) 39
lasagna (6) 25
lasciare (12) 19; (15) 6; (16) 20;
    (34) 4, 25; (36) 26; (48) 42
lassare (36) 13
lastricato (23) 10
latte (19) 12; (33) 5
lattuga (48) 42
lavare (15) 12; (43) 1; (47) 10
lavato (15) 1
lavorare (16) 21; (38) 3
Lavoro–Assiduità–Pigrizia (6)
lavoro (6) 1, 10; (27) 6
legame (16) 6
legato (43) 14
Legge–Giustizia (17)
legge (17) 1–6, 9; (18) 5; (30) 6; (42)
    7
leggiero (6) 5; (48) 22
legittimamente (17) 4
legna (13) 1

361

lenzuolo (25) 32

leone (13) 5; (34) 7; (46) 3; (48) 34

lepre (12) 29; (15) 6, 13; (24) 13; (36) 30; (44) 15; (45) 5

letame (21) 11

lettera (11) 15; (46) 7

letto (12) 4, 5; (18) 12; (27) 8; (38) 17

levar, levarsi (12) 5; (22) 9; (37) 7; (41) 14; (45) 5

libbra (3) 17; (19) 11; (48) 7

libertà (12) 25; (48) 7

libro (8) 7

licere (19) 10

limite (10) 16; (37) 13

lingua (1) 25, 28; (25) 3; (35) 9

lira (15) 9

lite (41) 8

litigante (41) 12

lodar, lodarsi (6) 13; (7) 4; (10) 30; (36) 3; (47) 12

lontano (2) 17; (9) 19; (22) 15; (30) 21, 22; (32) 7; (40) 1

losco (35) 10

lucere (4) 2

luna (13) 7; (15) 11; (31) 12

lungo (9) 17; (11) 20; (13) 9; (14) 12; (21) 13; (23) 5; (25) 32; (29) 2, 6; (33) 20; (34) 6; (38) 19; (39) 3; (47) 16; (48) 39

luogo (1) 22; (14) 5; (18) 5; (23) 9

lupo (1) 32; (5) 6; (12) 28; (15) 29; (16) 7; (38) 24; (39) 17; (43) 6; (48) 31

lustrare (46) 9

ma (13) 10

macinare (6) 7; (9) 24; (22) 7

madre (4) 18; (9) 15; (18) 4; (32) 1; (36) 11

maestro (6) 12, 13; (8) 5, 6, 13

maestro *(principale)* (48) 51

magagnare (13) 14

magari (14) 11

maggio (9) 29, 30; (40) 10

maggiore (11) 15; (22) 8; (26) 7; (31) 2; (35) 2; (47) 23

magione (20) 10

magro (6) 16; (19) 14; (38) 28; (41) 3

mai (1) 16, 17; (2) 20; (3) 24; (6) 15, 23; (8) 4, 12; (9) 11; (11) 16; (14) 7; (15) 10; (16) 13, 21; (19) 23; (21) 8; (30) 1; (33) 17, 22; (36) 20; (46) 19; (47) 16, 20; v. sempre mai

malanno (19) 23

malato (35) 16; v. ammalato

Male v. Bene

male (3) 7, 8; (6) 17; (9) 23; (13) 6, 25, 27; (16) 3, 9, 15; (19) 20, 24, 25; (20) 6; (25) 18; (26) 1; (27) 1; (31) 6; (33) 15; (36) 30; (38) 3; (39) 10; (46) 19

male *(infermità)* (13) 19; (33) 26; (35) 4, 8, 17

malizia (17) 5

malo (16) 11, 13; (32) 14

Mammona (22) 12

mancare (11) 24; (21) 1; (25) 24, 28

mandare (11) 26; (17) 17; (22) 5; (23) 4

mandorlo (38) 27

Mangiare v. Bere

mangiare (6) 21, 24; (12) 21, 27, 28; (23) 5; (29) 9, 12; (36) 30; (38) 1, 2, 14, 16; (39) 12, 13; (43) 17; (48) 31, 42

manico (12) 19

mano (5) 8; (6) 5; (7) 6; (12) 3; (26) 13; (30) 13; (31) 13; (36) 24; (38) 12; (43) 1, 14; (47) 9

mantenere (1) 8; (39) 5

Maometto (18) 18

marcio (12) 14, 16

mare (15) 34; (21) 7; (22) 17; (24) 22; (36) 3

marea (9) 4

marinaro (6) 14

marionetta (44) 2

maritarsi (31) 7, 9

maritato (31) 4

marito (31) 5

marmo (41) 4

martello (18) 15; (47) 9

matrigna (32) 10

mattina (20) 7

mattiniero (6) 9

matto (1) 7; (11) 13, 14, 16, 26; (19) 7

mattutino (40) 2

maturare (48) 37

me, meco (39) 9; (45) 7; (46) 12

medaglia (46) 11

medicina (15) 2

medico (9) 7; (35) 12, 15, 16; (47) 14

meglio (1) 25; (3) 2, 6; (9) 11; (10) 10, 11; (11) 3; (16) 8, 15; (18) 9, 11; (24) 7, 18, 20; (27) 8; (31) 9; (32) 9; (34) 7, 20; (35) 6, 10; (36) 32–37; (38) 8; (40) 1; (41) 3; (46) 2, 3; (48) 7, 55

mela (12) 16

membro (35) 14

memoria (27) 2

menare (33) 19

meno (34) 15; (45) 5

mente (2) 12; (11) 10; (35) 1; (48) 41

mentire (2) 12

mentitore (2) 13

mercante (7) 4; (45) 10

mercanzia (7) 3, 4

mercato (31) 15; v. buon mercato

merda (26) 4

mese (9) 25

messa (38) 19

messere (36) 18

Mestiere v. Commercio

mestiere (7) 5, 6, 8, 9; (47) 38

metà (10) 3

metro (13) 31

metter, mettersi (20) 11; (21) 7; (47) 9; (48) 41

mezzo (3) 11; (10) 4; (13) 21; (17) 8; (19) 20; (24) 21; (29) 1; (30) 24; (38) 29

mezzo *(metodo)* (48) 49

miele, mele (1) 31; (12) 15, 27; (15) 8; (19) 12; (36) 7

miglio (27) 12; (38) 15

migliore (3) 1; (9) 7; (27) 2; (35) 15; (36) 10; (46) 16

mille (25) 1

minaccio (4) 13

minore (16) 9

Mio e Tuo (28)

mio, miei (39) 6, 9; (43) 25; (46) 19

mirare (47) 19; (48) 25

misfatto (1) 2; (30) 14

misura, misurare (13) 31; (36) 5; (48) 13, 26

mitigare (9) 6

moderare (22) 6

modo (13) 28; (14) 10

moglie (31) 2

mole (46) 16

molle (48) 38

Molto–Poco–Niente (24)

molto (1) 9; (4) 13; (6) 5; (8) 7; (9) 16; (11) 21; (13) 3, 15; (24) 1, 9, 13, 27; (25) 14; (30) 15; (33) 8; (37) 5; (39) 11; (46) 21, 22

momento (9) 12

padella (13) 33; (19) 26

padre (6) 19; (8) 11; (32) 1, 3–5

padrone (27) 10; (28) 11–13; (29) 8; (44) 18; (46) 5

paese (9) 25; (19) 12; (29) 13; (44) 5, 8

pagare (27) 9, 10; (43) 24; (44) 17; (47) 39; (48) 30

paglia (13) 9; (18) 1, 12; (27) 6; (36) 28; (46) 22

pagliaio (14) 18

paiuolo (13) 33

pane (7) 6, 8; (11) 25; (24) 21; (25) 30; (34) 12; (37) 3; (38) 11, 14, 25; (41) 2; (42) 1; (43) 26; (48) 38, 40

panno (25) 33; (47) 10

papero (31) 15; (33) 19

paradiso (22) 11

pareggiare (34) 13

parentado (25) 16

Parenti e Figli (32)

parenti (25) 23; (39) 2

parere (1) 2; (4) 16; (11) 23; (28) 9; (32) 11

pari (31) 3; (43) 9

parlare (1) 5, 10, 12, 13, 15, 16, 20, 27, 33; (7) 5; (25) 3; (32) 13; (42) 7; (47) 38

parlatore (2) 13

parola (1) 6, 7, 14, 19, 21, 22, 26, 29, 30; (5) 1; (11) 4, 12; (16) 4; (25) 27; (36) 1

Parole e Fatti (1)

parte (7) 7

partorire (46) 8

pascere (37) 6; (44) 16

pasciuto (38) 13

Pasqua (9) 28

passare (9) 16; (13) 12

passeggiare (38) 15

passero (15) 28

passione (20) 10

passo (10) 8; (14) 12; (21) 13

paternostro (24) 29

patire (13) 34; (20) 12

patria (13) 21; (44) 10

Paura v. Volontà

paura (3) 4; (21) 6, 10, 12–14; (30) 4; (47) 19

Pazienza v. Speranza

pazienza (37) 11–14

pazzia (11) 11

pazzo (2) 6; (11) 12, 15, 18, 22, 25, 27, 29

peccare (3) 10; (17) 15; (47) 30

peccato (17) 8; (29) 4

pece (12) 3

pecora (12) 14, 28; (15) 29; (16) 17; (18) 11; (38) 18; (43) 10; (47) 17; (48) 31

peggio, peggiore (35) 8; (39) 14; (47) 41

pelle (5) 6; (13) 5; (15) 21; (26) 5; (35) 11; (36) 23; (41) 11

pellicceria (10) 23

pelo (16) 7; (20) 11

pena (17) 16; (43) 19

penetrare (22) 13

penitenza (29) 4

pensar, pensarsi (1) 12; (3) 14; (10) 12, 24; (17) 5; (32) 12; (33) 22; (45) 5

pensiero (20) 11; (25) 1; (36) 10; (48) 30

pentirsi (10) 24; (17) 14

pentola (12) 24; (13) 16

perdere (9) 10; (12) 20; (15) 12; (18) 11; (26) 10; (36) 24; (38) 18; (39) 11; (44) 9

perdizione (23) 9

perdonare (17) 8, 13; (41) 9

perduto (16) 1; (37) 7; (47) 28

perfetto (48) 33

pericolo (39) 1; (42) 5

perire (2) 3; (42) 3

perla (15) 26

perpetuo (44) 11

perso (9) 5; (39) 12; (47) 22

pesare (13) 9; (28) 1

pescare (3) 26; (6) 24

pesce (6) 24; (15) 20; (29) 12; (36) 31; (38) 10; (40) 8; (48) 45

peso (28) 15; (48) 26

pestare (15) 22

piacere (11) 27; (14) 9; (16) 1, 21; (28) 9; (30) 25

piaga (9) 6; (39) 10

piangere (20) 7, 8, 14; (32) 9

piano (9) 19; (36) 15

pianto (19) 29; (20) 2

piatto (15) 1

piazza (13) 17; (39) 7

piccino (29) 12

piccolo, picciolo (3) 19; (12) 1; (13) 16, 19; (24) 4; (32) 2, 13; (33) 21; (39) 5, 16; (46) 16

pidocchio (26) 5

piede, piè (1) 25; (19) 4; (28) 11; (35) 4

piegare (18) 9

piena (24) 26

pienezza (1) 10

pieno (38) 3, 4

pietra (12) 18; (13) 18

pigliare (6) 15; (13) 3; (14) 16; (15) 6, 13; (32) 16; (36) 7, 30; (47) 25; (48) 5

Pigrizia v. Lavoro

pigrizia (6) 20

pioggia (9) 26

piombare (22) 3

piovere (6) 7, 25; (12) 6

piovoso (9) 29

pipa (42) 2

più (1) 15, 28; (3) 22, 25; (4) 10; (8) 7, 12; (9) 5; (10) 7, 8; (11) 6, 13, 25; (13) 11, 37; (14) 12; (15) 18; (16) 4; (19) 11, 21; (22) 8; (24) 17, 21; (25) 4; (26) 9; (28) 2, 13; (32) 12; (34) 21; (36) 6, 7, 9, 21; (38) 5, 6, 9, 28; (39) 2, 16; (42) 1; (45) 4; (46) 4, 14, 18; (48) 9, 14, 21, 28

Poco v. Molto

poco (1) 5, 9, 13, 21; (10) 9; (11) 4; (24) 1, 7, 14, 27; (25) 15, 24; (28) 1; (38) 15; (46) 16, 21, 22; (47) 16; (48) 37, 38

poi (10) 24

pollo (48) 16

polvere (11) 19; (34) 27

ponte (4) 8; (9) 16; (42) 4

popolo (29) 7; (48) 4

porco (15) 26; (26) 3

porta (3) 10; (25) 7–9; (30) 23; (34) 14

portare (6) 4; (15) 32–34; (19) 17; (22) 5; (25) 8, 18; (28) 15; (33) 11, 15; (40) 3, 4, 9

posarsi (19) 14

possedere (26) 2; (36) 35

posto (44) 1, 9

potente (11) 6

potere (2) 3, 10; (4) 17; (6) 11, 23; (8) 1; (14) 1, 3–6, 9–13, 15, 17, 19; (16) 23; (18) 2, 7, 8; (21) 2; (22) 5, 12, 18; (23) 4; (24) 10, 19, 25; (30) 6; (32) 6; (33) 6, 8, 9; (37) 9; (39) 16; (41) 5; (45) 3, 12; (48) 18

Potere v. Dominio

povero (25) 27; (29) 4; (37) 3
Povertà v. Ricchezza
povertà (3) 6; (6) 20; (25) 20–23; (26) 7; (39) 11
pozzo (12) 19; (47) 22
pranzo (38) 15
praticare (43) 6
predicare (5) 9; (16) 3
preghiera (22) 13
premio (30) 7; (47) 40
prendere (12) 25; (15) 21; (26) 13; (27) 3, 4; (36) 31; (42) 3; (48) 41
presa (15) 18
presente (36) 37
presso (2) 10; (40) 1; (48) 38
prestamente (36) 12
prestanza (27) 4
prestare (27) 1
prestatore (27) 4
Prestito–Debito (27)
prestito (27) 3
presto (7) 3; (11) 18; (13) 16; (14) 8; (16) 12, 14; (30) 5; (33) 8; (34) 24; (38) 14; (45) 4; (47) 37; (48) 27, 37
presunzione (48) 44
prevedere (35) 6
prezioso (33) 12
prezzare (25) 24
prezzo (16) 2
prima (1) 12; (10) 20, 24; (15) 21; (36) 23, 30, 31; (39) 13
primavera (24) 5
primo (9) 24; (10) 7, 25; (28) 3; (30) 1; (42) 9; (46) 2; (48) 24
principe (17) 6; (29) 3, 6
Principio–Fine (10)
principio (10) 2, 5, 6, 10
Probità–Improbità (3)
processo (17) 17
prodigo (32) 4

profeta (5) 5; (13) 24
profondo (46) 18
proibito (3) 25
promessa (27) 11
promettere (1) 8, 9; (36) 33
pronto (48) 22
proporre (22) 1
proposta (1) 23
proprio (19) 1; (21) 14; (27) 12; (28) 1, 15; (44) 17; (45) 12
provvedere (22) 4; (35) 6
prudente (11) 6
pulce (12) 5; (38) 28
pulcino (32) 12
puledro (33) 12
punta (33) 11
punto (13) 11
pure (17) 16; (19) 18
puzzare (13) 14; (25) 11; (26) 4

qual(e)... tal(e)... (1) 23; (6) 1; (10) 5; (22) 16; (44) 13
qualche cosa, qualcosa (2) 20; (10) 29; (13) 26; (24) 18; (47) 19
qualche volta (7) 11
quattordici (7) 9
quattrino (24) 2; (25) 5, 17, 31
quattro (10) 21; (28) 13; (36) 9; (36) 16
quercia (33) 21
questione (34) 29
quiete (35) 15
quindici (7) 9
quinto (15) 3
qui(vi) (12) 13, 29; (19) 29; (48) 43

raccogliere (6) 2, 3; (12) 9; (47) 15
radice (26) 1
rado (1) 20
ragione (17) 11; (41) 15

senno (11) 1, 2; (19) 11; (38) 20
seno (5) 3
sentenza (36) 8; (41) 3
sentire (11) 8; (12) 10; (35) 14; (38) 22; (47) 11
separare (11) 18; (31) 11
sepolcro (23) 9
sepolto (25) 19
sepoltura (45) 9
seppellire (34) 25
sera (10) 30; (20) 7
sereno (9) 26; (31) 12; (45) 6
serpe (5) 2, 3
servare (17) 3
servire (14) 4; (22) 12; (36) 22; (47) 34; (48) 12
servitore (29) 8, 11; (46) 5
servizio (43) 4
servo (27) 4; (28) 13
seta (4) 12
sette (11) 13; (24) 23; (39) 13
sfondare (7) 10
sfortuna (30) 18
sfortunato (19) 15
sfuggire (45) 12
sicuro (36) 14
sicurtà (13) 6; (36) 11
siepe (13) 12; (40) 3
signore (13) 8; (14) 4; (29) 4, 7, 9; (36) 2; (40) 5
silenzio (1) 14
simile (29) 7; (35) 7; (43) 8
sino (48) 15
smuovere (22) 18
soffiare (47) 4
soffrire (13) 6
sogno (34) 2; (46) 1
solco (33) 13
soldato (42) 9
soldo (25) 12

sole (13) 7; (44) 1, 6, 7
Solidarietà–Reciprocità (43)
solo (16) 15; (19) 23; (31) 1; (34) 9, 12 (41) 10; (48) 11
soma (33) 25
somigliare (32) 7
sommità (2) 1
sonaglio (11) 27
sonata (13) 20
sopportare (18) 7
sopra (13) 1; (27) 5; (36) 28; (47) 4; (48) 20
sorcio (3) 4; (6) 15; (32) 16
sordo (47) 24
sorte (21) 3; (45) 13
sospirare (48) 25
sostenere (10) 27
soverchio (24) 16
spacciato (20) 9
spada (1) 28; (38) 6; (42) 3, 8
sparagnare (36) 34
spazzare (33) 27
specchio (15) 4; (48) 36
spegnere (16) 13
spendere (28) 7
Speranza–Pazienza (37)
speranza (37) 1–6
sperare (45) 4
spesa (11) 5; (15) 18; (28) 6
spesso (11) 24; (12) 23; (20) 7; (30) 26; (36) 24, 26, 29; (39) 3
spettare (23) 7
spettatore (13) 37
spezieria (46) 16
spezzato (2) 10
spilla (3) 17; (14) 18
spina (20) 13; (33) 11; (48) 56
spingere (37) 14
spirito (46) 7
splendere (13) 7; (44) 6

terzo (41) 12

testa (11) 24; (15) 12, 24; (27) 5; (36) 8; (38) 4

testimonio (36) 6

tingere (13) 33

tiraborsa (43) 15

tirare (15) 28; (19) 24; (28) 14; (47) 6; (48) 14

tirato (1) 19

toccar, toccarsi (12) 3; (46) 25; (47) 41

togliere (24) 26; (27) 6; (48) 52

tondo (25) 2

topo, topolino (12) 7; (21) 15; (46) 8; (48) 11

torbido (3) 26

tormento (20) 3, 5

tornare (1) 19; (2) 1; (9) 25; (12) 22

tornarsene (46) 23

torto (14) 19; (17) 12

tosato (22) 6; (46) 23

tosse (30) 5

tosto (17) 14; (33) 20; (48) 1

tradimento (16) 21

traditor (16) 21

trapiantato (33) 17

tratto (1) 4; (45) 15

tre (1) 12; (6) 22; (31) 14, 15; (33) 27; (36) 5, 12; (40) 8; (47) 31; (48) 32

trenta (14) 14

trino (48) 33

trionfe (10) 20

Tristezza v. Gioia

tristo (4) 3; (17) 13; (31) 10; (48) 11

tronco (32) 7; (36) 28

troppo (1) 5; (2) 10; (9) 21; (10) 9; (12) 2; (13) 17, 23; (19) 19; (24) 7, 15; (25) 30; (26) 11; (36) 29; (38) 7; (46) 6; (47) 19, 20

trottare (18) 6

trovar, trovarsi (1) 22; (7) 3, 6; (16) 2; (36) 25, 26; (45) 2; (48) 1

truffato, truffatore (3) 23

(il) Tuo v. (il) Mio

tuo (40) 4; (46) 19; (47) 38

tutta (34) 3; (38) 17

tutte (3) 2; (10) 22, 23; (18) 14; (23) 6; (25) 7, 9, 22; **(48) 32**

tutti (2) 19; (3) 14; (4) 5, 6; (6) 14, 19; (7) 8; (13) 13; (14) 9–11; (17) 1; (22) 10; (26) 1; (34) 8, 13, 27; (42) 3; (43) 10; (44) 1, 6; (48) 23

tutto (4) 2; (9) 30; (10) 14, 15; (13) 25; (24) 12; (25) 5; (26) 10; (30) 8, 15; (33) 28; (35) 10; (37) 11; (44) 5

ubriaco (38) 21

uccello (1) 27; (6) 9; (13) 3; (14) 16; (15) 14; (28) 10; (31) 8; (36) 32; (43) 9; (44) 12–14; (46) 10; (48) 35

uccidere (26) 12; (36) 23; (38) 6; (46) 7

udire (1) 11; (38) 23; (47) 24

udita (36) 6

uffizio (33) 4

ultimo (10) 17; (47) 41

umano (47) 29

umile (34) 14

umore (41) 14

un, una, uno (2) 15; (3) 16; (9) 13; (12) 4; (13) 8; (15) 6, 17; (17) 15; (19) 5, 6, 16; (24) 11, 12, 23; (28) 13; (32) 3; (34) 9; (36) 5–7, 32, 33, 37; (43) 1, 4, 10–13, 18; (45) 13; (46) 10, 19; (48) 21, 29

unghia (5) 1; (48) 34

unione (41) 1

universale (20) 6

unto (13) 22

Uomo e Donna (31)

uomo (1) 26; (3) 9, 15; (4) 11; (6) 18; (13) 6, 21, 36; (14) 3; (17) 17; (21) 10; (22) 1; (25) 31; (26) 6; (31) 1, 2, 8, 11, 14; (33) 2, 23, 24; (34) 12, 21; (39) 17; (44) 2; (45) 1; (47) 30

uovo (4) 14; (6) 26; (26) 12; (32) 14; (36) 14, 36

urlare (43) 6

usanza (24) 11

usare (17) 4

uscio (10) 8

uscire (14) 17; (15) 17; (34) 26

uso (17) 9

vagheggiare (30) 16

vaglio (15) 23

valere (1) 21; (10) 10, 26; (11) 3; (15) 2; (16) 3; (19) 11; (24) 21; (30) 6; (36) 6; (39) 2; (40) 1, 16; (42) 1

valle (46) 18

valore (46) 16

vano (30) 28

Varia (48)

varietà (2) 2

vaso (12) 15; (15) 33

vecchia (18) 6; (23) 4

vecchiaia (33) 4, 9, 10, 25, 26

Vecchiezza v. Gioventù

vecchiezza (33) 18

vecchio (8) 4; (14) 16; (23) 2; (30) 20; (32) 9; (33) 6, 8, 13–17, 20, 23; (36) 26; (39) 4

vedere (5) 8; (13) 37; (24) 10; (28) 13; (36) 9, 19; (37) 10; (39) 1; (43) 7; (47) 23

vendere (7) 12; (12) 25; (15) 21; (36) 23

vendetta (22) 3

venduto (13) 15

venire (2) 16, 17; (13) 25; (18) 18; (19) 9, 23, 25; (20) 3, 4; (30) 23; (33) 26; (34) 15; (35) 4; (37) 8; (38) 1, 30; (44) 11; (45) 4; (47) 21, 25

vento (6) 14; (12) 9; (15) 30; (18) 10; (21) 7; (22) 6; (25) 18; (39) 12

ventoso (9) 29

ventre (1) 29; (38) 4, 5, 23

ventura (21) 9; (31) 2

verde (9) 28

Verità–Bugia (2)

verità (2) 1–3, 5–10, 16

verme (6) 9

vero (2) 4, 14, 19; (16) 11; (25) 29; (39) 1; (47) 14

verso (28) 10

vescia (38) 10

vescovo (31) 4

veste (25) 33

vestimento (4) 11

vestire (4) 16

vestito (4) 12

vetro (19) 4; (24) 19; (47) 6

via (36) 26

viaggiando (8) 9

viaggio (13) 9; (21) 8

viandante (45) 10

vicinanza (40) 3, 4

vicinato (3) 24

Vicino–Ospite (40)

vicino (22) 8, 15; (40) 1, 2, 5; (47) 6

villano (25) 16; (38) 28

vincere (21) 4; (30) 8; (37) 11

vino (2) 5; (7) 2; (10) 19; (20) 9; (38) 20; (39) 4

vinto (29) 1

violenza (29) 2

virtù (18) 17; (33) 1; (47) 40
viso (12) 22; (18) 16
vista (4) 3; (36) 6
Vita e Morte (34)
vita (34) 1–3, 6, 20, 23; (37) 1; (46) 19
vitello (19) 8; (26) 14
vittoria (10) 20
vivere (6) 16; (8) 3; (11) 5; (22) 5; (22) 19; (25) 25; (33) 20; (34) 4, 5,
vivificare (46) 7
vivo (34) 7
vizio (6) 19; (16) 7; (25) 20; (26) 8; (33) 4
vizioso (24) 15
voce (15) 16; (48) 4, 6
voglia (48) 22
volare (36) 1
volentieri (44) 15
volere (1) 11; (5) 8; (6) 24; (10) 12; (14) 13; (18) 2; (21) 2; (22) 9; (23) 5; (24) 14; (25) 8; (26) 10; (31) 13, 16; (32) 6; (33) 3, 19, 20;

(36) 18; (37) 9; (38) 16, 26; (39) 4; (42) 6; (43) 25; (47) 2, 23, 24; (48) 2, 13, 27
Volontà–Coraggio–Paura (21)
volontà (21) 1
volpe (3) 12, 24; (5) 9; (6) 16; (10) 23; (13) 5
volpeggiare (3) 12
volta (1) 12; (3) 16; (12) 19; (24) 11; (25) 17; (33) 23; (34) 9; (36) 26; (37) 5; (47) 37; (48) 21; v. qualche volta
volto (1) 31
vuoto (38) 4; (46) 15

zampino (6) 27
zanzara (46) 17
zappa, zappare (42) 8; (48) 24
zecca, nuovo di zecca (33) 29
zio (43) 25
zoppo (17) 16
zuppa (36) 24; 38, 40

Español

A (10) 18
abad (14) 14
abandonar (21) 15
abarcar (26) 11
abierto (3) 10
abrazo (30) 17
abril (9) 29, 30
abrir (25) 7, 9
abultar (21) 12
abundancia (1) 10
acá (32) 11
acabar (10) 11, 14, 21; (19) 10
acción (15) 15
aceite (2) 1
aceituno (48) 38
acero (25) 8
acertar (8) 11, 14; (34) 18
aconsejar (48) 28
acordarse (33) 22
acostarse (12) 4, 5; (27) 8; (36) 18
acotar (46) 10
acreedor (27) 2
acto (24) 11
acudir (22) 8
Acuerdo–Discordia (41)
acusarse (12) 11
Adán (48) 24
adarme (35) 4
adelantarse (11) 6
adelante (47) 28
admirar (11) 23
admitir (17) 2
adolecer (46) 19
adonde (13) 12

adquirido (3) 7
adversidad (39) 1
afeitar (4) 16
afligido (13) 6; (48) 27
afortunado (30) 18
afuera (38) 21
agarrarse (18) 1
agosto (9) 18
agradar (11) 27; (28) 1; (33) 28; (47) 16
agraviado (41) 4
agravio (17) 13
agua (4) 8; (5) 10; (6) 24; (9) 16, 25; (13) 14; (15) 23, 34; (21) 10; (24) 22; (25) 18, 31; (28) 14; (36) 22; (38) 10; (45) 14; (46) 5, 28; (47) 18, 22
aguantar (2) 21
águila (12) 13; (32) 17; (48) 5
aguja (7) 4; (14) 18; (48) 56
agujero (48) 11
agujeta (3) 17
aguzar (18) 4
ahogado (2) 3
ahogarse (18) 1
ahora (33) 2
ahorcado (47) 7
ahorcar (3) 19
ahorrar (13) 19; (36) 34
aína (22) 9
aire (15) 27
ajeno (3) 8; (6) 27; (19) 21; (25) 30; (27) 12; (28) 5–8; (38) 12
ál *(otra cosa)* (7) 6

ala, alado (5) 7; (21) 13; (22) 9; (48) 22

alabanza (47) 12

alabar, alabarse (7) 4, 5; (10) 21; (19) 10

albarda (4) 17

alcanzar (21) 4; (25) 5; (37) 11

aldea (46) 2

alegrar (20) 12

alegría (20) 3, 4, 6; (35) 15; (37) 8

alejado (30) 22

alfiler (33) 29

algo (1) 15; (8) 3; (24) 14, 18; (27) 1 (47) 19

alguno (8) 11; (17) 4; (24) 28; (41) 11

aliviar (47) 34

alma (35) 1; (43) 12; (48) 36

almendra (38) 11

almohada (3) 3

almorzada (19) 11

alto (13) 17; (47) 19

alzar (25) 21; (39) 12

allá, allí (10) 23; (13) 33; (19) 29; (35) 9; (44) 15; (48) 43

amable (40) 7

amanecer (6) 25

amar (25) 14; (30) 1; (32) 8; (40) 3

amargar (2) 7; (38) 13

amargo (12) 15; (35) 5

amargura (20) 2

ambos (13) 2

amenazado (4) 13

Amigo y Enemigo (39)

amigo (5) 7; (25) 16, 23; (27) 7; (34) 24; (39) 1–4, 6–8, 12, 13; (40) 2; (41) 10; (43) 26

amistad (2) 8; (39) 1, 5, 10; (40) 3

amo (28) 11; (46) 5

Amor–Hermosura (30)

amor (26) 1; (30) 2–5, 7–11, 15, 18,

20, 22, 23; (48) 22

ancho (3) 21

andado (14) 1

andar, andarse (12) 3; (13) 32; (16) 15; (21) 8; (36) 15; (38) 8; (43) 6; (47) 1, 34

anegarse (45) 3

ansiedad (13) 6

anteojos (15) 4

ante(s) (1) 12; (3) 6; (9) 15; (10) 20, 21, 24; (15) 21; (17) 7; (18) 9; (31) 7; (33) 2; (36) 30; (46) 3; (47) 21

antojo (30) 19

añejo (39) 4

año (8) 7; (9) 12, 25, 27, 30; (11) 1

apaleado (19) 18

apariencia (4) 1, 3

Apariencias y Realidad (4)

apartar (11) 18; (31) 11; (36) 11

apellido (1) 30

apenas (29) 9

apetito (38) 1

apiadado (48) 55

aplacer (16) 21

aprender (8) 3, 4, 8, 12; (22) 17; (33) 15; (43) 6

apresurar (20) 11

apretar (26) 11; (47) 36

aprisa (9) 21

apriscar (21) 9

aprovechar, aprovecharse (13) 5; (41) 12

apuesta (15) 12

apurarse (20) 11

aquí (12) 29

arado (42) 8

arañazo (41) 11

arar (28) 13

árbol (6) 7; (13) 1; (16) 23; (24) 10;

costumbre (9) 14; (16) 16; (17) 9; (47) 32, 33

crecer (13) 23; (16) 14; (33) 17; (38) 30

creer (36) 4, 19; (48) 27

criado (29) 11

criar (5) 4; (32) 2; (38) 10; (48) 51

criatura (11) 28; (38) 9

cristal (19) 4

crujir (19) 29

cruz (5) 1; (19) 17; (23) 1

cual... tal... (22) 16; (29) 7; (32) 1, 14

cuanto... tanto... (18) 2; (19) 15; (30) 22; (46) 18

cuarenta (33) 29

cuatro (36) 9, 14

cuba (12) 10

cubrir (5) 7; (30) 14

cuco (3) 20

cuchara (23) 5

cuchillo (42) 11

cuenta (12) 26; (15) 31; (39) 3

cuerda (13) 11; (36) 21; (43) 21

cuerdo (11) 15

cuerno (1) 26; (4) 5

cuero (28) 5

cuerpo (12) 13; (35) 1; (43) 12

cuervo (5) 4; (32) 12, 14

cuestión (34) 29

cuévano (15) 1

cuidado (25) 1

culebra (6) 27

culinegro (13) 33

culo (36) 23

cumplir (1) 9

cuna (8) 12

cuña (13) 5

cuño (43) 22

cuquear *(azuzar)* (3) 20

cura (11) 16

curar, curarse (9) 6; (13) 7; (34) 26; (35) 6, 7, 11, 12

charlar (47) 34

chico (12) 1; (24) 4; (29) 12; (33) 21; (44) 13

chiquito (13) 16

chirriar (46) 14

chiva (33) 7

dañar (24) 7, 15

daño (1) 25; (47) 11

dar (1) 8; (4) 7, 17; (5) 3; (8) 7; (9) 20; (13) 15; (15) 29; (19) 26; (21) 13; (23) 7; (24) 14, 25; (26) 13; (33) 14; (36) 18, 33; (43) 2; (46) 4; (47) 3, 15, 37; (48) 1, 40

debajo (13) 3; (44) 7; (48) 20

deber (10) 18, 21; (11) 30; (27) 1, 5, 10; (42) 9; (43) 25; (47) 18

decir (1) 3, 11, 15; (2) 4, 6, 8, 9, 19, 20; (10) 18; (11) 6; (13) 17, 32, 33; (32) 11, 13; (36) 22, 37; (47) 1; (48) 23

declarado (48) 21

dedo (12) 3; (24) 6

defecto (13) 36

dejar (3) 8; (6) 11; (16) 20; (22) 3; (33) 6; (34) 4, 25; (36) 13, 26; (44) 9; (47) 4, 16; (48) 42

delante (15) 26; (33) 11

demasía (24) 16

demasiado (3) 21; (10) 9; (11) 21; (24) 15

dentro (4) 3

depender (48) 44

derecho (17) 2, 11; (33) 13

derramarse (33) 4

derribar (10) 25

desandar (14) 1

desatar (10) 5, 12
descansado (33) 10
descanso (6) 10
descarriado (16) 17
descendida (46) 18
descomponer (24) 23; (38) 7
desconfianza (36) 11
descubrir, descubrirse (3) 15; (11) 19; (48) 34
desdicha, desdichado (19) 15; (31) 2
deseado (3) 25
desear (31) 16; (34) 15; (36) 35; (48) 27
deseo (30) 25
desesperar (37) 5
Desgracia v. Felicidad
desgracia, desgraciado (3) 18; (19) 24; (20) 12; (30) 18
deshacer (39) 12; (40) 3
Deshonestidad v. Honestidad
deshonrado (34) 20
desierto (15) 16
desmemoriado (41) 4
desnudo (14) 3
despacio (36) 15
despertar (41) 7; (47) 35
después (3) 17; (9) 25; (15) 1; (23) 2; (36) 37; (38) 15; (41) 9; (46) 6
Destino v. Casualidad
destino (45) 12
detrás (23) 1; (43) 10; (44) 4; (48) 53
Deuda v. Empréstito
deuda (27) 8, 9, 11
deudor (27) 2
devanear (38) 17
devestir (48) 29
día (8) 3; (9) 17, 18; (10) 30; (20) 8; (40) 7, 8; (45) 8; (46) 27
Diablo–Infierno (23)
diablo (5) 1, 3; (6) 18; (23) 1–8; (32)

5; (41) 6; (47) 15
dicha (31) 2
dicho (1) 1, 2, 4; (2) 9
diente (2) 10; (16) 7; (19) 29; (43) 20; (47) 8
dieta (35) 15
diez (28) 13; (47) 33
diferente (14) 5
diferir (37) 7
difícil (10) 7; (36) 21
dignidad (34) 16
Diligencia v. Trabajo
diluvio (48) 53
dinero (1) 22; (9) 2; (11) 18; (24) 29; (25) 1, 2, 4, 5, 9–13, 19, 23, 31; (26) 1; (30) 15; (35) 2; (39) 7, 11; (44) 17
Dios–la Fe (22)
Dios (1) 24; (6) 8; (17) 16; (19) 8; (22) 1, 3–10, 12, 15; (26) 4; (31) 11; (38) 11; (39) 18; (47) 31; (48) 4
dioses (40) 9
discernimiento (15) 9
Discordia v. Acuerdo
discutidor (41) 11
discutir (15) 25
disponer (22) 1
disputa (13) 30
distinguir (34) 14
dividir (29) 1
dobla *(moneda)* (44) 16
doblado (11) 15; (32) 2
doblar (18) 9
doblez (36) 12
doctor (35) 15
doctrina (16) 4
doler (7) 12; (35) 9, 14; (48) 25
doliente (35) 13
dolor, doloroso (11) 2; (13) 23; (19) 21; (30) 3; (36) 2

fino (13) 11
flaco (19) 14; (38) 28
flojo (12) 2; (41) 16
flor (32) 11; (40) 10
florida (9) 28
florín (24) 2
fluir (19) 12
forjador (19) 1
fortaleza (11) 3
fortuna (19) 1–3, 6, 19; (20) 10; (21)
    5; (31) 12
frágil (19) 4
fraile (23) 2
frasco (46) 16
frío (15) 22; (21) 10; (30) 13; (38) 10
fruto (3) 25; (16) 23; (36) 27
fuego (12) 8; (46) 5
fuente (12) 19
fuera (20) 4; (31) 14
fuerte (11) 6; (30) 9; (34) 19, 26
fuerza (17) 11; (22) 5; (31) 13; (41)
    1, 2; (47) 33
fumar (42) 2

galgo (32) 15
gallina (4) 14; (6) 25; (24) 3; (26) 12;
    (31) 10; (36) 23, 30
gallinero (42) 1
gallo (21) 11; (31) 10
gana (21) 1
ganar (9) 13; (14) 3; (23) 6; (25) 19;
    (46) 19
ganso (31) 15
garbanzo (24) 23
garrido *(galano)* (38) 8
gastador (32) 4
gastar (15) 28
gata, gato (6) 15, 24; (7) 14; (12) 7,
    29; (13) 13; (21) 10; (32) 16; (34)
    23; (41) 13; (48) 11

generación (44) 11
generoso (26) 3; (28) 7
gente (8) 9; (41) 11; (44) 4
gloria (42) 5; (48) 47
golfo (44) 3
golondrina (24) 5, 6
golpe, golpear (10) 25; (15) 24
gordiano (10) 28
gota (12) 6; (24) 22; (36) 7
gotera (12) 18; (31) 14
gobernar (29) 1, 5
Gozo–Tristeza (20)
gozo (19) 20
gracia (30) 28
gracias (13) 15
gradar (14) 9
gran(de) (1) 4; (3) 19; (9) 22; (11)
    10; (12) 1; (14) 10; (17) 18; (19)
    16, 22; (24) 4; (29) 12; (30) 15; (33)
    21; (35) 17; (38) 5, 28; (46) 6, 18
grano (24) 3; (36) 31; (45) 2; (46)
    22; (48) 50
grey (22) 16; (29) 7
griego (29) 4; (39) 15
grillos (48) 8
guante (6) 15
guardado, guardador (25) 19; (32) 4
guardar, guardarse (5) 5; (25) 15, 17;
    (33) 9; (39) 18
guardia (15) 29
Guerra y Paz (42)
guerra (11) 26; (25) 10; (34) 21; (42)
    1, 6, 11
guiar (13) 2
gustar (30) 25; (38) 3; (44) 12
gusto (13) 29, 30; (14) 11; (47) 18

haba (44) 5
haber (1) 23; (2) 10; (7) 8; (14) 17;
    (19) 7; (23) 5; (27) 6; (29) 6; (32) 3;

manga (3) 21; (11) 11

mano (5) 8; (6) 27; (19) 15; (24) 6, 20; (25) 23; (26) 13; (28) 8; (30) 13; (36) 24, 32; (38) 12; (43) 1

manso (22) 6

manzana (12) 16

maña (21) 1

mañana (6) 9, 11; (20) 7; (36) 17, 36; (45) 7, 9, 10

mar (15) 34; (21) 7; (22) 17; (24) 22; (36) 3

marea (9) 4

María (31) 3

marido (31) 5

martillar (15) 22

más (1) 25, 28; (3) 22, 25; (4) 5, 13; (8) 10; (11) 13; (13) 11, 37; (16) 4; (20) 9; (22) 9; (24) 14, 17; (25) 1, 4; (26) 9; (27) 2; (28) 13; (30) 22; (32) 12; (34) 15, 24; (35) 3; (36) 7, 9, 10; (38) 5, 6; (45) 4; (46) 4, 14, 21; (47) 16, 33; (48) 6, 11, 14, 27, 28

más vale (1) 20; (3) 2; (9) 11; (10) 11; (16) 15; (18) 11; (19) 11; (24) 8, 18, 19, 21; (27) 8; (34) 20 (35) 6, 10; (36) 6, 32–34, 37; (38) 9; (39) 2, 7; (41) 3; (42) 1; (46) 2

matar (26) 12; (32) 16; (38) 6; (46) 7, 10; (48) 2

matorral (46) 10

mayo (9) 29, 30; (40) 10

mayor (10) 8; (20) 6; (22) 8; (25) 29; (30) 15; (31) 2; (43) 23; (46) 18

mear (31) 16

medalla (46) 11

médico (9) 7; (34) 18; (35) 12, 15, 16; (47) 14

medida (43) 19; (48) 13, 26

medio (3) 11, 12; (10) 4; (11) 4; (17) 8; (24) 21; (39) 13; (40) 3

medios (48) 49

medir (13) 31

medrar (33) 17

mejor (1) 15; (3) 1; (9) 7; (10) 10, 17; (11) 2, 3; (16) 8; (31) 9; (32) 9; (34) 7; (35) 15, 35, 36; (40) 1, 14; (48) 55

memoria (48) 47

memorioso (2) 12; (27) 2

Menester v. Necesidad

menester (2) 19; (7) 2; (23) 5

menesteroso (6) 20; (33) 18

menor (3) 19; (16) 9; (39) 16

menos (34) 17; (45) 4, 5

menospreciar (39) 16

menosprecio (48) 52

mentar (47) 7

mentir (2) 13

Mentira v. Verdad

mentira (2) 11, 15, 17

mentiroso (2) 12, 14, 18

mercado (31) 15

merced (12) 25

merecer (14) 13

mesa (39) 12

meter (15) 9; (19) 13; (29) 10; (35) 13; (47) 9

métrico (48) 26

mí (45) 7; (48) 53

Miedo v. Voluntad

miedo (3) 4; (21) 10, 12, 13; (47) 19

miel (1) 31; (12) 15, 27, 28; (15) 8, 32; (19) 12; (20) 1; (36) 7

mientes (16) 7

mientras (6) 7; (37) 1; (38) 30; (44) 18

mil (9) 25; (10) 19

milla (38) 15

(lo) Mío y (lo) Tuyo (28)

mío (47) 5

mirar (3) 5; (10) 12, 24; (13) 37;
   (28) 13; (30) 10; (31) 7; (47) 8, 19,
   28; (48) 18

misa (22) 14; (46) 26

Miscelánea (48)

mísero (37) 3

mismo (6) 22; (8) 2; (19) 19; (28) 3;
   (34) 27; (35) 12; (43) 14, 15, 24;
   (47) 40; (48) 21, 39, 40

mitad (10) 3

Mocedad–Vejez–Novedad (33)

mocedad (33) 3, 10, 18

modorro (16) 6

moho (13) 18

mojarse (38) 16

molar (47) 9

moler (43) 26

molinillo (43) 26

molino (15) 30; (28) 14

mona (4) 12

moneda (43) 24

monje (4) 4; (14) 14

montaña (18) 18

monte (21) 6; (22) 18; (38) 24; (44) 4;
   (45) 1; (46) 8

mordedura (35) 11

morder (4) 9; (5) 7; (43) 17; (47) 41

morir, morirse (16) 13; (33) 8; (34)
   8, 9, 11; (37) 6; (38) 30; (45) 14;
   (48) 16

moro (19) 16

mortaja (31) 4; (33) 4

mosca (12) 27, 28; (36) 7, 20; (48) 5

mosquito (46) 17

movedizo (13) 18

mover, moverse (16) 19; (38) 19

moza (48) 14

mozo (33) 2, 6, 8, 9; (38) 8

muchacho (29) 13

Mucho–Poco–Nada (24)

mucho **(1)** 5, 9, 13, 21; (2) 13; (4)
   14; (7) 10; (8) 7; (9) 16; (12) 15,
   24; (20) 3; (24) 1, 9; (25) 5, 24;
   (26) 11; (30) 15; (33) 20; (38) 20;
   (45) 8; (46) 15, 22; (48) 37

muchos (1) 16; (5) 8; (6) 5; (19) 20;
   (24) 1, 13, 27; (25) 14; (36) 5; (38)
   7; (46) 23

mudable (31) 12

mudar, mudarse (9) 8; (16) 7; (22)
   18; (39) 12

muela (35) 9; (38) 11; (47) 9

muelo (19) 21

Muerte v. Vida

muerte (20) 11; (26) 3; (30) 9; (34)
   5, 13–19, 26

muerto (12) 13; (15) 2; (19) 16; (34)
   7, 10, 21, 22, 24, 25

Mujer v. Hombre

mujer (20) 9; (23) 4; (31) 2, 5, 12–16;
   (36) 23

muladar (21) 11; (44) 15

mulo (13) 32; (14) 7; (21) 8; (26) 4

Mundo y Casa (44)

mundo (10) 15; (26) 4; (27) 5; (44)
   2, 3, 5; (47) 39

Mundología v. Ética

muro (14) 20

música (37) 2

músico (15) 9

nacer (2) 15; (8) 13; (13) 36; (14) 3,
   7; (15) 21; (32) 17; (33) 11; (34) 8,
   11; (43) 5; (44) 15; (45) 3; (46) 8

nación (41) 2

Nada v. Mucho

nada (6) 16, 17; (13) 14, 29; (17) 7;
   (24) 9, 18, 21, 24; (25) 4, 19, 28;
   (36) 20; (44) 7, 10; (45) 8; (46) 13

nadador (45) 14
nadar (2) 1; (5) 10; (44) 3; (45) 14
nadie (1) 29, 30; (3) 7; (8) 13; (10)
  21; (11) 9; (13) 24; (14) 2; (19) 10;
  (24) 25; (45) 12, 13; (48) 8
naipes (20) 9
nariz (28) 9
natural, naturaleza (19) 11; (47) 32;
  (48) 15
navegar (47) 18
Navidad (9) 28
Necedad v. Sabiduría
Necesidad–Menester (18)
necesidad (18) 3–6, 17; (22) 8; (35)
  16
necesitar (25) 28
necio (11) 12, 15, 27; (47) 3; (48) 20
negocio (7) 1; (10) 10
negro (49) 39
nervio (25) 10
ni... ni... (24) 6; (27) 12; (48) 45
nido, nidillo (44) 12–14
nieve (9) 27
ninguno (1) 16; (13) 36; (14) 4, 12;
  (15) 6; (19) 21; (20) 10; (24) 12,
  19; (34) 9; (38) 23; (39) 8; (44) 17;
  (48) 12
niño (2) 6; (32) 9, 13; (33) 23
no hay que... (34) 10; (36) 22, 30;
  (38) 2; (47) 7, 8
noche (9) 17; (13) 13; (38) 17; (46) 27
nombre (32) 10
nosotros (9) 8
notario (41) 6
Novedad v. Mocedad
novel (33) 28
nudo (10) 28; (43) 22
nueces (46) 21
nuera (33) 22
nuestro (37) 8; (39) 6

nueva (16) 11, 12
nueve (34) 23
nuevo (12) 10; (17) 6; (30) 20; (33)
  15, 27, 28; (36) 26; (44) 7
nunca (2) 3, 13; (8) 4; (9) 11; (11) 25;
  (13) 18; (14) 11, 15; (16) 1, 13; (17)
  12; (19) 6, 23; (23) 9; (25) 15, 21;
  (39) 10; (41) 4, 9; (47) 9, 20

obedecer (25) 6
obediencia (42) 9
obligado (14) 2
obra, obrar (1) 5; (6) 13; (10) 13
obrero (6) 12
ocasión (3) 9; (11) 9
océano (48) 6
ociosidad (6) 19
ocioso (6) 18; (33) 18
ocultar, ocultarse (5) 2; (30) 5
odio, odioso (41) 7; (48) 10
oficial (7) 6
oficio (7) 6, 8, 9
oídas (36) 6
oído (15) 17
oír (1) 11, 24; (11) 8; (32) 13; (38)
  23; (47) 11, 24; (48) 3
ojo (5) 4; (28) 11; (30) 21, 22; (36)
  9; (38) 5; (43) 20; (47) 19; (48) 25,
  36
oler (12) 10
olivo (48) 38
olor (25) 11
olvidar (17) 16; (18) 7; (30) 1, 20, 23;
  (48) 47
olvido (38) 14
olla (1) 29; (7) 5; (13) 10, 16; (18) 8;
  (24) 23; (38) 7
oración (15) 10; (22) 13; (38) 19
orar (22) 17
orégano (13) 10

oreja (6) 18
orejudo (13) 32
orgullo (48) 44
orín (12) 21; (16) 18
oro (1) 14; (3) 2; (4) 2; (25) 7, 8;
  (26) 12, 14; (48) 8
osado (21) 5
osar (21) 7
oso (15) 21
otorgar (1) 18
otro, otros (4) 3; (6) 23; (9) 14; (11)
  23; (12) 17; (13) 17; (15) 17; (19)
  24; (43) 1, 4, 5, 11, 17, 18, 23;
  (46) 10, 19; (47) 2; (48) 29
oveja (5) 6; (12) 14; (15) 29; (16) 17;
  (24) 13; (38) 18; (43) 10

Paciencia v. Esperanza
paciencia (37) 11–14
padrenuestro (1) 12
padre (6) 10; (32) 1, 3–5
Padres e Hijos (32)
pagador (27) 3
pagar (27) 6, 9, 10; (29) 4; (30) 3, 7;
  (36) 5; (43) 4, 24 (44) 17; (47) 27
país (13) 8
paja (13) 9; (27) 6; (36) 28; (46) 22;
  (48) 50
pajar (14) 18
pajarillo (44) 13
pájaro (14) 16; (36) 32; (44) 12; (46)
  10; (48) 35
palabra (1) 6, 14, 19, 25, 26, 28, 29;
  (11) 4; (25) 27
Palabras y Hechos (1)
Palacio (11) 17
palco (45) 10
palo (4) 16; (22) 7; (31) 13; (32) 7
paloma (32) 17
pan (18) 8; (24) 19, 21; (25) 30; (34)

12; (37) 3; (38) 8, 14, 25; (39) 12;
  (43) 25
panza (38) 3
paño (7) 3
papel (2) 21
papo (24) 3
par (14) 6; (43) 9; (46) 24
parar (12) 24; (30) 17
pardo (13) 13
parecer (4) 16; (36) 8
pared (15) 24; (18) 15; (40) 3; (48) 3
pariente (25) 16; (39) 2
parir (19) 8; (46) 8
parlero (31) 14
parte (7) 7; (11) 29
pasada (33) 10, 25
pasajero (48) 51
pasar (13) 12; (19) 13; (20) 12; (21)
  7; (31) 8
pasear (38) 15
pata (43) 14
patada (1) 25
patria (44) 10
Paz v. Guerra
paz (42) 1, 2, 6
pecado, pecador (17) 8, 15
pecar (17) 15
pecunia (24) 28; (25) 6
pecho (5) 1; (48) 22
pedir (23) 4; (24) 14; (47) 3
Pedro (46) 19
pegar (46) 24
pelar, pelarse (6) 7; (40) 4
pelear (3) 15; (15) 30
peligro, peligroso (4) 8; (39) 1; (40)
  5; (42) 5
pelo (19) 21; (35) 11
pelleja (1) 32; (24) 13
pellejero (10) 23
pena, penado (11) 5; (15) 18; (17)

15; (19) 22

pensamiento (36) 10; (48) 30

pensar (3) 14; (16) 22; (32) 12; (45) 5

peor (35) 8; (38) 12; (39) 14; (46) 14; (47) 23, 24

pequeño (39) 5, 16; (46) 16

perder, perderse (2) 8; (10) 9; (12) 16, 20; (13) 15; (14) 3; (15) 12, 15; (16) 1; (17) 11; (18) 11; (19) 21; (22) 9; (26) 10; (33) 6; (36) 24; (37) 7; (38) 18; (39) 11; (46) 19

perdición (23) 9

perdido (9) 5; (31) 10; (47) 22

perdonar (17) 8, 13

perecer (42) 3

Pereza v. Trabajo

perezoso (6) 20

perfecto (30) 4, 11

perla (15) 26

permanecer (44) 11

pero (13) 36

perra (19) 8

perro (4) 9; (12) 5; (15) 10, 11, 20; (19) 14; (24) 29; (31) 16; (33) 14; (34) 7, 22; (35) 11; (38) 29; (41) 10, 13; (46) 26; (47) 41; (48) 1, 2, 18, 42

perseverancia (21) 4

perseverar (47) 30

persona (33) 24

pesado (28) 1; (33) 25

pesar (13) 9; (20) 3, 8

pescado (48) 45

pescar (3) 26

peseta (25) 15

petaca (28) 8

pez, peces; (6) 24; (29) 12; (38) 10, 16; (40) 8

pez *(f)* (12) 3

picada (38) 28

pícaro (43) 23

pico (5) 7

pie (26) 13; (28) 4, 12; (34) 28; (35) 14; (41) 14; (48) 22

piedra (1) 19; (6) 14; (12) 18; (13) 18; (22) 7; (47) 6

piel (5) 6; (15) 21

pierna (2) 11; (11) 30; (25) 32

pillo (3) 12

pinchar (43) 16

pintar (23) 3

pipa (42) 2

pistola (46) 24

placer (20) 8

planta (33) 17

plata (1) 14; (3) 2; (25) 19; (42) 4

platón (6) 5

plaza (13) 17; (39) 7

pleitear (41) 12

pleito (17) 17; (30) 10

pobre (25) 27; (26) 7

Pobreza v. Riqueza

pobreza (25) 20–22

Poco v. Mucho

poco (1) 5, 9, 13, 21; (4) 14; (9) 19; (10) 9; (11) 25; (12) 15; (13) 26; (19) 7; (24) 1, 27; (25) 24; (26) 11; (30) 26; (36) 13; (38) 15; (46) 22; (48) 37

poder (2) 10; (4) 17; (6) 11, 23; (7) 12; (8) 1; (9) 29; (14) 1, 4–6, 9, 14, 17, 19; (16) 23; (18) 2, 7; (21) 2; (22) 12; (24) 10, 25; (29) 2; (30) 5; (32) 6; (33) 6, 8; (45) 12; (48) 18

Poder v. Dominio

poder, poderoso (30) 15; (40) 5; (41) 16

podrido (12) 16

polvo (34) 27

pólvora (11) 19; (15) 28

pollo (5) 9; (32) 12; (33) 19; (36) 36; (45) 2

poner, ponerse (1) 29; (4) 14; (18) 10, 16; (19) 15; (29) 10; (36) 30

porrada (11) 27

portal (32) 13

posada (10) 8

poseer (36) 35

postrero (36) 10; (47) 41

potro (33) 12

pozo (25) 31; (47) 22

precio (16) 2; (47) 40

predicar (5) 9

pregonero (7) 2

pregunta, preguntar (1) 23; (8) 10; (11) 13

prender (15) 6

prendido (33) 29

prepararse (42) 6

presente (36) 37; (39) 15

preso (10) 19

prestado (27) 4

prestar (27) 7

presto (16) 14; (17) 14; (33) 20; (36) 12; (38) 14; (47) 37; (48) 1, 11

prevenido (13) 21

prevenir (35) 6

pri(e)sa (9) 20, 22

primero (9) 24; (28) 2; (35) 2; (36) 10; (42) 9; (46) 2

primo (39) 2

príncipe (29) 3

Principio y Fin (10)

principio (10) 1–3, 10

probar (29) 9; (39) 1

profeta (5) 5; (13) 24

prometer (1) 8, 9; (13) 15

prometido (27) 11

pronto (12) 24; (14) 8; (24) 13; (45) 4

propio (19) 28; (44) 17; (47) 12

proponer (22) 1

provecho (1) 2

pueblo (48) 4

puente (9) 16); (42) 4

puerco (14) 15; (15) 26); (19) 8

puerta (3) 10; (25) 7, 9; (30) 23

pues (13) 7

pulga (12) 5; (19) 14; (38) 28; (48) 17

pulgar (47) 9

pulgarada (19) 25

punta (20) 10; (33) 11; (42) 10

puntada (13) 19

puñado (19) 11

puño (29) 10

qual... tal... (1) 23

quebrado (2) 10; (12) 2; (39) 10

quebran(tamien)to (46) 6; (47) 21

quebrantar (21) 3

quebrar, quebrarse (13) 10; (18) 9; (37) 14

quedar, quedarse (4) 12; (16) 22; (27) 10; (29) 9; (36) 1; (39) 11; (44) 15; (47) 28; (48) 43

quejarse (19) 22; (22) 3

querer (1) 11; (5) 8; (6) 22, 24; (12) 13, 23; (14) 10; (16) 5; (18) 2; (19) 8; (21) 2; (22) 17; (26) 9, 10; (27) 1; (28) 14; (30) 16; (32) 6; (33) 20; (35) 3; (38) 16; (39) 9; (41) 8, 9; (42) 6; (44) 15; (47) 2, 23, 24; (48) 8

quién (47) 1

quinientos (10) 19

quinto (15) 3

quitar, quitarse (13) 33; (20) 9; (24) 13; (47) 15

rabia (34) 22; (38) **29**; (48) 2

395

tiento (45) 2; (47) 26

tierra (13) 24; (19) 12; (29) 13; (36) 3; (44) 8, 11

tino (20) 9; (38) 20

tintín (24) 2

tirar (26) 5; (47) 6; (48) 14

tiznado (48) 39

tizón (9) 28

tocar (4) 5; (46) 25; (48) 54

todo (2) 16, 21; (4) 2, 10; (7) 7; (9) 6, 30; (10) 1, 7, 9, 15, 16; (13) 10; (19) 14; (21) 4; (24) 12; (25) 5; (26) 10; (27) 5; (30) 8, 15; (31) 8; (33) 28; (34) 17, 27; (36) 4; (37) 11; (38) 17, 27; (44) 2, 5, 10; (46) 11; (47) 31; (48) 10, 38

todos (1) 20; (2) 9, 20; (3) 14; (4) 6; (8) 3; (10) 22; (11) 9, 29; (13) 1, 12, 13; (14) 9–11; (17) 1; (22) 10, 14; (25) 3, 6, 7, 9; (26) 1, 8; (28) 7; (30) 14; (34) 13; (39) 8; (42) 3; (43) 9, 10; (44) 1, 6; (48) 13, 23

tomar (14) 13; (26) 13; (27) 4; (33) 16; (36) 33; (42) 3; (43) 2; (46) 10; (47) 25, 26

tonto (11) 18, 23, 25, 26

toparse (45) 1

torcido (14) 19

tornar, tornarse (9) 25; (34) 27

toro (47) 33

tortilla (6) 26

tos (30) 5

trabajar (6) 21

Trabajo–Diligencia–Pereza (6)

trabajo (6) 1, 4, 10, 12; (14) 10; (47) 34

traer (1) 2; (19) 24; (25) 18; (47) 14

tragar (46) 17

traición (16) 21

trampa (17) 5

tranquilidad (35) 15

tranquilo (44) 17

trapo (47) 10

tras (9) 26; (11) 1; (16) 10; (19) 18

traspuesto (33) 17

trasquilado (46) 23

tratar (4) 11

trecho (1) 4

trenta (14) 14

tres (31) 15; (36) 12; (40) 8; (48) 31, 33

triplicado (36) 21

Tristeza v. Gozo

tristeza (20) 4

tronco (36) 28; (43) 22

tropezar (36) 16, 28; (48) 21

trotar (18) 6

trote (33) 15

trucha (24) 20

trueque (7) 13

tu (47) 5, 38

tú (20) 7; (29) 9

tuerto (13) 8; (35) 10

tus (15) 20

(lo) Tuyo v. (lo) Mío

tuyo (40) 4

último (10) 17

un, una, uno (9) 13; (12) 4, 14; (13) 17; (15) 17; (16) 10; (19) 6; (24) 5, 6, 8, 12, 13; (28) 3; (31) 15; (32) 3; (34) 28; (36) 5, 7, 32, 33, 37; (41) 6, 8, 10; (43) 1, 10–12, 17, 18, 23; (46) 10, 19; (48) 29, 38

una vez (3) 16

unión (41) 1, 2

untar (13) 22

uña (13) 5; (43) 12; (48) 34

urinal (17) 17

usar (17) 4

болеть (19) 21; (24) 8; (35) 9, 14
болото (7) 5; (44) 12
болтать (38) 18
болтливый (19) 22
болтун (2) 13
больно, больнее (22) 3; (38) 28
больной (35) 3, 13, 16
больше (1) 13; (2) 14; (11) 13; (12) 2; (13) 23; (26) 9; (36) 7
большой (2) 13; (3) 19; (12) 1; (13) 9; (17) 17; (24) 1, 20; (29) 12; (32) 2, 13; (33) 21; (44) 3
борода (4) 7; (5) 1; (12) 22; (20) 11
борозда (33) 13
борьба (34) 1; (42) 11
бочка (12) 10, 15; (36) 34; (46) 15
боярский (36) 2
бояться (6) 13; (10) 11; (14) 3; (21) 6, 7, 10, 14; (38) 29
бражка (39) 11
браниться (30) 17
брат (20) 6; (35) 15; (40) 1; (41) 6
братство (25) 16
брать (1) 26; (21) 5; (24) 14; (27) 2, 3, 6; (30) 24; (34) 15; (46) 10; (48) 14
браться (7) 9
бревно (48) 39
бредить (48) 25
бремя (28) 15
бритьё (10) 4
брошен (45) 15
брюхо (1) 29; (38) 3, 5, 14, 23
будить (47) 35
будь (12) 27
буква (46) 7
бумага (2) 21; (11) 29
буря (12) 9; (46) 28
бутылка (46) 27
буян (41) 11

бывать (22) 14, 17; (24) 3; (34) 9; (35) 3; (37) 13; (38) 18; (39) 12
бык (1) 26; (3) 17; (26) 4; (33) 22
быстро, быстрее (13) 16; (48) 37
быть (9) 19; (10) 15; (14) 7; (30) 6; (31) 1; (33) 11, 20, 22; (34) 29; (37) 8; (45) 3, 11; (46) 2, 3; (47) 26
бычок (15) 19

валиться (19) 14; (36) 24
вариться (19) 28
ваши (5) 10
вблизи (40) 1
вводить (3) 9
вдали (40) 1
вдруг (14) 6
ведро (28) 5
везде (2) 1; (7) 7; (25) 31
век (4) 10; (8) 3; (31) 6; (37) 1; (44) 11
велено (33) 3
великий (11) 10; (17) 10; (21) 12; (25) 24
венец (10) 13
Вера см. Бог
вера (22) 18, 19
верблюд (46) 17
верёв(оч)ка (10) 15; (13) 11; (43) 14; (47) 7
верить, вериться (12) 23; (36) 6, 29; (48) 27
верно (36) 14
верста (1) 4; (48) 22
вертеться (3) 3; (38) 17
верхом (35) 4
весел, веселее (27) 10; (31) 8
веселье (31) 2
весна (24) 5; см. вешний
вести (10) 22; (13) 2
вестник (30) 19

29; (13) 5, 11; (17) 11; (20) 3;
(21) 1; (24) 13; (28) 12; (30) 19;
(37) 1; (42) 7; (44) 15

глава (31) 5

глаголати (1) 10

гладкий (1) 6

глаз (2) 7; (21) 12; (24) 17; (28) 11,
13; (30) 19, 21; (36) 6; (38) 5;
(43) 16, 20; (48) 25, 36

глас (15) 16; (48) 4

глодать (33) 9

глотать (29) 12

глупее (11) 24

Глупость см. Мудрость

глупость (11) 9, 22; (48) 44

глупый (2) 6; (26) 4; (33) 23

глухой (38) 3, 23; (47) 24

глядеть (47) 19

гнать (32) 10; (38) 24; (48) 14

гнев (41) 15

гнездо (44) 12–14

гнило (4) 3; (7) 10; (47) 12

гнить (13) 14

гнуться (18) 9

говорить (1) 5, 11–13, 16, 33; (2)
6, 19, 20; (10) 19, 21; (19) 10;
(25) 3; (32) 13; (35) 9; (47) 7

год (9) 12, 30; (16) 7

година (*время, час*) (34) 16

годиться (46) 9

годный (26) 3

гож (4) 15

голова (3) 3; (4) 7; (11) 28, 30; (12)
9; (24) 8; (35) 14; (36) 8; (38) 17;
(46) 3; см. глава

голод, голодный (18) 6; (25) 26;
(33) 18; (38) 18, 19, 23–30

голубки (6) 25

голый (24) 1

голь (18) 4; (25) 22

гонец (6) 23

гончая (24) 13

гоп (10) 21

гора (18) 18; (22) 18; (36) 13; (44) 4;
(45) 1; (46) 8

горб, горбатый (14) 19; (28) 4;
(32) 12

гордиев (10) 28

гордость (47) 21

горе (19) 20, 22; (20) 3–5; (29) 13;
(30) 3; (31) 2; (34) 26; (39) 11

гореть (2) 3; (3) 4

горка (10) 20

горло (24) 29

город (21) 5; (44) 8; (46) 2

городить (40) 3

горох (13) 32

горсть (40) 9

горчица (15) 1

горшок (13) 16, 33; (18) 3

горький (25) 30; (35) 5; (38) 13

горячий (30) 13

горячо (6) 6

господа (14) 4; (17) 6; (48) 12

господин (25) 6

Господство–Власть (29)

Господь (22) 6, 10

Гости см. Соседи

гость (9) 24; (28) 8; (40) 6–10;
(44) 16

готов, готовиться (26) 5; (42) 6

грабить (48) 29

граница (24) 16

греметь (46) 15

греть (38) 8

грех (3) 6, 9; (6) 17; (17) **15; (**19) 18;
(30) 14; (47) 6

грозить (4) 13; (40) 4

грозный (9) 17; (22) 8

гром (45) 6

грудь (5) 3
груша (31) 13
грызться (47) 9
грязь (12) 3
губ(к)а (6) 25; (33) 5
гуж (10) 19
гулять (6) 10; (33) 18
густо (45) 8
гусь (5) 9; (31) 15

да(ва)ть (1) 9; (4) 17; (11) 1; (12) 25;
    (13) 15; (24) 14; (26) 4, 13; (27) 1,
    2, 7; (34) 4; (46) 4, 5; (47) 13, 15,
    37; (48) 42
далеко (2) 17; (22) 15; (29) 2;
    (30) 22
дальше (9) 19
дано (25) 19
дарёный (47) 8
дарить (6) 8; (39) 15
даром (1) 22; (24) 28, 29
два, две (3) 15; (4) 10; (14) 4, 5, 20;
    (15) 6; (16) 9; (30) 20; (31) 15;
    (34) 9; (36) 9, 14, 18, 21, 32, 37;
    (39) 4; (41) 5, 10; (43) 13; (47) 31;
    (48) 12, 40; см. двое
двадцать (48) 40
дважды (36) 14; (47) 37
дверь (3) 10; (48) 14
двое (19) 20; (41) 5, 8; (48) 23
двор (40) 2
девица (30) 24
девки (20) 9
девятая (34) 23
девять (13) 19; (32) 3
дёготь (12) 15
дед (38) 12
действующий (35) 17
Дела см. Слова
делать, делаться (1) 5; (11) 9; (17)

14; (24) 5; (27) 4; (36) 10; (43) 5;
    (47) 2; (48) 17
дело (1) 2–4, 6, 8; (3) 5; (4) 15; (6)
    10, 13; (7) 1; (10) 4, 8, 10, 12, 13,
    26; (15) 25; (16) 1; (19) 16; (21) 9;
    (47) 29, 30
денежка (25) 9
день (4) 16; (9) 13, 17, 30; (10) 30;
    (40) 8
деньги (9) 2; (11) 18; (24) 28; (25)
    1–3, 5, 6, 11–13, 31; (26) 2; (28) 6;
    (30) 15, 23; (46) 10
деревня (46) 2
д(е)рево (4) 10; (13) 1; (16) 23; (24)
    6, 10; (33) 17; (36) 27; (48) 24,
    39, 43
дереть (24) 29
держать, держаться (11) 18; (25) 33
десять (11) 13; (38) 7
Дети см. Родители
дети (32) 3, 9, 11, 15; (33) 2
детки (32) 2, 4, 14, 16
дёшев, дёшево (7) 10, 11; (31) 16
дисциплина (42) 9
дитя, дитятко (4) 18; (32) 11, 12;
    (33) 7
длинный (4) 5; (23) 5; (39) 3
добела (15) 12
добиться (14) 14; (21) 2
добреть (28) 11
Добро и зло (16)
добро (3) 6; (13) 25, 26; (16) 20;
    (20) 5, 9; (25) 19; (28) 5; (38) 14;
    (40) 5; (43) 4, 5; (47) 39
добродетель (18) 17; (47) 40
добрый (1) 21, 22; (3) 2; (10) 3;
    (16) 1, 16, 23; (17) 4, 13; (31) 2;
    (32) 5; (39) 2; (41) 3
добыть (6) 16; (21) 9; (25) 18
доверять (36) 4

(33) 6
есть (6) 21; (12) 21; (14) 17; (18) 8;
(25) 24; (29) 9; (33) 9; (38) 2; (43)
17, 25; (48) 42
ехать (9) 19; (15) 32
ещё (26) 9; (31) 9

жаворонок (13) 3
Жадность–Скупость (26)
жадный (26) 6
жалеть (35) 13
жалость (48) 55
жар, жарить (6) 27; (36) 30
жать (*хлеб*) (6) 3
жать (*сжимать*) (47) 36
ждать (9) 4; (22) 3; (24) 23; (37) 5, 9;
(40) 5; (47) 39
желанный (40) 10
желать (26) 10; (36) 35; (47) 23, 24
железный (25) 8; (29) 10
железо (6) 6; (12) 21
Жена см. Муж
жена (31) 2, 4, 5, 13, 14
женить, жениться (31) 6, 7, 9; (32) 6
жених (31) 3, 8
женский (31) 12
женщина (44) 2
жеребёнок (33) 12
жёрнов (14) 20
жёсткий (14) 20
жив(ой) (19) 10; (22) 19; (34) 7, 12;
(45) 9
живот (38) 4, 19
животворить (46) 7
Жизнь и смерть (34)
жизнь (10) 30; (34) 1–3, 6, 20; (37) 1;
(42) 11; (47) 28
Житейская мудрость см. Этика
жить, житься (8) 3; (13) 17; (18) 2;
(20) 6; (25) 25; (28) 4; (34) 4, 5, 8;

(37) 1, 2; (38) 2; (43) 6, 12; (44) 4;
(47) 25, 26; (48) 55
жребий (45) 15
журавль (36) 33

забор (13) 12; (40) 3
забота (20) 10, 11
забы(ва)ть, забы(ва)ться (25) 16;
(30) 22; (33) 22; см. позабыть
заварить (12) 12
завистливый (16) 18
зависть (16) 18; (48) 55
завтра (6) 11; (36) 17, 36, 37; (45)
7–10
загнивать (12) 16
заговорить (25) 4
загонять (5) 9
загребать (6) 27
задний (11) 7
задолжать (27) 11
задорный (41) 11
Заём–Долги (27)
заесть (47) 41
заимодавец (27) 4
закал (33) 24
закидать (29) 9
Закон–Справедливость (17)
закон, законно (17) 1–6, 9–11; (18)
5; (42) 7
закрытый (36) 20
закрыть (10) 29
залезть (25) 16
заменить (1) 3
замиренный (39) 10
замки (15) 27
замуж (32) 6
заноситься (47) 21
запас (24) 7
запастись (23) 5
запеть (20) 7

(35) 15; (36) 11
махом (3) 8
мачеха (32) 10
мёд (1) 31; (12) 15, 27; (19) 12;
    (36) 7
медаль (46) 11
медведь (15) 21; (19) 27; (32) 10;
    (36) 31; (46) 10
медленно (9) 20
между (18) 15
мельница (15) 30; (28) 14
меньше, меньший (1) 13; (16) 9
меня (39) 9, 18; (43) 3; (46) 12
менять, меняться (9) 8; (16) 7;
    (48) 47
мера (24) 16; (43) 19; (48) 13
мереть (33) 8; (38) 6
мерить (13) 31
мёртвый, мертвец (34) 7, 22, 25
мести (33) 27; (47) 5
место (9) 24; (16) 11; (18) 6; (19) 15
    (22) 18; (44) 1, 9; (47) 28
месяц (*луна*) (15) 11
метать (15) 26
меткий (22) 7
метла (33) 27
меч (42) 3, 8
мешок (2) 16; (3) 21; (7) 14
мил, милый (30) 6, 17, 23–25; (32)
    11, 12; (48) 22
мило (4) 3; (7) 10; (28) 9; (33) 28
миловидность (30) 28
милостив (46) 1
мина (18) 16
миновать (34) 9; (45) 11; (47) 21
минуться (34) 26
мир (*свет*) (14) 9; (24) 1; (44) 2, 3;
    (47) 26
Мир см. Война
мир (31) 10; (41) 3; (42) 2, 6

мириться (18) 7
мне (45) 7
Много–Мало–Ничего (24)
много, многое (1) 5, 9; (4) 13, 14;
    (6) 5; (7) 3; (9) 16, 27; (12) 27;
    (18) 14; (23) 6; (24) 1, 9, 13, 14,
    27; (25) 1, 5, 14; (26) 3, 9; (34) 26;
    (37) 6; (38) 18; (41) 5; (46) 21, 22;
    (48) 28
могила (14) 19; (34) 28; (45) 9
можется (18) 2
можно (14) 14; (48) 21
мозг (6) 18
мокрый (9) 29; (14) 3; (19) 14
молва (16) 12
молебен (38) 19
молитва (22) 13
молиться (22) 17
молодцы (41) 12
молодо-зелено (33) 3
молодой (11) 24; (33) 8, 9, 11, 16
Молодость–Старость–Новизна
    (33)
молодость (8) 12; (33) 1, 6
молот, молоток (18) 15; (25) 8
молотить (15) 22; см. намолотить
молоть (12) 25
моло(ч)ко (15) 19; (19) 12; (21) 10;
    (33) 5
молочный (19) 12
молчаливый (19) 22
молчание (1) 14, 17, 18, 24
молчать (1) 15, 20, 33; (25) 3; (31
    12
монарх (29) 5
монах (4) 4; (23) 2
монета (43) 24
море (15) 34; (22) 17; (24) 4, 22;
    (36) 3
морковка (24) 19

насыщаться (1) 29
натолкнуться (6) 17
натура (47) 32
натягивать (12) 2
научать (11) 2
научить, научиться (8) 12; (18) 3, 14
находить (9) 23
Начало–Конец (10)
начало (10) 1–6, 10, 11
начаться (9) 25
начин, начинать (10) 8, 12
наш, наши (5) 10; (37) 8; (39) 6
неблагодарность (47) 39
небо (13) 3; (22) 11; (36) 33; (45) 6; (46) 27
невеста (31) 3
невестка (4) 17
Невозможность (14)
неволя (33) 26
негде (24) 25
недалеко (32) 7
недаром (2) 20
неделя (12) 25
недоверчивость (36) 11
недоволен (45) 13
недолгий (41) 15
недолговечный (30) 27
недостаток (13) 36
недоученный (11) 15
недруг (39) 15
незачем (15) 7
незванный (40) 6
незнание (17) 2
неймёт (20) 6
нельзя (18) 7; (46) 5
немного (2) 2
ненавидеть (41) 9
ненависть (2) 8; (41) 7
ненадёжен (39) 10

Ненадёжность см. Надёжность
ненасытим (23) 9
Необходимость см. Нужда
непойманный (36) 30
непочто (6) 23
неправда (3) 7
неправый (17) 12
неразлучный (48) 44
нести, несть (19) 17; (40) 9
нестись (*о птицах*) (19) 8
несущая (26) 12
несчастлив (30) 18
Несчастье см. Счастье
несчастье (13) 27
нет (14) 2; (24) 21, 25, 26; (39) 12; (46) 21; (48) 28
нечего (1) 15; (25) 24; (36) 30
Нечестность см. Честность
нечистая сила (23) 8
ни... ни... (48) 45
ни с кем (39) 8
низкий (13) 12
низко (46) 6
никак (17) 7
никогда (8) 4; (9) 11; (19) 23; (47) 20
никто (14) 4; (17) 2; (25) 27; (34) 21; (38) 29; (39) 11; (45) 13
нитка (24) 1; (36) 12
Ничего см. Много
ничего (1) 9; (7) 9; (9) 23; (10) 9; (21) 8; (24) 9, 18, 21, 24; (44) 7
ничто (21) 8
нищета (25) 21
нищий (26) 7
Новизна см. Молодость
новый (17) 6; (33) 27, 28; (39) 4; (44) 7
нога, ножка (1) 25; (2) 11; (5) 7; (11) 30; (19) 16; (21) 13; (25) 2, 32;

(34) 28; (36) 16; (41) 14; (47) 36
ножи (4) 5
нора (3) 24
норов (44) 8
нос, носок (6) 9; (31) 8; (37) 6; (46) 4; (48) 41
носить (15) 10
ночевать (36) 26
ночь (13) 13
ноша (13) 9; (28) 1
нрав, нравы (9) 14; (16) 7, 16
нравиться (30) 25
Нужда–Необходимость (18)
нужда (18) 3–6, 14, 17; (25) 28; (39) 1
нуждаться (26) 6; (35) 16; (47) 40
нужный (7) 12; (9) 22; (15) 4; (16) 21; (41) 7
нынче (36) 37
нюхать (15) 8

оба (13) 2, 33
обвинять (12) 11
обед, обедать (23) 5; (28) 8; (38) 12, 15, 18
обещать (1) 8, 9
обжечься (21) 10
обжигать (18) 3
обжорство (38) 6
обидеть (1) 17; (41) 9
облагаться (48) 30
обман (7) 13
обманчив (4) 1; (30) 28
обманывать (1) 7
обмен (7) 13
оборотный (46) 11
обсохнуть (33) 5
обход (17) 5
объяввлть (33) 11
обычай (17) 9

овечья (5) 6
овца (12) 14, 28; (13) 12; (18) 11; (22) 6; (32) 5; (41) 12; (43) 10; (48) 31
огонь (2) 3; (12) 8; (19) 26; (46) 5; (48) 33
огород (13) 10; (15) 29
одежда, одёжка (4) 11; (25) 32; (37) 3
одетый (33) 29
одеяло (14) 15
один (9) 13; (10) 25; (11) 13; (12) 16; (13) 19; (15) 6, 17; (19) 6; (24) 11, 12, 23; (31) 1, 2; (32) 3; (36) 5, 9; (41) 5; (43) 13; (46) 19; (47) 31; (48) 12, 26
одиночка (16) 15
одна (12) 14; (19) 23; (24) 5; (26) 3; (30) 20; (34) 9, 26, 28; (41) 10; (48) 11
одно (1) 8; (24) 1, 6; (30) 20; (36) 37; (48) 39
одолжать (47) 39
одураченный (37) 5
окно (48) 14
око (30) 19; (47) 19; см. очи
оковы (48) 8
околеть (38) 30
околица (48) 22
около (23) 1
омут (4) 8
опасность (40) 4
оправдывать (48) 49
Опыт см. Знание
опыт (8) 5
орало (*соха*) (42) 8
орёл (12) 13; (32) 17; (41) 12; (48) 5
орех (38) 11, 16
осёл (11) 17; (18) 12

различие (30) 10
разлучать (31) 11
Разное (48)
разрубить (10) 28
разрушить (41) 2
разум (11) 1, 3; (19) 19; (22) 9;
   (30) 26
разуметь (25) 26
рак (24) 20
ранний (6) 9
рано (20) 7
раньше (12) 10
расплохом (34) 15
располагать (22) 1
расправа (17) 15
распутье (21) 7
рассуждение (17) 14
рассчитать (15) 30
расти (13) 10; (14) 12; (16) 14; (38)
   30; (48) 51
раструсить (32) 4
расхлёбывать (12) 12
расход (25) 33
рать (41) 5
рвать, рваться (13) 11; (47) 41
ребёнок (32) 8
реветь (27) 1
ревность (30) 11, 12
редкий (40) 7
резвиться (12) 7
резвость (33) 1
река (19) 12
Ремесло см. Торговля
ремесло (7) 6–8
ремешки (28) 5
репа (38) 26
речь (1) 27, 32; (11) 4
решённый (10) 26
решето (15) 23
ржа, ржаветь (12) 21; (30) 1

Рим (10) 22
риск, рисковать (21) 8, 9; (42) 5
ровный (19) 15
рог, рогатый (1) 26; (26) 4
род (*поколение*) (44) 11
родины (34) 16
Родители и дети (32)
родить, родиться (2) 8; (8) 13; (19)
   11; (25) 12; (28) 12; (31) 3; (32) 5,
   17; (46) 8
родная (44) 17
родня (25) 23
родословный (48) 24
родственник (39) 2
рождаться (34) 11
Рождество (9) 28
рожь (23) 6
роза (20) 13
розга (32) 8
роса (6) 7; (38) 30
рот (13) 10; (25) 25; (36) 20, 24
рубаха, рубашка (24) 1; (28) 2
рубить (12) 6; (13) 1
рубль (24) 2; (25) 15; (39) 7
рука (3) 18; (5) 8; (6) 5, 23, 27;
   (12) 3; (26) 13; (29) 6, 10; (30) 13;
   (31) 7; (36) 32, 33; (43) 1
ручаться (13) 6
ручка (4) 18
рушиться (43) 23
рыбак (32) 15
рыб(к)а (3) 26; (6) 15, 24; (15) 20;
   (24) 20; (29) 12; (38) 10; (48) 45
рыж(ий) (11) 17
рыло (2) 10; (15) 8
рыть (12) 17

сад (24) 6
садиться (46) 6
сам, сама (6) 22; (7) 2, 8; (8) 2, 8;

423

Appendix

LATIN ORIGINS OF CERTAIN PROVERBS

Appendice

ORIGINES LATINES DE CERTAINS PROVERBES

Anhang

LATEINISCHE URSPRÜNGE MANCHER SPRICHWÖRTER

Appendice

ORIGINI LATINE D'ALCUNI PROVERBI

Apéndice

ORÍGENES LATINOS DE ALGUNOS PROVERBIOS

Приложение

Латинские источники некоторых посдовиц

(1)   1   Simul dictum, simul factum.

      3   Dicere et facere non semper eiusdem.

      4   Inter verba et actus magnus quidam mons est.

   11   Cum dixeris quod vis, audies quod non vis.

   17   Silendo nemo peccat.

   18   Qui tacet, consentire videtur.

   19   Et semel emissum volat irrevocabile verbum.

   25   Melius est pede quam labi lingua.

   27   Qualis homo ipse est, talis eius est oratio.

   28   Multo quam ferrum lingua atrocior ferit.

   29   Difficile est vacuo verbis imponere ventri.

   31   Mel in ore, fel in corde.

   32   Lupus in fabula.

(2)   2   Veritatis simplex est oratio.

      3   Veritas premitur, non opprimitur.

      5   In vino veritas.

      6   Stultus puerque vera dicunt.

      8   Veritas odium parit.

      9   Non omnia quae vera sunt, recte dixeris.

   12   Mendacem memorem esse oportet.

   14   Mendaci homini ne verum quidem dicenti credimus.

   17   Egregie mentiri potest, qui ex loco longe dissito venit.

   18   Mendax est fur.

   20   Publica fama non semper vana.

   21   Epistula non erubescit.

(3)   2   Melius est nomen bonum quam divitiae multae.

      5   Recte faciendo neminem timeas.

      7   Male parta male dilabuntur.

      8   Res parata furto durabit tempore curto.

      9   Occasio facit furem.

   11   Arte deluditur ars.

   13   Utrique sunt fures: et qui accipit et qui furatur.

   18   Parvus pendetur fur, magnus abire videtur.

   20   Difficillimum esse furari apud fures.

   26   Piscari in turbido.

(4) 1 Fallitur visus.
   Fronti nulla fides.
   2 Non omne est aurum quod splendet.
   4 Cucullus non facit monachum.
   5 Non est venator, quivis per cornua flator.
   7 Barba non facit philosophum.
   9 Canes qui plurimum latrant, perraro mordent.
   10 Malum vas non frangitur.
   11 Vestis virum reddit.
   12 Simia simia est, etiam si aurea gestat insignia.
   17 Qui asinum non potest, stratum caedit.

(5) 2 Latet anguis in herba.
   7 Cavendam esse felem quae a fronte lingat et a tergo laedat.
   8 Multi manum palpant, quam amputatam vellent.

(6) 1 Par praemium labori.
   2 Ut sementem feceris, ita metes.
   4 Sine labore non erit panis in ore.
   5 Multae manus onus levant.
   6 Dum ferrum candet, tundito.
   8 Aurora Musis amica.
   10 Labore peracto quies iucunda.
   12 Opus artificem probat.
   13 Opus laudat (commendat) artificem.
   19 Omnium malorum origo otium.
   20 Mendicitas ignaviae praemium.
   23 Ne quid expectes amicos quod tute agere possis.
   24 Felis amat pisces, sed aquas intrare recusat.
   25 Nulli per ventos assa columba volat.

(7) 2 Optimum vinum suspensa non indiget hedera.
   3 Proba merx facile emptorem reperit.
   6 Artem qui sequitur, raro pauper reperitur.
   9 Omnia qui temptat, nil apte perficit unquam.

(8) 1 Scientia potestas est.
2 Nosce te ipsum.
3 Vivere tota vita discendum est.
4 Nulla aetas ad discendum sera.
5 Experientia est magistra rerum.
6 Usus magister est optimus.
8 Docendo discitur.
11 Dubium sapientiae initium.
13 Nemo nascitur artifex.
14 Errando discitur.

(9) 1 Habent omnia tempora sua.
3 Tempus fugit.
7 Tempus dolorem lenit.
8 Tempora mutantur, et nos mutamur in illis.
11 Potius sero quam nunquam.
12 Saepe dat una dies, quod non evenit in anno.
13 Roma non fuit una die condita.
15 In nocte consilium.
18 Non semper sunt Saturnalia.
20 Festina lente.
23 Sero venientes, male sedentes.
24 Qui primus venerit, primus molet.
26 Post nubila Phoebus.

(10) 2 Boni principii bonus finis.
3 Bonum initium est dimidium facti.
5 Quale principium, tale et clausula.
6 Omne initium difficile.
12 Respice finem.
13 Finis coronat opus.
14 Si finis bonus est, totum bonum est.
20 Ante victoriam ne canas triumphum.
26 Post factum nullum consilium.
30 Diem vesper commendat.

Appendix Latina

(14) 1 Factum illud; fieri infectum non potest.

2 Ad impossibilia nemo obligatur.

5 Hic esse et illic simul non possum.

9 Nemo omnibus placet.

15 Asini cauda non facit cribrum.

20 Durum et durum non faciunt murum.

(15) 1 Post bellum auxilium.

2 Post mortem medicina.

4 Quid caeco cum speculo?

5 Caecus ne iudicet de colore.

6 Duos qui lepores sequitur, neutrum capit.

9 Asinus ad lyram.

12 Asini caput ne laves nitro.

16 Vox clamantis in deserto.

19 Ab asino lanam quaerere.

20 Piscem te natare doces.

23 Cribro aquam haurire.

25 De asini umbra disceptare.

29 Ovem lupo committis.

32 Noctuas Athenas afferre.

33 Ligna in silvam portare stultum est.

34 Mari aquam addere.

(16) 3 Verba movent, exempla trahunt.

7 Lupus pilum mutat, non mentem.

9 De duobus malis minus est semper eligendum.

13 Mala herba non interit.

14 Mala herba cito crescit.

19 Regula certa datur: bene qui stat, non moveatur.

(17) 2 Ignorantia legis neminem excusat.

5 Inventa lege, inventa fraude.

6 Novus rex, nova lex.

9 Consuetudo pro lege servatur.

10 Summum ius, summa iniuria.

11   Violentia praecedit ius.
13   Bonis nocet, qui malis parcet.

(18)   3   Magna vis necessitas.
       4   Mater artium necessitas.
       5   Necessitas non habet legem
       7   Optimum est pati quod emendare non possis.
      13   Aut bibat, aut abeat.
      14   Fames artium magister.
      17   Necessitatem in virtutem commutare

(19)   1   Suae quisque fortunae faber est.
       3   Fortuna caeca est.
       4   Fortuna vitrea est, tum quum splendet, frangitur.
       7   Fortuna favet fatuis.
       8   Dum fortuna favet, parit et taurus vitulum.
      10   Nemo ante mortem beatus.
      11   Vitam regit fortuna, non sapientia.
      19   Stultum facit fortuna, quem vult perdere.
      20   Solamen miseris socios habuisse malorum.
      21   Nemo claudicat alieno ex dolore.
      23   Nulla calamitas sola.

(20)   2   Post gaudia luctus.
       3   Laetitiae proximus fletus.
      10   Crux est generis omnis.
      12   Iucunda est memoria praeteritorum malorum.
      13   Inter vepres rosae nascuntur.

(21)   1   Volenti nil impossibile.
       4   Labor omnia vincit.
       5   Audentes fortuna iuvat.
       6   Folia qui timet, silvas non adeat.
      11   Gallus in suo sterquilinio plurimum potest.
      13   Pedibus timor addit alas.
      14   Umbram suam metuere.

(22)   1   Homo proponit, Deus disponit.

        7   Sero molunt deorum molae.

        9   Quem Deus vult perdere, prius dementat.

      13   Brevis oratio penetrat coelos.

      16   Qualis rex, talis grex.

      17   Qui nescit orare, pergat ad mare.

(23)   2   Daemon languebat, tum monachus esse volebat.

        3   Diabolus non est tam ater, ac pingitur.

      10   Undique ad inferos tantundem viae est.

(24)   1   De minimis granis fit magnus acervus.

        5   Una hirundo non efficit ver.

        6   Flos unus non facit hortum.

        7   Superflua non nocent.

      12   Unus vir, nullus vir.

      13   Multitudo canum mors leporis.

      15   Omne nimium nocet.

      18   Parum accipere plus est quam nihil omnino.

      24   Ex nihilo nihil fit.

      25   Nemo dat quod non habet.

      26   Ubi nihil est, Caesar iure suo excidit.

(25)   5   Pecunia impetrat omnia.

        6   Pecuniae oboediunt omnia.

           Pecunia regina mundi.

        7   Auro quaeque ianua panditur.

      10   Nervi bellorum pecuniae.

      11   Pecunia non olet.

      12   Nummus nummum parit.

      20   Paupertas non est vitium.

      22   Paupertas artis omnis perdocet.

      26   Plenus venter facile de ieiuniis disputat.

      28   Felix sua sorte contentus.

      29   Contentum suis rebus esse maximae sunt divitiae.

      31   Homo sine pecunia est imago mortis.

(26) 2 Non avaro divitiae, sed divitiis avarus servit.
    3 Avarus nisi cum moritur, nil recte facit.
    4 Nihil superbius paupere, dum surgit in altum.
    6 Semper avarus eget.
    8 Avaritia est radix omnium malorum.
    9 Qui multum habet, plus cupit.
   10 Qui totum vult, totum perdit.

(27) 2 Apud creditorem maior quam apud debitorem debiti memoria.
    9 Felix qui nihil debet.
   11 Promissio parit debitum.

(28) 2 Tunica propior pallio est.
    3 Proximus sum egomet mihi.
    5 Ex alieno corio lata secantur lora.
    7 De alieno liberalis.
    9 Suum cuique pulchrum est.
   11 Oculus domini saginat equum.

(29) 1 Divide et impera.
    2 Quod est violentum, non est durabile.
    4 Quidquid delirant reges, plectuntur Achivi.
    5 Rex regnat, sed non gubernat.
    8 Qualis dominus, talis et servus.
   11 Quot servi, tot hostes.
   12 Piscem vorat maior minorem.

(30) 1 Antiquus amor cancer est.
    2 Amor caecus.
    3 Ubi amor, ibi dolor.
    5 Amor tussisque non celatur.
    8 Omnia vincit amor.
   17 Amantium irae–amoris integratio est.
   19 Oculi sunt in amore duces.
   21 Procul ex oculis, procul ex mente.
   24 Formosa virgum est dotis dimidium.

(31) 4   Uxor, magistratusque dantur coelitus.

      13   Nux, asinus, mulier verbere opus habent.

      15   Tres mulieres faciunt nundinas.

(32) 1   Ut pater, ita filius; ut mater, ita filia.

       8   Qui bene amat, bene castigat.

       9   Melius est pueros flere quam senes.

      11   Noctuae pullus suus pulcherrimus.

      14   Mali corvi malum ovum.

      17   Aquila non generat columbam.

(33) 3   Iuventus, ventus.

      10   Quaere adolescens, utere senex.

      11   Urit mature quod vult urtica manere.

      16   Senectus primum consulenda.

      18   Senem iuventus pigra mendicum creat.

      19   Ante barbam doces senes.

      20   Mature fias senex, si diu vis senex esse.

      23   Bis pueri senes.

      25   Aetas senilis mala merx.

      26   Senectus ipsa est morbus.

      28   Grata rerum novitas.

(34) 1   Vivere militare est.

       5   Qualis vita, finis ita.

       6   Ars longa, vita brevis.

       7   Melior est canis vivus leone mortuo.

      10   De mortuis aut bene aut nihil.

      13   Omnia mors aequat.

      17   Contra vim mortis non est medicamen in hortis.

      19   Mors non accipit excusationes.

      22   Canis mortuus non mordet.

      26   Morborum medicus omnium mors ultimus.

(35) 1   Mens sana in corpore sano.

       2   Sani divitibus ditiores.

4 Citius venit malum quam revertitur.

5 In amaritudine salus.

7 Similia similibus curantur.

8 Sunt remedia saepe deteriora malis.

12 Medice, cura te ipsum.

14 Si caput dolet, omnia membra languent.

17 Extremis malis, extrema remedia.

(36) 1 Verba volant, scripta manent.

3 Fida terra, infidum mare.

4 Fide, sed cui, vide!

8 Quot homines, tot sententiae.

9 Plus vident oculi quam oculus.

10 Cogitationes posteriores sunt saniores.

13 Certa praestant incertis.

15 Tarde sed tute.

16 Errat interdum quadrupes.

19 Oculis magis habenda fides quam auribus.

22 Nemini dum vivit dicere licet: hoc non patiar.

25 Qui quaerit, invenit.

29 Ne omnibus crede.

32 Sola avis in cavea melior quam mille volantes.

(37) 1 Dum spiro, spero.

3 Spes servat afflictos.

5 Fallitur augurio spes bona saepe suo.

7 Quod differtur, non aufertur.

11 Patientia vincit omnia.

12 Doloris cuivis remedium patientia.

(38) 2 Edimus ut vivamus, non vivimus ut edamus.

3 Plenus venter non studet libenter.

13 Mus satur insipidam deiudicat esse farinam.

15 Post coenam stabis vel passus mille meabis.

16 Qui edere vult nucleum, frangat nucem.

20 Dum vinum intrat, exit sapientia.

23 Venter aures non habet.

24 Fames pellit lupum e silvis.

25 Cibi condimentum fames.

30 Expecta bos olim herba.

(39) 1 Amicus certus in re incerta cernitur.

3 Clara pacta, amicitia longa.

8 Amicus omnibus, amicus nemini.

9 Qui me amat, amet et canem meum.

10 Ab amico riconciliato cave.

11 Donec eris felix, multos numerabis amicos; tempora si fuerint nubila, solus eris.

15 Timeo Danaos et dona ferentes.

16 Hostis, etiamsi vilis, nunquam contemnendus.

17 Homo homini lupus est.

18 Ab inimicis possum mihi ipsi cavere, ab amicis vero non.

(40) 2 Cui bonus est vicinus, felix illucet dies.

5 Leonina societas.

6 Retro sedet ianuam, non invitatus ad aulam.

8 Post tres saepe dies vilescit piscis et hospes.

(41) 2 Concordia parvae res crescunt, discordia maximae dilabuntur.

5 Ne Hercules quidem adversus duos.

6 Fratrum concordia rara, discrepatio crebra.

10 Discordia duorum canum super ossa.

12 Duobus litigantibus tertius gaudet.

15 Ira furor brevis est.

16 Vana sine viribus ira est.

(42) 6 Si vis pacem, para bellum.

7 Inter arma silent leges.

(43) 1 Manus manum lavat.

6 Cum vulpe vulpinare.

7 Si fueris Romae, Romano vivito more.

8 Similis simili gaudet.

9 Concolores aves facillime congregatur.

11 Asinus asinum fricat.

15 Intelligunt se mutuo, ut fures in nundinis.

16 Corvus oculum corvi non eruet.

18 Clavum clavo pellere.

21 Par pari referre.

22 Duro nodo durus quaerendus est cuneus.

(44) 2 Fere totus mundus exercet histrionem.

7 Nihil novi sub sole.

8 Quot regiones, tot mores.

10 Ubi bene, ibi patria.

12 Sua cuique patria iucundissima.

16 Nullus est locus domestica sede iucundior.

17 Domus propria, domus optima.

18 Quilibet est rex in domo sua.

(45) 1 Occurrunt homines, nequeunt occurrere montes.

2 Invenit interdum caeca columba pisum.

3 Quem fata pendere volunt, non mergitur undis.

4 Insperata saepe contingunt.

7 Hodie mihi, cras tibi.

12 Inevitabile est fatum.

13 Nemo sua sorte contentus.

15 Alea iacta est.

(46) 2 Malo hic esse primus quam Romae secundus.

8 Parturiunt montes, nascetur ridiculus mus.

13 Aut Caesar, aut nihil.

14 Semper deterior vehiculi rota perstrepit.

15 Vasa inania plurimum sonant.

18 Quo altior mons, tanto profundior vallis.

19 Lucrum unius est alterius damnum.
Mors tua, vita mea.

21 Multum clamoris, parum lanae.

25 Extremitates, aequalitates.

(47) 2 Quod tibi fieri non vis, alteri ne feceris.

3 Ad consilium ne accesseris, antequam voceris.

7 Ne restim memores apud ipsum reste neccatum.

8 Noli equi dentes inspicere donati.

12 Non te laudabis: propria laus foetet in ore.

13 Honoratur arbor ob umbram.

16 Iocus dum optimus, cessandum.

18 Deridens alium non inderisus abibit.

24 Deterior surdus eo nullus qui renuit audire.

25 Tempori aptari decet.

28 Non progredi est regredi.

29 Errare humanum est.

32 Consuetudo est altera natura.

34 Facetus comes in via pro vehiculo est.

35 Irritare canem noli dormire volentem.

37 Bis dat qui cito dat.

38 Ne sutor supra crepidam.

39 Ingrati immemores beneficiorum esse solent homines.

(48) 4 Vox populi, vox Dei.

5 Aquila non captat muscas.

6 Multum valet communio sanguinis.

7 Libertas fulvo pretiosior auro.

10 Omne simile claudicat.

11 Miser est mus antro qui clauditur uno.

13 Est modus in rebus.

14 Natura plus trahit quam septem boves.

15 Quod natura dedit, tollere nemo potest.

17 Elephantum ex musca facere.

19 Habet et musca splenem.

24 Dum Adam agrum coleret et Eva neret, quis tunc nobilis?

25 Quod oculus non videt, cor non desiderat.

27 Libenter homines quod volunt, credunt.

29   Nudato Petro, Paulum tegere nefas.
     Altare spoliat, ut aliud operiat.
30   Liberae sunt nostrae cogitationes.
31   Lupus oves etiam numeratas devorat.
32   Omne trinum perfectum.
34   Ex ungue leonem.
36   Oculus animi index.
37   Cito maturum, cito putridum.
44   Inscitia mater arrogantiae.
45   Neque caro neque piscis esse.
46   Honos alit artes.
47   Honores mutant mores.
49   Cum finis est licitus, etiam media sunt licita.
52   Nimia familiaritas parit contemptum.
55   Praestat invidos habere quam misericordiam.

A List of Proverbs taken from the Bible

(1) 10 St. Matthew 12:34
     33 Ecclesiastes 3:7

(5)   5 St. Matthew 7:15

(6) 21 St. Paul
        (2 Thessalonians) 3:10

(10) 10 Ecclesiastes 7:8
     27 St. Matthew 10:22

(11) 3 Ecclesiastes 9:16

(12) 9 Hosea 8:7
     13 St. Matthew 24:28
     17 Proverbs of Solomon 26:27
     18 Job 14:19

(13) 2 St. Matthew 15:14
      6 Proverbs of Solomon 11:15
     24 St. Matthew 13:57

(14) 4 St. Matthew 6:24
     19 Ecclesiastes 1:15

(15) 16 St. Matthew 3:3
     26 St. Matthew 7:6

(16) 16 St. Paul
        (1 Corinthians) 15:33
     23 St. Matthew 7:18

(17) 4 St. Paul (1 Timothy) 1:8
      7 St. Paul
        (1 Corinthians) 4:5

(19) 12 Exodus 3:8
     29 St. Matthew 8:12

(20) 14 Ecclesiastes 3:4

(22) 12 St. Matthew 6:24
     18 St. Matthew 17:20
     19 St. Paul (Romans) 1:17

(23) 9 Proverbs of Solomon 27:20

(24) 27 St. Matthew 22:14

(25) 14 Proverbs of
        Solomon 14:20
     27 Ecclesiastes 9:16

(26) 1 St. Paul (1 Timothy) 6:10
     14 Exodus 32:4

(27) 4 Proverbs of Solomon 22:7

(28) 15 St. Paul (Galatians) 6:5

(29) 3 Psalms 146:3
     13 Ecclesiastes 10:16

(30) 4 St. John (1) 4:18
      9 Song of Solomon 8:6
     12 Song of Solomon 8:6
     14 Proverbs of
        Solomon 10:12
     28 Proverbs of
        Solomon 31:30

447